CROSSING THE LINE
THE NEW WOMAN OF THE FIN DE SIÈCLE

CROSSING THE LINE
THE NEW WOMAN OF THE FIN DE SIÈCLE

EDITED WITH AN INTRODUCTION BY
LOGAN E. GEE

WHITLOCK PUBLISHING
ALFRED. NY

First Whitlock Publishing edition 2018

Whitlock Publishing
Alfred, New York
www.whitlockpublishing.com

ISBN 978-1-943115-27-3

This book is set in Garamond on 55# acid-free paper that meets ANSI standards for archival quality.

Printed in the United States of America.

To Women

"In the name of your years of anguish,
    In the name of the curse and the stain,
By the strength of your sorrow, I call you
    By the power of your pain."

- Charlotte Stetson

INTRODUCTION

IN 19ᵀᴴ-CENTURY England, being a woman could be less than enjoyable. She had growing opportunities, such as the possibility of an education and more legal protections, but she was still a second-class citizen whose place was in the home. Societal norms dictated that her duties were tending to her children, to whom she had limited legal claim, serving her husband, and having no opinion on politics or any other matter outside of her domestic sphere. But true change arrived in the *fin de siècle* when a new type of woman made her first appearance in England's novels and periodicals.

The *fin de siècle*, a time of social and moral movements at the end of the 19ᵗʰ century in England, gave birth to women who challenged Victorian stereotypes. With her representation in novels such as *Story of an African Farm* (1883) by Olive Schreiner and *The Odd Women* (1893) by George Gissing, she was a character who was relatively unheard of in earlier Victorian fiction. She did not yet have a single name, but she had a clear message for English readers: the traditional roles of women needed to change.

While her presence was hard to miss in late Victorian fiction, these progressive women also made their way into periodicals throughout the country. In 1894, she was finally given her name, the New Woman, by Sarah Grand, a writer of New Woman novels such as *The Heavenly Twins* (1893) and *The Beth Book* (1897). In her article, "A New Aspect of the Woman Question" that appeared in *The North American Review* in March of 1894, Grand stated, "… but the new woman is a little above [man]…and proclaimed for herself what was wrong with Home-is-the-Woman's-Sphere." Grand was challenged by writers such as Maria Louise Ramé, who wrote under the pseudonym Ouida. Ramé believed that this New Woman was pompous and unrealistic in her aspirations to change the world. Following these negative comments, the mainstream media began morphing the New Woman into a manly caricature with delusional opinions and unfeminine desires. But the New Woman character and her reformist attitudes were met with open arms by women-run publications that featured her throughout their pages.

With the New Woman's presence in novels and other media, her influence easily made its way into Victorian society as women, specifically those in the middle class, adopted her ways and slowly found their voice in the public sphere by advocating for women's suffrage and, in some cases, temperance. She and her radical views lingered in English society until the very beginning of the twentieth century when she disappeared from newspapers and popular literature, but her agenda remained. In 1918 some women got the vote, and the changes the New Woman put in motion are still with us today.

CONTEXT FOR THE NEW WOMAN

EVEN BEFORE MARY Wollstonecraft's *A Vindication of the Rights of Women* in 1792, the question of where women belonged had been on the minds of both men and women. But the book inspired progressive women in the early and mid-1800s such as Harriet Martineua and Barbara Leigh Smith Bodichon who adopted and expanded upon Wollstonecraft's work by advocating for women's educational and employment opportunities. Causes such as these held through to the time of the New Woman and were incorporated into the shaping of her character.

Soon, rights to property and suffrage also weaved their way into early reformist platforms, and women were now starting larger campaigns for their rights. With these demands, change did come. The Divorce and Matrimonial Causes Act of 1857 allowed women to obtain a divorce if she could prove her husband's adultery, cruelty, desertion, or bigamy. Under this act, a man also had the right to divorce, but he only had to prove his wife's infidelity. Added later to the act was a clause stating that a woman could protect her own property and finances from her husband if she proved desertion.

With the passage of the Contagious Diseases Acts in 1864, English laws once again disempowered women. In an effort to stop the spread of venereal disease and protect the health of military men, the act allowed police officers to arrest suspected prostitutes in military towns. If a magistrate determined a woman was a prostitute, she was forced to undergo a medical examination. If she tested positive for venereal disease, she had to stay in a hospital for at least three months or risk imprisonment. Amendments to the act in 1866 and 1869 extended its range into other areas of England and increased the time of forced hospitalization for infected women.

Opposition arose when an effort against this act was launched by Josephine Butler, one of many figureheads in the growing women's movement. Butler argued that women who were accused of prostitution were not being treated fairly. She referenced previous documents, such as the Magna Carta which allowed for a fair trial before persecution, in an effort to support her arguments. In Parliament, liberal politicians William Fowler and James Stansfield also opposed the acts. Specifically, Stansfield believed the acts legalized prostitution.

Before Fowler lost his seat in the House of Commons, he stated that with no definition of prostitute in the act, arrests were made under pure speculation and that the examinations of these women's bodies were unjust and demeaning. Finally, in 1886, the Contagious Diseases Act was repealed. This marked a win for the women's movement and those fighting for women to be seen as respected and contributing members of society.

In 1870, the Married Women's Property Act further strengthened the independence of married women. The act allowed women who were married the right to maintain control over their own property. This included money or anything else with which she entered the marriage. Before this act, a wife's possessions became her husband's once married. In 1882, the act was expanded upon and women now had even more legal claim to what was theirs, similar to that of single women. These acts gave women rights distinct from their husbands, and they could be more than an accessory in the marriage rather.

Over the next twenty years, women gained more access to some freedoms that men had, but still lived with rigid restrictions. With such a demand for female education, universities slowly opened their doors to allow limited access to women, such as the University of London which began graduating women with Bachelor of Arts degrees in 1878. Women were also granted more rights over their children, but even with property and new rights, most women were still stuck in the domestic sphere. Soon though, starting the 1880s, the New Woman would shake up the status quo.

THE NEW WOMAN IN FICTION AND OTHER WRITING

BEFORE WOMEN-CENTERED publications and *Punch,* the New Woman was an unconventional character in Victorian literature. Throughout the 1880s and 90s, hundreds of New Woman novels, stories, and poems were published. A majority of these works have long since been forgotten, but were written mostly by women for women and became recognized as vehicles of social and political change. They imparted a clear call to action which was that the woman's role in the domestic and public spheres needed to be redefined. This is the same message that would soon be carried on by the New Woman of the woman's press and the female reformist parties of England.

In fiction, the New Woman followed mostly what became her stereotypical characteristics, such as her opinionated views and independent spirit, but depending on the writer, she could take on different attributes. In Olive Schreiner's *Story of an African Farm* (1883), for example, a New Woman-type character, Lyndall, obtains an education and advocates for the independence of women. Throughout the novel, she refuses marriage as a way of maintaining her own personhood, but she gets pregnant. This scandalous presentation of premarital sex received backlash from those who already criticized the New Woman and even some of those who supported her. But recognizing the sexual agency of women did add some dimension to the New Woman and radicalized her platform for women's issues surrounding marriage and independence.

George Egerton, the penname for Mary Chavelita Dunne, also used her story collections to explore the sexual freedoms of the New Woman. In Egerton's "A Cross Line," published in *Keynotes* in 1893, the female protagonist has an affair with a man who she meets while sitting by a tree on a spring day. She continues the affair until she finally decides to break off the relationship when she discovers that she is pregnant. Similar to Olive Schreiner's Lyndall, Egerton's New Woman character takes control of her sexuality and draws her own lines when it comes to relationships.

Both characters created by Schreiner and Egerton present a New Woman who decides for herself when and with whom she wants to have sex. While these representations present a woman who had control of herself in and out of marriage, she was *too* sexual for Victorian society. Those advocating for the New Woman did not want her to be seen as a purely sexual being, and critics believed that was what Schreiner and Egerton had created. But in time, the sexual agency possessed by the New Woman became a norm for her character, and those who supported her accepted it as a quality of progressive women.

Other New Woman writers, such as Sarah Grand and Mona Caird, often focused on the institution of marriage and the problems that can exist within a marital relationship. In her novels, Sarah Grand often critiques the position of women and men within bad marriages. Mona Caird also rejects the position of women within marriage, and in her essay "Marriage" (1897), Caird identifies the ways in which women fall into the submissive role under men who believe they have a right to dominate just because they are male. She uses examples such as the lack of legal guardianship a mother has over her children and the pains that a woman must endure throughout her life in an effort to rear children for her husband to illustrate the passive roles women were expected to take. Because these publications were less sexy than the works of Egerton and Schreiner, the messages these novels and essays brought to the table aligned more with those that were already part of the discussion and helped reinforce the change woman wanted to see.

Although plenty of New Woman literature was written by women, men also published on the subject and often received more attention for doing so. The New Woman genre provided men an opportunity to explore and play with female identity. In his novel *Jude the Obscure*, Thomas Hardy models his New Woman character, Sue Bridehead, after the liberal and intelligent New

Woman of the time and also focuses on unhappy marriages as one of the central elements to his plots. Another male writer, George Gissing, used his novel *The Odd Women* (1893) to examine independent women in the public sphere and their maneuvering in a male-dominated society.

For the most part, male writers supported the New Woman, but some published stereotypical representations that cast her in a negative light. For example, in *Dracula* by Bram Stoker, the heroine, Mina, writes in her diary, "If Mr. Holmwood fell in love with her [Lucy] seeing her only in the drawing-room, I wonder what he would say if he saw her now. Some of the 'New Women' writers will some day start an idea that men and women should be allowed to see each other asleep before proposing or accepting" (98). Because a woman who possessed any kind of sexual agency was looked down upon by Victorian English society, Mina's viewpoints align with societal norms. She is critical of the sexually free New Woman that she speaks of in this passage. She projects onto Lucy a hope that she will not be swayed to act like such a woman and will respect the rules of propriety. Here also it can be inferred that Stoker himself is attacking the sexual New Woman, though, throughout most of the novel he supports the independent and professional type of New Woman that is found in Mina.

In the 1890s when woman-focused periodicals and the mainstream newspapers began representing the New Woman, New Woman novels also flourished. More writers and novelists added to this period of women-centered works and it did not slow down until the 19th century came to a close and the New Woman character slowly exited English literature and society.

THE WOMEN'S PRESS AND THE MAINSTREAM PRESS

IN OCTOBER OF 1888, just after the New Woman began crossing between the spheres of domestic and public life, one of the first pro-women's suffrage publications appeared. Henrietta Muller, writing under the pseudonym Helen B. Temple, founded the *Women's Penny Paper* to address the marginalized position of women in mainstream publications. Other papers and leaflets that were woman-centered existed, such as *Aunt Judy's Magazine* (1866–1885) and *The Lady* (1885-), but these publications kept women in the roles of care givers and domestic partners rather than questioners of politics and public events. Other papers advocated for a more forward-thinking society, such as *Shafts* (1892-1900) and the *Woman's Gazette* (1881-1891), but it was the *Women's Penny Paper* that first included the New Woman.

Three years after its establishment, the *Women's Penny Paper* became the *Women's Herald* with the subtitle "The Only Paper Conducted, Written, and Published by Women." Soon after this name change, in April of 1892, Muller decided to leave the paper and Mrs. Frank Morrison took her place. With a new editor, the paper also took on new values that would satisfy its pro-suffrage readers while also grabbing the attention of those who were interested in politics, but still wanted to maintain their domestic and religious values. Reports on local-level and national-level politics became abundant in the pages, and soon after taking over, Morrison emphasized the paper's liberal leanings and echoed the agenda of the Women's Liberal Federation, a pro-woman's suffrage party.

About a year after its name change, the *Women's Herald* began featuring the New Woman as a way to create an image for the fair and respectable political woman that the paper was endorsing. This particular persona of the New Woman promised to reform English society and gain independence for women who wished to step out of their homes and have a say in the political arena while also keeping her domestic duties in mind and at heart. With her feminine touch, the New Woman's simple goal was to change the minds of those around her who believed that a woman's opinion did not belong in the public sphere.

When in 1893 the paper transitioned to a new editor, this time Lady Henry Somerset, it again changed names and became the *Woman's Signal*. This name stuck until the paper's final issue in 1899. The paper continued to feature and develop the characteristics and values of the New Woman. With her voice already calling for women's suffrage, the New Woman soon also advocated for a woman's right to an education, fair wages, and the opportunity to take part in discussions that involved the well-being of her country. The New Woman made clear that she would keep her womanly interests in mind as she applied her domestic skills to the management of public life.

With Somerset now as editor, the *Woman's Signal* disconnected itself from the Women's Liberal Federation and was no longer an explicitly liberal leaning paper, though it still supported women's suffrage. The paper moved away from its original coverage of national and local politics, and with the New Woman still alive within its pages, the paper used her as a figurehead for its focus on temperance and other social reform movements such as educational reform.

Other pro-woman papers also focused on the New Woman and spread her message throughout Europe and into the Americas. *Shafts*, for example, did its part in the woman's suffrage and rights campaign by creating a public forum where both men and women could write in to discuss current topics. Many other periodicals began doing the same, and soon men and women were promoting a better rounded identity for the New Woman. For example, published exchanges remarked on sexual agency and its connection with the New Woman characters in novels such as *Esther Waters* (1894) by George Moore and *Jude the Obscure* (1895) by Thomas Hardy. Debaters commented on the overwhelming fear that the New Woman's sexual drive would disrupt the image that reformers were trying to generate and that this sexual power would limit the influence that she had already gained.

These published debates also gave women an opportunity to speak freely about their feelings in a public forum with other women and men. At this time, women had few opportunities to debate social and political issues in public, but in these woman-focused publications, women's calls for change were finally being heard.

While the New Woman phenomena progressed in the women-focused press, her identity and what she symbolized in the mainstream media did not fare as well. Sarah Grand first introduced the idea of the New Woman in a debate between herself and English novelist Ouida in an American magazine, *The North American Review*, in 1894. The two women presented very different images of the New Woman of England and gave her both positive and negative attributes that would influence the American and English public perception of her. In her 1894 article titled "The New Woman," Ouida wrote as a response to Grand's piece, "The New Woman reminds me of an agriculturist who, discarding a fine farm of his own, and leaving it to nettles, stones, thistles, and wire-worms, should spend his whole time in demanding neighboring fields which are not his."

Due to a lack of favor in public opinion and controversies surrounding her activism, the New Woman character acquired both good and bad reputations. With the positive pushes produced by the women-focused periodicals and the negative pulls from mainstream press, the New Woman continued to be debated until the end of the 19th century. Even as she disappeared from the period's publications, she did not entirely disappear. Her fight evolved and permeated into the efforts of the women who continued to fight for their rights as the 20th century began.

THE NEW WOMAN VS. *PUNCH*

PUNCH MAGAZINE, SUBTITLED "The London Charivari," was first published on the 17th of July in 1841. Ebenezer Landells, a wood engraver, and Henry Mayhew, a writer, lifted the idea from *Le Charivari,* a satirical French publication. They decided that their version would be of a higher standard than other British Comic newspapers, most of which were for children. Being both satirical and radical, the weekly comics were unlike those of other magazines at the time such as the *Strand Magazine* and *Picture Post*. *Punch* persevered through decades, and in 1885 it began depicting a progressive woman.

Before 1885, the New Woman was without any kind of image. She was simply words and descriptions created by writers. *Punch,* as a publication that commented on everything both public and domestic, was quick to respond to the emerging challenges to gender norms. With its comics, *Punch* brought the New Woman to life by illustrating her body.

One of the first New Woman depictions appeared in the *Punch* comic titled "Things One Would Rather Have Left Unsaid," published July 18, 1885[1]. The comic features a man and woman who, it can be assumed by the rackets in their hands, have just finished playing a game of tennis. The size of the woman's shoes

1   See Image A on page xi

implies that she is unlike the stereotypical Victorian woman who was dainty and would certainly never sweat. And with women at this time just starting to play tennis competitively, it can be inferred that *Punch* was reinforcing the introduction a new type of woman who embraced physical fitness and competed in sports like men. Also worth noting is the comment about the man's pockets being too small for the woman's shoes. This reinforces her non-dainty size and again informs the reader that this is not a stereotypical Victorian woman.

One other detail worth noting regarding this image is that it depicts a solitary man and woman surrounded by the empty woods. They are alone together without a chaperone, a clear violation of the norms of Victorian propriety. The challenges to the status quo make the image typical of *Punch,* and even though the image was published just before the first issue of the *Women's Penny Paper,* it predicted the woman to come.

As the New Woman continued to evolve in European society, so did her presence in *Punch.* In contrast to the character in the *Woman's Signal, Punch's* New Woman began to reflect the bulky female of the mainstream press, which generally presented her as anything but a positive addition to English society. In its September 26, 1891[2] edition, *Punch* brings to the reader an image unlike that of its 1885 issue. Titled "The Sterner Sex," this comic illustrates two women, one of whom is wearing men's clothes, with a caption that reads, "Well—it makes you look like a young man, you know, and that's so effeminate." Here again *Punch* is depicting the New Woman with manly attributes, though not subtly in this case, and the non-New Woman character in the image is commenting on this manliness.

The manly New Woman became the norm for *Punch* magazine in the 1890s. She was often shown as aggressive, large, and more man than woman. In the comic "The New Woman" published June 15, 1895[3], a man chooses to take his tea with the female servants because, to him, the other women in his company are not female enough and he "can't get on without female society." Another illustration titled "Rational Costume," published June 13, 1896[4], took the manly New Woman caricature even further and shows two women who are dressed in bloomers and have just arrived at church. Because of their dress, a Vicar refers to the two women as men who should remove their hats before entering the church. In this comic, *Punch* has stripped all femininity from the New Woman and has placed her among not just men, but men who lack the proper conduct of a gentlemen.

Though *Punch* depicted a less than desirable version of the New Woman, it was still the first to depict her. With this illustrated body, the magazine portrayed her in both the positive light of a woman going against the norms of society, but also as a woman who was too manly because she was stepping far out of her proper place.

2   See Image B on page xii
3   See Image C on page xiii
4   See Image D on page xiii

THE NEW WOMAN AND THE FASHION MAGAZINE

DUE TO HIGHER literacy rates, lower taxes on print publications, and the invention of better printing equipment, women's fashion magazines gained popularity throughout the 19th century. With a focus on both high and everyday fashion, these magazines persuaded women to participate in consumer culture while also offering a voyeuristic escape for women who were trapped in the home. And though these magazines allowed women some advantages such as a heightened focus on individuality through dress, they negatively impacted the New Woman and her movement.

Fashion Magazines became more popular in the latter half of the 1800s, but one of the first, *Gallery of Fashion*, started in 1794 and ran for seven years. These magazines came and went, most of them having shorter runs than other types of periodicals. In the 1870s, fashion magazines began depicting more pointedly the roles of women in English society, specifically those who were middle-class and almost exclusively in the home. New fashion spreads included women out and about in the public sphere, which seems to align with the interests of the New Woman. However, these images were not doing the movement any favors.

While the New Woman advocated for a meaningful role in the public sphere, the editors of fashion magazines represented women in public as a way to objectify them. The focus of these advertisements and fashion plates was not what the woman was *doing* at the coffee shop or downtown, but rather what she was *wearing*. With fashionable dresses, women came to understand that they could communicate their husband's wealth and status while still appearing as nurturing mothers and wives. With images of objectified women being printed, it can be inferred that these magazines supported the patriarchal system that the New Woman was working against.

The escapes that fashion magazines seemed to offer were also incredibly superficial and could hardly mean anything in comparison to the New Woman campaigns of the time. Women were becoming mobile and acquiring agency that allowed them to travel into the public sphere with a voice. Most fashion magazines, on the other hand, still kept the woman in the home and offered no opportunity for a real escape. In fact, fashion magazines' promotion of consumer culture placed women farther under their husband's thumbs due to the financial dependence created by their material desires.

THE END OF THE 19TH-CENTURY NEW WOMAN

As THE *fin de siècle* came to a close, so did the radical New Woman character of England. Well known papers produced by the woman's press like *Shafts* and the *Woman's Signal* stopped printing just as the millennium turned, and *Punch* shifted its focus to more current events. Without a literary vehicle, the New Woman could no longer spread her ideals through English society. The personality that took years to create largely disappeared with her. The one thing that remained, though, was her message for reform.

Women were rallying together more and more in support of reform and suffrage. By the time the 20th century came around, women made up more than 51% percent of the population. This meant that there were roughly 1,178,317 more women than men in England, and with numbers such as this, it's no wonder women questioned why they could not have a say in what was going on in a country where they were the majority.[5]

By the 1900s, the National Union of Women's Suffrage Societies (NUWSS), an organization that had been formed in the late 1800s by 17 early suffrage societies, was gaining momentum, and in 1913 almost 500 suffrage societies made up the organization. These women came together with the goal of gaining the right to vote for women who owned property and were members of the middle class. Believing more would be accomplished if they presented themselves as intelligent individuals, the women were reasonable and non-violent when demonstrating.

Out of this group, Emmeline Pankhurt formed the Women's Social and Political Union (WSPU) in an effort to draw more attention to women's concerns and recruit working women to her cause. The WSPU turned out to be a much more violent group than the NUWSS, and the organization broke laws and went on hunger strikes to gain attention for their campaign. This group eventually split into two due to internal conflict, and separately the groups rallied on for the same cause.

When World War I broke out in 1914, the suffrage movement came to a halt and rallying for the woman's vote had to wait. But in 1918 with the passing of the Representation of the People Act, women over the age of 30 got the right to vote under the stipulation that they met property qualifications. The larger reason for passing the act, though, was that it cleared property qualifications for men who were returning from war and lowered the age to vote to 18. It was not until 1928 when the Equal Franchise Act was passed that men and women had the equal right to vote.

Throughout the early twentieth century, the New Woman continued on in spirit. Her message for equality and independence for English women was not forgotten and even carried on into other countries around the world. With her spunk, radical viewpoints, and desire for change, the New Woman movement left its mark on English society then, and still echoes on today.

The works in this collection were chosen to represent the many manifestations of the New Woman in late 19th-century British literature. Starting with Sarah Grand's "A New Aspect on the Woman Question," each essay, play, and short story brings to life the progressive female character that so many advocated for and against. The works reprinted here reveal the New Woman's desire for change, demand for public respect, and support of women's rights. Her reformist plots opened doors for women today, and with the reprinting of these works, contemporary readers can relive the efforts of the *fin de siècle* New Woman.

LOGAN E. GEE

---

5 Statesman's Year Book, 1911

IMAGES FROM *PUNCH*

THINGS ONE WOULD RATHER HAVE LEFT UNSAID.

She. "Would you mind putting my Lawn-Tennis Shoes in your Pockets, Mr. Green?"
He. "I'm afraid my Pockets are hardly big enough, Miss Gladys; but I shall be delighted to carry them for you!"

Image A: "Things One Would Rather Have Left Unsaid" published July 18, 1885

Image B: "The Sterner Sex!" published September 26, 1891

THE NEW WOMAN.

"You 're not leaving us, Jack! Tea will be here directly!"
"Oh, I'm going for a Cup of Tea in the Servants' Hall. I can't get on without Female Society, you know!"

Image C: "The New Woman" published June 15, 1895

RATIONAL COSTUME.

The Vicar of St. Winifred-in-the-Wold (to fair Bicyclists) It is customary for Men, I will not say Gentlemen, to remove their Hats on entering a Church!"
Confusion of the Ladies Rota and Iniona Bykewell.

Image D: "Rational Costume" published June 13, 1896

A Timeline for the New Woman

1792   Mary Wollstonecraft publishes *A Vindication of the Rights of Woman*

1841   July—*Punch*, The London Charivari is first published

1850   The Woman Question debate is featured in the writings of Harriet Martineau, an English essayist, journalist, and economic writer

1857   Divorce and Matrimonial Causes Act allows women conditional divorce

1864   The Contagious Diseases Acts are introduced into English Society

1867   The National Society for Women's Suffrage is founded

1870   Married Women's Property Acts allow women control over their earned income

1882   The Second Women's Property Act allows women the right to maintain control over their own property

1883   *Story of an African Farm* by Olive Schreiner is published

1886   The Contagious Diseases Acts are repealed

1888   October—The *Women's Penny Paper*, one of the first women-focused periodicals, is founded by Henrietta Muller

1892   April—The *Women's Penny Paper* becomes the *Women's Herald* and Mrs. Frank Morrison takes over as editor of the paper

1893   *Keynotes* by George Egerton is published

           The Odd Women by George Gissing is published

           The *Women's Herald* becomes the *Woman's Signal* and Lady Henry Somerset takes over as editor of the paper

1894   *Discords* by George Egerton is published

           March—The New Aspect of the Woman Question by Sarah Grand is published in *The North American Review*, Vol. 158 No. 448

           May—The New Woman by Ouida is published in *The North American Review*, Vol. 158 No. 450

1894   *The New Woman* by Sydney Grundy is produced
        Our Manifold Nature by Sarah Grand is published

1895   *The Notorious Mrs. Ebbsmith* by Sir Arthur W. Pinero is produced
        Jude the Obscure by Thomas Hardy is published

1897   *The Morality of Marriage and Other Essays on the Status and Destiny of Women* by Mona Caird is published
        Symphonies by George Egerton is published
        Dracula by Bram Stoker is published

1898   The National Union of Women's Suffrage Societies (NUWSS) formed by existing suffrage societies

1889   The final issue of the *Woman's Signal* is printed

1900   The *Fin de siècle* comes to an end and the New Woman character fades from English society

1901   Queen Victoria Dies

1903   The Women's Social and Political Union (WSPU) is formed

1914   World War I breaks out and disrupts the women's suffrage movement, but allows more women into the workplace

1918   The Representation of the People Act is passed and women over 30 are granted the right to vote

1928   The right to vote granted to women 21 and over

SELECTED BIBLIOGRAPHY

Collins, Tracy J. R. "Athletic Fashion, 'Punch', and the Creation of the New Woman." Victorian Periodicals Review, vol. 43, no. 3, 2010, pp. 309–335. JSTOR, JSTOR, www.jstor.org/stable/41038818.

Foster, Shirley, editor. *Victorian Women's Fiction: Marriage, Freedom and the Individual.* Totowa, Barnes & Noble Books, 1985.

Heilmann, Ann. *New Women Fiction: Women Writing First-Wave Feminism.* New York, St. Martin's Press, LLC., 2000.

MacPike, Loralee. "The New Woman, Childbearing, and the Reconstruction of Gender, 1880-1900." NWSA Journal, vol. 1, no. 3, 1989, pp. 368–397. JSTOR, JSTOR, www.jstor.org/stable/4315921.

Mangum, Teresa. *Married, Middlebrow, and Militant: Sarah Grand and the New Woman Novel.* Ann Arbor, University of Michigan Press, 1998.

Purdue, Melissa, and Stacey Floyd, editors. *New Woman Writers, Authority, and the Body.* Newcastle Upon Tyne, Cambridge Scholars Publishing, 2009.

Richardson, LeeAnn M. *New Woman and Colonial Adventure Fiction in Victorian Britain: Gender, Genre, and Empire.* Gainsville, University Press of Florida, 2006.

Sutherland, Gillian. *In Search of the New Woman: Middle-Class and Work in Britain 1870-1914.* Cambridge, Cambridge University Press, 2015.

Tusan, Michelle Elizabeth. "Inventing the New Woman: Print Culture and Identity Politics during the Fin-De-Siecle: 1997 VanArsdel Prize." Victorian Periodicals Review, vol. 31, no. 2, 1998, pp. 169–182. JSTOR, JSTOR, www.jstor.org/stable/20083064.

Walls, Elizabeth MacLeod. "'A Little Afraid of the Women of Today': The Victorian New Woman and the Rhetoric of British Modernism." Rhetoric Review, vol. 21, no. 3, 2002, pp. 229–246. JSTOR, JSTOR, www.jstor.org/stable/3093009.

Young, Emma and James Bailey. *British Women Short Story Writers: The New Woman to Now.* Edinburgh, Edinburgh University Press, 2015.

TABLE OF CONTENTS

CROSSING THE LINE
THE NEW WOMAN OF THE FIN DE SIÈCLE

NEW WOMAN ESSAYS

The New Aspect of the Woman Question

Sarah Grand

1894

IT IS AMUSING as well as interesting to note the pause which the new aspect of the woman question has given to the Bawling Brothers who have hitherto tried to howl down every attempt on the part of our sex to make the world a pleasanter place to live in. That woman should ape man and desire to change places with him was conceivable to him as he stood on the hearth-rug in his lord-and-master-monarch-of-all-I-survey attitude, well inflated with his own conceit; but that she should be content to develop the good material which she finds in herself and be only dissatisfied with the poor quality of that which is being offered to her in man, her mate, must appear to him to be a thing as monstrous as it is unaccountable. "If women don't want to be men, what do they want?" asked the Bawling Brotherhood when the first misgiving of the truth flashed upon them; and then, to reassure themselves, they pointed to a certain sort of woman in proof of the contention that we were all unsexing ourselves.

It would be as rational for us now to declare that men generally are Bawling Brothers or to adopt the hasty conclusion which makes all men out to be fiends on the one hand and all women fools on the other. We have our Shrieking Sisterhood, as the counterpart of the Bawling Brotherhood. The latter consists of two sorts of men. First of all is he who is satisfied with the cow-kind of woman as being most convenient; it is the threat of any strike among his domestic cattle for more consideration that irritates him into loud and angry protests. The other sort of Bawling Brother is he who is under the influence of the scum of our sex, who knows nothing better than women of that class in and out of society, preys upon them or ruins himself for them, takes his whole tone from them, and judges us all by them. Both the cow-woman and the scum-woman are well within range of the comprehension of the Bawling Brotherhood, but the new woman is a little above him, and he never even thought of looking up to where she has been sitting apart in silent contemplation all these years, thinking and thinking, until at last she solved the problem and proclaimed for herself what was wrong with Home-is-the-Woman's-Sphere, and prescribed the remedy.

1

What she perceived at the outset was the sudden and violent upheaval of the suffering sex in all parts of the world. Women were awaking from their long apathy, and, as they awoke, like healthy hungry children unable to articulate, they began to whimper for they knew not what. They might have been easily satisfied at that time had not society, like an ill-conditioned and ignorant nurse, instead of finding out what they lacked, shaken them and beaten them and stormed at them until what was once a little wail became convulsive shrieks and roused up the whole human househould. Then man, disturbed by the uproar, came upstairs all anger and irritation, and, without waiting to learn what was the matter, added his own old theories to the din, but, finding they did not act rapidly, formed new ones, and made an intolerable nuisance of himself with his opinions and advice. He was in the state of one who cannot comprehend because he has no faculty to perceive the thing in question, and that is why he was so positive. The dimmest perception that you may be mistaken will save you from making an ass of yourself.

We must look upon man's mistakes, however, with some leniency, because we are not blameless in the matter ourselves. We have allowed him to arrange the whole social system and manage or mismanage it all these ages without ever seriously examining his work with a view to considering whether his abilities and his motives were sufficiently good to qualify him for the task. We have listened without a smile to his preachments, about our place in life and all we are good for, on the text that "there is no understanding a woman." We have endured most poignant misery for his sins, and screened him when we should have exposed him and had him punished. We have allowed him to exact all things of us, and have been content to accept the little he grudgingly gave us in return. We have meekly bowed our heads when he called us bad names instead of demanding proofs of the superiority which alone would give him a right to do so. We have listened much edified to man's sermons on the subject of virtue, and have acquiesced uncomplainingly in the convenient arrangement by which this quality has come to be altogether practised for him by us vicariously. We have seen him set up Christ as an example for all men to follow, which argues his belief in the possibility of doing so, and have not only allowed his weakness and hypocrisy in the matter to pass without comment, but, until lately, have not even seen the humor of his pretensions when contrasted with his practices nor held him up to that wholesome ridicule which is a stimulating corrective. Man deprived us of all proper education, and then jeered at us because we had no knowledge. He narrowed our outlook on life so that our view of it should be all distorted, and then declared that our mistaken impression of it proved us to be senseless creatures. He cramped our minds so that there was no room for reason in them, and then made merry at our want of logic. Our divine intuition was not to be controlled by him, but he did his best to damage it by sneering at it as an inferior feminine method of arriving at conclusions; and finally, after having had his own way until he lost his head completely, he set himself up as a sort of a god and required us to worship him, and, to our eternal shame be it said, we did so. The truth has all along been in us, but we have cared more for man than for truth, and so the whole human race has suffered. We have failed of our effect by neglecting our duty here, and have deserved much of the obloquy that was cast upon us. All that is over now, however, and while on the one hand man has shrunk to his true proportions in our estimation, we, on the other, have been expanding to our own; and now we come confidently forward to maintain, not that this or that was "intended," but that there are in ourselves, in both sexes, possibilities hither to suppressed or abused, which, when properly developed, will supply to either what is lacking in the other.

The man of the future will be better, while the woman will be stronger and wiser. To bring this about is the whole aim and object of the present struggle, and with the discovery of the means lies the solution of the Woman Question. Man, having no conception of himself as imperfect from the woman's point of view, will find this difficult to understand, but we know his weakness, and will be patient with him, and help him with his lesson. It is the woman's place and pride and pleasure to teach the child, and man morally is in his infancy. There have been times when there was a doubt as to whether he was to be raised or woman was to be lowered, but we have turned that corner at last; and now woman holds out a strong hand to the child-man, and insists, but with infinite tenderness and pity, upon helping him up.

He must be taught consistency. There are ideals for him which it is to be presumed that he tacitly agrees to accept when he keeps up an expensive establishment to teach them: let him live up to them. Man's faculty for shirking his own responsibility has been carried to such an extent in the past that, rather than be blamed himself when it did not answer to accuse woman, he imputed the whole consequence of his own misery-making peculiarities to God.

But with all his assumption man does not make the most of himself. He has had every advantage of training to increase his insight, for instance, but yet we find him, even at this time of day, unable to perceive that woman has a certain amount of self-respect and practical good sense— enough at all events to enable her to use the proverb about the bird in the hand to her own advantage. She does not in the least intend to sacrifice the privileges she enjoys on the chance of obtaining others, especially of the kind which man seems to think she must aspire to as so much more desirable. Woman may be foolish, but her folly has never been greater than man's conceit, and the one is not more disastrous to the understanding than the other. When a man talks about knowing the world and having lived and that sort of thing, he means something objectionable; in seeing life he generally includes doing wrong; and it is in these respects he is apt to accuse us of wishing to ape him. Of old if a woman ventured to be at all unconventional, man was allowed to slander her with the imputation that she must be abandoned, and he really believed it because with him liberty meant license. He has never accused us of trying to emulate him in any noble, manly quality, because the cultivation of noble qualities has not hitherto been a favorite pursuit of his, not to the extent at least of entering into his calculations and making any perceptible impression on public opinion; and he never, therefore, thought of considering whether it might have attractions for us. The cultivation of noble qualities has been individual rather than general, and the person who practised it is held to be one apart, if not actually eccentric. Man acknowledges that the business of life carried on according to his methods corrodes, and the state of corrosion is a state of decay; and yet he is fatuous enough to imagine that our ambition must be to lie like him for our own benefit in every public capacity. Heaven help the child to perceive with what travail and sorrow we submit to the heavy obligation, when it is forced upon us by our sense of right, of showing him how things ought to be done.

We have been reproached by Ruskin for shutting ourselves up behind park palings and garden walls, regardless of the waste world that moans in misery without, and that has been too much our attitude; but the day of our acquiescence is over. There is that in ourselves which forces us out of our apathy; we have no choice in the matter. When we hear the "Help! help! help!" of the desolate and the oppressed, and still more when we see the awful dumb despair of those who have lost even the hope of help, we must respond. This is often inconvenient to man, especially when he has seized upon a defenceless victim whom he would have destroyed had we not come to the rescue; and so, because it is inconvenient to be exposed and thwarted, he snarls about the end of all true womanliness, cants on the subject of the Sphere, and threatens that if we do not sit still at home with cotton-wool in our ears so that we cannot be stirred into having our sympathies aroused by his victims when they shriek, and with shades over our eyes that we may not see him in his degradation, we shall be afflicted with short hair, coarse skins, unsymmetrical figures, loud voices, tastelessness in dress, and an unattractive appearance and character generally, and then he will not love us any more or marry us. And this is one of the most amusing of his threats, because he has said and proved on so many occasions that he cannot live without us whatever we are. O man! man! you are a very funny fellow now we know you! But take care. The standard of your pleasure and convenience has already ceased to be our conscience. On one point, however, you may reassure yourself. True womanliness is not in danger, and the sacred duties of wife and mother will be all the more honorably performed when women have a reasonable hope of becoming wives and mothers of men. But there is the difficulty. The trouble is not because women are mannish, but because men grow ever more effeminate. Manliness is at a premium now because there is so little of it, and we are accused of aping men in order to conceal the side from which the contrast should evidently be drawn. Man in his manners becomes more and more wanting until we seem to be near the time when there will be nothing left of him but the old Adam, who said, "It wasn't me."

Of course it will be retorted that the past has been improved upon in our day; but that is not a fair comparison. We walk by the electric light: our ancestors had only oil-lamps. We can see what we are doing and where we are going, and should be as much better as we know how to be. But where are our men? Where is the chivalry, the truth, and affection, the earnest purpose, the plain living, high thinking, and noble self-sacrifice that make a man? We look in vain among the bulk of our writers even for appreciation of these qualities. With the younger men all that is usually cultivated is that flippant smartness which is synonymous with cheapness. There is such a want of wit amongst them, too, such a lack of variety, such monotony of threadbare subjects worked to death! Their "comic" papers subsist upon repetitions of those three venerable jests, the mother-in-law, somebody drunk, and an edifying deception successfully practised by an un faithful husband or wife. As they have nothing true so they have nothing new to give us, nothing either to expand the heart or move us to happy mirth. Their ideas of beauty threaten always to be satisfied with the ballet dancer's legs, pretty things enough in their way, but not worth mentioning as an aid to the moral, intellectual, and physical strength that make a man. They are sadly deficient in imagination, too; that old fallacy to which they cling, that because an evil thing has always been, therefore it must always continue, is as much the result of want of imagination as of the man's trick of evading the responsibility of seeing right done in any matter that does not immediately affect his personal comfort. But there is one thing the younger men are specially good at, and that is giving their opinion; this they do to each other's admiration until they verily believe it to be worth something. Yet they do not even know where we are in the history of the world. One of them only lately, doubtless by way of ingratiating himself with the rest of the Bawling Brotherhood, actually proposed to reintroduce the Acts of the Apostles-of-the-Pavements; he was apparently quite unaware of the fact that the mothers of the English race are too strong to allow themselves to be insulted by the reimposition of another most shocking degradation upon their sex. Let him who is responsible for the economic position which forces women down be punished for the consequence. If any are unaware of cause and effect in that matter, let them read The Struggle for Life which the young master wrote in Wreckage. As the workingman says with Christ-like compassion: "They wouldn't be there, poor things, if they were not driven to it."

There are upwards of a hundred thousand women in London doomed to damnation by the written law of man if they dare to die, and to infamy for a livelihood if they must live; yet the man at the head of affairs wonders what it is that we with the power are protesting against in the name of our sex. But is there any wonder we women wail for the dearth of manliness when we find men from end to end of their rotten social system forever doing the most cowardly deed in their own code, striking at the defenceless woman, especially when she is down?

The Bawling Brotherhood have been seeing reflections of themselves lately which did not flatter them, but their conceit survives, and they cling confidently to the delusion that they are truly all that is admirable, and it is the mirror that is in fault. Mirrors may be either a distorting or a flattering medium, but women do not care to see life any longer in a glass darkly. Let there be light. We suffer in the first shock of it. We shriek in horror at what we discover when it is turned on that which was hidden away in dark corners; but the first principle of good housekeeping is to have no dark corners, and as we recover ourselves we go to work with a will to sweep them out. It is for us to set the human household in order, to see to it that all is clean and sweet and comfortable for the men who are fit to help us to make home in it. We are bound to raise the dust while we are at work, but only those who are in it will suffer any inconvenience from it, and the self-sufficing and self-supporting are not afraid. For the rest it will be all benefits. The Woman Question is the Marriage Question, as shall be shown hereafter.

THE NEW WOMAN

OUIDA

1894

IT CAN SCARCELY be disputed, I think, that in the English language there are conspicuous at the present moment two words which designate two unmitigated bores: The Workingman and the Woman. The Workingman and the Woman, the New Woman, be it remembered, meet us at every page of literature written in the English tongue; and each is convinced that on its own especial W hangs the future of the world. Both he and she want to have their values artificially raised and rated, and a status given to them by favor in lieu of dessert. In an age in which persistent clamor is generally crowned by success they have both obtained considerable attention; is it offensive to say much more of it than either deserves? Your contributor avers that the Cow-Woman and the Scum-Woman, man understands; but that the New Woman is above him. The elegance of these appellatives is not calculated to recommend them to readers of either sex; and as a specimen of style forces one to hint that the New Woman who, we are told, "has been sitting apart in silent contemplation all these years" might in all these years have studied better models of literary composition. We are farther on told "that the dimmest perception that you may be mistaken, will save you from making an ass of yourself." It appears that even this dimmest perception has never dawned upon the New Woman.

We are farther told that "thinking and thinking" in her solitary sphynx-like contemplation she solved the problem and prescribed the remedy (the remedy to a problem!); but what this remedy was we are not told, nor did the New Woman apparently disclose it to the rest of womankind, since she still hears them in "sudden and violent upheaval" like "children unable to articulate whimpering for they know not what." It is sad to reflect that they might have been "easily satisfied at that time" (at what time?), "but society stormed at them until what was a little wail became convulsive shrieks"; and we are not told why the New Woman who had "the remedy for the problem," did not immediately produce it. We are not told either in what country or at what epoch this startling upheaval of volcanic womanhood

7

took place in which "man merely made himself a nuisance with his opinions and advice," but apparently did quell this wailing and gnashing of teeth since it would seem that he has managed still to remain more masterful than he ought to be.

We are further informed that women "have allowed him to arrange the whole social system and manage or mismanage it all these ages without ever seriously examining his work with a view to considering whether his abilities and his methods were sufficiently good to qualify him for the task."

There is something deliciously comical in the idea, this suggested, that man has only been allowed to "manage or mismanage" the world because woman has graciously refrained from preventing his doing so. But the comic side of this pompous and solemn assertion does not for a moment offer itself to the New Woman sitting and aloof in her solitary meditation on the superiority of her sex. For the New Woman there is no such thing as a joke. She has listened without a smile to her enemy's "preachments"; she has "endured poignant misery for his sins," she has "meekly bowed her head" when he called her bad names; and she has never asked for "any proof of the superiority" which could alone have given him a right to use such naughty expressions. The truth has all along been in the possession of woman; but strange and sad perversity of taste! she has "cared more for man than for truth, and so the whole human race has suffered!"

"All that is over, however," we are told, and "while on the one hand man has shrunk to his true proportions" she has, all the time of this shrinkage, been herself expanding, and has in a word come to "fancy herself" extremely. So that he has no longer the slightest chance of imposing upon her by his game-cock airs.

Man, "having no conception of himself as imperfect," will find this difficult to understand at first; but the New Woman "knows his weakness," and will "help him with his lesson." "*Man morally is in his infancy*." There have been times when there was a doubt as to whether he was to be raised to her level, or woman to be lowered to his, but we "have turned that corner at last and now woman holds out a strong hand to the child-man and insists upon helping him up." The child-man (Bismarck? Herbert Spencer? Edison? Gladstone? Alexander III.? Lord Dufferin? the Duc d'Aumale?) the child-man must have his tottering baby steps guided by the New Woman, and he must be taught to live up to his ideals. To live up to an ideal, whether our own or somebody else's, is a painful process; but man must be made to do it. For, oddly enough, we are assured that despite "all his assumption he does not make the best of himself," which is not wonderful if he be still only in his infancy; and he has the incredible stupidity to be blind to the fact that "woman has self-respect and good sense," and that "she does not in the least intend to sacrifice the privileges she enjoys on the chance of obtaining others."

I have written amongst other *pensées éparses* which will some day see the light, the following reflection:

> *L'école nouvelle des femmes libres oublée qu'on ne puisse pas a la fait combattre l'homme sur son propre terrain et attendre de lui des politesses, des tendresses et des galanteries. Il ne faut pas aux même moment prendre de l'homme son chaise à l'Université et sa place dans l'omnibus; si on lui arrâche son gagnepain, on ne peut pas exiger qu'il offre aussi sa parapluie.*[1]

The whole kernel of the question lies in this. Your contributor says that the New Woman will not her present privileges; *i.e.*, she will still expect the man to stand that she may sit; the man to get wet through that she may use his umbrella. But if she retain these privileges she can only do so by an appeal to his chivalry, *i.e.*, by a confession that she is weaker than he. But she does not want to do this: she wants to get the comforts and the concessions due to feebleness, at the same time as she demands the lion's share of power due to superior force alone. It is this overweening and unreasonable grasping at both positions which will end in making her odious to man and in her being probably kicked back roughly by him into the seclusion of a harem.

Before me lies an engraving in an illustrated journal of a woman's meeting; whereat a woman is demanding in the name of her sovereign sex the right to vote at political elections. The speaker is middle-aged and plain of feature; she wears an inverted plate on her head tied on with strings under her double-chin; she has balloon-sleeves, a bodice tight to bursting, a waist of ludicrous dimensions in proportion to her portly person; she is gesticulating with one hand, of which all the fingers are stuck out in ungraceful defiance of all artistic laws of gesture. Now, why cannot this orator learn to gesticulate and learn to dress, instead of clamoring for a franchise? She violates in her own person every law, alike of common-sense and artistic fitness, and yet comes forward as a fit and proper person to make laws for others. She is an exact representative of her sex.

Woman, whether new or old, has immense fields of culture untilled, immense areas of influence wholly neglected. She does almost nothing with the resources she possesses, because her whole energy is concentrated on desiring and demanding those she has not. She can write and print anything she chooses; and she scarcely ever takes the pains to acquire correct grammar or elegance of style before wasting ink and paper. She can paint and model any subjects she chooses, but she imprisons herself in men's *atéliers* to endeavor to steal their technique and their methods, and thus loses any originality she might possess. Her influence on children might be so great that through them she would practically rule the future of the world; but she delegates her influence to the vile school boards if she

1   "The new school of liberated women forgets that you may not battle a man on his own turf and still expect his politeness, his affections, his gallantry. You needn't s multaneously remove a man from his chair at the university and his seat on the bus; if you steal his livelihood, you can't demand that he offer his umbrella."

be poor, and if she be rich to governesses and tutors; nor does she in ninety-nine cases out of a hundred ever attempt to educate or control herself into fitness for the personal exercise of such influence. Her precept and example in the treatment of the animal creation might be of infinite use in mitigating the hideous tyranny of humanity over them, but she does little or nothing to this effect; she wears dead birds and the skins of dead creatures; she hunts the hare and shoots the pheasant, she drives and rides with more brutal recklessness than men; she watches with delight the struggles of the dying salmon, of the gralloched deer; she keeps her horses standing in snow and fog for hours with the muscles of their heads and necks tied up in the torture of the bearing rein; when asked to do anything for a stray dog, a lame horse, a poor man's donkey, she is very sorry, but she has so many claims on her already; she never attempts by orders to her household, to her *fournisseurs*, to her dependents, to obtain some degree of mercy in the treatment of sentient creatures and in the methods of their slaughter.

The immense area which lies open to her in private life is almost entirely uncultivated, yet she wants to be admitted into public life. Public life is already overcrowded, verbose, incompetent, fussy, and foolish enough without the addition of her in her sealskin coat with the dead humming bird on her hat. Woman in public life would exaggerate the failings of men, and would not have even their few excellencies. Their legislation would be, as that of men is too often, the offspring of panic or prejudice; and she would not put on the drag of common-sense as man frequently does in public assemblies. There would be little to hope from her humanity, nothing from her liberality; for when she is frightened she is more ferocious than he, and when she has power more merciless.

"Men," says your contributor, "deprived us of all proper education and then jeered at us because we had no knowledge." How far is this based on facts? Could not Lady Jane Grey learn Greek and Latin as she chose? Could not Hypatia lecture? Were George Sand or Mrs. Somerville withheld from study? Could not in every age every woman choose a Corinna or Cordelia as her type? become either Helen or Penelope? If the vast majority have not either the mental or physical gifts to become either, that was Nature's fault, not man's. Aspasia and Adelina Patti were born, not made. In all eras and all climes a woman of great genius or of great beauty has done what she chose; and if the majority of women have led obscure lives, so have the majority of men. The chief part of humanity is insignificant, whether it be male or female. In most people there is very little character indeed, and as little mind. Those who have much never fail to make their marks, be they of which sex they may.

The unfortunate idea that there is no good education without a college curriculum is as injurious as it is erroneous. The college education may have excellencies for men in its *frottement*, its preparation for the world, its rough destruction of personal conceit; but for women it can only be hardening and deforming. If study be delightful to a women, she will find her way to it as the hart to water brooks. The author of *Aurora Leigh* was not only always at home, but she was an invalid; yet she became a fine classic, and found her path to fame. A college curriculum would have done nothing to improve her rich and beautiful mind; it might have done much to debase it.

The perpetual contact of men with other men may be good for them, but the perpetual contact of women with other women is very far from good. The publicity of a college must be odious to a young girl of refined and delicate feeling.

The "Scum-woman" and the "Cow-woman," to quote the elegant phraseology of your contributor, are both of them less of a menace to humankind than the New Woman with her fierce vanity, her undigested knowledge, her over-weening estimate of her own value and her fatal want of all sense of the ridiculous.

When scum comes to the surface it renders a great service to the substance which it leaves behind it; when the cow yields pure nourishment to the young and the suffering, her place is blessed in the realm of nature; but when the New Woman splutters blistering wrath on mankind she is merely odious and baneful.

The error of the New Woman (as of many an old one) lies in speaking of women as the victims of men, and entirely ignoring the frequency with which men are the victims of women. In nine cases out of ten the first to corrupt the youth is the woman. In nine cases out of ten also she becomes corrupt herself because she likes it.

It is all very well to say that prostitutes were at the beginning of their career victims of seduction; but it is not probable and it is not provable. Love of drink and of finery, and a dislike to work, are the more likely motives and origin. It never seems to occur to the accusers of man that women are just as vicious and as lazy as he is in nine cases out of ten, and need no invitation from him to become so.

A worse prostitution than that of the streets, *i.e.*, that of loveless marriages of convenience, are brought about by women, not by men. In such unions the man always gives much more than he gains, and the woman in almost every instance is persuaded or driven into it by women – her mother, her sisters, her acquaintances. It is rarely that the father interferes to bring about such a marriage.

In even what is called a well-assorted marriage, the man is frequently sacrificed to the woman. As I wrote long ago, Andrea del Sarte's wife has many sisters. Correggio dying of the burden of the family, has many brothers. Men of genius are often dragged to earth by their wives. In our own day a famous statesman is made very ridiculous by his wife; frequently the female influences brought to bear on him render a man of great and original powers and disinterested character, a time-server, a conventionalist, a mere seeker of place. Woman may help man sometimes, but she certainly more often hinders him. Her self-esteem is immense and her self-knowledge very small. I view with dread for the future of the world the power which modern inventions place in the hands of woman. Hitherto her physical weakness has restrained her in a great measure from violent action; but a woman can make a bomb and throw it, can fling vitriol, and fire a repeating revolver as well as any man can. These are precisely the deadly, secret, easily handled modes of warfare and revenge, which will commend themselves to her ferocious feebleness.

Jules Ruchard has written:

> *J'ai professé de l'anatomie pendant des longues années, j'ai passé une bonne partie de ma vie dans les amphithéâtres, mais je n'en ai pas moins éprouvé un sentiment penible en trouvant dans toutes les maisons d'education des squilettes d'animaux et des mannequins anatomiques entre les mains des fillettes.*[2]

I suppose this passage will be considered as an effort "to withhold knowledge from women," but it is one which is full of true wisdom and honorable feeling. When you have taken her into the physiological and chemical laboratories, when you have extinguished pity in her, and given weapons to her dormant cruelty which she can use in secret, you will hoist with you own petard—your pupil will be your tyrant, and then she will meet with the ultimate fate of all tyrants.

In the pages of this REVIEW as physician has lamented the continually increasing unwillingness of women of the world to bear children, and the consequent increase of ill-health, whilst to avoid child-bearing is being continually preached to the working classes by those who call themselves their friends.

The elegant epithet of Cow-woman implies the contempt with which maternity is viewed by the New Woman who thinks it something fine to vote at vestries, and shout at meetings, and lay bare the spines of living animals, and haul the gasping salmon from the river pool, and hustle male students off the benches of amphitheatres.

Modesty is no doubt a thing of education or prejudice, a conventionality artificially stimulated; but it is an exquisite grace, and womanhood without it loses its most subtle charm. Nothing tends so to destroy modesty as the publicity and promiscuity of schools, of hotels, of railway trains and sea voyages. True modesty shrinks from the curious gaze of other women as from the coarser gaze of man.

Men, moreover, are in all except the very lowest classes more careful of their talk before young girls than women are. It is very rarely that a man does not respect real innocence; but women frequently do not. The jest, the allusion, the story which sullies her mind and awakes her inquisitiveness, will much oftener be spoken by women than men. It is not from her brothers, nor her brother's friends, but from her female companions that

2   "I've taught anatomy for many years, I've spent a good part of my life in operating theatres, but I have nothing but the most painful reaction to finding, in all the halls of learning, animal skeletons and anatomical mannekins in the hands of young girls."

she will understand what the grosser laugh of those around her suggests. The biological and pathological curricula complete the loveless disflowering of her maiden soul.

Everything which tends to obliterate the contrast of the sexes, like your mixture of boys and girls in your American common schools, tends also to destroy the charm of intercourse, the savor and sweetness of life. Seclusion lends an infinite seduction to the girl, as the rude and bustling publicity of modern life robs woman of her grace. Packed like herrings in a railway carriage, sleeping in odious vicinity to strangers on a shelf, going days and nights without a bath, exchanging decency and privacy for publicity and observation, the women who travel, save those rich enough to still purchase seclusion, are forced to cast aside all refinement and delicacy.

It is said that travel enlarges the mind. There are many minds which can no more be enlarged, by any means whatever, than a nut or a stone. The fool remains a fool, though you carry him or her about over the whole surface of the globe, and it is certain that the promiscuous contact and incessant publicity of travel, which may not hurt the man, do injure the woman.

Neither men nor women of genius are, I repeat, any criterion for the rest of their sex; nay, they belong, as Plato placed them, to a third sex which is above the laws of the multitude. But even whilst they do so they are always the foremost to recognize that it is the difference, not the likeness, of sex which makes the charm of human life. Barry Cornwall wrote long ago:

As the man beholds the woman,
    As the woman sees the man;
Curiously they note each other,
    As each other only can.

Never can the man divest her
    Of that mystic charm of sex;
Ever must she, gazing on him,
    That same mystic charm annex.

That mystic charm will long endure despite the efforts to destroy is of orators in tight stays and balloon sleeves, who scream from platforms, and the beings so justify abhorred of Mrs. Lynn Lynton, who smoke in public carriages and from the waist upward are indistinguishable from the men they profess to despise.

But every word, whether written or spoken, which urges the woman to antagonism against the man, every word which is written or spoken to try and make of her a hybrid, self-contained, opponent of men, makes a rift in the lute to which the world looks for its sweetest music.

The New Woman reminds me of an agriculturist who, discarding a fine farm of his own, and leaving it to nettles, stones, thistles, and wire-worms, should spend his whole time in demanding neighboring fields which are not his. The New Woman will not even look at the extent of ground indisputably her own, which she leaves unweeded and untilled.

Not to speak of the entire guidance of childhood, which is certainly already chiefly in the hands of woman (and of which her use does not do her much honor), so long as she goes to see one of her own sex dancing in a lion's den, the lions being meanwhile terrorized by a male brute; so long as she wears dead birds as millinery and dead seals as coats; so long as she goes to see an American lashing horses to death in idiotic contest with velocipedes; so long as she curtsies before princess and emperors who reward the winners of distance-rides; so long as she receives physiologists in her drawing-rooms, and trusts to them in her maladies; so long as she invades literature without culture and art without talent; so long as she orders her court-dress in a hurry; so long as she makes no attempt to interest herself in her servant, in her animals, in the poor slaves of her tradespeople; so long as she shows herself as she does at present without scruple at every brutal and debasing spectacle which is considered fashionable; so long as she understands nothing of the beauty of meditation, of solitude, of Nature; so long as she is utterly incapable of keeping her sons out of the shambles of modern sport, and lifting her daughters above the pestilent miasma of modern society—so long as she does not, can not, or will not either do, or cause to do, any of these things, she has no possible title or capacity to demand the place or the privilege of man.

MARRIAGE

MONA CAIRD

From THE MORALITY OF MARRIAGE AND OTHER ESSAYS ON THE
STATUS AND DESTINY OF WOMEN 1897

PART I - THE PIONEER OF CIVILISATION

*"Now I could multiply witness upon witness . . . I could go back into the mythical
teaching of the most ancient times, and show you how . . . that great Egyptian
people, wisest then of nations, gave to their Spirit of Wisdom the form of a woman;
and into her hand for a symbol, the weaver's shuttle; and how the name and
form of that spirit adopted, believed, and obeyed by the Greeks, became that
Athena of the olive-helm and cloudy shield, to whose faith you owe, down to this
date, whatever you hold most precious in art, in literature, or in types of national
virtue."*—RUSKIN, "Sesame and Lilies."

THERE IS NO social philosophy, however logical and farseeing on other points,
which does not lapse into incoherence, as soon as it touches the subject of woman.
The thinker abandons the laws of reasoning which he has obeyed until that fatal
moment; he forgets every principle of science previously present to his mind,
and suddenly descends to a lower intellectual plane, making statements that any
schoolboy might scorn. Our philosopher—once so strict in logical inference—
takes the same view of women as certain Indian theologians took of the staple
food of their country. "The Great Spirit," they said, "made all things, except the
wild rice, but the wild rice came by chance."[3] Women are the wild rice of the
modern philosophical world. They are treated as if they alone were exempt from
the influences of natural selection, of the well-known effects upon organs and
aptitudes of continued use or disuse—effects which every one has exemplified in
his own life, which every profession proves, and which is freely acknowledged in
the discussion of all questions except those in which woman forms an important
element. "As she was in the beginning, is now, and ever shall be . . ."

There is a strange irony in this binding of women to the evil results, in their
own natures, of the restrictive injustice which they have suffered for generations.

---

3 Tylor's "Primitive Culture."

15

We chain up a dog to keep watch over our home; we deny him freedom, and in some cases, alas! even sufficient exercise to keep his limbs supple and his body in health. He becomes dull and spiritless, he is miserable and ill-looking, and if by any chance he is let loose, he gets into mischief and runs away. He has not been used to liberty or happiness, and he cannot stand it.

Humane people ask his master: "Why do you keep that dog always chained up?"

"Oh! he is accustomed to it; he is suited for the chain; when we set him free he runs wild."

So the dog is punished by chaining, for the misfortune of having been chained, till death releases him.

In the same way, we have subjected women for centuries to influences which called forth a particular set of activities; we have rigorously excluded (even punished) every other development of power; and we have then insisted that the consequent overwrought instincts and adaptations of structure are, by a sort of compound interest, to go on adding to the distortions themselves, and at the same time to go on forming a more and more solid ground for preserving the restrictive system. We *chain*, because we *have chained*. The dog must not be released, because his nature has adapted itself to the misfortune of captivity.

He has no revenge in his power; he must live and die, and no one knows his wretchedness. But the woman takes her unconscious vengeance, for she enters into the inmost life of society. *She* can pay back the injury with interest. And so she does, item by item. Through her, in a great measure, marriage becomes what Milton calls "a drooping and disconsolate household captivity," and through her influence over children she is able to keep going much physical weakness and disease which might, with a little knowledge, be readily stamped out; she is able to oppose new ideas by the early implanting of prejudice; in short, she can hold back the wheels of progress, and send into the world human beings likely to wreck every attempt at social reorganisation that may be made, whether it be made by men or by gods.[4]

---

4   Gibbon, in speaking of the effect of continued bondage and contempt upon a particular class, says that such conditions appear to degrade the character and to have rendered them "almost as incapable as they were supposed to be of conceiving any generous sentiment, or of performing any worthy action."

Indeed, it needs no Gibbon to tell us this. The effect upon the human being of consistent discouragement and contempt can be studied daily, if we care to open our eyes.

A child can be made actually stupid by incessantly assuring him that he is so, and nothing is easier than to deprive a person of the ability to perform a task by surrounding him with a penetrating atmosphere of discouragement, and unbelief in the possibility of his achievement. It is true that, in the case of certain individuals, the contemptuous discouragement may have the effect of inciting to stronger effort. But this can scarcely be the case with a whole class, still less with a whole sex, for the chances of breaking through the ramparts of human obstructiveness grow less and less, in proportion to the largeness of the class which is suffering the obstruction. For example: Suppose, in a Protestant land, a bigoted Roman Catholic

Seeing, then, that women are not a sort of human "wild rice," come by chance or special creation, no protest can be too strong against the unthinking use of the hackneyed arguments against their emancipation, arguments into which are packed an unmanageable host of begged questions.

Having made this protest, I propose to trace as carefully as is possible in the space of this and the three following articles (1) The part played by woman as the pioneer of civilisation; (2) the nature of her position in marriage and out of it, at the time of transition between mediaeval and modern times; and (3) her position at the present day.

Through improved means of communication, and facilities for learning, the swiftness with which social movements make way among modern communities has much increased. It is for this reason that any institution that now lags far behind quickly grows intolerable.

family subjected to petty domestic persecution a member converted to the Reformed Church. His position would be extremely unpleasant, without doubt; but still he could always find support and sympathy among his co-religionists, and could break through the thin walls of his immediate surroundings, and find asylum from the intolerance of his home in the outside world. Public opinion would be with him.

Take, again, the unlucky case of the son of wealthy parents, who insisted that, as it was unnecessary for the young man to make his living, it was his clear duty to remain at home by the fireside, playing chess with his father in the evenings, soothing his mother's declining years with pleasant chat about her neighbours, walking or driving with her in the afternoons, making knitted mittens for his sisters, paying afternoon calls, shopping, and writing innumerable letters to relations all over the world, in order to explain to them how his interesting family was passing its time.

Suppose, in short, that this young man is required to make himself generally useful and agreeable to everybody at every time, in forgetfulness of self and with untiring devotion to his appointed duties. If that young man failed to take the view of his duty insisted on by his parents, he would find no difficulty in refusing to comply with their demands. And he would find this facility, not by any means because the demands were preposterous, but because they were unusual. No parent, however angry, would be really heartbroken at the refusal of a son to dance attendance on the family at the domestic hearth, and the young man could refuse the office without feeling that he was dealing a real blow to affectionate and devoted relatives by so doing. After all, nobody really expects such conduct from a son, and therefore does not grieve if he acts otherwise.

But now take the case of a daughter in such a position. The scene instantly changes! Could *she* refuse to dedicate herself to the family, without inflicting a real and deadly wound on the hearts of her parents? Could *she* break through the prejudice of her home, and find friends, relatives, a whole public outside ready to support and approve her action? So far from finding support, she would have the whole body of average people dead against her, as well as her own training, fears, and the self-distrust bred of years of education in the school of feminine submission.

Instead of her brother's frank and flat refusal to comply with preposterous demands, the woman has to wait, to use tact, compromise, subterfuge, perhaps; to eat her heart out through years of fruitless efforts to gain a modicum of freedom without causing sorrow in the process. What miserable conflicts with tyrannous opinion, with selfish affection; what reproaches, wounded feelings, and heartache all this involves, could be told by many a woman of to-day, who has known the bitterness of these years of slow decay; of seeing her health, nerve, ability, hope, fretted to death in this cruel and baffling conflict with conditions which she is assured are only waiting to reward talent and determination!

It was impossible that the demand of women for freedom should become a feature of modern life, without the marriage-relation, as at present understood, being called in question. Their claim for freedom included—whether all who made it so intended or not—a claim for a modified marriage.

In the preceding articles, its varying primitive forms have been glanced at. No one who has convinced himself of the facts thus set forth will be able to believe in the finality of any particular form. He will be forced to recognise that the relationship between the sexes holds intimate connection with other social conditions. He will see that the subjection of a sex which may be maintained while that sex is economically dependent, can never be permanently established after that disadvantage is removed. He will then be also forced to recognise that our present ideas regarding marriage are founded on the fact of the pecuniary dependence of women—a dependence which has been the result rather of human injustice than of any natural disabilities of woman.

The legends and traditions of all ages and peoples go to show, that even as regards physical strength, women are by no means aboriginally inferior to men.[5] How the idea of their inferiority has arisen, in the face of so much

5   As for their personal valour, every reader of history knows that when occasion and opportunity concurred, women have shown themselves to possess this quality in the highest degree, and as rulers they have a brilliant record. It is difficult to find any country, principality, or city that has borne a great part in history which does not prove, on research, to have been founded, saved, or advanced in fortune by the influence of some remarkable woman. The history of Switzerland, for example, teems with instances of wise women rulers. Among these may be instanced the following:—The famous "Spinning Queen" Bertha, wife of the King of Burgundy (then a Swiss principality), is remembered with reverence, and called by the French Swiss "Mother of our Liberties." Hadwig, wife of Burkhardt of Rhoetia, was celebrated for her valour, learning, beauty, and goodness. Queen Agnes of Königsfelder was called in as umpire to decide the differences between Duke Albrecht of Habsburg and the Perpetual League, "this wondrously shrewd and quick woman who had for thirty years swayed the Habsburg politics." The Lady Abbess of Zurich, the Duchess of Wiirtemberg, and many other notable women have assisted in establishing the fortunes and liberties of Switzerland.

As for the remarkable women of Roman history, especially in later times, when more liberty was enjoyed by this sex, their names occur incessantly, and it is a striking fact that in almost every case when the affairs of State were guided by a woman, the Empire entered upon a period of comparative prosperity, and its downward impetus was for the time perceptibly slackened. Gibbon, who has a sovereign and frequently expressed contempt for women, yet is bound to give testimony to this fact. In illustration of this disdain of the historian for all women, the following may be instanced:—He first describes the admirable and vigorous administration of the great Queen Zenobia, who raised Palmyra almost to the position of a rival of Rome; he shows, moreover, that this had been accomplished at a time when the neighbouring states of Asia were sunk, one and all, in feebleness and corruption. Gibbon then adds: "Her sex alone rendered her an object of contempt." Not the most palpable and towering superiority could remove that eternal stigma of sex! Gibbon quotes the saying of Tacitus regarding the ancient German tribe: " The Silures are sunk even below servitude; they obey a woman."

The women of the Renaissance are of course proverbial for their brilliant learning and attainments, and many of the female saints enjoy a similar reputation. Catherine of Siena is perhaps the most widely celebrated among her sister martyrs. In the well-known picture at the Vatican St Catherine is represented as "appearing before the Emperor Maximilian, and carrying away by her knowledge a whole areopagus of philosohpers assembled to dispute with her."

evidence to the contrary, is not easy to understand. The notion is probably confined to those communities that we call civilised. It does not seem likely that savage tribes, whose hard work is done, and whose burdens are carried by their women, share this idea of the native physical weakness of the working half of their community. The King of Dahomey, whose most formidable regiment is composed of fierce Amazons, can scarcely regard women as inferior in respect to muscle and sinew, whatever he may think of their disposition. In Egypt, Spain, Germany, at different epochs, we have records which amply prove Dr. Richardson's contention, that physical strength, in either sex, depends on the method of training in early life, and that there is nothing to prevent women, in the course of a few generations, from recovering the physical power which their mode of existence, and the ill-usage suffered during the long patriarchal ages, have combined to destroy. Even in one generation improved conditions and training can work miracles. The pressure under which women have lived, throughout these centuries of bondage, has been inconceivably great; indeed, until the burden is lifted, few will understand how crushing was its weight. So consistent and all-pervading has been the impact on body, mind, and character, that a uniform pressure has even been mistaken by many of the sufferers for no pressure at all, or rather for the inevitable misery entailed, as they believe, by existence itself. The absence of complaint among many women, of which we hear so much, often springs from sheer lack of experience of that sense of fresh, unrestricted, unfatigued power with which every human creature ought to start on the journey of life. To stand thus erect, with only the natural resistance of atmosphere and gravitation to offer a fulcrum for the living forces of the body and brain, this is what the women of civilised Christendom cannot hope to understand until they have learnt to realise that the unnecessary burden is not laid upon them by "Nature," but by their fellows.

Researches of recent years have brought to light the remarkable fact that woman, as the first agriculturist, the first herbalist, the initiator of the art of medicine, the discoverer of the most ancient of human lore, is, as Karl Pearson says, "the pioneer of all civilisation." So far from being the receptive and adaptive creature of popular imagination, she, in fact, holds the position of leader and originator in all the arts of industry: the prophetess and teacher of humanity from the beginning of its upward career.[6]

---

6   Elie Reclus regards woman as the first architect. "Amongst our Hyperboreans, as amongst a great number of primitive people, such as the Tartars, and, for the most part, the negroes, the construction of dwellings is, as a matter of course, the business of women, who take the entire charge of it, from the foundation to the top, the husbands only assisting by bringing the materials to the scene of action. . . . I. . . see ... in this an argument in favour of the hypothesis that woman was the first architect."

"It is to woman, I think, that mankind owes all that has made us men. Burdened with the children and the baggage, she erected a permanent cover to shelter the little family;. . . She laid

The transition from the matriarchal to the patriarchal system, as we have observed in the far Past, has created many anomalous ideas, as may be seen from the strange contradiction occurring in ancient myths and legends, as regards the estimation in which women were held, in bygone ages. As goddesses, as priestesses, as something powerful, mysterious, and sacred on the one hand! as things, as chattels, as temptations to sin, as necessary evils, as dependents, slaves, ministers of pleasure, play things, child-bearers, on the other, have women been regarded in different eras.[7] It is not difficult, indeed, to find representatives of

---

there the firebrand, from which she never parts, and the hut became illuminated, the hut was warmed, the hut sheltered a hearth. Has not Prometheus been called the Father of Men, to make us understand that humanity began with the use of fire? Now, whatever has been the origin of fire, it is certain that women have always been the guardians and preservers of this source of life."

Reclus goes on to show how the woman, rearing and taming some of the wild animals of the forest about her home—perhaps some fawn whose mother has been slain by the hunters—becomes the foundress of pastoral peoples.

"And this is not all . . . the woman . . . collected eggs, seeds, and roots. Of these seeds she made a store in her hut; a few that she let fall germinated close by, ripened, bore fruit. On seeing this she sowed others, and became the mother of agricultural peoples.

"In fact, among all uncivilised men, cultivation may be traced to the housewife. Notwithstanding the doctrine which holds sway at present, I maintain that woman was the creator of the primordial elements of civilisation."

In the times of the Empire, as Gibbon informs us, "all the linen and woollen manufactures . . . spinning, weaving, and dyeing were executed chiefly by women of servile condition for the use of the palace and army," and he mentions also "a gynecium or manufacture at Winchester."

Thus the word *gynecium*—which implies that women are the workers employed—is used apparently as a synonym for *manufacture*.

Again, concerning the city of Carthage, Gibbon writes: "The picture of Carthage, as it flourished in the fourth and fifth centuries, is taken from the Expositio Totius Mundi. ... I am surprised that the *politia* should not place either a mint or an arsenal at Carthage, but only a gynecium or female manufacture."—"Decline and Fall of the Roman Empire."

Though we hear so little about the lives of the poorer and servile classes of women in these Imperial times, there is little doubt that a vast share of the real burden of all that magnificence fell on their shoulders.

Prophetesses, sibyls, witches are found in all lands and among all races of the earth. For instance, the responses of the Delphic oracle were given by a woman. Examples will occur in swarms to every reader.

Even the Moors had their prophetesses, as we learn at the time of their conflict in Africa with Belisarius, who (himself inspired, according to his own testimony, by the presence, counsels, and courage of his wife) went forth against a people who were led to battle by women. Under this command they held out against the Roman arms—and when Belisarius was the military commander—with astonishing persistence, and for a surprisingly long time.

In works of mercy it is seldom denied that women have been preeminent, but their power of initiation, even in these departments, is often disputed. Yet it is to a woman, Fabiola, the beautiful and penitent descendant of the race of the great Fabius, that we owe the foundation of the first regular hospital that the world has ever known. It was erected at Ostia at the expense and under the management of this lady in the early ages of Imperial Christianity (Woy's "Rome," p. 366)

7   The Fathers of the Church are loud and unanimous in their opposition to feminine influence, in spite of the large and courageous part that women played in its creation during the ages of persecution. From beginning to end of its career the Church has owed to this sex more than can

each and all of these views among our civilised contemporaries. The incongruity is explained when we realise that the history of woman has been chequered even to the extent betrayed by these contradictory views; that, at different epochs in her career, her "nature" has been regarded in all these varying lights, and that, in every case, that most astonishing "nature" has been supposed to be immutable, inherent, and divinely ordained from the beginning.

To condense the essential history of women after the introduction of patriarchal rule, into a sentence, we may say that woman originally became the property of man by right of capture; now the wife is his by right of law.

Yet for many centuries we continue to see evident traces, of the old age of mother-rule, Karl Pearson finding even in the witch-persecutions of the Middle Ages remnants of the old belief in the woman's mysterious power and knowledge, and of man's determination to extinguish it. The awe remained (according to this writer) in the form of superstition, but the old reverence was turned into antagonism. There was a struggle for supremacy between the sexes, and in early literature this struggle is evident, as well as the sentiment that women are all evil creatures, thirsting for unholy power, and must be resisted by all good and valiant men.

Part II - Marriage Before and After the Reformation

"There is no sort of vexation which among civilised peoples man cannot inflict upon woman with impunity."—Diderot.

On the spread of Christianity and the ascetic doctrines of its later teachers, feminine influence had received a severe check.[8] "Woman"! exclaims Tertullian with startling frankness, "thou art the gate of hell"! This is the key-note of the

---

possibly be calculated (see note, p. 45, Emancipation of the Family, Part II.), yet it has consistently treated them with contempt and aided in their oppression. Accepting their bounty and support, it has ever delighted in their humiliation.

Its attitude is illustrated almost comically in the Church of *Sta Croce in Gerusalemme* in Rome, a *Basilica* founded by Helena, the mother of Constantine. She brought from Jerusalem a reputed piece of the True Cross, and built the Church as a noble casket for the relic. Now the Chapel of St Helena which holds this relic is divided into two halves by a grating, and this grating, so it is decreed, "women cannot pass without incurring excommunication." Women are thus excluded from the sanctuary of a chapel dedicated to a woman, in a church built by a woman, and forbidden to approach the sacred relic placed there by a woman, that relic being the very reason why the Basilica of Sta Croce in Gerusalemme has any existence.

The question almost suggests itself: was it done for a joke?

8   It is usual to trace all improvements in the position of women to Christianity. Whatever may be thought regarding the ultimate influence of this faith on social relations, its first effect was hostile to female interests. That is to say, it arrested the very marked movement that was going on under the influence of Justinian in the direction of bestowing greater freedom on women. This freedom was at once denounced by the Christian teachers as the cause of the corruptions of society. The agent of the devil let loose among men for their destruction: such was the early Christian estimate of woman.

Lecky attributes their upward movement in the age of Justinian to the more mystical Oriental philosophies which had superseded Stoicism.

monastic age. Woman was an ally of Satan, striving to lead men away from the paths of righteousness. She appears to have succeeded very brilliantly! We have a century of almost universal chaos, ushering in the period of the minnesingers and the troubadours, or what is called the age of chivalry. Chaotic, however, as was this era, it brought forth some of the most beautiful conceptions of conduct which the human heart has ever created.

Perhaps it is idle to attempt to imagine what would have happened if some particular influence had been absent, at a particular historical juncture; yet it is difficult to avoid speculating as to the probable line of European development, if mediaeval chivalry had not arisen to provide humanity with a set of ideals which, to this day, represent all that is generous and honourable in conduct, and all that is noble and courteous in manners. Nearly all writers agree in tracing to the romantic spirit of this institution, the development and fixing of those sentiments of reverence for weakness, and contempt for cowardly aggression, which tend to keep society healthy and possible, to this day. The spirit that we call chivalrous arose in an age of barbarism, almost like a miracle, for no really adequate cause appears to be traceable for its advent, in the midst of so much that was dark and brutal.[9]

Yet out of that darkness the beautiful conceptions of chivalry sprang into being, giving rights to the weak, demanding mercy from the strong, and founding the ideal of manliness on that of pity and of service. It is difficult to conceive an ideal more opposed to that of the Scandinavian ancestors of the Germanic peoples, among whom, nevertheless, chivalry took its rise. These fierce northern savages, who lived only to slay, looked upon mercy as another name for feebleness, and on service as degrading to the dignity of the warrior, who alone among men was worthy of respect.

It has been observed by thoughtful writers, that in the age of chivalry arose an entirely new sentiment, the sentiment of love as it is understood by modern civilised peoples; love, with an element of idealism and reverence, as distinguished from the passion as represented in all literature before the Middle Ages. Out of what unpromising soil this new flower of the spirit came forth is perhaps most readily seen by recalling one of the elements of that feudal state, which yet must be given the credit of having produced it.

> "The suzerain," says Guizot, "had also the right of marriage, that is to say, the right of offering a husband to the heiress of a fief, and of obliging her to choose among those offered to her. . . . The woman could only escape

---

9   "I am not sure that we could trace very minutely the condition of women for the period between the subversion of the Roman Empire and the first Crusade . . . there seems, however, to have been more roughness in the social intercourse between the sexes than we find at "a later period."—Hallam, "Europe during the Middle Ages."

    "Courtesy had always been the proper attribute of knighthood, protection of the weak its legitimate duty; but these were heightened to a pitch of enthusiasm when woman became their object."—Hallam.

accepting one of the husbands, by paying the seigneur a sum equal to that which they had offered him to have her as a wife, for he who desired the hand of the inheritor of a fief, thus bought it of the suzerain."

When we see that such a custom existed at the time when the ideals of chivalry were coming into existence, we are forced to realise how enormous is the force of human sentiment, as distinguished from mere physical force, or even from fixed institutions. Chivalry not only bestowed upon the woman perfect freedom in the disposal of hand and heart, but required of the knight who should win her, devoted and lengthened service. It is, of course, easy to destroy the fairness of this picture, by dwelling upon a thousand points at which practice fell short of the exquisite theory. It is the beauty of the theory that is here insisted on, and its effects upon civilisation, to this day. Perhaps the fashion of sentiment has changed, for the moment, and the ideals of chivalry no longer excite enthusiastic admiration. At any rate, few people seem fully to realise how noble a type of character was actually developed during this age; how fine a combination of qualities distinguished the best of the knights and the minnesingers. The songs and poetry of the latter are full of sweetness, and redolent of all the stirring romance that clings, for ever, to this era. With the quaint antique verses in which they celebrate their ladies and their love, many a picturesque scene of mediaeval life seems to float back across the centuries, from grim, high-roofed, moss-stained German castles, such as perch, to this day, on the top of some inaccessible rock, looking down, in their loneliness, upon fields and plains at their foot, and dreaming—one might almost fancy—of the never-returning days, when the sounds of war and song used to fill the old halls with tumult, breaking the dead silence of the hill-top, which now broods there in mournful fashion, while it enhances the sadness and the beauty of these most convincing relics of a brilliant and generous era.

The stories of the vocal contests of the minnesingers in these old castles, before the counts and landgraves and their guests, have become part of familiar history. The very names of the minstrels carry with them a sweet savour from that epoch of gentle knighthood and "faire courtesie."

Walther von der Vogelweide, perhaps more than any other singer of his time, has this power of summoning back to us the epoch which he graced:—

"A man such as one would like to have for a friend, so bright in all his being, so gentle, for all his light and pleasing form, so inwardly earnest and firm; merry with the gay, sad with the mourners; full of hope from childhood on, and unwearying in striving after high goals; fresh and cheerful even in time of need; thankful for good fortune. Somewhat gloomy, indeed, in old age, and with good cause; for spring and summer were over for the minnesingers, and Walther foresaw the approach of autumn."

Alas, the autumn that the troubadour foresaw for himself and his fellow-minstrels has overtaken his country and all the civilised world! Sterner times were at hand for the merry land that he loved with so true a patriotism. Paradox though it seems, the Reformation was to sweep away all tolerance and urbanity from the war-tormented Empire, and Germany was no longer a fitting place for a man who had the assurance to assert that "Christians, Jews, and heathen serve one and the same God."[10]

The character of Martin Luther affords a singularly dramatic contrast to that of Walther von der Vogelweide, a type of the best outgrowth of German chivalry. Luther's influence served to modify, for ever, the effects of that institution, and to combine with other powerful influences of the Sixteenth Century, to initiate that particular condition of social life, which we may, broadly speaking, describe as modern, as distinguished from mediæval.

The great commercial development of this epoch, the increased navigation and discoveries of travellers, the growth of cities, and the sentiments which accompany wealth when divorced from mental cultivation, all played their part in producing the society of to-day, and the spirit that we call *bourgeois*. It was out of these materials that marriage, as at present interpreted, grew into definite form. It was at this time that immense stress began to be laid on outward sanctions, while sentiment and spiritual considerations of all kinds were increasingly ignored. This society became more staid and outwardly respectable. The obvious abuses of the chivalric era gradually lessened and disappeared; but the change can scarcely be regarded as indicating a genuine advance in moral perceptions. In fact, in some respects, it indicates a backward movement. With all the licence of the preceding age, sentiment and romance had been dominant; whereas, in the *bourgeois* age, a materialistic view begins to prevail. Forms and conventions are substituted for more romantic tests of right and wrong; the inward and spiritual is judged by outward and visible signs or labels; and in course of time, all question of the inward and spiritual has been forgotten, and attention becomes fixed exclusively on the labels. If the badge is satisfactory, its wearer is accredited without further question; if it be absent, or dubious, archangels may not hope for admission into respectable circles. Fortunately, there are few things in human fate that are wholly evil. This worship of mere form, this Apotheosis of the Label has doubtless had its uses in the training of mankind to obedience; a blind and stupid sort of obedience, but still valuable as discipline, in the absence of a better kind of education. It may, perhaps, be compared to the drudgery of mere parrot-learning, which can never inspire the intelligence of the child, and often annihilates it, but may be of service—*faute de mieux*—in forcing the errant will to the discipline of application. Or, to regard the matter from a slightly different aspect, it may also be said that since the majority of mankind are not brilliantly intelligent, nor gifted with great moral

10   "History of Germany in the Middle Ages."—Ernest F. Henderson.

insight, formal signs and labels must always be their safest guides, and that these alone can be trusted to keep them from straying into one knows not what bogs and quagmires. And this is true, so far as it goes; only we must not forget that the same shepherding power over the multitudes can be claimed for *any* idols of wood or stone or custom, provided only that they possess a sufficiently terrifying aspect to scare their votaries into submission. A broomstick set on end might become a valuable civilising agent, if only the cultus of the broomstick could be brought to the point of commanding real terror. We may, in fact, be said to have ourselves reached that happy stage which might be impartially described as the Broomstick Era.

It is usual to take for granted that the institution of marriage, as at present interpreted, works in the direction of training mankind in self-control; that, in fact, it is at once a terrifying and an elevating Broomstick. Yet the reformers of the Sixteenth Century preach a very different doctrine. They, in fact, teach the *impossibility* of self-control, *instead of its necessity*, and regard marriage *not* as a sacrament or a spiritual union, but merely as a concession to human weakness. Luther is most explicit on this point. Indeed, it is difficult to see how the Father of Evil himself, in his most inspired moments could have devised a means of placing marriage on a more degrading basis than that on which it was placed, of malice aforethought, by the great reformer. Those, in our day, who talk so much about the "sacredness" of marriage, can know but little about its history. Luther deprived it of all the spiritual significance which the Catholic Church had been so careful to emphasise, and reduced it to something little above a licensed sin. His celebrated sermon on matrimony leaves no doubt as to his point of view. It is, according to him, a necessary sin, which Heaven will forgive, because of the feeble nature of mankind. He lays enormous stress on the command to "increase and multiply," and obviously regards women simply and solely in relation to their powers of carrying out this exhortation. He hands over the whole sex—of course without consulting them in the matter— to a life-work which was, by his own showing, entirely physical; a work which doomed them to the existence of a docile and overworked animal, scarcely relieved by any other activities than those which might be expected to conduce to a more approved fulfilment of those duties.

And in all essentials, this is precisely the view that we hear reiterated in our own day by the orthodox, though their language, of course, is less "plain." Surely we need seek no more convincing proof than this, that time and familiarity will endear *anything* to humankind! If marriage, as the reformers conceived it, be sacred, then nothing is profane![11]

Luther's doctrine was somewhat inconsistent as well as materialistic. For, while regarding marriage as a necessary sin, he also seems to regard it as a *duty*,

11 "Abraham... believed God's word, wherein was promised him that from his unfruitful and as it were dead wife, Sarah, God would give him seed."—Martin Luther.

condemning the celibate life with much acerbity, doubtless through a spirit of opposition to the monastic teachings of the Church. His views on this point have probably confirmed, if not exasperated, the perilous force of primitive passions. He has done much to hold back progress in particular directions.

Karl Pearson[12] takes a most uncompromising view of Luther's teaching, and sees apparently nothing but evil in the effects of the Reformation on the social relations. Bebel[13], on the other hand, believes that its results were on the whole beneficial, chiefly, it appears, because Luther attacked the ascetic doctrines of the Church; while Lecky[14] says: "Protestantism, by purifying and dignifying marriage, conferred a great benefit upon women."

In this last utterance, may one not trace the influence upon the writer of those very doctrines whose enormous power over our own civilisation we have just been considering?

Lecky assumes, apparently as proved, that Protestantism dignified marriage; and it is difficult to avoid the inference, that he too has been taught to regard the prevalence of labels as trustworthy indications of a higher standard. It would, it is true, be difficult to show that society was really in a worse condition after the Reformation than immediately before it, nor is this task here attempted. But it is undeniable that the doctrine which influenced the relations of men and women at that epoch, was of a nature to degrade rather than to elevate those relations. If a better condition, nevertheless, followed this crisis, other influences must have been at work, and the improvement took place *in spite of*, and not in consequence of, the new doctrines. Other influences, in fact, *were* at work. This appears to be what Lecky has in his mind when he speaks of Protestantism having dignified marriage; for he goes on to draw a picture of the greater liberty of thought and government, the general improvement and progress wherein marriage must, more or less, have shared.

In breaking the back of the ecclesiastical tyranny, Protestantism undoubtedly did one great service to women, for up to this time, their fate had been largely determined by the Canon law, which (as Lecky puts it) "has always treated them with signal injustice and contempt."

Still, all improvements being allowed for, the woman's position, as established at this epoch, was one of great degradation. She could scarcely claim the status of a separate human being. She was without influence, from the dawn of life to its close, except such spurious kinds as could be stolen or snatched. The old chivalrous feeling for woman seems to have faded out with the romance of the Middle Ages. She figured as the legal property of man, the "safeguard against sin," the bearer of children *ad infinitum*.

12   "Ethics of Free Thought."
13   "Woman."—Bebel.
14   "History of European Morals."

Whether or not there was less real corruption than in earlier times, much real corruption now nourished under the cloak of respectability. Married life offered grand opportunities for tyrannical men; for the general sentiment supported them in their tyranny, and sternly demanded absolute submission on the part of their wives. A man might indeed be a tyrant in his own home, in the devout belief that he was doing no more than exercising his just rights, nay, performing his bounden duties as ruler of the household.

Another striking characteristic of this epoch must be noted—viz., the concurrence of a more rigid marriage convention with the existence of a class of women who now (according to many writers) became organised, for the first time, into a definite professional body, not unlike the trade-guilds which form so striking a feature of the period. The open corruptions of the preceding age were thus exchanged for a sort of orderly licence. The outcast class was formed into a strictly regulated band, subject to special laws, while the "honest" women were gathered into another fold and dedicated equally to the service of man, but under different conditions. They, too, were to wear out their lives in a bitter service, but this service, as their masters were pleased to consider, was suited beyond all others to the inborn "nature" of women—a service, in fact, that good women must regard as the most blessed and sacred; epithets, by the way, which seem to be always employed when something peculiarly degrading is to be recommended, and when there really is absolutely nothing else that *can* be said to recommend it.

The whole social system thus built itself up, with order and decorum. The purity of society, about which there was much concern, was protected by punishing the delinquencies of the female half of it with extreme severity, in order, presumably, to make a good average of punishment, when taken in combination with the entire exemption from penalty enjoyed by the corresponding male offenders.

This arrangement was made easier by the growth of that professional class of women, who were at once imperiously demanded and sternly punished by the community, their offence being their response to the demand. This class, while obeying that social behest, without which they could never have existed, formed a convenient scapegoat on whom the penalties of transgression and the contempt of the virtuous could be freely showered, through whom, moreover, the sacredness of the home and the security of property, in duly wedded wives, could be thoroughly provided for. The arrangement was more than convenient. It secured from a friendless class enormous services (or at least it secured that which society demanded); it afforded the woman who had become the legal property of one man, the satisfaction of looking down on a position which she was able to consider more despicable than her own—wherefore, has never yet been explained—and thus helped to reconcile her to social arrangements which told so heavily against her.

These despised women, who preferred, of the two alternatives offered to them by society, the degradation outside marriage to the slightly different and more approved form of degradation within it, were, in many cases, driven by misfortune and poverty to their lot; the destruction of the nunneries, at the time of the Reformation, having deprived many a lonely woman of a place of refuge. Anyone who realises the conditions of life at that time, cannot fail to understand what must have been the fate of such unfriended women.

At best—or at what would be considered best—a woman became the drudge and child-bearer of a man, in "respectable" wedlock, wives being bought and sold as if they were cattle, and educated at the same time, with what can only be called ferocity, to do their "duty" patiently, silently, devotedly, and to remain thus meek and submissive under the severest provocation.[15] Carried off by the highest bidder, they were solemnly exhorted to obedience and purity, to a life of God-fearing service, and untiring devotion to their lords, in life and in death. To drive a hard bargain and to sermonise one's victims at the same time, is a feat distinctly of the Philistine order. Indeed, these well-to-do burghers, with their commercial and practical instincts, were the true ancestors of our modern Philistine, to whom they have handed down, almost intact, their system of marriage and their sentiments regarding women.

Bebel speaks of Luther as the interpreter of the "healthy sensualism" of the Middle Ages. Any "healthy sensualism," however, which did not make itself legitimate according to Luther's ideas, was liable to severe penalty, women offenders being subject to truly terrible forms of punishment. But whether they offended, or whether they conducted themselves according to the regulations, their lives appear to have been hard and pitiful enough. Society was inventive as to punishment, but showed little imagination as regards rewards. Bebel says that—

"the married woman's duties were so manifold that a conscientious housewife had to be at her post early in the morning till late at night to fulfil them, and even then it was only possible to do so with the help of her daughters. . . . Not only had she the usual household cares of the modern housewife, but she had to spin, weave, and bleach, to make all the linen clothes, to boil soap, to make candles, and brew beer ... to work in the fields and garden, to attend to the poultry and cattle."[16]

Not indeed that hard work in itself is a grievance, but *hard work without its rightful recompense of independence*—that is the definition of slavery.

At this time, history is strangely silent on the subject of women and their occupation and status. Except from accidental references, and what may be read between the lines, it is difficult to gain an insight into the real condition of the negligible half of humanity. Their lives are to us a closed chapter, full

15   See Story of Griselda, of Marzia of Cesena, p. 204—ect., ect.
16   "Woman." –Bebel.

of mystery; full, too, of moment, for silently and certainly, in those obscure side-scenes of existence, all that we call modern civilisation was growing into form: all the sentiments and habits, even the very instincts that determine the calibre of our present life, were shaping themselves, with the unerring movements of crystal-atoms, as they obey the strange internal impulses that drive them to their inevitable devices. And thus, while women were ignored in the obvious course of human affairs, and history soared above their bowed heads, the material of that very history was forming under their hands. In those shrouded homes, where the minds of children received their life-long stamp from the mothers of the race, all the determining elements of human sentiment were initiated and fashioned, in that mysterious process of spiritual crystallisation, which it is our habit to call Fate.

Meanwhile, the reformers were busy laying down rules, and proclaiming duties for the sex that is always expected to fall in pleasantly with any scheme of life which masculine philosophy may evolve—for "negligible" though they be, it is clear that no social order could be carried out if women refused to bear their humble part therein. And so, with loud voice and one accord, the reformers proclaimed that a woman's main duty and privilege was to bear children without limit; that death and suffering were not to be considered for a moment, in the performance of this duty; that for this end she had been created, and for this end—and the few others just enumerated—she must live and die. Even the gentle Melancthon, on this subject, says as follows:—"If a woman becomes weary of bearing children, that matters not: let her only die from bearing, she is there to do it."

Of course this doctrine is by no means obsolete. It is the prevailing view of our most respectable classes; those who hold the scales of public morality in their hands, and whose prerogative appears to be to judge, in order that they be not judged. Remembering this, we cannot be surprised at Luther's teachings. Why should a coarse-fibred monk of the Sixteenth Century consider sufferings which are overlooked by tender-hearted divines of the present era?

As an instance of the way in which an exceptionally good man of our own age can regard this subject—his goodness notwithstanding—we may turn to the introduction, by Charles Kingsley, to Brook's *Fool of Quality*, which Kingsley edited. A short account is given of the life of Brook, who flourished (in a very literal sense) at the time of the Restoration, and who was saved, as his biographer points out in joy and thankfulness, from the vices of that corrupt age, by an early marriage. Kingsley goes on to describe the home where all that is commendable and domestic reigned and prospered. He dwells lovingly on that pleasant picture of simple joys and happy cares, upon the swarms of beautiful children who cluster round their father's knee, and help to rescue him from the dangers of a licentious age. Kingsley mentions, just in passing, that the young wife watches the happy scene from a sofa, having become a confirmed invalid from the number of children she has borne during the few years of her married life. But what of that? What of the anguish and weariness, what of the thousand painful disabilities which that young woman has suffered before her system yielded to the strain—disabilities which she will have to bear to her life's end? Has not the valuable Brook been saved from an immoral life? (Of course, Brook could not be expected to save himself!—we are not unreasonable.) Have not Propriety and Respectability been propitiated? And the price of all this? Merely the suffering and lifelong injury of one young woman, in a thoroughly established and "natural" manner; nothing more. Kingsley feels that it is cheap at the price. *Brook is saved!* Hallelujah!

In order to understand how it happens that a good man can think in this way without knowing his cruelty (and that is the cruellest part of the matter!), it is necessary to study the history of the Middle Ages and the transition from that epoch to modern life. In that study we shall come upon all the "forbears" of Charles Kingsley's views, and realise that even good men are the result of their antecedents, and that only in special directions have our thinkers emancipated themselves from the thraldom of established prejudice. And it is for this reason that the progress of the world is so slow: since even those to whom we have to look for reform go on giving their support to all the old abuses, except just those particular ones whose evil they have themselves detected. And so the world goes on, decade after decade, with its needless miseries, its needless wrongs, which the amiable and the distinguished conspire with the cruel and the selfish to perpetuate. Year after year, women are ruined, in body and soul, inside and outside the pale of society, the ruin in both cases being essentially the same in nature, and springing from the same cause. A religious rite or a legal form is, for a woman, to mark the whole difference between irredeemable sin and absolute duty. From this significant fact it is easy to infer the nature of the married woman's position, and to see that—unless human laws have some supernatural power of sanctification—her position is, *per se*, degrading.[17] Women resent this assertion, not unnaturally, since most of them have to accept the position as it stands. Yet nothing is gained by blinking the fact, and much is lost by this refusal to look matters squarely in the face.

Female education has indeed been devised to discourage any such boldness. If women had not been trained to regard facts as more or less improper— especially facts that affect themselves—society would be, at this moment, many centuries further forward on its path of progress.

From the system of purchase—which has been shewn to be the real foundation of our marriage system—arose our strange and inconsequent ideas of "honour" for man and woman. How many have realised that "honour" or

---

17   It is of course merely the abstract status of marriage in its legal and social aspects which is here alluded to, and not marriage as it may be and often is. See *Married Life, Present and Future*, p. 138.

"virtue" in a woman did not originally take its rise from any sense of personal self-respect, but from the fact of her position as the property of her husband? This is assuredly no attempt to undervalue the quality itself, but to point out that the woman has actually been forced to develop her moral standards, not under the guidance of her own individual conscience, but *in accordance with the conditions of her servitude to man.* Just as a pointer acquires his peculiar powers through hereditary adaptation to his master's convenience, so, in very fact, women have acquired certain qualities, and, above all, certain standards of conduct, through hereditary training in *their* master's service. Undoubtedly, by this means, valuable qualities have been acquired (the pointer can boast no less). But it is not a little significant that they have been acquired exactly in the same way as traits useful to man have been acquired by domesticated animals. Thus women's virtues are not absolute but relative: relative, that is, to man.

A little thought will show how this is now, and has been, since the days of the patriarchate, the one standard by which female virtues take their measure.

It is thus, in fact, that the woman's chastity became the watch-dog of the man's possession; it is thus that the dual moral standard for the two sexes has arisen. *The woman must protect the man's property in herself,* and failure in this duty is held as an unpardonable offence against the holder of the property.[18] To ask the man to develop the same quality that he demands in the woman seems to the vast majority, even now, very much as if some upstart "new" pointer should suddenly shoulder the gun and expect the sportsman to point the game!

The ugliness of all this, and of the facts on which it depends, is not the fault of those who *perceive* it, but of those who created it, and who now uphold it; a distinction which the justice of the British public is not always ready to admit.

The ugliness, indeed, is largely modified by many over growths of nobler sentiment and chivalrous custom. Nevertheless, the origin of woman's virtue is very obvious to all careful observers, in the attitude of the public mind on this subject. The idea that a man's honour can be injured by his wife's infidelity is indeed a most naïve proclamation of the theory of proprietorship. It can be explained on no other assumption. Like many other incongruous ideas, this barbaric view of the marriage relation has grown into the very fibre of human existence, and has become associated with its closest affections. It is for this reason that its hold on mankind is so powerful, although it would puzzle most people to give an account of their faith that would be worth a second's consideration.

18   There is a significant parallel to this attitude of mind in the story of the African slave, who, having been thrown into a river by a captious friend, broke out into furious imprecations, and ended with the culminating outburst: "You dam' blackguard—you see what you do ! You drown massa's black nigger!" And, in the same way, when the predatory lover prowls round, and seeks to lure away an indignant and well-trained wife, she exclaims in effect, though in far superior words: "You dam' scoundrel! you see what you do—you want to carry away massa's white wife!" (e.g., "Sir, you insult me! What right have I ever given you to suppose that I should be lax in protecting my husband's honour? Would you betray his trust in you? Leave me, sir!").

Probably few persons, whose attention had not previously been warned, would feel any shock of surprise or disgust in reading the following sentence from Lord Shaftesbury's "Characteristicks," a work bearing the date 1714.

The author is speaking of love-affairs in cases where the woman is married, and he describes the lovers in such cases as "Pretenders who, through this plea of irresistible necessity, make bold with what is another's. . . but the law makes bold with them in its turn, as with other invaders of property."

It is doubtful whether this very bald and frank description of the wife as "property" would startle an assembly of the orthodox. Why, indeed, should it, since that is, after all, precisely their own unformulated view of the matter? When some divorce case makes the British public double its consumption of newspapers and express itself in horror and surprise, it is *au fond*, the invasion of property that causes the consternation.

The husband feels, in some mystic fashion, dishonoured by his loss, albeit it is the wife and not he who, on his own showing, has committed the crime.

Is it possible to be really dishonoured by any action except one's own? One may be pained, injured, thrown into despair by another person; but, in the name of reason, how dishonoured? Obviously this idea, that has so strong a hold in current morality, betrays some forgotten origin that once accounted for it rationally, but which now lies latent and unavowed among the dearest of our prejudices.

We have seen how the nebulous outlines of our social faiths were hardened, in Germany, during the time of the Reformation and the development of the great cities. During the same period, the England that her sons called "merry" was also on her deathbed, and modern England was born amidst the storm of that momentous epoch—a shadowed and care-worn land, full of toil and gloom and sorrow. One wonders for how long that strange, driven look has rested on the faces of her people, as they hurry through her brimming cities, eternally pursuing the means of existence, forgetful of its ends. True children of the Reformation, these grey and grim and business-driven hordes of men and women, enduring, in dull patience, the weariness of their lives, rigid in the observance of custom, but tolerant of the miseries that rage within and without the citadel of their conventions.

And now, looking back over the rough track that we have traversed, in the effort to obtain a general view of social history, it is easy to pick out the prominent features and to realise in what manner our present England has grown up. The result of such a bird's-eye view is not cheering. The factors are (roughly) as follows:—strict marriage, prostitution, the cultus of external sanctions, irrespective of spiritual facts; commercialism and competition in the most exaggerated forms, the subjection of women, with their consequent purchase by men, under differing names and conditions throughout society; and finally, the (also consequent) dual moral standard for the two sexes.

We need no ghost come from the grave to tell us that from elements such as these it is morally impossible to produce a healthy society.

Part III - The Lot of Woman Under the Rule of Man

" *There was no shame on earth too black to blacken*
    That much-praised woman's face."—Charlotte Stetson.

Perhaps it may be said without much exaggeration, that the cure for social ills is the clear realisation of their existence. But the prescription seems simpler than it really is. People are indeed ready enough to cry out against the innumerable progeny of evils that spring out of some great fundamental wrong; but it sometimes takes centuries before a whole nation comes to recognise that parent-wrong, in its relationship with its vast and objectionable family. The individuals of that family differ among themselves, and differ according to the conditions of their age, so that in (say) the fifteenth century, they will be fathered on one institution, and in the sixteenth, mankind will find some other contemporary abuse on which to lay the blame of their birth. Meanwhile, the guilty ancestor of them all lies cherished in the very heart of the society that it ruins. We have seen that among these patriarchs of evil, the subjection of women must be classed. As in the case of a sufferer from blood-poisoning, some of the symptoms may be mitigated, but new distresses will follow the supposed cures, until the poison itself is driven out of the system.

It has often been objected: "Granting that these evils are born of that particular parent, how can they be cured?" And the answer simply is: They can be cured only by making mankind *en masse* recognise that they are the offspring of that parent. The rest follows inevitably, if sometimes rather slowly.

It is with the view of tracing the career of this parent evil (viz., the relation of man to woman) that these essays have been written. To reveal the ferocious creature, in his true colours, is to deprive him of claws and fangs and all the paraphernalia of destruction; but the overwhelming difficulty lies in the revealing.

It is now proposed—with exactly the same object in view—to take instances from history illustrating the condition of women; and by reminding ourselves of these well-known facts, to show how unmistakable is the ancestry of these conditions whose horror is realised in succeeding centuries, but never to the same extent in their own.

It is the habit of most people to read the chronicles of the Past as if some mystic barrier separated that by gone period from our own enlightened times. To read thus is to lose one of the most valuable lessons of history.

The following instances are taken from Gibbon, whose impartiality on this subject cannot be questioned.

After the defeat of the Goths by the Emperor Claudius (who, nevertheless, was very anxious to improve the discipline of his troops), the Gothic women were divided into groups and allotted to the Roman soldiers—two or three to each. This proceeding was thus officially recognised, nay, ordered in one of the best-disciplined of the imperial armies, and from this much may be inferred. If the true internal history of warfare could be written, it would surely be found that the full horror of this scourge of mankind had fallen upon women.

A chief of the Roxolani had deserted the standard of Hermanric, King of the Goths, into whose power the luckless wife of the traitor chief afterwards fell. In order to revenge himself upon her husband, Hermanric ordered her to be torn asunder by wild horses. To ill-treat the property of his enemy, let it be observed, was to gratify his thirst for vengeance.

During the Gothic invasion of Greece, under Alaric,

"the beautiful women were driven away with the spoil and cattle of the flaming villages." "The female captives," Gibbon adds, "submitted to the laws of war . . . beauty was the reward of valour, and the Greeks could not reasonably complain of the abuse which was justified by the example of heroic times."

The next instance carries us to the fifth century, and to the scene of the mighty conflict between the Franks and Huns in Central Europe. The Thuringians, who served in the army of the Huns under Attila,

"massacred their hostages as well as their captives; 200 young maidens were tortured with exquisite and unrelenting rage; their bodies were torn asunder by wild horses; or their bones crushed under the weight of rolling waggons; and their unburied limbs were abandoned on the public roads, as a prey to dogs and vultures."

Without sharing in any of the excitement, the glory, or the rewards of war, women have always had to accept its worst risks, and to endure its most terrible insults.

In times of peace, men were able to defend their possessions, wives included. To dispute a monopoly in the latter kind of property has always been, and still is, the unpardonable offence. But as soon as the country was disturbed by war, houses and cities were plundered, and woman shared the fate of the rest of man's possessions.

In the "Institutes of Manu" we find precisely the same view set forth with authority; though here, there are some faint traces of the mother-age; as in the asserted "venerableness" of a mother, who surpasses in that quality "a thousand fathers." However, her extreme venerableness appears to avail the Indian woman but little.

"But they term the Daiva rite, the gift of a daughter, after having adorned her, to a sacrificial priest, rightly doing his work. . . ." "That is" (adds the translator in a note),"the priest who performs a sacrifice receives a maiden as part of the fee."[19]

The author of the "Institutes" makes the following assertions:—

"Houses which women, not honoured, curse; those, as if blighted, perish utterly. . . ." Also: "Where women grieve, that family quickly perishes."

19   "Institutes of Manu." Translated by Dr. Burnell.

Here, again, is a faint glimpse of the ancient faith. Yet the real trend of the teaching of Manu, in common with the teaching of all prophets until this day, has been of a kind to cause women to grieve and to curse most bitterly. Perhaps that is why so many "houses" and nations have indeed utterly perished.

> "Though of bad conduct and debauched" (Manu continues in his more patriarchal vein), "or even devoid of good qualities, a husband must always be worshipped like a god by a good wife."

Most English readers indignantly exclaim against this maxim; nevertheless this is precisely the doctrine that English wives have been taught from time immemorial, though in language which veils the admonition in a manner necessary for the protection of modern sensibilities. We like to have our survivals of barbarous old doctrine expressed with true refinement. Submissive deference to the husband, simply because he *is* the husband, by the wife, simply because she *is* the wife, still remains a defended canon of feminine morality. "Of course, my dear, if your husband approves—" is a familiar phrase on the lips of women of the last generation, nor is it by any means obsolete to-day. Doubtless there is an instinctive desire on the part of many women, who were brought up in the old faith, to prevent their sisters from moving beyond the lines that bounded female existence in the earlier half of the century. The idea is entirely modern that the wife has a right to choose her own mode of existence, without waiting for her husband's permission. An amiable couple would be likely to consult one another's wishes, within reason, but the idea of "approval," in the old interpretation, belongs unmistakably to the order of sentiment which Manu set forth for the guidance of the women of India; a sentiment which there led to child-marriage, suttee, and the ill-treatment of widows.

> "For women," says Manu, "there is no separate sacrifice, nor vow, nor even feast. If a woman obeys her husband, for that she is exalted to heaven."

Translate this into current terms, and we have a most familiar homily: "The true woman has no interests separate from those of her home" [no "separate vow nor feast" for *her!*] "Her highest ambitions and her noblest vocation are to be found in that sacred circle—" and so on, *ad libitum*. As for the last quoted sentence of Manu: ("If a woman obeys her husband, for that she is exalted to heaven"), Annie S. Swan gives a ready-made modern version.

"And I further hold," she says, "that having undertaken the duties and responsibilities matrimony involves, God will require at her hands an account of that stewardship before any other." (The claims of the stewardship seem to be too manifold to leave much time for the construction of sentences; the one just quoted recalling the following example of similar formation: " Replying in the affirmative, the coffin-lid was again closed").

Volumes might, of course, be filled with facts gleaned from all times, illustrating the same underlying idea in its different manifestations, mild or terrible, according to the general state of civilisation of the country and the age.

There are, indeed, but few homes in England at this moment, that do not offer examples of the kind; though in many—probably in most cases—the idea on which they rest has found its least degrading and least obvious form of manifestation. Yet it is a fact, and a somewhat startling one, that the tacit beliefs on which the best of English homes are founded (setting aside, of course, unorthodox exceptions), are those which render possible and law-protected, the outrages suffered by women in the very worst.

In Mongolia, there are large cages in the market-place, wherein condemned prisoners are kept and starved to death. The people collect in front of these cages to taunt and insult the victims as they die slowly, day by day, before their eyes. In reading the history of the past, and the literature of our own day, it is difficult to avoid seeing, in that Mongolian market-place, a symbol of our own society, with its iron cage, wherein women are held in bondage, suffering moral starvation, while the thoughtless gather round to taunt their lingering misery. Let any one who thinks this exaggerated, note the manner in which our own novelists, for instance, past and present, treat all subjects connected with women, marriage and motherhood, and then let him ask himself if he does not recognise at once its ludicrous inconsistency, and its insults to womanhood, open and implied. The very respect, so-called, of man for woman, being granted solely on condition of her observing certain laws dictated by him, conceals a subtle kind of insolence. It is really the pleased approval of a lawgiver at the sight of obedient subjects.

Woman has certainly been the Ugly Duckling of society; hunted, insulted, threatened or cajoled by her masters; scouted, scolded, admonished, betrayed; suffering all the evils of her age and country, while enjoying not a tithe of its compensating privileges; held in tutelage, yet punished for all sins and errors with a ferocity and a persistence specially reserved for the sex which is called weak; and specially directed against those who are held incapable of the responsibilities of freedom and of citizenship. Truly the fate of woman, in its injustice, its debasement and humiliating pain, is a tragedy such as Shakespeare never wrote nor Æschylus dreamt of.

PART IV - A MORAL RENAISSANCE

"So each new man strikes root into a far-fore time."—MATTHEW ARNOLD.

UP TO THE present day, the sentiments naturally attendant on the purchase system of marriage have received no serious check.

In strict accordance with hereditary preconceptions, civilised women have been carefully trained, while the ideas of young men are developed on lines that accurately correspond, so that the type of conduct and sentiments to which the young girl is educated, is exactly that which the young man has learnt to expect;

or if it is not always *quite* so exact as he might wish, the difference is scornfully set down to the discredit of the rebel; and when such differences become too numerous, loud lamentations arise, and prophecies become frequent of the approaching collapse of society.

However, on the whole, the young man has had little reason to complain. Departures from the antique pattern of feminine excellence have been rare indeed, considering the rigidity of that pattern, and the tremendous forces which it at once concealed and rendered futile. The model has been accepted with scarcely a murmur, and followed, perforce, for centuries with such fidelity that no other design has seemed even possible to most of us, much less preferable.

To the preservation of orthodoxy on these subjects, our conditions have of course brought powerful assistance. While marriage remained practically the only means of livelihood for women, there was little danger of their seeing too clearly the seamy side of the arrangement; for to see *that* would be to stand helpless and open-eyed between the alternatives of selling themselves for a livelihood, and starvation; or, in milder cases, between the alternatives of social failure, and a marriage which, without being altogether worldly, would yet never for a moment, have been thought of in the entire absence of the worldly motive.

If the position was to remain tolerable at all, obviously it must not be looked in the face. Therefore the pretence must be cherished that the mere form of marriage makes the purchased condition an honourable one. Thousands of respectable women feel in their heart of hearts its real nature, but for that very reason, they try to buttress their self-respect by angry denial.

Kirke White's *Ode to Thought* is singularly expressive of their condition of mind. Thought, indeed for women, has ever been a vindictive companion!

> "Hence, away, vindictive Thought!
> Thy pictures are of pain;
> The visions through thy dark eye caught,
> They with no gentle charms are fraught,
> So prithee back again,
> I would not weep,
> I wish to sleep,
> Then why, thou busy foe, with me thy vigils keep?"

Of what avail, then, is it to inveigh against mercenary marriages, however degrading they may be, when a glance at the position of affairs shows that there is, for the average woman, no reasonable alternative? We cannot expect, even if we ask, every woman to be a dauntless heroine, and to choose a hard and thorny path when a comparatively smooth one (as it seems) offers itself, and, moreover, when the pressure of public opinion urges strongly in that direction. A few braver natures will resist, to swell the crowd of worn-out, underpaid workers, but the majority will take the voice of Society for the voice of God, or, at any rate, of wisdom, and our common respectable marriage—upon which the safety of all social existence is supposed to rest— will remain, as it is now, the worst, because the most hypocritical form of woman-purchase.

Few people, when brought face to face with the problem, can be found to approve of mercenary unions. They blame, however, not the social order, but the *victims* of that order: the unfortunate girls whose horizon is as limited as their opportunities, whose views of life are cribbed, cabined, and confined by their surroundings, whose very right and wrong, just and unjust, are chosen for them. They act as they are taught to act, behaving precisely as every average person behaves—viz., in exact obedience to the public opinion of his little world.

"Yes, marriage is often a failure," say the orthodox reproachfully; "it is entered into too early, too thoughtlessly, without (on the part of the wife) a knowledge of cooking and the domestic arts, without a flawless temper, without absolute immunity from headaches. Society and the institution of marriage are not to blame, only the faulty individuals who marry."

Alas, for much instructed, much badgered, much be laboured individuals! Like the absent, they are always in the wrong! The last person who could be justly blamed for the marriage failure is the girl who acts according to universal example and precept.

It is impossible for an outsider to realise the restrictions and narrowness of the average girl's life. We are too near to the result to be able to see it. When some one points out that the education has been distorting, we, on our side, point beamingly to some of its disastrous consequences, and say, "Behold, the Eternal has so willed it. Thus was the young person designed by Nature from the beginning."

And this is the bewildered being, stunted in intelligence, in self-respect; with a swollen, unwholesome conscience, spreading in all directions like some rankly-growing gourd, increasing not in harmony with, but at the expense of the other sides of the nature—this is the ill-treated being who is held responsible for the failure of marriage, the victim to whom a logical society says: "Marry, and ask no questions; who are you that you should criticise an institution which has lasted for centuries? Marriage is your natural career, your own highly-developed conscience must tell you so. If you do not adopt it, well, we fear you will find cause to regret your decision. If you can't secure a husband, we can but regard you as a failure, a supernumerary who has no proper place in the world." So the bewildered being turns an alarmed ear to the counsel that greets her on every side, in one form or another, open or disguised; for it is not only from the lips of worldlings that these warnings issue. People know better than to appeal merely to the self-interest of a being possessing such a magnificent overgrowth of conscience. The being can be led; she need not be driven. Society appeals to her gourd and wins an easy victory. But alas, for the poor Young Person! With all her dutiful submission, her marriage is not happy. There is no real community of thought between the pair. The wife means well—what else has she a gourd for?—but of what avail is this, if the best that she can do is to obey her husband? There are few men who do not deserve something more, and none who would not tend to deteriorate under such temptations to egotism. The wife meanwhile suffers, as she feels her husband drifting from her, but she says nothing. He is the last person to guess how lonely and how sad her life is. "Until a woman cries, men never think she is suffering; bless their block-headism!" exclaims Mrs. Carlyle.

And all this springs, not in the main from the faults of the individual, but from the fault of the tradition, which thus inspires the wife, when most desirous of doing her duty, to suppress all that is individual in herself, while it encourages the husband to expect such deference as his right.[20] This idea that the wife should subordinate her dominant interests is perhaps one of the most frequent causes of colourless and monotonous homes. "There's no place like home—and a good thing, too!" some contributor to *Punch* recklessly exclaims. Out of such homes springs a second crop of bewildered beings, whose only sin is obedience, but upon whose shoulders is piled almost all the blame of our unsuccessful marriages. Not only the absent but the sinned-against are always in the wrong. To encourage a child to put a lighted match to a train of gunpowder and then to punish him because he has caused a disastrous explosion is neither wise nor just.

On the other hand, if a woman remains single, her lot, under present social conditions, is often a very sad one. Bebel is eloquent upon the sufferings of unmarried women, which must be keen indeed for those who have been prepared for marriage and for nothing else, whose emotions have been coloured solely by pictures of domestic happiness. To the eye that is trained in so one-sided a fashion as to be able to see the colour red and no other, grey indeed will the universe appear if all red objects be withdrawn from it.

Mrs. Augusta Webster amusingly points out the inconsistencies of popular notions on this subject. She says:—

> "People think women who do not want to marry unfeminine; people think women who *do* want to marry immodest: people combine both opinions by regarding it as unfeminine for women not to look forward longingly to wifehood as the hope and purpose of their lives, and ridiculing and contemning any individual woman of their acquaintance whom they suspect of entertaining such a longing. They must wish and not wish; they must by no means give and they must certainly not withhold encouragement—and so it goes on, each precept cancelling the last, and most of them negative."

20 "Instead of boiling up individuals into the species, I would draw a chalk line round each individuality and preach to it to keep within that and to preserve and cultivate its identity at the expense of ever so much lost gilt of other people's 'isms'."—Mrs. Carlyle.

There are, doubtless, equally absurd prejudices which hamper a man's freedom by teaching girls and their friends to look for proposals of marriage, instead of regarding signs of interest in a more wholesome spirit. It is certain that we shall never have a world really worth living in, until men and women can show interest in one another without being driven either to marry, or to forego altogether the pleasure and the profit of frequent meeting. Nor will the world be really a pleasant world while it continues to make friendship between persons of opposite sexes wellnigh impossible, by insisting that they *are* so, and thereby, in a thousand direct and indirect ways, bringing about the fulfilment of its own prophecy. All this false sentiment, with the restrictions it implies, makes the ideal marriage—that is, a union prompted by harmony of nature and by friendship—almost beyond the reach of this generation.

It may be worth while to quote here a typical example of some letters written to Max O'Rell, on the publication of *The Daughters of John Bull*. One lady of direct language exclaims fiercely, "Man is a beast!", and she goes on to explain in gleeful strains that, having been left a small fortune by a relative, she is able to dispense with the society of "the odious creature." (Of course Max O'Rell warmly congratulates the "odious creature.")

"At last," another lady bursts forth, "we have some one among us with wit to perceive that the life which a woman leads with the ordinary sherry-drinking, cigar-smoking husband is no better than that of an Eastern slave. Take my own case, which is that of thousands of others in our land. I belong to my lord and master, body and soul. The duties of a housekeeper, upper nurse, and governess are required of me. I am expected to be always at home, at my husband's beck and call. It is true that he feeds me, and that for his own glorification he gives me handsome clothing. It is also true that he does not beat me. For this I ought, of course, to be duly grateful; but I often think of what you say on the wife and servant question, and wonder how many of us would like to have the cook's privilege of being able to give warning to leave."

If the wife feels thus, we may be sure the husband thinks he has his grievances also; and when we place this description side by side with that of the unhappy plight of bored husbands commiserated by Mrs. Lynn Linton, there is no escaping the impression that there is something very "rotten in the state of Denmark." Amongst other absurdities, we have well-meaning husbands and wives harassing one another to death, for no reason in the world but the desire of conforming to current notions regarding the proper conduct of married people. These victims are expected to go about perpetually together, as if they were a pair of carriage-horses; to be for ever holding claims over one another, exacting or making useless sacrifices, and generally getting in one another's way, with a diligence and self-forgetfulness that would be admirable were it not so supremely ridiculous. The man who marries finds that his liberty has gone, and the woman exchanges one set of restrictions for another.

She thinks herself neglected if the husband does not always return to her in the evenings, and the husband and society think her undutiful, frivolous, and so forth, if she does not stay at home alone, trying to sigh him back again. The luckless man finds his wife so *very* much confined to her "proper sphere," that she is, perchance, more exemplary than entertaining. Still, she may look injured and resigned, but she must not seek society and occupation on her own account, bringing new interest and knowledge into the joint existence, and becoming thus a contented, cultivated, and agreeable human being. No wonder that, while all this is forbidden, we have so many unhappy wives and bored husbands. The more admirable the wives, the more profoundly bored the husbands.

Doubtless there are bright exceptions to this picture of married life, but we are not dealing with exceptions. In most cases, the chain of marriage frets and chafes, if it does not make a serious wound; and where there is happiness—as we are so often assured that there is—it is dearly bought, and is not often on a very high plane. For husband and wife are then apt to forget everything in the narrow interests of their home, to depend entirely upon one another, to steep themselves in the same ideas, till they become mere echoes, half-creatures, useless to their kind, because they have let individuality die. There are few things more stolidly irritating than a very "united" couple. The likeness in appearance and gesture that may often be remarked between married people, is a melancholy instance of this communal form of degeneration. This condition, be it observed, is the very antithesis of that deep and real unity of two individualities, which are harmonious just because they are *not* identical—as two colours, for example, may be exquisite in harmony, where a mere repetition of the same tint, in two nominally separate objects, would create nothing but a tiring monotony.

The tyrannical spirit has little or no check under present conditions of married life, for the despot—male or female—knows that the victim must bear whatever has to be borne without hope of relief on this side the grave; except when the grievance is of such a nature as to come within the reach of the law; a wide enough margin to give scope to sufficiently serious cases of tyranny, as probably nobody would attempt to deny.

This tyranny takes various forms; many of them—and these are perhaps the most difficult to deal with—being based upon pleas of love and devotion; a devotion which claimants have no weak idea of presenting gratis. Often the tyranny expresses itself profitably by appeals to the pity and the conscience of the victims; by threats of the suffering that will ensue to the despot, if his wishes are heartlessly disregarded. Should these measures fail, more drastic methods are adopted. There are stern or pathetic reminders of indisputable claims, accusations of selfishness, of failing duty, and so forth. Between married people, this system is carried to its extreme, and derives much of its power from the support of popular sentiment.

Upon the legal bond is founded every sort of sentimental tie, till at last the couple so bind and entwine themselves with multitudinous restrictions, that every vestige of freedom disappears, and obligation enters into the very citadel of the heart. All spontaneity must and does evidently depart, and if feelings so bullied and pinioned show the tendency of all prisoners to escape, then loud are the wailings of the injured one, who has succeeded at last in worrying affection to death. The luxury of a grievance is the sole remaining consolation. It seems strange that, with so long an experience behind them, human beings have not yet learnt that, though they may obtain dominion by making large demands, they are likely to win regard in inverse proportion to their claims; and that, in any case, it is a little absurd to set up an injured and fretful demand for affection, as if it could be laid on with the gas and the water, and kept going in regular quarterly supplies. Even when such conduct does not destroy attachment, it does what perhaps is worse; it destroys individuality.

There must be a perpetual surrender of tastes and opportunities, in deference to the affectionate selfishness of the devoted partner, who is unable to realise that what may seem trivial to him is a matter of importance to some one else. The husband cannot bear to be parted from his wife for a single evening; therefore unselfishness dictates that the wife shall sacrifice her innate love of—say the drama (which he energetically loathes), and forego every opportunity of gratifying her taste. The adoring wife, on the other hand, who hates to leave home, feels deserted and miserable if her husband is absent for more than twenty-four hours, and she either complains mournfully when he returns, recounting her sufferings, or perhaps, in eloquent silence, intimates to him that he is a brute.

He, therefore, feels it his duty to curb his predilection for travel, restricting his wandering soul to a dash down to the sea or the river, sandwiched between prologue and epilogue of apologies, except at such times as the martyr's crown stirs his wife's ambition, and she bravely accompanies him on a painful little pleasure excursion.

Thus each one of this estimable couple has to give up what is most prized, in deference to the feelings of the other, who becomes a sort of amiable vampire, draining the life-blood from its willing prey.

This process of mutual injury is carried on in most marriages that are called happy. In marriages that are called unhappy, one of the pair has ordinarily proved recalcitrant, resisting the effacing process which the other sought to enforce—*hinc illæ lacrimæ!*

Perhaps, on the whole, happy marriages of this order are more disastrous than unhappy ones, for the united pair finally succeed at large cost and trouble, in inflicting upon one another the greatest loss that a human being—as such— can sustain, since he misses his inheritance: his own development, the peculiar experiences that await him in the domain of his slumbering personality, the peculiar contributions that humanity might have won from him. Thus both he and the community are defrauded, since man can possess and enjoy only so much of the universe of things as he can perceive; or in other words, the rank and the nature of human life are determined mathematically by the extent and the character of individual consciousness. All that tends to narrow and stunt this, narrows and stunts the life of the whole race, and retards its growth. Popular sentiment is busy at this stunting process. Thus we find the system almost reducing itself to absurdity in orthodox family life, wherein—speaking roughly—all approved persons are conducting their existence, not according to their own convictions, but according to those of some affectionate relative. In short, every estimable person is acting vicariously on the motives of somebody else.

We come to the conclusion, that the present form of marriage—exactly in proportion to its conformity with orthodox ideas—is a failure. If certain unconscious heretics, ignoring the teachings of orthodoxy, have given us inspiring examples of what marriage might be and can be, such instances afford no argument in favour of the institution as it is at present interpreted. Just to the extent to which a union follows that popular interpretation, is it a degrading bondage.

These are hard words, yet many more years will not pass away before most thinking people admit them to be justified.

The coercive element in marriage, be it observed, has been introduced as a crude corrective to the utter helplessness to which law-aided custom has reduced women. Wives (as it is even now argued) would be deserted by their husbands and left to starve, unless the law compelled the latter to remain with them. To place women in such a position that they need no longer chain unwilling husbands to their side from sheer dread of starvation, does not appear a particularly shocking proposition, when looked at calmly. When we are assured that marriage is really for the protection of the woman, there is indeed some truth in the assertion. She has been brought to a position which obliges the law to come to her aid, now and then. Her capital (as so many men have naively pointed out, without the faintest suspicion of the terrible wrong implied by the fact) consists in her youth, beauty, and attractions. She must invest it in marriage, and Society offers a guarantee for the payment of the interest. Such is the protection that marriage offers to women!

There are many signs that this arrangement is ceasing to be satisfying to either sex. They both more or less chafe against the commercial element, which social conditions still prevent them from either abolishing or ignoring. An increasing number of women are refusing a life of comparative ease in marriage, rather than enter upon it as a means of livelihood, for which their freedom has to be sacrificed. As this sentiment grows general, men and women cannot fail to recognise, as a mere truism, that so long as affection and friendship remain between a married couple, no bonds are necessary to hold them united; but that when these cease, the tie becomes intolerable, and no law ought to have power to enforce it. It need scarcely be added that there are, in these days, a growing number who insist that there must be complete acknowledgment of the right of the woman to possess herself, body and soul, in absolute independence. It has been part and parcel of her slave's position that this right has hitherto been denied her, by the sentiment of her contemporaries, nay, until the decision in the Jackson case, by force of law.

As the monogamic ideal becomes more and more realised and followed, not from force but from conviction, increasing freedom in the form of marriage must—paradox as it sounds—be looked for among a developing people. Greater respect for the liberties of the individual would alone dictate a system less barbaric, and would secure it from danger of abuse.

It must not be forgotten that all these anticipated changes cannot but be dependent on the educating influences that are brought to bear on the younger generation. Instead of separating girls and boys during their early years, we shall learn to educate them together, and thus lay the foundation, from the very beginning, of a wholesome community of interests, without which no marriage can be otherwise than disappointing.

It is our present absurd interference with the civilising influences of one sex upon the other, that initiates and enhances many of the dangers and difficulties of our social life, and gives colour to popular fears.

Anyone who imagines that he can destroy a social fact by attacking its figure-head, is hopeful rather than wise. It is not marriage *per se*, but the whole social drift with which it is at present co-related, that constitutes the evil. We must look not for destruction, but for re-birth. The essential wrongs on which I have been insisting—being wrongs of thought and sentiment—are destined to give way before a vigorous moral Renaissance, which has already begun. Few close observers can have failed to recognise, amidst the remarkable tumult of thought during the last few years, signs and wonders which seem to herald an awakening of this nature. These new ideas—like waves on an iron-bound coast—create not a little clamour as they beat upon the granite of age-long creed and custom. That clamour attests their reality and their strength.

That this change should be hotly opposed for a season is not a matter for regret. Ideas on which the fate of humanity may depend, could not be safely admitted without at least some preliminary processes of threshing, by which one may hope the chaff may be separated from the grain. The majority still believe, and must continue to believe for a long time to come, that there is nothing but danger in any doctrine which disturbs, by one hairsbreadth, the present conceptions of the conjugal relations. That majority will continue their work on the threshing-floor, perhaps helping rather than hindering that which they desire to oppose. The new ideal must submit to the process for the appointed years of its probation.

The changes suggested here, involve an immense increase of complexity, a widening of the human horizon. We are, in fact, contemplating a stupendous step of racial progress. There is a whole world yet to explore in the direction of social developments, and it is more than probable that the future holds a discovery in the domain of spirit as great as that of Columbus in the domain of matter.

A Defence of the "Wild Women"

Mona Caird

From The Morality of Marriage and Other Essays on the Status and Destiny of Women 1897

"What a great deal of trouble it would save the human race if once and for ever the predominant male would wake up to see that he has no more right to say what a woman shall or shall not do than a woman has to say what a man shall or shall not do."—Anon.

The first impulse of women whom Mrs. Lynn Linton calls "wild," is, probably, to contradict the charges that she makes against them in the course of three ruthless articles in the *Nineteenth Century*; but reflection shows the futility as well as the inconsequence of such a proceeding. After all, those who have lost faith in the old doctrines are not so much concerned to prove themselves, as individuals, wise and estimable, as to lead thinking men and women to consider popular sentiments with regard to the relation of the sexes, and to ask themselves whether the social fiat which for centuries has forced every woman, whatever be her natural inclination or powers, into one avocation, be really wise or just; whether, in truth, it be in the interests of the race to deprive one half of it of all liberty of choice, to select for them their mode of existence, and to prescribe for them their very sentiments.

To the task of opposing the conclusions of Mrs. Lynn Linton, her adversaries must bring considerable force and patience, and for this singular reason, that she gives them nothing to answer. One cannot easily reply to strings of accusations, levelled against the personal qualities of women who venture to hold views at variance with those at which the world arrived, at some undefined, but happy and infallible epoch in its history. The unbeliever finds himself thrown back upon the simple schoolroom form of discussion, consisting in flat contradiction persistently repeated until the energies give out. As this method appears undignified and futile, it seems better to let most of the charges pass in silence, commenting only on one or two here and there. It is of no real moment whether Mrs. Lynn Linton's unfavourable impression of the women who differ from her in this matter, be just or unjust. The question is simply: Are their views nearer or farther from the truth than the doctrines from which they dissent? As regards their personal qualities, it must, in fairness, be remembered that the position of the advocate of an unpopular cause is a very trying one. The apostles of a new faith are generally driven, by the perpetual fret of opposition and contempt, to some rancour or extravagance; but such conduct merely partakes of the frailty of human nature, and ought not to prejudice a really impartial mind against the views themselves.

Such a mind will consider principles and not persons; and although the absurdity of its champions may tell against the spread of a new doctrine amongst the mass, it certainly ought not to retard it among thinkers and students of history, who must be well aware that the noblest causes have not been able to command infallible advocates, nor to protect themselves from perilous friends.

It would be interesting to make a collection from the writings of Mrs. Lynn Linton, of all the terrific charges that she has brought against her sex, adding them up in two columns, and placing, side by side, the numerous couples that contradict each other. At the end of this sad list, one might place the simple sentence of defence, "No, we are not!" and although this would certainly lack the eloquence and literary quality of Mrs. Lynn Linton's arguments, I deny that it would yield to them in cogency.

There is nothing that is mean, paltry, ungenerous, tasteless, or ridiculous, of which the woman who repudiates the ancient doctrines is not capable, according to this lady; unless, indeed, they are such abject fools that they have not the energy to be knaves. The logic is stern: either a woman is a "modest violet, blooming unseen," unquestioning, uncomplaining, a patient producer of children, regardless of all costs to herself; suffering "every one's opinion to influence her mind," and "all venerable laws hallowed by time ... to control her actions,"—either this, or a rude masculine creature, stamping over moors with a gun, that she may ape the less noble propensities of man; an adventuress who exposes herself to the dangers of travel, simply that she may advertise herself in a book on her return; a virago who desires nothing better than to destroy in others the liberty that she so loudly demands for herself.

There is, according to Mrs. Lynn Linton, no medium between Griselda and a sublimated Frankenstein's monster, which we have all so often heard of and seldom seen. Mrs. Lynn Linton's experience, in this respect, appears to have been ghastly. This is greatly to be regretted, for it has induced her to divide women, roughly, into two great classes: the good, beautiful, submissive, charming, noble, and wise, on the one hand; and on the other, the bad, ugly, rebellious, ill-mannered, ungenerous, foolish, and liberty-demanding. The "wild women" are like the plain and wicked sisters in a fairy tale, baleful creatures, who go about the world doing bad deeds, and oppressing innocence as it sits rocking the cradle by the fireside. It seems hard for the poor elder sisters to be told off to play this dreadful role, amid the hisses of the gallery; and they deserve some sympathy after all, for truly, the world offers temptations to evil courses, and innocence at the cradle can be desperately exasperating at times! It has a meek, placid, sneaky, virtuous way of getting what it wants, and making it hot and uncomfortable for unpopular elder sisters.

After all, in spite of Mrs. Lynn Linton, there is no more finished tyrant in the world than the meek sweet creature who cares nothing for her "rights," because she knows she can get all she wants by artifice; who makes a weapon of her womanhood, a sword of strength of her weakness, and does not disdain to tyrannise over men to her heart's content by an ungenerous appeal to their chivalry. She is a woman—poor, weak, helpless, and her husband may not call his soul his own! Tears are a stock-in-trade, and nerves a rock of defence. She claims no rights—she can't understand what all this absurd talk is about—she is quite satisfied with things as they are. Personal dignity she has none; it would sadly interfere with her successful methods of insinuating herself through life, in serpentine fashion. She gets what she can as best she may, living by her wits; a mere adventuress, after all, in spite of her unblemished character; appealing to men's frailties, chivalry, as every member of a subject class has to appeal, if any great success, or even a bare livelihood is to be hoped for.

But far be it from me to affirm, in simple opposition to Mrs. Lynn Linton, that all women of the old school are of this kind. My object is not to bring a counter-charge, but to point to the type which power on the one side, and subordination on the other, tend to produce. There are thousands, however, of the time-honoured school, who never dream of attempting this unconscious retaliation. Many of them neither demand rights nor win their way by artifice. They accept their lot, exactly as it is, in a literal spirit, being just enough developed to see the meanness of trading upon the chivalry of men, and not enough so to resent being placed in a position which makes them dependent, utterly and hopelessly, upon masculine favour. These women—the most pathetic class of all—have been so well drilled to accept their position without question, that they launch their complaints only at Fate and Nature, if ever they are moved to complain at all. Their conscience and their generosity forbid them to make use of the usual weapons of a dependent race: artifice and flattery. They are thus denied even this redress, which less sensitive women enjoy without stint. These half-developed women respond loyally to the stern demands made upon them by public sentiment. They are martyrs to "duty" in its narrowest sense; they turn a meek ear to society when it addresses homilies to them. It does not strike them as unjust, nor do they even enjoy the sad consolation of perceiving the humour of the situation, when their stern monitors, in all the pomp and circumstance of arbitrary authority, demand of them the loftiest principles, burden them with the heaviest responsibilities, while continuing to deprive them of all corresponding rights.

In short, the women of the old order and the women of the new, have faults and virtues, each after their own kind, and it is idle to make general affirmations about either class.

It is well, therefore, to check the inherent instinct to contradict, when Mrs. Lynn Linton says that women of the new faith are all evil and ugly. One must say, rather, that this is a mere matter of opinion, formed from the impression that each person gathers from individual experience, and from the bias with which that experience is met. Let, however, the impression be as unfavourable to the "wild women" as it may, it is neither fair nor philosophic to refuse to consider their claims. The liberal-minded will remember that the claims of a class hitherto subordinate always seem preposterous, and that the more complete has been their exclusion, the more ridiculous will appear their aspirations. We can accurately measure their degree of subjection by the loudness of the popular outcry against their claims. Yet, the inclination to treat with derision any new demand for liberty, stands on a level with the instinct of the street urchin to jeer at anything to which he is unaccustomed, as, for example, any person in foreign garments, though the latter excel a thousand times, in dignity and comeliness, the natives of the country.

It is not very surprising if some of the apostles of the new faith, irritated by the most powerful hindrances of law, sentiment, tradition—baffling, subtle, unceasing as these are—have made the mistake, as I think, of seeking to emphasise their demand for the liberty that men enjoy, by imitating men's habits and manners, and by seizing every occasion to take part in the fierce battle for existence, as if that were a desirable thing in itself, instead of an unhappy necessity. They are not alone in their error, however; they are not singular when they fail to see that the life that men now lead, in the effort to "earn a living and to succeed," is perilous to themselves and to the race. To add to that great body of struggling men, another body of struggling women would, evidently, by itself, not mend matters; and it is clear that the hopes which we may hold for the future of the race, through the emancipation of women, cannot rest on the prospect of their entering the tumultuous arena of competition. Undeniably, it would be wiser if women would use their influence to render the conflict less fierce, to slacken the greed for money, success, display, and to turn the ambitions of men to more rational and fruitful ways.

But however true all this may be, it is unluckily also true that women have to live, and that even those who possess a father or a husband have, at most, food and shelter; they have not independence. The wife among the less prosperous of the middle classes, who takes upon her shoulders at least half the burden of the household—to put it very mildly—may toil all her life and grow worn with anxiety and worry, but she will still be as dependent upon her husband's will or caprice as if she were an idler, living upon his bounty.

Women are beginning to feel this, more or less distinctly, and to desire to earn a little money for themselves, so that they may possess some means of subsistence that is really their own, small though it may be. This is surely natural enough, however evil may be the consequences of an inrush of women workers into the labour market. Since the work of women in their homes, is not of a kind to give them independence, they are beginning to seek for employment of a sort that is recognised as deserving of reward, knowing that their pecuniary position eternally stands in the way of any improvement, as regards their legal and social status, and that it often obliges them to submit to a thousand wrongs and indignities which could not otherwise be placed upon them.

A certain number of rebels are bending all their energies to the removal of this invincible hindrance, and to attain this end they are forced to join, more or less, in the struggle for a livelihood. It will be a happy day for humanity when a woman can stay in her own home without sacrificing her freedom. Short-sighted is the policy which would keep the wife and mother helpless in the hands of the man whose home she sustains and holds together, which would give her but a meagre share of right to the children which have cost her so much to bear and tend, while burdening her with fullest responsibility regarding them. To this point I would especially call the attention of that large portion of the community who are convinced of the importance of the fireside and the home, who believe that in every other locality the woman is out of her sphere. Would they not use their influence most wisely, from their own point of view, in seeking to remove some of the heavy penalties that are attached to the enjoyment of home and fireside, and to make these sanctuaries deserve a little better all the sentiment that has been lavished upon them?

It is easy, indeed, to see the peril to the well-being of the race that lies in the labour of women outside the home; that peril can scarcely be exaggerated. But if women demand the natural human right to take their share of the opportunities, such as they are, which the world has to offer—if they desire the privilege of independence (a privilege denied them, work as they will, within the home), by what right does society refuse their demand? Men are living lives and committing actions, day by day, which imperil the well-being of the race; on what principle are women only to be restrained? Why this one-sided sacrifice, this artificial selection of victims for the good—or supposed good—of humanity? The old legends of maidens who were chosen every year, and chained to a rock on the shore, to propitiate gods or sea-monsters, seem not in the least out of date.

Sacrifices were performed more frankly in those days, and nobody tried to persuade the victims that so far from constituting a grievance, it was an enjoyable and blessed thing to be devoured. They did not talk about "woman's sphere" to a maiden chained to a rock within sight of the monster, nor did they tell her that the "true woman" desired no other destiny. They were brutal, but they did not add sickly sentiment to their crime against the individual. They carried out the hideous old doctrine of vicarious sacrifice—which is haunting us like an evil spirit to this day—in all good faith and frankness, and there was no attempt to represent the monster as an engaging beast when you got to know his inner self.

Society is unjust in exacting these sacrifices; every member of it must stand equal in its sight, if it would claim the name of a free state. On the soil of such a state, there must be no arbitrary selection of victims for the general good, made from a certain class, or, still worse, from a certain sex. One can imagine the heaven-assaulting howl that would go up, were it proposed to deal in this way with a particular body of men. Loud would be the protest of this hapless band, picked out for sacrifice, should they be denied the right, common to all others, of seeking their fortunes as might seem good to them! No argument about the welfare of the race would reconcile a nation of free-born men to such a proposal. Yet this is the argument that free-born men do not hesitate to employ, as a plea for making an arbitrary exception to the disadvantage of women.

The attempt to force upon these any sacrifice, on the sole ground of their sex; to demand of them a special act of renunciation of rights and privileges on that account, gives us an exact analogue of the old tribute to the gods of a nation which chose its victims, not by fair hazard from the population, but from a class set apart for the iniquitous purpose. Such actions are subversive of all social life, for the existence of a community depends, finally, upon its respect for the rights of its individual members. Upon these rights society is built; without them, nothing is possible but an aggregation of tyrants and slaves, which does not deserve the name of a society, since it is bound together by force, and the union between its members is accidental, not organic. On what rests, finally, my safety and freedom as a citizen, but on the understanding that if I leave your rights intact, you will also respect mine?

But further: the argument which takes its stand upon the danger to the community of the freedom of women, besides being unfair (since it would select a whole sex for the propitiatory victims), is, on its own ground, fallacious. True, indeed, is it that if all women were to rush into the labour market and begin to compete with men and with one another, the result would be evil; but it is *not* true that if they were to be placed on an equality with men in the eye of the law, if in marriage they were free from all artificial disability, if in society they had no special prejudices to contend with—it is not true in *that* case that the consequence of this change in their position would be detrimental to the real interests of the common wealth. On the contrary, its influence would be for good, and for more good than perhaps anyone now dares to believe. And among the many causes of this beneficent result we may number this: that women would be able to choose the work for which they were best suited. We should have fewer governesses who loathed teaching, fewer wives who could do most things better than look after a house, and fewer mothers to whom the training of children was an impossible task. Moreover, Society would rejoice in more of that healthy variety among her members which constitutes one of the elements of social vitality. There is room for all kinds of women, did we but realise it; and there is certainly no reason why the present movement should sweep away all those of the ancient type in whom Mrs. Lynn Linton takes delight. They have their charm, but it must be acknowledged that, for all their meekness, nothing would please them better than tyrannically to dictate to their less chastened sisters, what mode of life and what kind of sentiments they shall adopt. By what charter or authority does the domestic woman (like the person in the train who wants the window up) attempt to restrict, within her own limits, women who entirely disagree with her in opinion and in temperament?

Granted, for the moment, that Mrs. Lynn Linton and her followers are justified of Heaven in their views, and that it always was and always will be necessary for women to dedicate themselves wholly to the production of the race; still, this truth—if such it be—must be left to demonstrate itself without any tyranny, direct or indirect, from those who realise it; otherwise they violate the conditions of social liberty, and even their own principle is jeopardised, through being forced upon the unconvinced. The history of all persecutions, religious or other, ought to warn us against the danger of allowing the promulgation of a faith, true or false, by forcible means, and I include among forcible means all forms of coercive prejudice and sentiment, for often these are far more powerful than legal enactments. Let us not forget the glorious privilege of the citizen of a free state to be in the wrong, and to act upon his error until the torch-bearers of truth shall be able to throw light upon his pathway. That once accomplished, his adherence will be worth having.

The demand that all women shall conform to a certain model of excellence, that they shall be debarred from following the promptings of their powers,—whatsoever be the pretext for the restriction,—is the outcome of an illiberal spirit, and ought to be resisted as all attacks on liberty ought to be resisted. The fact that the attack is made on liberties which, as yet, are only candidates for existence, is the sole reason why Englishmen do not resent the aggression.

Let it be remembered, for the consolation of those who fear the results of this new movement, that if modern women are lapsing from the true faith, if they are really insurgents against evolutionary human nature, instead of being the indications of a new social development, then their fatal error will assuredly prove itself in a very short time. Should some harm be suffered in the proving, that is merely the risk that has to be taken, in all free states, in order to secure the possibility of progress.

These, then, are the principles upon which women of the new faith claim tolerance for their views, be they right or wrong. Having demanded these initial rights, they then proceed to give their reasons for holding such views, and for the rebellion which they preach against the old order.

To the time-honoured argument that Nature intended man to be anything and everything that his strength of muscle and of mind permitted, while she meant woman to be a mother, and nothing else, the rebels reply that if a woman has been made by nature to be a mother, so has a cow or a sheep; and if this maternal capacity be really an infallible indication of principal function, there is nothing to prevent this reasoning from running downhill to its conclusion, namely, that the nearer a woman can become to a cow or a sheep the better.

If popular feeling objects to this conclusion, and yet still desires all women to make maternity their chief duty, it must find another reason for its faith, leaving nature's sign-posts out of the question. On these sign-posts man himself is privileged to write and re-write the legends, though of this power he seems at present to be unconscious, persistently denying it, even while his restless fingers are busy at their work.

This dear and cherished appeal to nature, however, will never be abandoned by the advocates of the old order, while breath remains to them. But if they use the argument, they ought not to shrink from its consequences, nor, indeed, *would* they, but that it happens that women, as a matter of fact, have by this time, in spite of so much discouragement, risen above the stage of simple motherhood, thus accustoming their critics to attributes distinctively human. These newer attributes, having become familiar, no longer seem alarming or "unnatural." In our present stage of development, we demand of a woman that she shall be first of all a mother, and then that she develop those human qualities that best harmonise with her position as such. "Be it pleasant or unpleasant," Mrs. Lynn Linton says, "it is none the less an absolute truth—the *raison d'être* of a woman is maternity...the cradle lies across the door of the polling-booth and bars the way to the Senate."

We are brought, then, to this conclusion: that if there be any force in what is commonly urged respecting Nature's "intentions" with regard to woman, her development as a thinking and emotional being, beyond the point where human qualities are superficially useful to her children, is "unnatural" and false, a conclusion which leads us straight away to Oriental customs and to Oriental ethics. Moreover, another consideration confronts us. Nature, besides designing women to be mothers, designed men to be fathers: why, then, should not the man give up his life to his family in the same wholesale way? "The cases are so different," it will be said. Yes, and the difference lies in the great suffering and risk which fall solely to the share of the mother. Is this a good reason for holding her, for her whole life, to this painful task, for demanding that she shall allow her tastes and talents to lie idle, and to die a slow and painful death, while the father, to whom parenthood is also indicated by "nature," is allowed the privilege of choosing his own avocations without interference? Further, if woman's functions are to be determined solely by a reference to what is called nature, how, from this point of view, are we to deal with the fact that she possesses a thousand emotional and intellectual attributes that are wholly superfluous to her merely maternal activities? What does Mrs. Lynn Linton consider that "nature intends" by all this?

In the present order of society, speaking roughly, a woman, to whom maternity seems unsatisfying or distasteful, has either to bring herself to undertake, to the exclusion of all other interests, that one task for which she is unfitted, or to deny her affections altogether. To man, the gods give both sides of the apple of life; a woman is sometimes permitted the choice of the halves,—either, but not both. In thousands of cases she is offered neither.

Yet every new development of society, every overthrow of ancient landmarks, tends to prove more and more conclusively that this fetish "Nature," who is always claimed as the patroness of the old order, just when she is busy planning and preparing the new, has *not* separated the human race into two distinct sections with qualities entirely and eternally different. If this were so—if women were, in fact, the only beings under heaven not modifiable by education and surroundings, then we should be forced to reconstruct from the foundation our notions of natural law, and to rescind the comparatively modern theory that it is unwise to expect effects without causes, or causes without effects. We should live once more in a world of haphazard and of miracle, in which only one fact could be counted upon from age to age—viz., the immutable and stereotyped "nature" of women.

Unless we are prepared for this antique and variegated creed, we cannot consistently pronounce, as Mrs. Lynn Linton so authoritatively pronounces, what is the sphere or *raison d'être* of either sex, and what it must be for evermore. It seems, indeed, safe to predict that women will continue to bear children, but it is far from safe to prophesy to what extent that function will in the future absorb their energies. We know that although men have been fathers from the beginning of human history, they have not made fatherhood the key-note of their existence. On the contrary, it has been an entirely secondary consideration. They have been busy in influencing and fashioning a world which their children are to inherit—a world that would be sorrier than it is, if men had also made the fact of parenthood the central point of their career.

The disastrous consequences of such conduct on the part of women have been dwelt upon at length elsewhere in this volume. It is impossible to exaggerate these evils, and impossible to insist on them too strongly, seeing the misery that springs from them, and the stubborn prejudice that still perseveres in denying their existence. The dedication of a whole sex to this exhausting function has gone far to destroy the healthy balance of the racial constitution, physical, mental, and moral. It has thrown work on to unfit shoulders, formed a sort of press-gang of the most terrible kind, inasmuch as unwilling motherhood is worse than unwilling military service. It has deprived the very children, on whose behalf this insane cruelty has been wrought, of the benefit of possessing really efficient mothers. They have been doomed to grow up under the influence of tired-out, half-educated women who can scarcely manage their own weary lives, much less guide the growth of young souls and bodies during the critical and fate-deciding years of childhood and early youth. It may seem paradoxical, but is none the less true, that we shall never have really good mothers, until women cease to make motherhood the central idea of their existence. The woman who has no interest larger than the affairs of her children is not a fit person to train them.

For the sake of men, women, and children, it is to be hoped that women will come to regard motherhood with new eyes; that the force of their artificially fostered impulses will become less violent, and that there may be an increase in them of the distinctly *human* qualities and emotions in relation to those that are merely maternal. It is this *change of proportion* in the force of human qualities that virtually creates a new being, and makes progress possible. Once more, in the light of this truth, how false are all the inferences of phrases such as "Nature intends," "Nature desires." She intends and desires nothing—she is an abject slave. *Man* intends, *Man* desires, and "Nature," in the course of centuries, learns to obey.

This worship of "Nature" is a strange survival in a scientific age of the old image-worship of our ancestors. She is our Freya or Hertha, a personal will who designs and plans. This is a subtle form of superstition which has cunningly nestled among the folds of the garment of Science, and there it will lurk, safe and undetected, for many years, to discourage all change, to cast discredit on all new thought, to hold man to his errors, and to blind him to his own enormous power of development.

It is this insidious superstition that prevents intelligent people—nay, persons of scientific training—from recognising the effect upon women of their circumstances. Professions are known to leave their mark on men, although the influence of a man's profession is not so incessant and overwhelming as are the conditions of women's lives, from which there is no escape from the cradle to the grave. Yet it is always grudgingly and doubtfully admitted, if at all, that this fact offers an explanation of any bad quality in the feminine character. No one seems to realise how, age after age, women have been, one and all, engaged in the same occupations, subjected to the same kind of stimulus and training; how each individual, of infinitely varying multitudes, has been condemned to one function for the best years of life, and that function an extremely painful and exhausting one. No one seems to understand that these causes *must* produce effects, and that they have produced, among others, the effect in women of certain tyrannous and overwrought instincts, which we say, reverentially and obstinately, "Nature has implanted in woman." We might more accurately say: Suffering, moral and mental starvation, physical pain, disease induced by the over-excitement of one set of functions—these have fostered impulses which we have the assurance to call sacred.

At the present time, some very interesting researches are being carried on, which tend to show, so far as they have gone, that the constitution of women has been literally destroyed by the centuries of ill-usage, often unwitting, which public sentiment has forced them to submit to; whilst their training, in combination with their absolute dependence on men, has induced them often to endure their fate as if it were the will of Heaven.

These researches show that through these ages of overstrain of every kind—physical, emotional, nervous—one set of faculties being in perpetual activity while the others lay dormant, woman has fallen into a state that is more or less ailing and diseased; that upon her shoulders has been laid the penalty of the injustice and selfishness of men.[21]

21   Ellis Ethelmer, the author of a remarkable pamphlet called "Life to Woman" (obtainable from Mrs. Wolstenholme Elmy, Buxton House, Congleton, Cheshire), brings forward evidence which proves this point. One or two instances given may here be quoted, the reader being reminded that an immense body of similar evidence lies behind that which is adduced in this most interesting pamphlet.
The writer first points out how marriage has been the subject of legislative enactments and religious ordinances, and always seemingly with the same end in view—increasing of the population. For this purpose, such agencies have employed "injunctions and allurements—threats of infamy and perdition for infertility, and bribes of worldly comfort or eternal Paradise for the begetting of a progeny." "These," says Ellis Ethelmer, "have been held out by rulers, spiritual and temporal, in Church or State, throughout all ages, to induce the populace to 'increase and multiply' (that the ruler's own property and power might be swollen in the process)." . . . Evidence on this point might be adduced ranging from the Mosaic injunction, "increase and multiply," and the ancient Greek, Roman, and Oriental honours or civic privileges conferred on fathers of large families, down to the modern national or colonial bounties offered to inhabitants or immigrants similarly qualified. Malthus says: "The customs of some nations, and the prejudices of all," have acted in some degree like a bounty on the getting of children. ("On Population," i. 8.) Inducement to propagation has been a studied object of both religious and civil precept; appeals to man's nobler aspiration or baser sensuality, as either seemed likely to prove the more effective for the object in view. The patriarch of the Jewish nation is represented as being prompted by the promise of a progeny "as the sand which is upon the sea-shore" for multitude; and each male scion was spurred by the assurance of wealth and happiness to him who had his "quiver full " of children. The evident bearing of the teaching was that the begetting of a multiplicity of children was a religious as well as a civic duty, *to be performed even in default of personal impulse.* This factitious and double-stringed appeal has been played upon in a hundred different ways in the history of all nations. Higher honours were decreed to prolific fathers by the State during life, and greater bliss was promised them after death by the Church."

Have we not gone far enough along this path of destruction; or must women still make motherhood their chief task, accepting the old sentiment of subservience to man, until they drive yet further into the system the cruel diseases that have punished the insanities of the past; diseases which are taking vengeance upon the victims of ill-usage for their submission, and pursuing their children from generation to generation with relentless footsteps? Such is the counsel of Mrs. Lynn Linton and her school. Upon the consequences of all this past ill-treatment is founded the pretext for women's disabilities in the present. They are physically

"In Corea, the male human being who is unmarried is treated with the greatest indignity." "In India," according to the Laws of Mann, "marriage is the twelfth Sanskara, and thus a religious duty incumbent upon all." (Westermarck, "History of Marriage," p. 41.) The Abbé Reynal says of these Hindu laws: "Population is made a primitive duty, so sacred a command of nature that the law permits to cheat, to lie, and to commit perjury in trying to bring about a marriage." "According to the Talmud, the authorities can compel a man to marry, and he who lives single at the age of twenty is accursed by God almost as if he were a murderer." (Westermarck, "Marriage," p. 141.)

"A Mahommedan is in some degree obliged to polygamy, from a principle of obedience to his prophet, who makes one of the greatest duties of man to consist in procreating children to glorify the Creator." (Malthus, "On Population," i. 7.) "Zoroaster declared propagation a meritorious act; enjoined multiplicity of children; made the 'obedience' of wives to their husbands a great matter of duty; and commanded that every woman should be a wife. He took a sure way to tempt or frighten an ignorant people into propagation, by announcing that 'children were the glory of the celestial spirits, and helped their parents after death over the bridge that joined the heaven to the earth.'" (Bryant Barrett, "Code Napoleon," vol. i. p. 87.)

"At Sparta, the obligation of marriage was legal, like the military service." (Letourneau, "Evolution of Marriage," p. 195.)

Aristotle says: "A man who had three sons was exempt from the night-watch, and he who had four enjoyed a complete immunity from public burdens." ("De Kepublico," lib. ii. c. 6.)

In Roman legislation, as Alexander, the mediaeval writer, summarises: "Moreover, the old Romans bestowed Prætorships, Quæstorships, and Consulships, and honours and magistracies on none but the parents of many children." (Bk. iv. chap. 8.)

Sir P. Colquhoun ("Summary of the Roman Civil Law," par. 571, 573) says: "*Liberti* (manumitted slaves) were freed from servitude, and freemen from the burden of tutorship, in virtue of a number of children. The first places in the theatres were reserved to those who exceeded in the number of their issue. Further, those who living at Rome had three children, in Italy four, or in the provinces five, were exempted from personal public duties."

In China: "A woman's sole chance of any happiness in a future life is made contingent on her maternity; though, again, in this labour a daughter is not to count. Only as a mother of a son, as the continuator of the direct line of a family, can a woman escape from her degradation." (See "Woman Free," p. 68.)

In India: "To the widow of high caste a hint of the Vedic reward of the 'world of life' is held out; while, in lower conditions, the woman is too much a slave for inducement (other than injunction and threat) to be deemed of any necessity; her bodily servitude and sexual abuse from early youth is almost beyond belief." (See "Woman Free," p. 71 *et seq.)*

"To die in giving birth is accounted martyrdom."

In Rome, certain civic privileges were given to the mother of more than three children. The old festivals, and many ancient religious observances, are adduced in support of the author's contention, namely, that there has been enormous over-stimulus on one side of the nature and faculty.

weak, nervous, easily unstrung, and for this reason, it is urged, they must continue to pursue the mode of life which has induced these evils. This is strange reasoning.

The suffering of women to-day is built upon their suffering of yesterday and its consequences. It is surely a rather serious matter to cut off a human being from whatever the world has to offer him, in this short life, even if the vocation appointed be of the most desirable.

From this point of view, what force or meaning have Mrs. Lynn Linton's taunts and accusations against her sex, even though they were all perfectly just? It is probable that women, in virtue of their susceptible physical constitution and nervous system (a quality, by the way, which distinguishes the man of genius from the ordinary being) are more responsive than men are to their surroundings. Therefore, all that Mrs. Lynn Linton says, if true, about the wildness of ignorant women in times of excitement—she cites for an example the *tricoteuses* of the French Revolution—might perhaps be explained on this ground. A quick response to stimulus is *not* the mark of a being low in the scale of existence, though it may lead to extravagant deeds when untutored. But Mrs. Lynn Linton will not look at this question philosophically. She hurls accusations at her sisters, as if it pleased her to add another and yet another insult to those which the literature of centuries—with that exquisite chivalry which we are so often warned our freedom would destroy—has never tired of flinging at the defenceless sex. It does not strike Mrs. Lynn Linton to inquire into the real causes that underlie all these problems of a growing human nature; she prefers the finger of scorn, the taunt, the inexpensive sneer.

Why does she so harshly condemn the results of the system of things which she so ardently approves? If all has really been so well in the State of Denmark, how is it that women (according to her showing) have become such ridiculous and contemptible idiots, that they are to be held fitted only for the purposes of race production? To make her position more difficult to understand, Mrs. Lynn Linton dwells, with some insistence, on the effects upon her sex of their training. She speaks of "ideal qualities which women have gained by a certain amount of sequestration from the madding crowd's ignoble strife. . . . Are the women at the gin-shop bar," she demands, "better than the men at the gin-shop door, the field-hands in sun-bonnets more satisfactory than those in brimless hats?" This is to prove that women have no real moral superiority. Elsewhere, however, is asked: "Can anyone point out anywhere a race of women who are superior to their conditions?" All this is strange reasoning from one who takes her stand on the fiats of "Nature," as distinguished from the influences of surroundings.

One might ask: "Can anyone point out anywhere a race of *men* who are superior to their conditions?" But this possible question never seems to strike Mrs. Lynn Linton, for she exposes herself all through the article to the same form of demand, and she nowhere attempts to meet it. Her mode of warfare is indeed bewildering; for she attacks from both sides, makes double and antagonistic use of the same facts, and she does not at all object to assertions clearly contradictory, provided they are separated in time and space by the interval of a paragraph or two.

Her arguments, when formidable, mutually and relentlessly devour each other, like so many *plus* and *minus* quantities, which, added together, become cancelled and leave a clean *zero* between them.

Unconscious, however, of this cannibalism among her legions, the authoress finds herself at the close of her article with a gigantic and robust opinion which nothing—not even her own arguments—can disturb.

As an instance of this strange suicidal tendency of her reasoning, we may compare the already quoted paragraphs, setting forth the effects of environment upon the woman's temperament, with the even more determined assertion of its eternal, unalterable, and God-ordained nature. Confront these two statements, and what remains? Mrs. Lynn Linton seems to half surrender her position when she says that ". . . there are few women of anything like energy or brain-power who have not felt in their own souls the ardent longing for a freer hand in life"; but the following sentence seems to run still further into the jaws of the enemy: "Had Louis the Sixteenth had Marie Antoinette's energy and Marie Antoinette Louis's supineness, the whole story of the Reign of Terror, Marat, Charlotte Corday, and Napoleon might never have been written." What doctrine of Mrs. Lynn Linton's does it even *seem* to support?

In unblushing contradiction of this sentiment, Mrs. Lynn Linton asserts that political women have always been "disastrous," and that even Mme. Roland "did more harm than good when she undertook the manipulation of forces that were too strong for her control, too vast for her comprehension."

Were the forces of the French Revolution within the grasp of any one person, and does it tend to prove woman's inability for any but the domestic sphere, that Madame Roland did not stem the tide of this great movement which had been preparing for centuries beforehand, and which proved intractable to many of the sterner sex, as well as to the "disastrous" Madame Roland?

"Women are both more extreme and more impressionable than men," Mrs. Lynn Linton says; "and the spirit which made weak girls into heroines and martyrs, honest women into the yelling *tricoteuses* of the blood-stained saturnalia of '92, still exists in the sex, and among ourselves as elsewhere."

In short, when a "weak" girl espouses martyrdom, she is prompted thereto by a sort of hysteria, male heroism alone being heroic.

While admitting, nay emphasising, on the one hand, the fact of the remodelling force of circumstances, Mrs. Lynn Linton denies that feminine character and intelligence can ever be altered by one hairsbreadth, except—and here comes the third and crowning contradiction—except for the worse.

Among the many other minor points which this writer has touched upon, are several which call for special comment, from the point of view opposed to hers. For example, we are asked to believe that the peace of the home practically depends on the political disabilities of woman; or, in other words, that a man is unable to endure in his wife opinions differing from his own. I do not believe that men are quite so childish and petty as all this; but if they are, it is indeed high time that they should learn the lesson of common courtesy and tolerance.

The device of keeping peace between two persons, by the disarmament of one of them, is ingenious and simple, but there is a temptation to think that such peace as that, if peace it can be called, would be well exchanged for strife. Does peace, indeed, mean the stagnation that arises from the relationship between the free and the fettered, or does it mean the generous mutual recognition of the right of private judgment? The denial of political power to women, if it ever does prevent dissension, achieves at best, on the part of the wife, unreasoning acquiescence, and not rational agreement.

Mrs. Lynn Linton says that "amongst our most renowned women are some who say with their whole heart, 'I would rather have been the wife of a great man, or the mother of a hero, than what I am—famous in my own person.'" That is a matter of taste, but it seems strange that these famous women should not have acted upon their predilections. Against the following sentence I cannot refrain from expressing a sense of revolt; but the revolt is on behalf of men rather than of women. "But the miserable little manikin who creeps to obscurity, overshadowed by his wife's glory, is as pitiful in history as contemptible in fact. The husband of the wife is no title to honour; and the best and dearest of our famous women take care that this shall not be said of them and theirs."

Are men, then, to be treated as if they were a set of jealous schoolboys, or superannuated invalids, whom the discreet person allows to win at chess, because they have a childish dislike to being beaten?

It is consoling to remember that the ideas on which such feelings rest are giving way, slowly but surely, in all directions. It is only when the rebellion is extended over evidently new ground that Mrs. Lynn Linton and her followers begin to sound the tocsin, assuring the rebellious woman that she shows "a curious inversion of sex, disdaining the duties and limitations imposed on her by Nature." As a crowning taunt, Mrs. Lynn Linton says: "All women are not always lovely, and the wild women never are." This reminds one of the exasperated retort of an angry child who has come to the end of his invention—a galling if somewhat inconsequent attack upon the personal appearance, which is generally the last resort of outraged juvenile nature.

Nothing perhaps can better show the real attitude of this lady and her followers on this question, than her irritation against those who are trying to bring a ray of sunlight into the harems and zenanas of the East.

"Ignorant and unreasonable," she says, "they would carry into the sun-laden East the social conditions born of the icy winds of the North. ... In a country where jealousy is as strong as death, and stronger than love, they would incite women to revolt against the rule of seclusion, which has been the law of the land for centuries before we were a nation at all. That rule has worked well for the country, inasmuch as the chastity of Hindu women and the purity of the family life are notoriously intact."

If Mrs. Lynn Linton approves of the relation of the sexes in the East, and looks upon it with an eye of fondness, because it dates back into ages whose savagery breaks out in the blood of civilised men to this day, then she may well set herself in opposition to the rebellion, among modern women, against the less intolerable injustice which they suffer in the West. Did we happen to be living in harems in South Kensington or Mayfair, with the sentiment of the country in favour of that modest and womanly state of seclusion, it is easy to imagine with what eloquence Mrs. Lynn Linton would declaim against the first hint of insurrection—although in that case, by the way, the strictly unfeminine occupation of writing articles would be denied her.

The really grave question raised in this lady's work, is that of the effect of the political and social freedom of women upon the physical well-being of the race; for while past conditions have been evil, future ones may conceivably be equally so, though they could with difficulty be worse. This is, indeed, a serious problem, which will require all the intelligence of this generation to solve. But first, I would suggest what appears to be a new idea (strange as this may seem), namely, that the rights of the existing race are at least as great as those of the coming one. There is something pathetically absurd, in the sacrifice to their children, of generation after generation of grown people. Who were the gainers by the incessant surrender? Of what avail was all that renunciation on behalf of those potential men and women, if, on their attainment of that degree, they too have to abandon the fruits of so much pain, and so many lost possibilities, and to begin, all over again, the weaving, *ad infinitum*, of this singular Penelope's web? The affairs of the present are carried on by the adult population, not by the children; and if the generations of adults are going to renounce, age after age, their own chances of development—resigning opportunities of intellectual progress for the sake of their children—how, in the name of common sense, will they benefit humanity? For those children also, when their minds are ripe for progress, must, in accordance with this noble sentiment, immediately begin, in *their* turn, to renounce, and resign, and deny themselves, in order to start another luckless generation upon the same ridiculous circle of futility.

I fear that it is not unnecessary to add that I do not here inculcate neglect of children, but merely claim some regard for the parent whom it cost previous parents so much to bear, and rear, and train. I protest against this insane waste of human energy, this perpetual renunciation for a race that never comes. When and where will be born that last happy generation, who are to reap all the fruit of these ages of sacrifice? Will they wallow in the lost joys of sad women who have resigned ambitions, and allowed talents to die in this thankless service? Will they taste all the experience that their mothers consented to forego? Are all these things stored up for them, like treasure that a miser will not spend, though he perish in his garret for lack of warmth and nourishment?

Not so; but rather, for every loss suffered by the fathers, the children will be held debtors.

As regards the fears that are entertained, on all sides, at the prospect of women taking part in political life, or in any occupation which custom has not hitherto recognised as feminine, the advocates of freedom might ask: why nobody has hitherto felt the least alarm about the awful nervous strain which the ideal submissive woman has had to undergo, from time immemorial. Why has nobody considered the danger involved in the bearing and rearing of vast families, and the incessant cares of a household, under conditions, perhaps, of straightened means? Is there anything in the world that causes more nervous exhaustion than such a combination of duties? Doctors are, for once, agreed that worry is the most resistless of all taxes upon the constitution. Monotony of life has the same tendency, and a lack of variety in interests and thought undeniably conduces to the lowering of the vitality. Yet nobody has taken fright at the fatal combination of all these nerve-destroying conditions, which belong essentially to the lot of woman under the old *régime*.[22]

The one sort of strain which seems to be feared for the feminine constitution is that of brain-work, although, as a matter of fact, mental effort, if not too prolonged and severe, enhances and does not exhaust the vitality.

It is true, it cannot be carried on simultaneously with great physical exertion. To go on having children, year after year, superintending them and the home while doing other work outside, would indeed have disastrous consequences, but who would wish to see women doing anything so insane? Such a domestic treadmill is stupid and brutal enough, without the addition of the mental toil. It is the treadmill that calls for modification.

If the new movement had no other effect than to rouse women to rebellion against the madness of large families, it would confer a priceless benefit on humanity.

We are accustomed to hear a great deal about the mother's joys, especially from male enthusiasts, on this ever-popular theme; but there are, here and there, evidences of sentiments of another nature on the part of mothers; and,

22   "The idea of the pilgrimage (to the hill-top) was to get away from the endless and nameless circumstances of every-day existence, which by degrees build a wall about the mind, so that it travels in a constantly narrowing circle. . . . *This is all—there is nothing more*; this is the reiterated preaching of house-life . . . the constant routine of house-life, the same work, the same thought in the work, the little circumstances daily recurring will dull the keenest edge of work."—"The Story of My Heart," by Richard Jefferies.

significantly enough, in those most spontaneous expressions of feeling—ancient folk-songs and lullabies. The Athenæum of August 1895, in reviewing a collection of lullabies, says of the authoress:—

> " She has chosen very pretty ones, though many of them are not so much cradle-songs proper ... as expressions of the mother's weariness and longing for the moment when the child, which has been more or less of a burden to her all day, will sleep and let her rest.

'O haste thee, babe, that so I too
May get at last to sleep,'
            says the Italian mother."[23]

These sentiments are not often expressed, but no keen observer can fail to see that they are very wide-spread, even among the orthodox.

Let any reasonable woman expend the force that, under the old order, would have been given to the production of, say, the third, fourth, or fifth child, upon work of another kind, and let her also take the rest and enjoyment, whatever her work, that every human being needs. It is certain that the one or two children which such a woman might elect to bear, would have cause to be thankful that their mother threw over "the holiest traditions of her sex," and left insane ideas of woman's duties and functions to her grandmothers.

But there are many modern women, who in their own way, are quite as foolish as those grandmothers, for they are guilty of the madness of trying to

---

23   It may be worth while to give the other examples, as they are somewhat striking. The Welsh mother (as the reviewer remarks) is still more explicit:—

"'Tis I that nurse the babe, and rock
His cradle to and fro,
'Tis I that lull and lullay him
Unceasingly and low.

"On this day's morn, alack! he cried
From midnight until three,
But it is I that lose my sleep,
The care is all on me,"

and so on in the same strain; but her complaint is nothing to that of the Scotch mother, who sings:—

"Hee O! wee O!
What wad I do wi' you?
Black is the life
That I lead wi' you.

"Ower mony o' you;
Little for to gie you;
Hee O! wee O!
What wad I do wi' you? " &c.

These verses at least reveal the existence, from very ancient times, of a certain lack of appreciation of "a woman's crowning joy."

live the old domestic life without modification, while entering, at the same time, upon a larger field of interests, working simultaneously body and brain under conditions of excitement and worry. This insanity, which one might indeed call by a harsher name, will be punished, as all overstrain is punished. But the cure for these evils is not to immerse women more completely in the cares of domestic life, but to simplify its methods, by the aid of a little intelligence, and by means which there is no space to discuss here. The present waste of energy in our homes is simply appalling.

Surely the distortion of the faculties of one sex would be a ruinous price to pay for the physical safety of the race, even if it secured it, which it does not, but, on the contrary, places it in peril. If it were really necessary to sacrifice women for this end, then progress would be impossible. Society would nourish within itself the germ of its own destruction. Woman, whose soul had been (by supposition) sacrificed for the sake of her body, must for ever constitute an element of reaction and decay, which no unaided efforts of man could counteract. The influence, hereditary and personal, which women possess, secures to them this terrible revenge.

But there is another consideration in connection with this point, which Mrs. Lynn Linton overlooks. If the woman is to be asked to surrender so much because she has to produce the succeeding generation, why is the father left altogether out of count? Does *his* life leave no mark upon his offspring? Or does Mrs. Lynn Linton, perhaps, think that if the mother takes precautions for their welfare to the extent of surrendering her whole existence, the father may be safely left to take no precautions at all?

"The clamour for political rights," this lady says, "is woman's confession of sexual enmity. Gloss it over as we may, it comes to this in the end. No woman who loves her husband would usurp his province." Might one not retort: No man who loves his wife would seek to hamper her freedom? But in fact, nothing could be more false than the assertion that the new ideals imply sexual enmity. On the contrary, they contemplate a relationship between the sexes which is more close and sympathetic than any relationship that the world has yet seen.

Friendship between husband and wife, on the old terms, was almost impossible. Where there is power on the one hand and subordination on the other, whatever the relationship that may arise, it is not likely to be that of friendship.

Separate interests and ambitions, minds moving on different planes—all this tended to make strangers of those who had to pass their lives together, hampered eternally by the false sentiment which made it the right of one to command, and the duty of the other to obey. But now, for the first time in history, we have come within measurable distance of a union between man and woman, as distinguished from a common bondage. Among the latest words that have been said by science, on this subject, are the following from the "Evolution of Sex," by Professors Geddes and Thompson—

"Admitting the theory of evolution, we are not only compelled to hope, but logically compelled to assume, that those rare fruits of an apparently more than earthly paradise of love, which only the forerunners of the race have been privileged to gather, or, it may be, to see from distant heights, are yet the realities of a daily life to which we and ours may journey."

As for Mrs. Lynn Linton's accusations against the "wild women," as regards their lack of principle and even of common honesty, they are surely themselves a little "wild."

The rest of her charges are equally severe, and they induce one to wonder through what unhappy experiences the lady has passed, since she appears never to have encountered a single good or generous woman outside the ranks of her own followers—unless it were a born idiot here and there! Even the men who disagree with her, are either knaves or fools!

I would exhort the "wild women" to be more tolerant than this, and to admit that they number many able opponents, as well as many wise and generous supporters, among both men and women. The matter is too serious to be wrangled about. The adversaries of the "wild woman" have hit upon not a few truths in their time, and have done much service in forcing the opposite party to think their position out, in all its bearings. From the "wild" point of view, of course, the conclusions of Mrs. Lynn Linton and her school seem false, because they deal with facts, when they find them, without sufficiently comparing and balancing them with other facts, perhaps rather less obvious; and, above all, without taking into account the one very significant fact: that the human constitution is as sensitive as a weather-glass to its conditions, and susceptible of infinite modification.

Mrs. Lynn Linton expresses herself with indignation against the mothers who allow their daughters to have a certain amount of freedom; "they know," she says, "the dangers of life, and from what girls ought to be protected. If they disregard the wisdom of experience, on whose soul lies the sin? Is the wolf to blame who passes through the open fence into the fold?"

Yes, certainly he is; the negligence of the shepherd does not turn the wolf into a lamb. But, as a matter of fact, the illustration is not a true one. The social "wolf" attacks the lambs only if the lambs exceed the limits of what society expects of them, as regards liberty. A girl, walking alone in London, meets with no trouble, whereas in Paris or Vienna she might run the risk of annoyance. It is clearly in the interests of every one that those limits should be, as much as possible, extended. The greater the number of girls who are allowed this independence, the less the risk, and the less the hindrances and difficulties for all concerned. The burden on mothers of a host of daughters who cannot stir from their homes without a bodyguard, is very severe. Mrs. Lynn Linton does her best to check the tendency to a greater self-reliance among girls, and would throw society back upon its path towards its abandoned errors.

The quarrel, in fact, between Mrs. Lynn Linton and her opponents is simply the time-honoured quarrel between yesterday and to-day, between reaction and progress, between decaying institutions and the stirrings of a new social faith.

There was a time when Mrs. Lynn Linton had ardent sympathies with the struggle of a soul towards a new hope, but that is all over; and she has no sympathy left for any belief which is not "hallowed by time;" for any attitude of mind (at least in her own sex) that is not unquestioning and submissive.

The world will occupy itself in this conflict for a long time to come; and the issue must entangle itself with the great economic problem that this age has to solve, the whole matter of the relation of the sexes being therein involved.

If this generation is wise, it will conduct these two movements in a fashion new to history. Taking warning by the experience of the past, it will avoid the weak old argument of violence, as a strong and intelligent teacher avoids the cowardly and senseless device of corporal punishment. It will conduct its revolution by means of the only weapon that has ever given a victory worth winning—intelligence.

Mankind has tried blood and thunder long enough; they have not answered. The counter-stroke is as strong as the original impetus, and we expiate our error in the wearisome decades of a reaction. No revolution can be achieved to any purpose, that is not organic; it must rest upon a real change in the sentiment and constitution of humanity. We are not governed by armies and police, we are governed by sentiment; and this power that lies in human opinion is becoming strengthened with every advance that we make in civilisation, and in the rapidity with which ideas are communicated from man to man, and from nation to nation. The whole course of progress tends towards the dethronement of brute force in favour of the force of thought. Let women lead the way in preferring calm argument to excited vituperation, even when vituperation might be well deserved by its object; let them at least strive to conduct their movement as, on the whole, it may be claimed to have been conducted hitherto, in a steady, philosophic, and genial spirit; regarding the opposition that they receive, as much as possible from the point of view of the student rather than of the partisan, realising that in this greatest of all social revolutions, they must expect the fiercest resistance; that men, in opposing them, are neither better nor worse than all human beings of either sex have shown themselves to be, as soon as they become possessors of power over their fellows. The noblest can scarcely stand the test, and of average men and women it makes bullies and tyrants. If this general fact be borne in mind throughout the struggle, it will be easier to avoid these feelings of bitterness and rancour which the sense of injustice infallibly creates. It will remind those engaged in the encounter to regard it in the historic spirit, while not abating, in the smallest degree, their enthusiasm for the cause of justice and of progress. It will teach them not to be too much dismayed, if the change for which they have striven so hard must be delayed until long after they are dead, and all those who would have rejoiced in it are no longer there to see the sun rise over the promised land. It will teach them, too, to realise more strongly than most of us are inclined to do, that men and women are brothers and sisters, bound to stand or fall together; that in trying to raise the position of women, they are serving at least as much the men who are to be their husbands or sons; that, in short—to quote the saying of Hegel—"The master does not become really free till he has liberated his slave."

NEW WOMAN PLAYS

The New Woman
An Original Comedy in Four Acts

Sydney Grundy

1894

Characters.

Gerald Cazenove.	Margery.
Colonel Cazenove.	Lady Wargrave.
Captain Sylvester.	Mrs. Sylvester.
James Armstrong.	Miss Enid Bethune.
Percy Pettigrew.	Miss Victoria Vivash.
Wells.	Dr. Mary Bevan.

Servants.

Acts 1 and 2: *At Gerald Cazenove's.*

Act 3: *Drawing-room at Lady Wargrave's.*

Act 4: *An Orchard at Mapledurham.*

The New Woman.

Act 1.   Gerald Cazenove's *Chambers. A sitting-room, somewhat effeminately decorated. The furniture of the boudoir type, several antimacassars and a profusion of photographs and flowers. The main entrance, R. at back, in the flat. Doors, R. and L., window, L. of flat.*

A knock is heard off, as curtain rises. Enter Wells, L., *crosses stage and opens door in flat. Enter* Colonel Cazenove *and* Sylvester.

COLONEL. Is my nephew at home?

WELLS. No, Colonel; but I expect him every moment.

COLONEL. Very well; I'll wait. [*Exit* WELLS, *door in flat.*] Bah! what a stench of flowers! [*Opens window and throws out a bunch of lilies standing on the table below.*] Sit down, Sylvester—if you can find a chair to carry twelve stone.

SYLVESTER. Really, I feel a sort of trespasser.

COLONEL. Sit down.

SYLVESTER [*sits*]. I don't know Cazenove very well—

COLONEL. I'm much in the same case. Since he came up to town, I've only called upon him once before. By Jove, it was enough. Such a set as I met here!

SYLVESTER. I understood that he was up the river.

COLONEL. Came back yesterday. Hope it's done him good. After all, he's my nephew, and I mean to knock the nonsense out of him.

SYLVESTER. Colonel, you're very proud of him; and you have every reason to be. From all I hear, few men have won more distinction at Oxford.

COLONEL [*pleased*]. Proud of him? My dear Sylvester, that boy has more brains in his little finger than I have—gout. He takes after his aunt Caroline. You remember Caroline?

SYLVESTER. Oh, I remember Lady Wargrave well.

COLONEL. Wonderful woman, sir—a heart of gold—and a head—phew! Gerald takes after her. At Oxford, he carried everything before him.

SYLVESTER [*laughing*]. And now these women carry him behind them!

COLONEL. But he's a Cazenove! He'll come right side up. We Cazenoves always do. We may go under every now and then, but we come up again! It's in the blood.

SYLVESTER. According to my wife—and Agnes is a clever woman in her way—

COLONEL. Don't know her.

SYLVESTER. His cultivated spirit and magnetic intellect are one of the brightest hopes for the social progress of our time—[*Laughs.*] whatever that may mean!

COLONEL. Does it mean anything? That is the sort of jargon Gerald was full of, when I saw him last. But he'll get over it. Intellectual measles. Oxford's a fine place, but no mental drainage.

SYLVESTER. I can form no opinion. I hadn't the advantage of a university training.

COLONEL. I had. I was rusticated. We Cazenoves always were—till Gerald's time. But he'll redeem himself. We Cazenoves have always been men, except one. That's my sister, Caroline; and, by Jove, she's the next best thing—a woman.

[*Rising, in his enthusiasm—the antimacassar slips on to the seat.*]

SYLVESTER. A real woman.

COLONEL. Caroline's a heart of gold—

SYLVESTER. Yes, so you said.

COLONEL. Did I? I beg your pardon. [*Sits on the antimacassar, instantly springs up, and flings it into a corner. Points to that covering* SYLVESTER's *chair.*] Throw that thing away!

SYLVESTER. All right. I'm used to 'em. We grow 'em at our house. [*Looks round.*] I might be sitting in my wife's boudoir! Same furniture, same flowers, same photographs—hallo, that's rather a pretty woman over there!

[*Crosses.*]

COLONEL. A pretty woman, where? [*Crosses.*] No, not my style!

SYLVESTER. Ha! ha!

COLONEL. What are you laughing at?

SYLVESTER. My wife! I didn't recognize her.

[*Goes about examining photographs.*]

COLONEL. Ten thousand pardons! I had no idea—

SYLVESTER. Bless me, my wife again!

COLONEL [*looking*]. That's better. That's much better.

SYLVESTER. It's an older photograph. Agnes was quite a woman when I married her, but she grows more and more ethereal. Philosophy doesn't seem very nourishing.

COLONEL. She's a philosopher?

SYLVESTER. Haven't you read her book? "Aspirations after a Higher Morality."

COLONEL. The old morality's high enough for me.

SYLVESTER. I've tried to read it, but I didn't succeed. However, I've cut the leaves and dropped cigar ash on the final chapter. Why, here she is again!

COLONEL. *Three* photographs? And you're not jealous?

SYLVESTER. My dear Colonel, who am I to be jealous?

COLONEL. Her husband, aren't you?

SYLVESTER. Yes, I am Mrs. Sylvester's husband. I belong to my wife, but my wife doesn't belong to me. She is the property of the public. Directly I saw her photograph in a shop-window I realized the situation. People tell me I've a wife to be proud of; but they're wrong. Mrs. Sylvester is not my wife; I am her husband.

COLONEL [*taking up a book*]. This is what comes of educating women. We have created a Frankenstein. "Man, the Betrayer—A Study of the Sexes—By Enid Bethune."

SYLVESTER. Oh, I know her. She comes to our house.

COLONEL. And has a man betrayed her?

SYLVESTER. Never. Not likely to.

COLONEL. That's what's the matter, perhaps?

SYLVESTER. Her theory is, that boys ought to be girls, and young men should be maids. [COLONEL *throws down the book*.] That's how she'd equalize the sexes.

COLONEL. Pshaw! [*Takes up another book.*] "Ye Foolish Virgins!—A Remonstrance—by Victoria Vivash."

SYLVESTER. Another soul! She's also for equality. Her theory is, that girls should be boys, and maids should be young men. Goes in for latchkeys and that sort of thing.

COLONEL [*throws down the book*]. Bah! [*Takes up a third.*] "Naked and Unashamed—A Few Plain Facts and Figures—by Mary Bevan, M.D." Who on earth's she?

SYLVESTER. One of the plain figures. She comes to our house, too.

COLONEL [*reads*]. "The Physiology of the Sexes!" Oh, this eternal babble of the sexes! [*Throws book down.*] Why can't a woman be content to be a woman? What does she want to make a beastly man of herself for?

SYLVESTER. But my wife isn't a woman.

COLONEL. None of them are, my boy. A woman, who is a woman, doesn't want to be anything else. These people are a sex of their own, Sylvester. They have invented a new gender. And to think my nephew's one of them!

[*Strides up and down, seizes another antimacassar and flings it into another corner.*]

SYLVESTER. Oh, he's young. Don't despair!

COLONEL. I don't despair! Do you suppose this folly can continue? Do you imagine that these puffed-up women will not soon burst of their own vanity? Then, the reaction! then will come *our* turn! Mark my words, Sylvester, there'll be a boom in men!

[*Rubbing his hands.*]

Enter GERALD, *door in flat.*

GERALD. Good afternoon. I'm sorry to have kept you waiting.

[*Shakes hands with* COLONEL.]

COLONEL. Here you are, at last.

GERALD [*shaking hands with* SYLVESTER]. How's Mrs. Sylvester?

SYLVESTER. I was just going to ask you. You see more of her than I do.

GERALD. We are collaborating.

COLONEL. In the Higher Morality?

SYLVESTER. How are you getting on?

GERALD. Oh, we are only on the threshold. I finished the first chapter about daybreak.

COLONEL. That's how you waste the precious hours of night? Gad, sir, when I was your age—

GERALD. That was thirty years ago. Things have changed since then.

COLONEL. And they haven't improved.

GERALD. That is a question.

COLONEL. Oh, everything's a question nowadays! Nothing is sacred to a young man fresh from Oxford. Existence is a problem to be investigated; in my youth, it was a life to be lived; and, I thank Heaven, *I* lived it. Ah, the nights I had!

SYLVESTER. Would it be impertinent to inquire upon what subject my wife is engaged?

GERALD. Our subject is the Ethics of Marriage.

SYLVESTER. Of my marriage?

GERALD. Of marriage in the abstract.

COLONEL. As if people married for ethics! There is no such thing, sir. There are no ethics in marriage.

GERALD. That is the conclusion at which we have arrived.

COLONEL. You are only on the threshold, and yet you have arrived at a conclusion?

GERALD. So much is obvious. It is a conclusion to which literature and the higher culture inevitably tend. The awakened conscience of woman is already alive to it.

COLONEL. Conscience of woman! What are you talking about? I've known a good many women in my time, and they hadn't a conscience amongst 'em! There's only one thing can awaken the conscience of woman, and that is being found out.

GERALD. I am speaking of innocent women.

COLONEL. I never met one.

GERALD. Yet—

COLONEL. Tut, tut, sir; read your Bible. Who was it had the first bite at the apple? And she's been nibbling at it ever since!

GERALD. Well, well, uncle, you don't often come to see me; so we won't argue. Can I prevail on you to stay to tea?

COLONEL. To stay to *what*, sir?

GERALD. Tea. At five o'clock, I have a few friends coming. Mrs. Sylvester— [SYLVESTER *puts down photograph and turns*]—Miss Bethune—Miss Vivash—

SYLVESTER. And Dr. Mary Bevan?

GERALD. Yes, I expect Miss Bevan.

COLONEL. "Naked and Unashamed?"

GERALD. They may bring Percy with them.

COLONEL. Percy?

GERALD. Percy Pettigrew.

COLONEL. A man? An actual man? A bull amongst that china?

SYLVESTER. Well, hardly!

COLONEL. You know him, Sylvester?

SYLVESTER. They bring him to our house.

GERALD. Nobody has done more for the Advancement of Woman.

SYLVESTER. By making a public exhibition of the Decay of Man.

GERALD. Sylvester, you're a Philistine. I won't ask you to stay.

SYLVESTER. Man the Betrayer might be dangerous, amongst such foolish virgins.

COLONEL. The danger would be all the other way. I am not sorry *I* shall have protection. My sister, Caroline, will be here at five.

GERALD. Aunt Caroline! [*A little nervously.*]

COLONEL. I came to announce her visit.

SYLVESTER. Lady Wargrave has returned to England?

COLONEL. After ten years' absence. She has been travelling for her health, which was never too robust; and since Sir Oriel's death, she has been more or less a wanderer.

GERALD. I knew she had arrived, but I postponed presenting myself till I was summoned. My aunt has the kindest of hearts—

COLONEL. A heart of gold, sir.

GERALD. And a pocket too. Nobody knows that better than I do. Since my parents' death, she has been father and mother, as well as aunt, to me. But there was always something about aunt that made one keep one's distance.

COLONEL [*in a milder voice than he has yet used*]. And there is still, Gerald.

GERALD. Then I'm glad I've kept mine.

COLONEL. You acted very wisely; I happen to know she wished her arrival kept secret and to descend upon you like a *dea ex machinâ*. Caroline always had a sense of dramatic effect. But how the deuce did you know of her return?

GERALD. Oh, very simply. Margery told me.

COLONEL. Margery!

GERALD. Aunt wrote to summon her to resume her duties.

COLONEL. But Margery's at Mapledurham. Caroline was stopping with some friends in Paris, and Margery was sent on to her father's.

GERALD. Six weeks ago.

COLONEL. Why, you know all about it.

GERALD. Yes, I was staying there when she arrived. I have been rusticating for the last six weeks. It's so much easier to write in the fresh air.

SYLVESTER. You have been writing down at Mapledurham?

GERALD. That's what I went for.

COLONEL. For six weeks?

GERALD. Six weeks.

COLONEL. And you have only finished the first chapter?

GERALD. It's so difficult to write in the fresh air. One wants to go out and enjoy oneself. And then old Armstrong's such a jolly old boy.

SYLVESTER. Armstrong, of Mapledurham? The farmer? Oh, I know him well. I go there for the fishing.

COLONEL. Then, do you know Margery?

SYLVESTER. Margery? No.

GERALD. How that girl sculls!

COLONEL. Oh, Margery was rowing?

GERALD. Do you know, uncle, she can almost beat me?

COLONEL. But what an arm she has!

GERALD. And when she feathers—

[*Pantomime.*]

COLONEL. Ah! when she feathers—

[*Double pantomime.*]

GERALD. What a voice, too!

COLONEL. Hasn't she!

GERALD. So musical! When she sings out, "Lock, ho!"

COLONEL [*imitating*]. "Lock, ho!"

GERALD. No, not a bit like that—more silvery!

COLONEL. Not a bit! more silvery!

BOTH [*pantomiming*]. "Lock, ho!"

SYLVESTER. Who's Margery?

COLONEL. Oh, my dear fellow, just your sort—*my* sort—well, hang it, every man's sort! Margery is—oh, how can I explain? If I'd seen a Margery thirty years ago; well, I should never have been a bachelor! Margery is—come, Gerald, what *is* Margery? Margery is a woman, who— Well, Margery's a woman! That's all Margery is!

GERALD. Old Armstrong's daughter. We grew up together. When I was very young, I was considered delicate, and I was sent to the farmhouse at Mapledurham. When I went to Eton, Lady Wargrave took Margery into her service. There she has remained—

COLONEL. And she is coming with your aunt to-day.
[*Knock at door in flat. Re-enter* WELLS, *followed by* MRS. SYLVESTER, *with a small portfolio.*]

WELLS. Mrs. Sylvester!

[*Exit, door in flat.*]

MRS. SYLVESTER [*stops short on seeing* SYLVESTER.]. Jack!

SYLVESTER. This is an unexpected pleasure. [*A cold matrimonial kiss.*] Colonel Cazenove—my old Colonel. Mr. Cazenove I think you know.

MRS. SYLVESTER. Well, of course, Jack! How ridiculous you are! Should I be here if I didn't know Mr. Cazenove?

SYLVESTER. I haven't the least notion. I only know you wouldn't be at home.

MRS. SYLVESTER. I was in all the morning.

SYLVESTER. I had business at the Horse Guards. I shall be home to dinner, though.

MRS. SYLVESTER. Oh dear, I wish I had known that. There's only mutton.

SYLVESTER. The same mutton?

MRS. SYLVESTER. What do you mean by same?

SYLVESTER. I mean the mutton I had yesterday.

MRS. SYLVESTER. Did you have mutton yesterday?

SYLVESTER. No matter; I'll dine at the club.

MRS. SYLVESTER. Thank you, dear.

SYLVESTER. Good-bye. [*Kiss.*] Good-bye, Mr. Cazenove.

COLONEL. I will come with you. [*To* GERALD.] I am due at your aunt's.

GERALD. But I shall see you again presently?

COLONEL. If I am visible behind Caroline. Madam, your servant. [*Aside to* SYLVESTER.] Cheer up, Sylvester! I'll join you at the club, and we will wind the night up at the Empire.

[*Exit after* SYLVESTER, R. *of flat*].

MRS. SYLVESTER. That is so like a man! Doesn't say he's coming home, and then expects six courses and a savoury!

GERALD. There is a difference between cold mutton and six courses, to say nothing of the savoury.

MRS. SYLVESTER. It is a fine distinction, and in no way affects the validity of my argument.

GERALD [*smiling*]. You mean, of your statement.

MRS. SYLVESTER. Husbands are all alike. The ancient regarded his wife as a slave, the modern regards her as a cook.

GERALD. Then they are *not* alike.

MRS. SYLVESTER [*emphatically*]. A man thinks of nothing but his stomach.

GERALD. That is another proposition.

MRS. SYLVESTER. You're very argumentative to-day. I haven't seen you for six weeks, and you've come home in a nasty, horrid temper!

GERALD. I have been working so hard.

MRS. SYLVESTER. Why is your face so brown?

GERALD. Well, of course, I went out.

MRS. SYLVESTER [*takes his hand*]. And why are your hands blistered?

GERALD. I had a few pulls on the river; and being out of training—

MRS. SYLVESTER [*innocently*]. Were you stroke?

[*Holding his hands.*]

GERALD. Not always.

[*Bites his lip.*]

MRS. SYLVESTER. On, then you weren't alone?

GERALD. I met an old friend up the river.

MRS. SYLVESTER. Now I understand why you didn't write to me.

[*Drops his hand and turns away pettishly.*]

GERALD. About the book? [*She gives him a quick glance.*] Oh, I had nothing to say, except that I was getting on all right. I've written the first chapter.

[*Produces MS.*]

MRS. SYLVESTER. And I've written the last. [*Opening portfolio.*] Connoting the results of our arguments.

GERALD. But where are the arguments?

MRS. SYLVESTER. We'll put those in afterwards. [GERALD *looks at her.*] That's how Victoria always writes her novels. She begins at the end.

GERALD. But this is a work of philosophy.

MRS. SYLVESTER [*pouting*]. Oh, you *are* disagreeable!

GERALD [*putting MS. aside*]. Don't let us talk philosophy to-day. I want to talk to you about something else.

MRS. SYLVESTER [*cheerfully*]. Yes!

GERALD. I have something to tell you.

MRS. SYLVESTER. Interesting?

[*Smiling.*]

GERALD. I'm in love.

MRS. SYLVESTER. Oh!

[*From this point her manner changes.*]

GERALD. Yes, in love, Mrs. Sylvester—in real love.

MRS. SYLVESTER. What do you call real love?

GERALD. Something quite different from what we had supposed. We've been on the wrong tack altogether. We have imagined something we have labelled love; we have put it into a crucible, and reduced it to its elements.

MRS. SYLVESTER. And we have found those elements to be, community of interest and sympathy of soul.

GERALD. But unfortunately for our theory, the thing we put into the crucible wasn't love at all.

MRS. SYLVESTER. How do you know?

GERALD. I didn't, till last week.

MRS. SYLVESTER. It was at Mapledurham you made this discovery?

GERALD. At Mapledurham.

MRS. SYLVESTER. And your friend?

GERALD. She was the revelation.

MRS. SYLVESTER. I thought it was a woman.

GERALD. That word just describes her. She is a woman—nothing more or less. Away went all my theories into air. My precious wisdom was stripped bare before me, and in its nakedness I saw my folly. Not with laborious thought; but in one vivid flash I learned more than I ever learned at Oxford.

MRS. SYLVESTER. Really?

GERALD. A woman! that is what one wants—that's all. Birth, brains, accomplishments—pshaw! vanities! community of interest—sympathy of soul? mere dialectics! That's not love.

MRS. SYLVESTER. What *is*, then?

GERALD. It defies analysis. You can't put love into a crucible. You only know that there is something empty in you; and you don't know what fills it; but that's love. There's no mistake about the real thing.

MRS. SYLVESTER. Is she good-looking?

GERALD. In *my* eyes.

MRS. SYLVESTER. A lady?

GERALD. In social station, beneath me. But what's social station?

MRS. SYLVESTER. This is infatuation. Some riverside coquette—

GERALD. Simplicity itself.

MRS. SYLVESTER. Of course you think so; but you don't know women. The simple woman hasn't yet been born. This isn't love, Mr. Cazenove. This is the temporary victory of the baser side of your nature. The true alliance is the union of souls.

GERALD. Of man and woman.

MRS. SYLVESTER. But of soul and soul; not a mere sensual temptation.

GERALD. Nor is this. A week ago I thought so. I know better now.

MRS. SYLVESTER. Happily the weeks are not all over yet. In a few more you will have forgotten her as completely as she will have forgotten *you*.

GERALD. In a few more, I hope that she will be my wife.

MRS. SYLVESTER. You contemplate a *mésalliance?*

GERALD. There is no *mésalliance* where there's love.

MRS. SYLVESTER. You, of whom everyone expects so much, to throw away your opportunities, and to begin your life hindered and hampered by a foolish marriage.

GERALD. If she will only marry me.

MRS. SYLVESTER [*looks at him, pained*]. I may still be your friend?
[*Offers him her hands, which he takes a little reluctantly.*]

Re-enter WELLS.

WELLS. Lady Wargrave.

[*Exit.*]

Enter LADY WARGRAVE *leaning on the* COLONEL'S *arm. She walks with a crutch-stick, and is followed by* MARGERY, *who carries a cushion.* MRS. SYLVESTER *retires up, so that she is not immediately seen by* LADY WARGRAVE.

GERALD [*a little tentatively*]. My dear aunt!

[*They shake hands.*]

LADY WARGRAVE. You may kiss me.
[*He kisses her, then casts a glance of gratitude at* MARGERY. *Meanwhile* MARGERY *has prepared a chair for her, into which she is placed by* GERALD *and the* COLONEL, *who is now subdued and deferential, in marked contrast to his last scene.* MARGERY *takes up her position in the background.*]

COLONEL. I was so fortunate as to meet the carriage.

LADY WARGRAVE. Theodore was late as usual.

COLONEL. Only ten minutes, Caroline; but, as you know, time, tide, and your aunt wait for no man.

LADY WARGRAVE. Now, Gerald, let me look at you. Your face to the light, please. [GERALD *stands for inspection. She takes a long look through her eye-glass.*] I don't like that necktie.

GERALD [*smiling and bowing*]. It shall be changed to-morrow, aunt.

LADY WARGRAVE. To-day. [GERALD *bows. She takes another look.*] That will do, Gerald.

[GERALD *salutes. She drops her glasses.*]

COLONEL. Stand at ease! Dismiss!

LADY WARGRAVE. Theodore, this is not a barracks!

COLONEL. True. [*Bows.*] Peccavi!

LADY WARGRAVE [*addressing* GERALD]. I need hardly say with what pleasure I have followed your career at Oxford. It is worthy of a Cazenove.

COLONEL. Brilliant—magnificent!

LADY WARGRAVE. It is worthy of a Cazenove; that is all.

[COLONEL *subsides, bowing.*]

GERALD. Yes, aunt, I flatter myself—

LADY WARGRAVE. Don't do that. You did your duty. Nothing more.

GERALD. By the way, did you receive my poem?

LADY WARGRAVE. Poem?

GERALD. That won the Newdigate. I sent you a copy—to Rome.

LADY WARGRAVE. Ah, I remember; I received the document. Tell me, were there many competitors?

GERALD. A dozen or so.

LADY WARGRAVE. Is it possible that Oxford can produce eleven worse poems than yours?

GERALD. My dear aunt!

[COLONEL *turns aside, chuckling, and finds himself face to face with* MARGERY, *laughing; both become suddenly serious.*]

MRS. SYLVESTER [*advancing*]. It is a work of genius—none but a true poet—

LADY WARGRAVE [*half rising.* MARGERY *steps forward to help her*]. I ask your pardon. Gerald, you haven't introduced me!

GERALD. Forgive me, Mrs. Sylvester—forgive me, aunt, but in the excitement of seeing you—

LADY WARGRAVE. Sylvester!

COLONEL. Wife of my old lieutenant. Captain now.

LADY WARGRAVE. Wife of Jack Sylvester! I am pleased to meet you. I have known your husband almost from a boy. But I don't see him.

[*Looking round.*]

GERALD [*confused*]. He has just gone.

[LADY WARGRAVE *looks from one to another. Slight pause.*]

MRS. SYLVESTER. Mr. Cazenove and I are collaborating.

LADY WARGRAVE. Oh! Captain Sylvester's wife is collaborating with *you*?

GERALD. On the ethics of marriage.

Mrs. Sylvester. Viewed from the standpoint of the higher morality.

Lady Wargrave. Ah! [*Drops back into her seat, helped by* Margery.] That will be a very interesting work. [Margery *retires up.*] Did you do very much down at Mapledurham?

Gerald. Not *very* much, I'm afraid.

Mrs. Sylvester. Mr. Cazenove met a friend up the river.

Lady Wargrave. A friend? Margery, you didn't tell me that.

Margery [*advancing, and with a slight curtsey*]. I didn't know, my lady.

Mrs. Sylvester. An old friend.

Colonel. Perhaps the old friend was Margery herself?

Mrs. Sylvester [*perplexed and curious*]. Your maid was at Mapledurham?

Lady Wargrave. Her father lives there. Theodore, don't you think Margery looks all the better for her holiday?

Colonel [*with enthusiasm*]. If it is possible—

Lady Wargrave. Theodore! [*Aside to him, stopping his mouth with her fan.*]

Colonel [*subsides*]. Peccavi! [*Sotto voce.*]

Lady Wargrave. Doesn't she look brown?

Gerald. Well, up the river everybody does. It was hot weather, too.

Lady Wargrave. It must have been. You should have seen her hands. They were all over blisters.

Colonel. Ah, that was the rowing!

[*Pantomime as before.*]

Lady Wargrave. Margery! [Margery *casts down her eyes.*] You were rowing?

Margery. Sometimes, my lady.

Mrs. Sylvester. Stroke. [*Looking at* Gerald.]

[Lady Wargrave, *watching* Mrs. Sylvester, *motions to* Margery, *who retires up.*]

Colonel [*aside to* Lady Wargrave]. Caroline, you took the water very neatly.

Lady Wargrave [*aside to* Colonel]. The higher morality has caught a crab.

Mrs. Sylvester [*gathers up MS. into her portfolio*]. I will not trespass any longer, Mr. Cazenove. No doubt, your aunt has much to say to you.

Gerald. But won't you stay to tea?

Mrs. Sylvester. Thanks. Captain Sylvester dines early.

COLONEL [*aside*]. At the club!

MRS. SYLVESTER. Good day to you, Lady Wargrave. [LADY WARGRAVE *is about to rise.*] Pray don't rise. [*Bows to the* COLONEL *and goes to door in flat where* GERALD *is waiting for her.*] Don't trouble; I know my way.

[*Exit.*]

LADY WARGRAVE. Poor Sylvester! He was such a nice boy! [GERALD *comes down.*] Gerald, can Margery wait in the next room?

[GERALD *opens door* R. *Exit* MARGERY R.]

GERALD [*returning*]. And how have you been, aunt? You never mentioned your health in your letters. Are you better?

LADY WARGRAVE. I mustn't complain; but Providence is really most unjust. Here am I, who have lived a life of temperance, in my old age—

COLONEL. Middle age, Caroline!

[*Bowing.*]

LADY WARGRAVE [*smiling*]. A chronic invalid; while this old transgressor who has denied himself nothing [COLONEL *grins*], and committed every sin in the Decalogue [COLONEL *chuckles*], is as hale and as hearty as I am infirm.

COLONEL. Never felt better, never!

LADY WARGRAVE. But how have *you* been, Gerald? We belong to the past—

COLONEL. Caroline!

LADY WARGRAVE. *You* belong to the future, and the future belongs to you.

GERALD. Oh, I've been all right!

[*A little recklessly.*]

LADY WARGRAVE. Quite sure you suffer from nothing?

GERALD. What do you mean?

LADY WARGRAVE. Your letters have told me a great deal—more than perhaps you know; but I have read them very carefully; and when you asked me to come home—

GERALD. I didn't, aunt.

LADY WARGRAVE. Between the lines.

GERALD [*laughing*]. What did I say to you between the lines?

[*Kneeling by her.*]

LADY WARGRAVE. You told me that you had learned everything Oxford has to teach worth learning, and that you were in danger of becoming—well [*laying her hand on his head*]—shall we say, *tête montée*?

COLONEL. Yes, Caroline! I should certainly say, *tête montée*.

LADY WARGRAVE. Cure yourself, Gerald. Knowledge is not wisdom [*stroking his head*]. Forgive me, dear; but I have known so many men who have never survived the distinctions of their youth, who are always at Oxford, and even in their manhood play with rattles. Now, forget Oxford—go into the world—lay books aside, and study men.

COLONEL. *And* women.

LADY WARGRAVE. Yes—and *women*.

[*Knock without.*]

GERALD [*rising*]. Just what I'm doing!
[*Female voices in altercation. Re-enter* WELLS, *door in flat.*]

WELLS. Miss Bethune, Miss Vivash.
Enter EDIN *and* VICTORIA, *in hot argument. They take opposite sides of the stage and continue the discussion without taking the slightest notice of anybody.* LADY WARGRAVE *looks from the one to the other in amazement. Exit* WELLS, *door in flat.*

EDIN. I can't agree with you! Say what you will, I can't agree with you!

VICTORIA. That doesn't alter the fact. A woman has just as much right to a latchkey as a man.

EDIN. But a man has no right to a latchkey.

VICTORIA. That's ridiculous!

EDIN. Rudeness is not argument!

VICTORIA. Why make distinctions?

EDIN. I make no distinctions. I admit that a woman has just as much right to come home with the milk as a man: but I say, a man has no right to come home with the milk; and I say more—no woman who respects herself has any *desire* to come home with the milk!

VICTORIA. Bother the milk! It isn't a question of milk. It's a question of making artificial distinctions between the sexes.

EDIN. I say that there ought to be *no* distinction! Why should a man be allowed to commit sins—

VICTORIA. And woman not be given an opportunity?

EDIN. Then do you *want* to commit sins?

VICTORIA. I want to be allowed to do as *men* do.

EDIN. Then you ought to be ashamed of yourself; there!

VICTORIA. I only say, I ought to be allowed.

EDIN. And *I* say that a man, reeking with infamy, ought not to be allowed to marry a pure girl—

VICTORIA. Certainly not! *She* ought to reek with infamy as well.

EDIN. Victoria!

[Knock without.]

VICTORIA. What is the difference between man and woman?

EDIN. There is *no* difference!

Re-enter WELLS, door in flat.

WELLS. Dr. Mary Bevan.

[Exit Wells.]

Enter DR. MARY BEVAN.

VICTORIA. Why should a woman have children and a man have none?

EDIN. But a man *has* children!

DOCTOR. Only vicariously.

VICTORIA. Here's Dr. Mary!

[Rushing up to DOCTOR. EDIN has rushed up to the other side of her.]

DOCTOR [*pragmatically*]. But I am not without hope that, when the attention of science is directed to the unequal incidence of the burden of maternity, some method of re-adjustment may be devised.

LADY WARGRAVE [*who has risen*]. Pardon me, ladies; but if you are about to consult your physician, you would no doubt prefer to be alone.

[They turn and see her for the first time.]

VICTORIA. Pray, don't move.

GERALD. My aunt, Lady Wargrave. Colonel Cazenove.

DOCTOR. These matters are best discussed openly. A morbid modesty has too long closed our eyes. But the day of awakening has come. Sylvester, in her "Aspirations after a Higher Morality," Bethune, in her "Man, the Betrayer," Vivash, in her "Foolish Virgins," have postulated the sexual problem from every conceivable point of view; and I have myself contributed to the discussion a modest little treatise—

EDIN. No, no, not modest!

VICTORIA. Profound!

DOCTOR. "Naked and Unashamed!"

EDIN. Man has done all the talking up to now—

VICTORIA. He has had things all his own way—

DOCTOR. And a nice mess he's made of them!

EDIN. Now it is our turn.

VICTORIA. We mean to put things right!

DOCTOR. Man has departed. Woman has arrived.

LADY WARGRAVE. Excuse my ignorance, but I have been away from England for so many years. Can this be the New Woman I have read about?

COLONEL. Everything's New nowadays! We have a New Art—

EDIN. A New Journalism—

VICTORIA. A New Political Economy—

DOCTOR. A New Morality—

COLONEL. A New Sex!

LADY WARGRAVE [*smiling*]. Ah!

DOCTOR. Do you object to modernity?

LADY WARGRAVE. I've only one objection to new things; they are so old.

VICTORIA. Not the New Woman!

LADY WARGRAVE. No; *she* is generally middle-aged.

> [COLONEL *turns to* GERALD, *to hide his chuckles.*]

EDIN. Then, do you take Man's part in the discussion?

LADY WARGRAVE. I take no part in it.

DOCTOR. Do you deny that Woman has arrived, Man has departed?

LADY WARGRAVE. I don't wonder at it. But Man has an awkward habit of coming back again.

TRIO. Never!

LADY WARGRAVE. Then Woman will go after him.

> [COLONEL *roars out aloud—the Women survey him with disgust.*]
>
> *Re-enter* WELLS, L., *and whispers to* GERALD.

GERALD. Tea is quite ready, ladies!

EDIN. Ah! a cup of tea!

> [*Exit* L., *followed by* VICTORIA, DOCTOR MARY *and* WELLS.]

LADY WARGRAVE. Theodore, your arm. These ladies interest me. Besides, they sadly want a chaperone.

COLONEL. They want a husband—that's what *they* want, badly!

LADY WARGRAVE. Gerald, call Margery. [GERALD *goes to door* R.] Well, they are looking for one.

[Glancing after GERALD.]

COLONEL. And they've found *you*, Caroline.
> [*Exeunt both, laughing, L. Each time the door, L., is opened, a babel of female voices is heard from within, and such phrases as "Peter Robinson's," "Swan and Edgar's," "Stagg and Mantle's," are distinctly audible above the clink of teacups, etc.*]

Re-enter MARGERY, R.; *she goes straight to* LADY WARGRAVE'S *chair, and is about to carry the cushion into the room, L., when* GERALD, *who has stood back, watching her, advances.*

GERALD. Margery! [MARGERY *drops the cushion and turns.*] Thank you! God bless you!

MARGERY. For what, sir?

GERALD. You have not told my aunt.

MARGERY. Of course I haven't told her! [*Slight pause.*] May I go?

GERALD. Not yet. Margery, can you ever forgive me?

MARGERY. For being a man? Oh yes!

GERALD. Can you ever respect me again?

MARGERY. I do respect you, sir.

GERALD. Not as I do you, Margery. You don't know what you did for me that day. If you had rounded on me, I should not have cared—but to be silent—to do nothing—to forgive me!

MARGERY. I had a reason for forgiving you.

GERALD. What?

MARGERY. That's my business.

GERALD. But, Margery, you do forgive me?

MARGERY. Don't let's talk about it.

GERALD. *Really* forgive me?

MARGERY. Really!

GERALD. Prove it to me.

MARGERY. How can I?

GERALD [*still holding her*]. Be my wife!

MARGERY [*recoiling*]. Mr. Cazenove!

GERALD. My name is Gerald.

MARGERY. Mr. Gerald!

GERALD. Gerald! Call me so, Margery.

MARGERY. I couldn't, sir. Don't ask me!

GERALD. Then you refuse me? [MARGERY *is silent—he turns away.*] Well, I don't deserve you.

MARGERY [*approaching him*]. Oh, don't think I mean that! Do you suppose you are the only man that's ever made love to me? It's a man's business to make love; and it's a woman's business to stop him—when he makes love too hard. But if we can't be lovers, Mr. Gerald, we can be friends.

GERALD. It's got past friendship with me, Margery. Since I came back to town, everything's changed. My pursuits all feel so empty and so meaningless; every woman I meet seems different from what she was: and oh, how different from *you*!

MARGERY. Gentry *are* different. We're different breeds. That's why we can't be lovers.

GERALD. We can be man and wife!

MARGERY. Isn't that being lovers?

GERALD. In my case, it would be!

MARGERY. Hush! Mr. Gerald, that's impossible. My lady will be asking for me. Let me go!

GERALD. Not till I've told you how I love you, Margery. Seeing you again is breathing the pure air. It seems a younger and a sweeter world, now you have come again. Nothing else matters. All my life beside appears a folly and a waste of time. My real life was lived with you down yonder, out in the fields, and rambling through the woods and listening to the music of the weir. The life that we began together so pleasantly, cannot we live together to the end? I was quite honest when I said I loved you. And couldn't you love *me*,—just a little bit?

MARGERY. You oughtn't to ask that!

GERALD. I mean to have an answer.

MARGERY. Please, Mr. Gerald, don't! It makes it very hard for me—

GERALD. Answer me! Could you love me, Margery?

MARGERY. Oh, what's the use of asking? You only want to make me tell a lie.

GERALD. Answer me!

MARGERY. I *have* answered you!

GERALD. Margery, then you do!

MARGERY. That is what made it easy to forgive you. Now let me go.

GERALD. Not till you've said that you will be my wife.

MARGERY. Oh, Mr. Gerald.

GERALD. Gerald! say Gerald!

MARGERY. It's no use. I can't!

GERALD. Say you will marry me!

MARGERY. If you will let me call you "Mr. Gerald."

[*Embrace.*]

COLONEL [*off, opens door* L.]. Margery! where are you?

Re-enter L., *just as* MARGERY *is withdrawing from* GERALD's *arms, stands thunderstruck. Exit* MARGERY, L.

GERALD. It's all right, uncle.

COLONEL. All right, you call it? Look here, you young cub! None of your higher morality with Margery!

GERALD. I tell you, it's all right. Margery's going to be your niece—my wife.

COLONEL. Margery, your wife! [*Slight pause.*] You're a damned lucky dog!

GERALD. That I am, uncle!

COLONEL. 'Gad, sir, you're a man; and I thought you were a monkey. I congratulate you!

GERALD [*shaking hands*]. *You* don't object then?

COLONEL. I thought a Cazenove would come right side up.

GERALD. But what will aunt say?

COLONEL [*suddenly collapses*]. I was forgetting Caroline!

GERALD. She must be told.

COLONEL. But cautiously. Courage! I'll back you up!

GERALD. I'll tell her now!

COLONEL. Stay! Don't do anything rash! I wouldn't risk a private interview. Safety in numbers.

GERALD. I will tell them all!

COLONEL. Sht! what a bomb-shell! Courage!

GERALD. Courage, yourself! You're shaking all over.

COLONEL. No matter. I'll stand by you!

LADY WARGRAVE [*opening door*, L.]. Gerald!

COLONEL. Form square! Prepare to receive cavalry!

[*Retires up.*]

Re-enter LADY WARGRAVE, L.

LADY WARGRAVE. Where are you? Why have you deserted me? To leave me at the mercy of that crew! My poor, dear, Gerald! however did you get into this set?

GERALD. It was my poem did it.

LADY WARGRAVE. I thought, that crime would bring its punishment. Now, they're upon the marriage service! As though *that* concerned them! Gerald, if you marry any of that tribe, you'll really break my heart!

[COLONEL *comes down* R. *of* GERALD.]

GERALD. I hope I shall never do that!

LADY WARGRAVE. Marry a *woman*, whatever else she is.

COLONEL [*aside to* GERALD]. Courage!

GERALD. Or isn't, aunt!

[*Effusively.*]

COLONEL [*aside to* GERALD]. Caution!

[*Retires up.*]

LADY WARGRAVE. Or isn't!

The door L. *is thrown open, and re-enter* DR. MARY, EDIN, *and* VICTORIA, *all talking, followed by* MARGERY, *who takes up her original position at the back.*

DOCTOR. "Obey," forsooth!

VICTORIA. To promise to love is ridiculous, for how can one control the mysterious expansions of the heart?

DOCTOR. It is the brain that loves. A still more complicated mechanism.

EDIN. It is impossible to honour a man who has invariably lived a revolting, ante-nuptial life—

VICTORIA. But to "obey!"

[COLONEL *works down stage, interested.*]

DOCTOR. Lady Wargrave, even *you* surely wouldn't promise to "obey" a man?

LADY WARGRAVE. Not till he asked me, certainly.

COLONEL. Ha! ha!

[*The trio turn on him; he retires up.*]

LADY WARGRAVE. Gerald, I must be going.

DOCTOR. So must I.

EDIN. And I.

DOCTOR. I have a clinical lecture—

VICTORIA. I have an engagement.

GERALD. One moment, ladies! Stay one moment, aunt! Before you go I want to tell you all of *my* engagement.

LADY WARGRAVE. Your engagement, Gerald?

GERALD. Yes, I am going to be married.

[*Pause.*]

EDIN [*with jealousy*]. To Agnes Syl—? Oh, I forgot; she's married.

LADY WARGRAVE. To whom?

[*All stand expectantly.*]

GERALD. To Margery.

[*All stand transfixed. Exit* COLONEL, *door in flat.*]

DOCTOR. Mr. Cazenove, I offer you my congratulations. Having a clinical lecture to deliver, you will excuse me if I say good afternoon.

EDIN. Wait for me, Doctor. [*Exit* DR. MARY, *door in flat.*] You have my best wishes.

[*Exit, door in flat.*]

VICTORIA. And thank you for the plot of my next novel.

[*Exit, door in flat.*]

LADY WARGRAVE. Gerald, is this a trick?

GERALD. No, aunt; it is the truth.

LADY WARGRAVE. And you, a Cazenove! It is out of the question! I won't permit it! I forbid it, Gerald!

GERALD. But, my dear aunt, you said only just now—

LADY WARGRAVE. No matter!

GERALD. Marry a woman—

LADY WARGRAVE. Don't repeat my words! A Cazenove marry Margery! Ridiculous!

GERALD. But, aunt—

LADY WARGRAVE. Silence! You said just now, you hoped that you would never break my heart. Well, Gerald, you have broken it. A Cazenove!

[*Exit, door in flat.* MARGERY *takes up the cushion, and is about to follow.*]

GERALD. Put that thing down. [*She puts it down.*] You are mine now; not hers.

MARGERY. Yes, Mr. Gerald.

GERALD [*sits, drawing her to him*]. For better, for worse, Margery.

MARGERY. For better, for worse.

GERALD. You are not frightened?

MARGERY. Not now, Mr. Gerald.

GERALD. Then call me, Gerald.

MARGERY. Gerald!

[*Dropping on her knee by his side.*]

GERALD. You're not afraid to make those promises!

MARGERY. No, Gerald!

GERALD. To love—to honour.

MARGERY. And obey!

[*Looking up at him.*]

ACT 2.   *Twelve months have elapsed. Study at* GERALD's *opening upon a little boudoir, through curtains which are drawn across part of the stage at back. Doors, R., and L.U.E. Mantelpiece, between doors, R.*

GERALD *discovered, seated at a writing table, with his back to the curtains, writing busily.* MARGERY's *head appears through the curtains, which she holds closely round it, so that only her face is visible. She watches* GERALD *for a few moments, with a broad smile on her face.*

MARGERY. Bo!

[*Withdraws her head.*]

GERALD [*starts and looks round*]. Margery, of course!

[*Resumes his writing. A peal of laughter behind the curtains, and* MARGERY's *head reappears, laughing.* GERALD *throws down his pen.*]

MARGERY [*running in*]. Did I startle you?

GERALD. Not much; I'm getting used to it.

MARGERY. Well, don't be cross!

GERALD. I'm not cross, dear; but these repeated interludes make composition rather difficult.

MARGERY. Oh, bother! you've been all the morning at that stupid book, and I'm so happy, I can't help it. Kiss me, and say that you forgive me!

GERALD. Of course I forgive you!

MARGERY. Kiss me, then!

GERALD. My dear—

MARGERY. Gerald! will you kiss me?

GERALD [*kisses her*]. How many times does that make?

MARGERY. Only three this morning. You used to like kissing me.

GERALD. Yes, dear, but—

MARGERY. What?

GERALD. This isn't writing my book.

MARGERY. No, but it's being happy, and that's worth all the books that ever were written.

GERALD. Yes—being happy—that's the great thing.

[*Sighs.*]

MARGERY. Why do you sigh?

GERALD. Did I sigh?

[*Smiling.*]

MARGERY. Yes.

GERALD. I didn't know I sighed. Writing's hard work.

MARGERY. Then put the book away! [*Thrusts the MS. aside.*] I've such news for you!

GERALD. News?

MARGERY. Such good news. Guess what it is. I'll give you three tries.

GERALD [*deprecatingly*]. Margery!

MARGERY. You'll never guess!

GERALD. Then what's the use of trying?

MARGERY. Because I want you to guess wrong.

GERALD. I shan't do that!

MARGERY. You will! I'm sure you will!

GERALD. I'm sure I shan't, because I am not going to guess at all.

MARGERY [*grimaces*]. Cross again! You'd better not be, or you know the penalty!

GERALD. Come! what is the good news?

MARGERY. That's the good news.

[*Gives him a card.*]

GERALD [*with real pleasure*]. Margery!

MARGERY [*pouting*]. You might have guessed!

GERALD. A card from Lady Wargrave! And addressed to you!

MARGERY. Asking us to a party at her house.

GERALD. Don't say a party, Margery!

MARGERY. Well, isn't it a party?

GERALD. Call it an At Home.

MARGERY. Oh, that's another lesson! Never call things by their right names, it's vulgar!

GERALD. This is an olive-branch, and no mistake! So aunt is thawing at last.

MARGERY. Stop a bit, Gerald!

GERALD. Wait a moment, Margery!

MARGERY. Is that another lesson? Never use one syllable when two will do? Very well, Gerald, I'll remember that. But what do you mean by olive-branch?

GERALD [*looks at her, and sighs again*]. Oh, never mind!

MARGERY. Yes, tell me. I want to make sure as I go along.

GERALD. An overture—a sign of reconciliation—like holding out your hand.

MARGERY. Ah, now I understand! But what a funny thing to call it—olive-branch!

[*Bursts into a peal of laughter.*]

GERALD [*shivers slightly and goes over to the mantelpiece. Aside*]. It didn't sound like that in Mapledurham! [*Conquering himself, returns to her.*] I'm so glad aunt's come round. You don't know how it's worried me—her estrangement.

MARGERY. They've all come round now. They've all recognized me. Oh, I'm so happy, Gerald! It isn't half as hard to be a lady as I thought!

GERALD [*thoughtfully*]. Of course you'll have to answer this!

MARGERY. Of course!

GERALD. Show me the answer when you've written it!

MARGERY. Oh, I shan't spell it wrong!

GERALD. No, dear, but—

MARGERY. I know what you mean. I might use all short words instead of long ones. [GERALD *laughs.*] Don't be afraid: I'll pick the longest in the dictionary. [*Kisses him.*] Ah, Gerald, dear! short words were good enough for you once!

[*Archly.*]

GERALD. I dare say.

MARGERY. Yes; when you said, "I love you, Margery!" Say it again!

GERALD. Margery, what nonsense!

MARGERY. That's what I like—nonsense. Say it again!

GERALD [*with effort*]. I love you, Margery. [*Sits, and resumes his pen.*] Now, let me get on with my work!

MARGERY [*goes L. Aside*] Somehow it didn't sound like that in Mapledurham. [*Brightly.*] Well, I suppose his head's full of his book. I wish mine was of mine. Oh, those French verbs! and what's the use of them? Why isn't English good enough for England?

Enter WELLS, L.

WELLS. Captain Sylvester.

[GERALD *flings down his pen in despair. Exit* WELLS, L.]

Enter SYLVESTER.

MARGERY. Ah, I'm so glad you've come! [*Crosses to him.*] I wanted somebody to talk to. Gerald's so busy!

[*Takes* SYLVESTER's *hat and stick.*]

SYLVESTER. Busy? then I'm afraid I intrude.

GERALD [*resignedly*]. Oh, not at all! [*Sees* MARGERY *at back, who has put* SYLVESTER's *hat on, very much askew, and is marching up and down with the stick under her arm.*] Good gracious, Margery!

[MARGERY *laughs.* SYLVESTER *laughs.* GERALD *goes up, snatches the hat and stick, and turns to put them down.*]

MARGERY. Cross again! [*As* GERALD *turns again, he finds himself face to face with her, holding her mouth out.*] Penalty!

GERALD. It is for Captain Sylvester to forgive you.

SYLVESTER. Anything. Mrs. Cazenove can do no wrong. [*Bows.* MARGERY *curtseys.*] But where's Agnes? Happening to pass this way, I thought I might perhaps give her a lift home.

MARGERY. Oh! Gerald expects Mrs. Sylvester—

GERALD. Later on, later on!

SYLVESTER. Then may I wait for her?

GERALD. Oh, certainly! [*Taking up MSS.*] If you'll excuse me going on with my work. I've been a good deal interrupted.

[*Goes to door*, R.]

SYLVESTER. By all means, if I may talk to Mrs. Cazenove!

[GERALD *bows stiffly and exit*, R., *watched by* MARGERY, *who makes a grimace to audience.*]

MARGERY. I believe Gerald's jealous!

SYLVESTER [*laughing*]. Of *me*?

MARGERY [*laughs*]. Just fancy anyone being jealous of *you*! [*Laughs loudly, then stops suddenly.*] Hush! I forgot! We mustn't make so much noise. Clever people don't like noise.

SYLVESTER. Music is noise to some people. I like it!

MARGERY. Ah, but then you're not clever!

SYLVESTER [*laughing*]. I'm afraid not!

MARGERY. There's a pair of us!

SYLVESTER. And what a pleasure it is to meet somebody who's not clever. Mrs. Cazenove, I think cleverness is the most boring thing in the world. This planet would be quite a pleasant place but for the clever people.

MARGERY. Do you mean my husband?

SYLVESTER. I was thinking of my wife; she's one of them. I'm not. I'm only Mrs. Sylvester's husband.

MARGERY. Are you sure you're that?

SYLVESTER. I have always been under that impression.

MARGERY. A husband who isn't master of his wife isn't half a husband.

SYLVESTER. I am content to be a fraction!

MARGERY. But you're a cipher.

SYLVESTER. You're frank, Mrs. Cazenove.

MARGERY. I only say to your face what everybody says behind your back.

SYLVESTER. What do they say?

MARGERY. That Mrs. Sylvester's too much alone.

SYLVESTER. Never. She's always with your husband!

MARGERY. Well?

SYLVESTER. As long as *you* don't object—

MARGERY. Object? Not I! But that's a very different thing!

SYLVESTER. How so?

MARGERY. I am my husband's wife, and I am not afraid of any woman in the world.

SYLVESTER. You have no need to be. [*With admiration.*] And in your preeminence resides my safety, Margery.

MARGERY. I'm not Margery now!

SYLVESTER [*seriously*]. I ask Mrs. Cazenove's pardon. [*In a casual tone*] You don't object to the collaboration, then?

MARGERY. I think it's fun! They are so serious over it. As if the world depended on a book! As if there were no Providence or anything, and they two had to keep creation going by scratching upon little bits of paper! I love to watch them, biting at their pens, and staring at that little crack up there. [*Looking at the ceiling.* SYLVESTER *looks also.*] I often think to myself, you may well look—there's something there that'll keep the world going round, just as it is, long after your precious book is dust and ashes.

SYLVESTER. Then you do watch them, Margery—Mrs. Cazenove?

MARGERY. Oh, often, from my room. [*Indicates curtains.*] But I can scarcely keep from laughing all the time. Some day I mean to have such fun with them! I mean to steal in here, [*business*] and put my head out, so—and just when they are putting the world right, say Bo!
[*Runs back, and bursts into a peal of laughter.* SYLVESTER *laughs also.*]

Re-enter WELLS, L.

WELLS. Miss Vivash!
[*Exit* WELLS, L.]

Enter VICTORIA.

VICTORIA. Good morning, dear. [*Kisses* MARGERY.] What! Captain Sylvester! you here, and Agnes not?

MARGERY. Mrs. Sylvester is coming!

VICTORIA. No need to apologize! A wife is just as much entitled to entertain another woman's husband as a husband to entertain another man's wife. You're getting on, dear. That's philosophy!

MARGERY. Gerald is in the next room!

VICTORIA. Then it's not philosophy!

MARGERY. I'll go and wake him up.
[*Exit*, R.]

VICTORIA. Humph! [*Sits.*] Well, how long do you give it?

SYLVESTER. Do you mean philosophy?

VICTORIA. The Cazenove *ménage*. Another six months? These love-matches are honeymoon affairs. When once that's over, there's an end of everything.

SYLVESTER. But is it over?

VICTORIA. Everybody's talking. Cazenove is bored to death.

SYLVESTER. I don't think his wife is.

VICTORIA. Ah, that will come in time; and when it does, I mean to take Margery in hand. She is neglected shamefully. *She* hasn't discovered it yet, but all her friends have.

SYLVESTER. They're generally first in the field.

VICTORIA. If a husband ignores his wife, the wife is entitled to ignore her husband. What would a man do under the same circumstances?

SYLVESTER. Is not the question rather, what a man *ought* to do?

VICTORIA. That is Utopian. We must take the world as we find it.

SYLVESTER. I'm afraid Mrs. Cazenove won't be an apt pupil.

VICTORIA. No spirit—no proper pride. But things can't go on as they're going long. Margery is on the edge of a volcano. I give it six months.

SYLVESTER. Is it as bad as that?

VICTORIA. Never at home—and when he is—"in the next room." Never takes her anywhere, and I don't wonder at it. Margery is too *gauche* for anything. But what could be expected, when a man throws himself away in that manner? Bless me, there were other women in the world!

SYLVESTER. Oh, plenty, plenty.

VICTORIA. Unluckily, he's found that out. [*Aside.*] That's one for *him*!

SYLVESTER. Indeed!

VICTORIA [*gives him a glance of contempt, and produces a cigarette case*]. Do you mind tobacco?

SYLVESTER. Not at all. I like it. [*Re-enter* MARGERY, R.] If Mrs. Cazenove—

MARGERY. Gerald's so busy, will you please excuse him?

VICTORIA. Certainly. Will you join me?

[*Offers case.*]

MARGERY. Thank you, I can't smoke.

VICTORIA. Then you should learn at once. [*Puts a cigarette in her mouth.*] Could you oblige me with a light? [SYLVESTER *strikes a match.*] Thanks.
[*Lights up at the wrong end of a gold-tipped cigarette.* MARGERY *stands, arms akimbo, surveying her.*]

MARGERY. Do you like smoking?

VICTORIA. No, but I smoke on principle!

SYLVESTER. On the wrong principle!

VICTORIA. I beg your pardon. Men smoke cigarettes.

SYLVESTER. Yes, but they light them at the other end.

> [VICTORIA *takes the cigarette out of her mouth and looks at it.* MARGERY *and* SYLVESTER *burst out laughing. She throws it away viciously.*]

Re-enter WELLS, L.

WELLS. Miss Bethune.

> [*Exit* WELLS, L.]

Enter EDIN.

EDIN. How are you, dear? [*Kisses* MARGERY.] Victoria!

> [*Goes to* VICTORIA, *who presents her cheek.*]

SYLVESTER [*to* MARGERY]. Now you have company, I'll say good-day. I've waited for my wife quite long enough!

MARGERY [*with outstretched hand*]. But you will come and see me again soon?

> [EDIN *and* VICTORIA *exchange glances.*]

SYLVESTER [*holding her hand, and in a lower voice*]. Shall you be in to-morrow?

MARGERY [*frankly*]. Yes. [SYLVESTER *smiles and presses her hand; she sees her mistake.*] If Gerald is.

> [EDIN *and* VICTORIA *are exchanging whispers.*]

SYLVESTER [*drops her hand; aside*]. Women are like Bradshaw—a guide and a puzzle!

> [*Exit*, L.]

EDIN. Does Captain Sylvester often call, my dear?

MARGERY. He has done lately.

EDIN. Quite a change for him! He must occasionally meet his wife!

VICTORIA [*who has gone to the mantelpiece for a match*]. Now that that man has gone—

> [*Lights another cigarette.*]

EDIN. Victoria!

VICTORIA [*offering case to* MARGERY]. Can't I prevail on you?

MARGERY [*takes one*]. Well, I don't mind trying.

> [*Lights hers from* VICTORIA's, VICTORIA *putting the case on the table.*]

EDIN. How *can* you, Margery? I call it shocking! To take a nasty, evil-smelling thing like this [*taking a cigarette out of* VICTORIA's *case*]—and put it to your lips—brrh! [*Shudders, but puts it in her mouth.* MARGERY *presses her burning cigarette against it till it is alight.*] Don't, Margery, don't! I call it horrid—most unladylike!

MARGERY. Now puff!

> [*All three sit and puff vigorously.* MARGERY *perched on table.*]

VICTORIA. Well, dear, and how are you getting on?

MARGERY. Oh, famously!

EDIN. I hope you've taken my advice to heart!

VICTORIA. And mine! Have you a latch-key yet?

MARGERY. Oh, yes!

EDIN. Margery, you shock me!

MARGERY. Well, you're easily shocked!

VICTORIA. You have a latch-key?

> [*Triumphantly.*]

MARGERY [*simply*]. Yes, we have a latch-key!

BOTH [*in different tones*]. *We?*

MARGERY. What would Gerald do without one?

VICTORIA [*with contempt*]. Gerald!

MARGERY. When he comes home late.

EDIN. *Does* he come home late?

VICTORIA. All men do!

EDIN. *Before* marriage. Would that were *all* they did. [*Mysteriously.*] Has he told you everything?

MARGERY. He's told me everything I've asked him.

VICTORIA [*with curiosity, putting down cigarette*]. What have you asked him?

MARGERY. Nothing!

EDIN. Margery! [*rises*] it's such women as you on whom men prey!

> [*Turns off.*]

VICTORIA [*rises*]. And it's such men as him that women marry!

> [*Turns off.*]

MARGERY. When they get the chance! [*Grimace at audience.*]

> *Re-enter* WELLS, L.

WELLS. Colonel Cazenove.

> [EDIN *hides her cigarette behind her back;* MARGERY *flings hers away, jumps down and runs to meet him. Exit* WELLS, L.]

> *Enter* COLONEL.

MARGERY. Uncle!

> [*Flings her arms round his neck, and gives him three smacking kisses.* COLONEL *smiles all over his face.* EDIN *and* VICTORIA *exchange shrugs.*]

COLONEL. Bless me! what a smell of tobacco! [*Looks about, sniffing, sees* VICTORIA.] Ah, the foolish—beg pardon!—Miss Vivash! [*Bow.*] Dear me, something burning!

> [*Sniffs.* VICTORIA *sits again.*]

EDIN [*confused*]. Yes, Mr. Cazenove—the next room

COLONEL [*seeing her*]. Man the Be— Miss Bethune, I think?

> [*Holds out his hand.* EDIN *has to change the cigarette into her left hand behind her back; shakes hands, then turns to wipe the nicotine from her lips, unconsciously presenting the turning cigarette to* COLONEL'S *eyeglass.* MARGERY *laughs.* COLONEL *grins at audience.*]

COLONEL. I thought something was burning. [EDIN *throws cigarette into the grate, and covers her face.* COLONEL *lifts his finger.*] And you said Mr. Cazenove!

EDIN. Well, it wasn't a story. He *is* in the next room.

COLONEL. So man has not a monopoly of the vices!

EDIN. We're none of us perfect!

COLONEL. No, [*rubbing his hands*] thank Heaven! It's the spice of the old Adam that makes life endurable!

MARGERY [*again embracing him*]. Oh, I'm so happy, uncle!

EDIN [*aside*]. Wish she wouldn't do that!

MARGERY. Oh, so happy!

COLONEL. So am I, Margery. What did I always say? Caroline's a heart of gold. I knew she would come round. I always said I'd stand by you and Gerald.

MARGERY. Uncle!

COLONEL. I always said so!

MARGERY. You ran away!

COLONEL. Yes, but I said so. Then you have got her card?

MARGERY [*nodding her head*]. Yes!

> [*Jumps up and gives him another kiss.*]

EDIN [*aside, jealously*]. I do wish she wouldn't!

COLONEL. My doing, Margery—my doing!

EDIN. I have a card as well!

COLONEL. My doing, Miss Bethune!

EDIN. I've just been ordering my gown!

COLONEL [*gallantly*]. I trust it will be worthy of the wearer.

[*Bows.* EDIN *smiles.*]

MARGERY. Have *you* a card, Miss Vivash?

VICTORIA [*who has sat very quietly, now rises*]. If you'll excuse me, dear, I'll say good-morning!

MARGERY [*shakes hands*]. Must you go?

[*Exit* VICTORIA, L.]

MARGERY. Excuse *me*, uncle. Gerald doesn't know you're here!

[*Exit*, R.]

COLONEL. Miss Vivash—?

EDIN. Don't trouble, Colonel! She resents an escort. I have no patience with Victoria. Trying to be a man!

COLONEL. And making only a *succès d'estime!*

EDIN. I like a woman to be womanly!

COLONEL [*aside*]. The best of 'em.

EDIN. I don't mean weak—like Agnes. She goes to the other extreme. Do you know, I'm getting very anxious about Agnes!

COLONEL. Mrs. Sylvester?

EDIN. Haven't you noticed anything? Of course not! You men never do!

COLONEL. I am afraid I must plead guilty!

EDIN. Haven't you observed how much she and your nephew are together?

COLONEL. But they're collaborating.

EDIN. Ah, Colonel, when a man collaborates with a woman, a third person ought always to be present.

COLONEL. To protect the man?

EDIN [*tapping him, playfully*]. You are incorrigible!

COLONEL [*cheerfully*]. I always was, and at my age reformation is out of the question!

EDIN. Oh, you are not so old as all that!

COLONEL. Guess.

EDIN. Fifty!

COLONEL [*pleased*]. Add six to it!

EDIN. Six!

COLONEL [*aside*]. She might add eight.

EDIN. I don't believe it, Colonel.

COLONEL [*aside*]. *Quite* the best of 'em! [*Sits.*] So you have appointed yourself the third person?

EDIN. It's time someone did.

COLONEL. A sort of Vigilance Committee, eh?

EDIN. I simply take the interest of a friend in Agnes.

COLONEL. And what is the result of your observations?

EDIN. I have come to a terrible conclusion.

COLONEL. You alarm me!

EDIN. That she is a poor, tempted creature.

COLONEL. Bless me! I never regarded her in that light before. I thought the boot was on the other leg. [*Corrects himself hurriedly.*] Foot!—foot! [*Indicating* EDIN's, *which she is carefully showing; aside.*] Very neat foot she has!

EDIN. Men always stand by one another, so should women. Agnes must be protected against herself!

COLONEL. Then it's herself, after all? I thought you meant my nephew.

EDIN. So I do. She is the moth—he is the candle.

COLONEL. Really!—

EDIN. Oh, you men, you men! You're all alike—at least, I won't say all!

COLONEL. Say all, say all! It really doesn't matter!

EDIN. No, no, I won't say all!

COLONEL. You say so in your book!

EDIN [*pleased*]. You've read my book?

COLONEL [*evading the question*]. "Man, the Betrayer?"

EDIN. Well, you know, Colonel, one has to paint with a broad brush.

[*Pantomime.*]

COLONEL. Yes, when one paints with tar! [*Aside.*] Very nice arm, too! [*Aloud.*] Look at your title!

EDIN. "Man, the Betrayer!"

COLONEL [*aside*]. Don't know any more!

EDIN. A mere figure of speech!

COLONEL [*admiring her*]. Figure?

EDIN. Mere figure!

COLONEL. Damned fine figure, too!

> [*To himself, but aloud.*]

EDIN. Colonel!

COLONEL. Ten thousand pardons! I was thinking of something else. Pray forgive my bad language!

EDIN. Oh, I'm used to it! Victoria's is much worse!

COLONEL. Miss Vivash!

EDIN. Vulgar-minded thing! Learned French on purpose to read Zola's novels. I don't suppose that even *you* have read them.

COLONEL. Oh, haven't I? Every one!

EDIN. I don't believe it, Colonel!

COLONEL. I'm a shocking old sinner! I never professed to be anything else!

EDIN. I simply don't believe it! You men exaggerate so! You make yourselves out to be so much worse than you are. Whereas we women pretend to be so much better. That's the worst of us! We are such hypocrites! Oh, if you knew as much about women as *I* do—

COLONEL [*aside, much interested*]. Now I'm going to hear something. [*Meanwhile* MARGERY *has crept in*, R., *behind them. She flings her handkerchief over the* COLONEL's *eyes, and ties it in a knot behind his head, then skips away from him. Rising.*] You rascal! It's that Margery! I know it is! Where are you? [*Groping about*, MARGERY *evading him, and in shrieks of laughter.*] Margery, if I catch you!

MARGERY. But you can't!

> [EDIN *has risen to evade the* COLONEL, *who is groping all over the room—a sort of blind man's buff—all laughing.*]

COLONEL [*seizing* EDIN]. I've got you!

> [*Kisses her.* EDIN *shrieks.* MARGERY *roars.* COLONEL *tears off the handkerchief and stands aghast.*]

Re-enter WELLS, L.

WELLS. Lady Wargrave.

> [*Sudden silence. Exit* COLONEL, R. EDIN *runs out*, C., *in confusion.*]

Enter LADY WARGRAVE, L., *and comes down.*

[*Exit* WELLS, L. EDIN *re-appears* C., *and runs across stage behind* LADY WARGRAVE, *and off*, L. MARGERY *stands confused, not knowing how to greet* LADY WARGRAVE.]

LADY WARGRAVE [*putting out both hands*]. Margery! [*Holding both* MARGERY'S *hands*].

MARGERY. Oh, Lady Wargrave!

LADY WARGRAVE. Aunt. I've called to make amends to you.

MARGERY. Amends?

LADY WARGRAVE. For my neglect. [*Kisses her.*] Forgive me, Margery, but your marriage was a shock to me. However, I've got over it. Perhaps, after all, Gerald has chosen wisely!

MARGERY. Thank you for your kind words. I knew you had got over it.

LADY WARGRAVE. Of course! you had my card.

MARGERY. I knew from uncle, too. How good of him to bring it all about!

LADY WARGRAVE. Theodore!

MARGERY. I mean, to reconcile you!

LADY WARGRAVE. My dear Margery, your uncle has never presumed to mention the subject?

MARGERY. Oh, what a story he has told us! he said it was *his* doing.

LADY WARGRAVE. No doubt. When you know Theodore as well as I do, you will have learnt what value to attach to his observations!

MARGERY. Won't I pay him out?

[*Shaking her fist.*]

LADY WARGRAVE. Never mind your uncle. Tell me about yourself—and about Gerald. I hope your marriage has turned out a happy one.

MARGERY. Yes—we're as happy as the day is long.

LADY WARGRAVE. That is good news. Then you haven't found your new position difficult?

MARGERY. Oh, I'm quite used to it! I'm not a bit shy now. Of course I put my foot in it—I make mistakes sometimes; but even born ladies sometimes make mistakes.

LADY WARGRAVE. Yes, Margery. [*Bending her head slightly.*] And Gerald?

MARGERY. Is the best husband in the world to me. Of course, he's very busy—

LADY WARGRAVE. Busy?

MARGERY. With his book; and sometimes I can't help annoying him. That's nothing. We haven't had a real cross word yet.

LADY WARGRAVE. Does he write very much?

MARGERY. Oh, morning, noon, and night. He's always got a pen in his hand. I often say I wonder he doesn't wear the ceiling out with looking at it.

[*Laughs.*]

LADY WARGRAVE. That isn't writing, Margery.

MARGERY. No, but it's thinking—and he's always thinking.

[*Falls into a reverie.*]

LADY WARGRAVE. Do you go out much?

MARGERY. We went out a good deal at first, but we got tired of it. I like home best; at any rate, Gerald does. I rather liked going out. Oh, I'm quite a success in society.

LADY WARGRAVE. Indeed?

MARGERY. Of course, aunt, I'm not clever; but I suppose I'm witty without knowing it!

LADY WARGRAVE. Witty?

MARGERY. At any rate, I make the people laugh. Isn't that being witty? Then *I* laugh as well, although I don't know what I'm laughing at, I'm sure! [*Laughs.*] Oh, everybody laughs at me—but Gerald. And he's thinking of his book!

LADY WARGRAVE. Do you have many visitors?

MARGERY. Oh, yes! Miss Vivash—Miss Bethune—Dr. Mary—Mrs. Sylvester—and uncle. They're often coming. As for Mrs. Sylvester, she almost lives here!—oh, and Captain Sylvester, he's taken to calling lately!

LADY WARGRAVE. In future, dear, you'll have another visitor. I see I have neglected you too long. And you must come and see me. We'll go out together.

MARGERY. Oh, that *will* be nice! Then you have *quite* forgiven me?

LADY WARGRAVE. But not myself!

MARGERY [*embracing her*]. Oh, why is everyone so good to me?

Re-enter GERALD, R., *followed by* COLONEL.

GERALD. Aunt, this is kind of you! but you were always kind.

LADY WARGRAVE. Not always. I ought to have paid this visit earlier. I made a mistake, Gerald, and I have come to acknowledge it.

COLONEL [*laying his hand on* LADY WARGRAVE'S *shoulder in an access of enthusiasm*]. Caroline, you're a trump!

LADY WARGRAVE. Theodore!

COLONEL. No other word for it! I always said you'd come round!

LADY WARGRAVE. Never!

COLONEL. Always!

LADY WARGRAVE. Theodore, you *never* said so!

COLONEL. To myself.

[*Turns off.*]

GERALD. Better late than never, aunt. And thank you for the card for your At Home.

[*Talks to* LADY WARGRAVE.]

MARGERY. Oh, uncle, you're a shocking old story, aren't you?

COLONEL. What have I been saying now?

MARGERY. You said it was *your* doing!

COLONEL. So it was!

MARGERY. Aunt vows you'd nothing to do with it at all!

COLONEL [*taking* MARGERY *aside*]. Caroline's a heart of gold; but your aunt must be managing! So I let her manage, and I manage *her*.

MARGERY. You?

[*Smiling.*]

COLONEL. But I do it quietly. I influence her, without her knowing it. Sheer force of character. Chut! not a word! [*Backing away from her, signalling silence; backs into* LADY WARGRAVE.] Ten thousand pardons!

[*Bows profusely.*]

LADY WARGRAVE. Really, Theodore!
[MARGERY *goes up, stifling her laughter; he shakes his handkerchief at her.*]

Re-enter WELLS, L.

WELLS. Mrs. Sylvester!

Enter MRS. SYLVESTER; *she hesitates, on seeing* LADY WARGRAVE. *Exit* WELLS, L.

GERALD. Pray come in, Mrs. Sylvester. You know my aunt.

MRS. SYLVESTER. I think we've met before.

LADY WARGRAVE. Yes, at my nephew's chambers. I remember perfectly. You were engaged upon some work or other.

GERALD. It's not finished yet. I am so interrupted!
[*Glancing at* MARGERY *who has crept down behind* COLONEL.]

MARGERY [*whispering in* COLONEL'S *ear*]. Who kissed Miss Bethune?
                                [COLONEL *starts guiltily*; MARGERY *roars*.]

GERALD [*angrily*]. Margery!
                                                    [MARGERY *runs out*, L.]

LADY WARGRAVE. Not finished yet!

MRS. SYLVESTER. But we have made great progress.

LADY WARGRAVE. And are you satisfied with what you have done?

GERALD. It is certainly interesting.

LADY WARGRAVE. It is not enough for me that a work of my nephew's should
    be interesting! Tell me, as far as you have gone, do you think it is worthy
    of a Cazenove?

GERALD. It is the work of my life.

MRS. SYLVESTER. And of mine!

LADY WARGRAVE. As far as you have gone. But what is to be the end of it?

GERALD. Ah, we've not got there yet.

LADY WARGRAVE. Would you admit a third collaborateur?

MRS. SYLVESTER [*alarmed*]. Who?

LADY WARGRAVE. An *old* woman.

GERALD. Lady Wargrave's joking!

LADY WARGRAVE. Oh, I could put an end to it, I think!

MRS. SYLVESTER. We don't know what the end will be ourselves.

LADY WARGRAVE. There I have the advantage. If I can help in any way, my
    experience is always at your service. Meanwhile, I fear I am another
    interruption. Theodore, your arm!

GERALD [*follows them to door*, L.]. Thank you so much for coming.
                                                    [*Holding his hand out*.]

LADY WARGRAVE [*taking it*]. And for going?
                                        [*Exit with* COLONEL, L.]

MRS. SYLVESTER. What does she mean?

GERALD. Thank her for going?

MRS. SYLVESTER. And the end of it?

GERALD. Aunt always talks in riddles!

MRS. SYLVESTER. Is it a riddle?

GERALD [*avoids her eyes*]. Come, let us get to work. I've done hardly anything today. It's first one interruption, then another.

[*Sits.*]

MRS. SYLVESTER. We should be quieter at our house.

GERALD. There's your husband!

MRS. SYLVESTER. Always a husband!

GERALD. Or a wife. Ah, me!

[*Sits with his head between his hands, staring at vacancy;* MRS. SYLVESTER *watching him sympathetically.*]

MRS. SYLVESTER [*comes and kneels by him*]. Gerald! [*He starts slightly.*] You are not happy. You have realized the truth.

GERALD. What truth?

MRS. SYLVESTER. Your marriage was a mistake from the beginning.

GERALD. Not from the beginning. It started right enough, but somehow it has taken the wrong turn.

MRS. SYLVESTER. It was wrong from the first. Mine was the true ideal. The thing that you thought love was a mere passion—an intoxication. Now you have come back to your better self you feel the need of sympathy.

GERALD. No, no; my love was real enough, and I love Margery still; but love doesn't seem to bear the wear and tear of marriage—the hourly friction—the continual jar.

MRS. SYLVESTER. There is no friction in true marriage, Gerald. You say you love your wife, and it is good and loyal of you to deceive yourself; but you can't deceive me. Haven't I made the same mistake myself? I was a thoughtless, inexperienced girl, Jack was a handsome, easy-going man. We married, and for a year or two we jogged along. But I grew up—the girl became a woman. I read, I thought, I felt; my life enlarged. Jack never reads, never thinks—he is just the same. [*Rising.*] I am not unhappy, but my soul is starved—[*goes to mantelpiece and stands looking at him*]—as yours is!

[*Pause.* MARGERY's *face appears between the curtains at the back, wearing a broad smile. She grimaces at them, unobserved, and remains there; then looks at* GERALD *with a long face of mock sympathy.*]

GERALD. Well, we must make the best of it!

MRS. SYLVESTER. Yes, but what *is* the best? [MARGERY *grimaces at her.*] Is our mistake so hopeless, irremediable? After all, is not true loyalty loyalty to oneself?

GERALD [*looks at her*]. You think so?

MRS. SYLVESTER. Or what becomes of our philosophy?

GERALD. Yes, what becomes of it?

> [*Another pause.* MARGERY *laughs almost audibly. During the next passage the laugh subsides into an expression of perplexity.*]

MRS. SYLVESTER. What is a promise when the heart's gone out of it?

GERALD. Surely it is a promise.

MRS. SYLVESTER. To an empty phrase must one sacrifice one's life? Must one stake everything on the judgment of one's youth? By the decision of a moment must one be bound for ever? Must one go through the world "with quiet eyes unfaithful to the truth?" Does one not owe a duty to oneself? There can be but one answer!

GERALD [*absently*]. Margery! [MARGERY *winces as if struck—quite serious now. Then with energy.*] But, Agnes, Margery is impossible! She's no companion to me! I am all alone! Her very laughter grates upon me! There's no meaning in it! It is the laughter of a tomboy, of a clown! And she will never learn! She's hopeless, Agnes, hopeless! [MARGERY *drops back horror-struck, but her face disappears only by degrees.* MRS. SYLVESTER *lays her hand on him. Another pause. The curtains close.*] What is one to do?

> [*Rising.*]

MRS. SYLVESTER. We are face to face with the problem! Let us confront it boldly. Gerald, do you love me?

> [*A thud behind the curtains.* GERALD *starts guiltily. Pause. They stand looking at one another.*]

GERALD [*in a whisper*]. What was that? [*Goes up cautiously and draws curtains back, discovering* MARGERY *stretched senseless on the floor.*] Margery!

ACT 3. *A Fortnight Later. Drawing-room at* LADY WARGRAVE'S. *Main entrance C., Conservatory R. Entrance, L., to an inner room. Fireplace, R., up stage, near which is* LADY WARGRAVE'S *chair, with the cushion of Act I.*

The stage is discovered half-filled with Guests, who stand and sit in groups, including COLONEL, CAPTAIN *and* MRS. SYLVESTER, *and* GERALD. LADY WARGRAVE *is receiving her guests. A buzz of general conversation; and a band is heard playing in the inner room, loudly at first, but softly after the picture is discovered.*

SERVANT [*at entrance C.*].

Miss Vivash and Mr. Pettigrew!

Enter VICTORIA, *followed leisurely by* PERCY, *a very young man who is always smiling to himself, unconsciously.*

VICTORIA [*going straight to* LADY WARGRAVE *and grasping her hand*]. Good evening, Lady Wargrave, I have taken the liberty of bringing a friend whose name is no doubt known to you—Mr. Percy Pettigrew.

[PERCY *bows distantly, smiling.*]

LADY WARGRAVE. Pettigrew, did you say?

PERCY. Percy Bysshe Pettigrew.

[*Smiling.*]

LADY WARGRAVE. Of course! *two* of your names are *quite* well known to me; it is only the surname that is unfamiliar.

PERCY [*smiling*]. Pettigrew!

[*Turns off.*]

GERALD. One of my Oxford friends.

LADY WARGRAVE [*aside to him*]. One of those who are always at Oxford?

VICTORIA. His "Supercilia" are quoted everywhere.

LADY WARGRAVE. His—?

GERALD. A column Percy does for "The Corset."

VICTORIA. A newspaper devoted to our cause.

GERALD. "The Corset" is Percy's organ.

LADY WARGRAVE. Ah, his rattle!

SERVANT. Dr. Bevan.

DR. BEVAN [*shakes hands with* LADY WARGRAVE]. I hope I am not late; but I was detained at the hospital. Most interesting case, unhappily unfit for publication.

SERVANT. Miss Bethune.

[*Exit* SERVANT.]

Enter EDIN.

COLONEL [*to* SYLVESTER]. The best of 'em! [EDIN *shakes hands with* LADY WARGRAVE.] Ah, what a pity, what a pity, Sylvester!

SYLVESTER. What is a pity, Colonel?

COLONEL. That such a figure should be wasted!

SYLVESTER [*in a matter of course voice*]. I prefer Mrs. Cazenove's.

[*Turns off.* COLONEL *eyes him curiously. The other Guests should be so arranged that each man is surrounded by a little group of women.*]

PERCY [*the centre of one group, lolling lazily, always smiling with self-complacency, suddenly sits up and shivers*]. No, no! don't mention it. It bores me so.

[*Shivers.*]

CHORUS. And me!

[*All shiver.*]

VICTORIA. The stage has ever been Woman's greatest foe.

GUEST. For centuries it has shirked the sexual problem.

SYLVESTER [*who has strolled up*]. But doesn't it show signs of repentance?

PERCY. The theatre is dying.

SYLVESTER. Death-bed repentance, then. That's the one problem it discusses.

GUEST. It is the one problem in life.

PERCY. The theatre is dying! Dixi!

[*Leans back again.*]

DOCTOR. The novel will sweep everything before it.

SYLVESTER. You mean, the female novel?

DOCTOR. Nothing can stop it.

SYLVESTER. No, it stops at nothing.

DOCTOR. Nor will it, till the problem is solved. That solution, I venture to predict, will be on the lines of pure mathematics.

SYLVESTER. Really?

[*Smothering a yawn.*]

DOCTOR. I put the proposition in this way. The sexes are parallel lines.

SYLVESTER. Which are bound to meet.

DOCTOR. I must not be taken to admit, that there is any physiological necessity.

VOICES. Certainly not.

DOCTOR [*to* LADY WARGRAVE, *who is passing*]. I am sure, Lady Wargrave must agree with us.

LADY WARGRAVE. What is that, Doctor?

DOCTOR. That there is no physiological necessity—

LADY WARGRAVE. To discuss physiology? I am quite of your opinion.

[*Passes on.*]

EDIN [*who is in a group surrounding* COLONEL]. That's where we differ. What is *your* view, Colonel?

COLONEL. My dear Miss Bethune, there is no occasion for Man to express *any* view, when Woman expresses them all. First, you must reconcile your internal differences.

VOICE. But we can't.

COLONEL. To begin with, you must make up your minds whether you wish to regenerate us or to degrade yourselves.

EDIN. Regenerate you, of course.

COLONEL. Miss Vivash prefers the alternative.

EDIN. That is Victoria's foible.

COLONEL [*gallantly*]. I can admit no foible in a lady.

EDIN. At any rate, we are agreed on the main point—the equality of the sexes.

COLONEL. That, alas, is impossible.

VOICE. Impossible?

COLONEL. Whilst Woman persists in remaining perfect.

VICTORIA. Cannot Man emulate her?

COLONEL. I am afraid his strength is only equal to the confession of his unworthiness.

EDIN. You would confess that? Then you agree with me, that a woman is entitled to know the whole of a man's past?

LADY WARGRAVE [*who has joined them*]. Would it not be more useful if she knew something of his future?

EDIN. Women have futures; men have only pasts.

DOCTOR [*still in* SYLVESTER's *group*]. It stands to reason—pure reason—there ought not to be one law for women and another for men.

SYLVESTER. You mean, that they ought both to be for women?

DOCTOR. I mean, that the institution of marriage is in urgent need of reconsideration.

SYLVESTER. The sooner, the better.

DOCTOR. I am glad you think so.

SYLVESTER. When the institution of marriage is reconsidered, man will have another chance.

[*Exit*, R.]

LADY WARGRAVE [*who has joined* PERCY's *group*]. What do I think of the New Woman? There is no New Woman; she is as old as Molière.

[*Stands listening, amused.*]

CHORUS. Molière!

VICTORIA. A pagan!

PERCY. A frank pagan. For pure art we must go to Athens.

CHORUS. Athens!

PERCY. Or the Music Halls. Have you seen Trixy Blinko?

CHORUS. Trixy—oh, charming—sweet!

PERCY. In her alone I find the true Greek spirit. What were the prevailing characteristics of Hellenic culture? [*A sudden silence.*] Breadth and centrality, blitheness and repose. All these I find in Trixy.

CHORUS. Little dear!

LADY WARGRAVE. Somewhat *risquée*, isn't she?

PERCY. To the suburban mind.

> [LADY WARGRAVE *bows and turns off.*]
>
> SERVANT *enters*, L.

SERVANT. Signor Labinski has arrived, your ladyship.

> [*Exit*, L. LADY WARGRAVE *speaks to one or two of the Guests, and the company disperse, most of them going off,* L., *but a few,* C., *and others into the conservatory. During this general movement, the music off, is heard louder.* COLONEL *is left with* DR. MARY.]

COLONEL. Nonsense, my dear Doctor— The fact's just this. The modern woman is prostrated by the discovery of her own superiority; and she is now engaged in one of those hopeless enterprises which *we* have regretfully abandoned. She is endeavouring to understand *herself.* I offer her my respectful sympathy.

> [*Bows and sits,* C.]

DOCTOR [*sits by him*]. The truth amounts to this: the one mitigating circumstance about the existence of Man is, that he occasionally co-operates in the creation of a Woman.

COLONEL. His proudest privilege! The mystery to me is, that you ladies haven't found it out before.

> *Re-enter* EDIN, C.

DOCTOR. Yes, but you shirk the question!

> [COLONEL *is fanning himself, helplessly.*]

EDIN [*aside*]. A man in distress! I must help him! [*Advancing sweetly.*] What were you saying, Doctor?

> [*Sits on the other side of* COLONEL.]

COLONEL [*aside*]. Bethune! the best of 'em!

DOCTOR. You know, from your own experience, that marriage is not a necessity.

COLONEL. No, it's a luxury—an expensive luxury.

EDIN. Oh, surely that depends upon the wife.

DOCTOR. It is she who has to associate with him.

EDIN. And considering what his past has been—

COLONEL. Suppose it hasn't!

DOCTOR. But it always has!

EDIN. I should be sorry to think that.

DOCTOR. Take the Colonel's own case.

COLONEL [*alarmed*]. Doctor!

DOCTOR. Do you deny that you have had a past?

COLONEL. Oh, a few trifling peccadilloes!

EDIN. Then you must never marry.

COLONEL. Am I to have no chance of reformation?

EDIN. It is your own fault.

DOCTOR. Entirely.

COLONEL. One moment, my dear ladies! Excuse me pointing out, that, in the last resort, there must always be a female accomplice!

EDIN. Poor, tempted creature!

COLONEL. *Tempted* by a *man*!

DOCTOR. We all have our weak moments.

[*Sighs.*]

EDIN. All of us!
[*Sighs. As the pair sit with their eyes cast down, silent,* COLONEL *looks from one to the other in dismay, then steals off,* R.]

COLONEL [*at door*]. Getting dangerous!
[*Exit,* R. *When they look up, each with a languorous glance, they find themselves languishing at one another; both rise.*]

EDIN [*putting her arm round* DOCTOR's *waist*]. My dear, we are missing the music!
[*Exeunt,* L.]

Re-enter MRS. SYLVESTER *and* GERALD, C. *Movement of other Guests across stage, during music.*

MRS. SYLVESTER. Where have you been? I have seen nothing of you. What have you been doing?

GERALD. Thinking.

MRS. SYLVESTER [*jealously*]. Of whom?

GERALD. Of Margery.

[*Movement of* MRS. SYLVESTER.]

MRS. SYLVESTER. Has she said anything?

GERALD. No, not a word.

MRS. SYLVESTER. Of course, she heard?

GERALD. What did I say? What did I do? What must she think of me? I can't bear this suspense. For the last fortnight, she's been another woman. So grave—so thoughtful—so unlike herself. There is no laugh to grate upon me now. What would I give to bring it back again?

MRS. SYLVESTER. Is it she only who has changed?

GERALD. Ever since I saw that figure on the ground, I can see nothing else. And it is I who brought it to the dust—I, who had sworn to cherish it. Yes, you are right; I too am different; I see things from a different point of view. And when I think of Margery's young life, so full of hope and joy—Margery, who never asked to be my wife—Margery, whom I compelled to marry me—with all the joy crushed out of her—I feel too much ashamed even to ask forgiveness. And as I watch her move about the house—silent and sorrowful—I ask myself, how much did Margery give up for me? I took her from the station of life in which she was born, and in which she was happy. I set her in another and a strange one. Was mine the only sacrifice? How much of friendship and of old association did she resign for my sake? My life continued as it was before—I had my old friends and my old pursuits. What had she? Nothing—but my love. And I took it away from her. Because she made a few mistakes, and a few people laughed—a few more didn't call—and I mistook a light heart for an empty head. What do all these things matter? what is a man worth who sets such things above a love like hers?

MRS. SYLVESTER. This is pure pity, Gerald.

GERALD. Pity for myself.

MRS. SYLVESTER. She was no wife for you. She could be no companion.

GERALD. If she was no companion, did I make her one?

MRS. SYLVESTER. Need you tell *me* all this?

GERALD. Yes, Mrs. Sylvester, it's best I should. I came to tell it you.

MRS. SYLVESTER. Not Agnes now!

GERALD. Forget my folly, and forget your own.

MRS. SYLVESTER. Mine was no folly. I, at least, was sincere; the love that isn't based on sympathy is a mere passion.

GERALD. And the love that has no passion in it, isn't worth the name!

MRS. SYLVESTER. That's your idea?

GERALD. And what is yours? Let us be frank.

MRS. SYLVESTER. Oh, frankness, by all means.

GERALD. Forgive me; but we're face to face with truth. Don't let us flinch from it. We have both made the same mistake—not in our marriages, but in despising them. What we want in a partner is what we lack in ourselves. Not sympathy only, but sex. Strength requires gentleness, sweetness asks for light; and all that is womanly in woman wants all that is manly in man. You think your husband is no mate for you. What I have missed in Margery, have you not missed in him?

MRS. SYLVESTER [*after a pause*]. I understand you. It is over.

GERALD. It is for you to say. We have gone too far together for either of us to turn back alone. I have not only made my own hearth desolate, but yours. I owe you all the reparation I can make. I only want you to know the truth. What is left of my life you may command, but my heart is not mine to bestow.

MRS. SYLVESTER [*turns up, to hide her emotion, and tries to go into the room,* L., *but half-way she falters and puts out her hand*]. Gerald!
 [*He goes to her and offers her his arm. Exeunt* GERALD *and* MRS. SYLVESTER, L. *Other Guests cross the stage. Enter* MARGERY, C. *Finding herself opposite* LADY WARGRAVE'S *chair, takes a long look at it, then moves the cushion, and gradually gets into her old position behind it. Music heard off, softly, during this passage.*]

MARGERY. Yes, this is how it ought to be. It looks a different world altogether—the real world—the world, when Gerald loved me!
 [*Comes down and sits, in a reverie.*]

Re-enter SYLVESTER, R.

SYLVESTER. Alone, Mrs. Cazenove? It isn't often that I find you alone. I've seen nothing of you lately. You've always been out when I've called.

MARGERY. I was in once.

SYLVESTER. Only once.

MARGERY. It was enough.

SYLVESTER. You are cruel.

MARGERY. Are you looking for your wife?

SYLVESTER [*laughs*]. Agnes and I go very different ways.

MARGERY. I think you're going the same way, both of you.

SYLVESTER [*still laughing*]. But in opposite directions. Mrs. Cazenove, you're quite a philosopher. Why have you grown so serious all at once?

MARGERY. I'm older than I was.

SYLVESTER. Only a fortnight since you were all vivacity.

MARGERY. One can live a long time in a fortnight.

SYLVESTER. I hope these ladies haven't converted you.

MARGERY. Yes; I am a new woman.

SYLVESTER [*laughs*]. Your husband has been reading you his book!

MARGERY. A good deal of it.

SYLVESTER. What is it all about? If I am not too curious.

MARGERY. It's about love.

SYLVESTER. I thought it was about marriage.

MARGERY. Aren't they the same thing? He says they are, and I agree with him. And then he says [*half to herself*] that, when the love is gone, so is the marriage—and I think he's right!

[*Loses herself in thought.*]

SYLVESTER [*gazes at her for some moments, then unable to restrain himself*]. Ah, Margery! if Heaven had given me such a wife as you—

MARGERY [*rises*]. Heaven didn't, and there's an end of it.

SYLVESTER [*rises*]. Forgive me! how can I help admiring you?

MARGERY. Can't you admire me without telling me? It's well to make the best of what we have, instead of trying to make the worst of what we haven't.

SYLVESTER. I must be silent!

MARGERY. Or not talk in that way.

[*Moves away.*]

SYLVESTER [*following, in an outburst*]. Gerald doesn't love you [*movement of Margery*]—oh, you said that just now! you mayn't know that you said it, but you did! My wife doesn't love me—I don't love my wife—and yet I must say nothing.

MARGERY. What's it to me that you don't love your wife?

SYLVESTER. I love *you*, Margery.

MARGERY. I knew that was coming.

SYLVESTER. Honestly love you! I admired you always. It was an empty admiration, perhaps—the admiration a man feels for twenty women—but it grew solid; and the more you repulsed me, the more you attracted me. You mayn't believe me, but at first I *wanted* you to repulse me; then it got past that; and when I saw you sitting there alone—living over in your mind your wasted life—I loved you, and the words sprang to my lips. Nothing could keep them back! I love you, Margery—nobody but you! Why should your life be wasted? Why should mine?

MARGERY. Well, have you finished?

SYLVESTER [*seizing her*]. No!

MARGERY. I can guess the rest. You say Gerald doesn't love me, you don't love your wife, and your wife doesn't love *you*; but you forget one thing—that *I* don't love you either.

SYLVESTER. Not now, but by-and-by. Margery, I would make you love me—I would teach you!

MARGERY. So, I'm to *learn* to be unfaithful, is that it? As one learns music? No, Captain Sylvester! Suppose two people are so much in love that they can't help it, Heaven is their judge, not me. But to *begin* to love when they *can* help it—not to resist—to *teach* themselves to love—that's where the wrong is, and there's no gainsaying it.

SYLVESTER. Suppose your husband left you?

MARGERY. I would have no other!

SYLVESTER. Why not?

Re-enter GERALD, L.

MARGERY. Because I love him, and I don't love you!
        [MARGERY'S *back is towards* GERALD, *so that she doesn't see him; but* SYLVESTER *is facing him and sees him.*]

GERALD [*coming down to* MARGERY]. What has he said?

MARGERY. Nothing for your ears!

SYLVESTER. Yes, for all the world's! I'll tell you!

MARGERY. I forbid you! Leave me with my husband.
                [SYLVESTER *hesitates a moment, then exit*, C.]

GERALD. Margery, speak! I have a right to know.

MARGERY. You have no right!

GERALD. You will not tell me?

MARGERY. No!

GERALD. Then *he shall!*

[*Advances on her.*]

MARGERY. Stand back! You shall not go!

GERALD. What, you defend him?

MARGERY. Against you, I do! Who are you to question him? Are your own hands clean?

GERALD [*drops back as if struck*]. Margery!

MARGERY [*holding out her hand*]. Good-bye!

GERALD. Good-bye?

MARGERY. I'm going home.

GERALD. To Mapledurham?

MARGERY. We'll say good-bye now.

GERALD. Here—Margery?

MARGERY. You needn't be afraid. There'll be no scene; I've done with tears.

GERALD. You're [*chokes*] going to leave me?

MARGERY. Yes.

GERALD. For a few days, you mean?

MARGERY. I mean, for ever. Gerald, I've had enough of half a home and only half a heart. I'm starving, withering, dying here with you! They love me there! Let me go back to them! Oh, what a world it is! To think that one can get the love of any man except the man one loves!

GERALD. You have it, Margery!

MARGERY [*fiercely*]. I haven't.

GERALD. If you only knew—

MARGERY. I know I haven't! what's the use of words? Do you think a woman doesn't know when she's not loved, or is? When you first said you loved me, down in the fields yonder, do you suppose you took me by surprise? You had no need to swear. I knew you loved me, just as certainly as I know now you don't!

GERALD [*much moved*]. Oh, what a scoundrel I was, Margery!

MARGERY. No man's a scoundrel to the woman he loves. Ah, it was easy to forgive your loving me. But I'll do something that is not so easy. I will forgive you for *not* loving me. It's been a struggle. For the last fortnight I haven't said a word, because I wasn't master of myself, and I didn't want to speak till I'd forgiven you. I wasn't listening, Gerald. Heaven knows I would have given all the world not to have heard a word; but when you spoke my name, I couldn't move. The ground seemed slipping underneath my feet, and all the happiness of all my life went out of it in those three words, "Margery's hopeless, hopeless!"

GERALD. Don't! don't! you torture me!

MARGERY. Yes, Margery *is* hopeless. Every scrap of hope has gone out of her heart. I heard no more. It was enough. There was the end of all the world for me. [Gerald *groans*.] But it was well I heard you. I should have gone blundering along, in my old madcap way, and perhaps not found it out till I had spoilt your life. It's well to know the truth; but, Gerald dear, why didn't you tell it *me* instead of her? Why didn't you tell me I was no companion? I would have gone away. But to pretend you loved me, when you didn't—to let me go on thinking you were happy, when all the time you were regretting your mistake—not to tell *me*, and to tell someone else—oh, it was cruel, when I loved you so!

GERALD. How could I tell you, Margery?

MARGERY. How could you tell *her*? How could she listen to you? I forgive *you*, Gerald—I didn't at first, but now I understand that there are times when one's heart is so sore, it must cry out to somebody. But *she*—

GERALD. It was my fault!

MARGERY. You are mistaken there. It was your voice that spoke them, but the words were hers. It's she who's robbed me of your love! It isn't I who've lost it; she has stolen it!

GERALD. No, no!

MARGERY. Be careful, or she'll steal your honour too. Don't trust to her fine phrases. She deceives herself. She wants your love, that's what that woman wants: not to instruct the world—just to be happy—nothing more or less; but she won't make you happy or herself. If I am no companion, she's a bad one!

GERALD. You wrong her, Margery—indeed, you do! *I* was the culprit—

MARGERY. Have some pity on me! Don't let the last words I shall hear you say be words defending her! Think what she's done for me! Think how you loved me when you married me—think what our two lives might have been, but for her—think what mine *will* be! for mine won't be like yours. Your love is dead, and you will bury it, but mine's alive—alive!

[*Breaks down.*]

GERALD. And so is mine!

MARGERY [*springs up*]. Don't soil your lips with lies! I've borne as much as I can bear. I can't bear that!

GERALD. If you will only listen—

MARGERY. I have heard too much! Don't speak again, or you will make me hate you! My mind's made up. I have no business here! You are above me. I'm no wife for you! I'm dragging you down every day and hour.

GERALD. Margery! you shall not go!

MARGERY [*flinging him off*]. To-night and now! Good-bye!

[*Rushes into conservatory*, R.]

GERALD. What right have I to stop her?

[*Goes up, leans upon chair. Re-enter* SYLVESTER, C.]

SYLVESTER. Now, Mr. Cazenove, I am at your service.

GERALD. You are too late.

[*Exit*, C.]

SYLVESTER. So, he won't speak to me. But I will make him. If he thinks I am caught, like a rat in a trap, he's made a mistake. There'll be a scandal—well, so much the better! Better that they should know the truth all round.

Re-enter MRS. SYLVESTER, L.

MRS. SYLVESTER. Ah, you are here! I've been looking for you everywhere.

SYLVESTER. Looking for *me*?

MRS. SYLVESTER. I want you to take me home.

SYLVESTER. I've something to say to you. Sit down.

MRS. SYLVESTER. Not to-night. I'm tired.

SYLVESTER. Yes, to-night. What I'm going to say may be everybody's property to-morrow. I choose that you should know it now.

MRS. SYLVESTER. I don't understand you.

SYLVESTER. But you shall. I've often heard you say that a loveless marriage is no marriage. Well, ours is loveless enough, isn't it?

MRS. SYLVESTER. It has been.

SYLVESTER. It is! I've never understood you; and if there was any good in me, you've never taken the trouble to find it out.

MRS. SYLVESTER. I can't bear this now.

SYLVESTER. You must. Don't think I'm going to reproach you. I take all the blame on myself. What if I were to tell you that you've made a convert to your principles where you least expected it?

MRS. SYLVESTER. What do you mean?

SYLVESTER. That it's best for us both to put an end to this farce that we're living. I mean, that I love another woman.

MRS. SYLVESTER [*rising*]. You!

SYLVESTER. Perhaps that seems to you impossible. You thought, perhaps, that I was dull and stupid enough to go on with this empty life of ours to the end. I thought so too, but I was wrong. I love this woman, and I've told her so—

MRS. SYLVESTER [*with jealousy*]. Who is she?

SYLVESTER. And I would tell her husband to his face—

MRS. SYLVESTER. Then she is married?

SYLVESTER. As I tell *you*.

MRS. SYLVESTER. Who is she, I say?

SYLVESTER. Margery.

MRS. SYLVESTER. Margery! Are you all mad, you men? What is it in that woman that enslaves you? What is the charm we others don't possess? Only you men can see it; and you all do! You lose your senses, every one of you! What is it in her that bewitches you?

SYLVESTER. What you've crushed out of yourself—your womanhood. What you're ashamed of is a woman's glory. Philosophy is well enough in boots; but in a woman a man wants flesh and blood— frank human nature!

MRS. SYLVESTER [*laughing, hysterically*]. A mere animal!

SYLVESTER. A woman.

MRS. SYLVESTER. Well, you have found one.

SYLVESTER. Yes.

MRS. SYLVESTER. Take her, then! go your way!

SYLVESTER. I will.

[*Exit*, C.]

MRS. SYLVESTER. This world was made for such as you and her! We have no place in it—we who love with our brains! we have no chance of happiness!

Re-enter MARGERY, R., *cloaked*.

MARGERY. What chance have we? we, who love with our hearts! we, who are simply what God made us—women! we, to whom love is not a cult—a problem, but just as vital as the air we breathe. Take love away from us, and you take life itself. You have your books, your sciences, your brains! What have we?—nothing but our broken hearts!

MRS. SYLVESTER. Broken hearts heal! The things that *you* call hearts! One love is dead, another takes its place; one man is lost, another man is found. What is the difference to a love like yours? Oh, there are always men for such women as you!

> *By degrees re-enter omnes, R., L., and C., gradually, except* GERALD.

MARGERY. But if the love is not dead? if it's stolen? what is our lot then—ours, whose love's alive? We, who're not skilled to steal—who only want our own—

MRS. SYLVESTER. Not skilled to steal! have you not stolen mine?

MARGERY. I have one husband, and I want no other!

> [*Murmurs.*]

LADY WARGRAVE [*restraining her*]. Calm yourself, dear!

MARGERY. I have been calm too long!

LADY WARGRAVE. Remember, you are my niece.

MARGERY. That's what I do remember! [*Murmurs continue.*] I am Gerald's wife! That's what she doesn't forgive me! [*Addressing* MRS. SYLVESTER.] You call yourself a New Woman—you're not New at all. You're just as old as Eve. You only want one thing—the one thing every woman wants—the one thing that no woman's life's worth living without! A true man's love! Ah, if we all had that, there'd be no problem of the sexes then. I had it once. Heaven help me, I have lost it! I've done my best—it isn't much, but it's the best I can. I give it up! If you have robbed me of his love, my own is left to me; and if the future's yours, the past is mine. He loved me once, and I shall love him always!

> [*Exit, C.*]

ACT 4.   *A Month Later. An orchard at Mapledurham. Farmhouse at back, C. Paths off, R. and L. front. A cluster of trees, R., at back. A few stumps of trees to serve as seats.*

> MARGERY *discovered, standing on a ladder placed against one of the trees, gathering apples, which she throws into a basket below. She is dressed in peasant costume.*]

> *Enter* ARMSTRONG, C.

ARMSTRONG. Margery!

MARGERY. Yes, dad!

ARMSTRONG [*comes underneath the tree and roars with laughter*]. Here's a slice of luck! That fellow in London wants the grey mare back again!

MARGERY [*who has come down*]. The grey mare, father?

ARMSTRONG. Old Dapple! you remember her?

MARGERY. Of course! but what about her?

ARMSTRONG. Bless me, haven't I told you? I sold old Dapple to a chap in London.

MARGERY [*reproachfully*]. You sold old Dapple?

ARMSTRONG. She's too good for hereabouts. True, she's a splint on the off leg, but what's a splint? I sold her without warranty, and buyer took her with all faults, just as she stood.

MARGERY. Well, dad?

ARMSTRONG. Darn me, if the next day he didn't cry off his bargain!

MARGERY [*thoughtfully*]. Poor Dapple!

ARMSTRONG. Oh, says I, if you're not satisfied with her, I am. So, there's your money; give me back my mare. An Armstrong doesn't stand on warranties.

MARGERY. No, daddy dear, and you don't mind the splint?

ARMSTRONG. But Margery, you should have seen the screw he got in place of her! Ha, ha! she was *all* splints!

MARGERY. He's found that out?

ARMSTRONG. And wants the old mare back! at my own price!

MARGERY. This *is* good news! For we were getting hard up, weren't we, father?

ARMSTRONG. Ay, farming isn't what it used to be; and now that you won't let me take in visitors—

MARGERY. I never stopped you.

ARMSTRONG. How about Captain Sylvester?

MARGERY. Oh, him!

ARMSTRONG. He's an old customer; and always seemed a civil-spoken gentleman enough.

MARGERY. Too civil!

ARMSTRONG. That's more than you were, Margery. You'd scarce say a word.

MARGERY. He came for no good.

ARMSTRONG. There's no harm in trout fishing—unless it's for the trout.

MARGERY. I was the trout.

ARMSTRONG. You? Go on! That's the way with you girls! You think all the men are after you. I'm sure he said nothing to hurt you.

MARGERY. But he has written since.

ARMSTRONG [*scratches his head*]. I didn't know he'd written.

MARGERY. Nearly every day.

ARMSTRONG. Those letters were from *him*? I thought they were from—

[*Hesitates.*]

MARGERY. No! From Captain Sylvester.

ARMSTRONG. Of course you haven't answered them?

MARGERY. Only the last.

ARMSTRONG. I shouldn't have done that.

MARGERY. Yes, you would, dad!

ARMSTRONG. Well, you know best. You always went your own way, Margery, and it was always the right road.

MARGERY. Where shall I put these apples?

ARMSTRONG. Nay, I've the broadest shoulders. Give me a hand; I'll take 'em.
[MARGERY *helps him to put the basket on his shoulders. Exit*, C.]

MARGERY. Dear old dad! We leave our parents, and we return to them; they let us go, and they take us back again! How little we think of their partings, and how much of our own!

[*Sits*, R.]

Enter SYLVESTER, L. *front.*

SYLVESTER. I saw you in the apple-tree, and took a short cut.

MARGERY. You got my message then?

SYLVESTER. How good of you to send for me! So then my letters have had some effect?

MARGERY. I sent for you because I want to speak to you.

SYLVESTER. And I to you. Margery, I've left my wife.

MARGERY. Yes, so I heard.

SYLVESTER. She was no wife to me. For years our marriage has been a mockery, and it was best to put an end to it. Now I am free.

MARGERY. Because you've left your wife?

SYLVESTER. It's no use beating about the bush. Things have gone too far, and I'm too much in earnest. She loves your husband. It is common talk. I've shut my eyes as long as possible, and you've shut yours; but we both know the truth.

MARGERY. That you've deserted her!

SYLVESTER. What if I have?

MARGERY. Go back.

SYLVESTER. Back to a wife who is no wife!

MARGERY. Back to the woman you promised to protect, and whom you left when she most needed you.

SYLVESTER. Because I love you, Margery!

MARGERY. That love won't last long. Love can't live on nothing!

SYLVESTER. There is no hope for me?

MARGERY. No, not a scrap!

SYLVESTER. Then what do you propose? To sacrifice your life to an idea—to be true to a phantom? You owe no faith to one who is unfaithful. Think! You are young— your real life lies before you—would you end it before it's begun? A widow before you're a wife?

MARGERY. I *am* a wife, and I shall not forget it. If I have lost my husband's love, at least I'll save his honour. A public scandal mayn't mean much to *you*, but it means your wife's ruin—it means Gerald's. Gerald shall not be ruined! You shall go back to her!

SYLVESTER. Is it a challenge?

MARGERY. Challenge or not, you *shall*! It is ignoble to desert her so! You are a coward to make love to me! If her love was unworthy, what is yours? Is it for you to cast a stone at her? See! Read your letters! [*Producing a packet.*] Letters to me—love-letters! Letters to a woman you didn't respect in her grief and persecuted in her loneliness—a woman who would have none of you—who tells you to your face you're not a man! Your love's an insult! take the thing away!

[*Turns off. Pause.*]

SYLVESTER. Do you propose to send those to my wife?

MARGERY. No! but I want to make you realize you need more mercy than you show to her. These letters were written for my eye alone; to open them was to promise secrecy.

SYLVESTER. Why have you kept them, then?

MARGERY. To give them back to you.

> [*Gives him the packet. Another pause.*]

SYLVESTER. Margery, everything you say and do makes it more hard to go away from you.

MARGERY. You're going, then?

SYLVESTER. Your words leave me no choice.

MARGERY. Where are you going? to her?

SYLVESTER. I don't know yet. I don't know if I'm welcome.

> [*Playing with the packet, mechanically.*]

MARGERY. That rests with you. You say, she's been no wife to you; but have you been a husband to her?

SYLVESTER. Why do you take her part? She's injured you enough.

MARGERY. Yes; she *has* injured me; but now I know what it is to live without love, and to want it, I can pardon her. Can't you? [*Goes to him and gives him both her hands.*] Forgive her, Captain Sylvester—freely as I do you—give her the love that you have offered me—and you will find your wife's a woman just as much as I am.

SYLVESTER. Margery—I may call you "Margery?"

MARGERY. I'm "Margery" to everybody now.

SYLVESTER. If there were more women like you, there would be fewer men like me.

> [*Exit*, L.]

MARGERY [*looks after him, then goes*, R. *front and looks again*]. He'll go back to his wife; and if she isn't happy, it's her fault.

> [*Exit*, R.]

Re-enter ARMSTRONG, *showing out*, C., LADY WARGRAVE *and the* COLONEL.

ARMSTRONG. This way, my lady. I'll send Margery to you.

> [Exit ARMSTRONG, R.]

COLONEL. This must be put right, Caroline.

LADY WARGRAVE. I mean to put it right.

COLONEL [*severely*]. A Cazenove living apart from his wife!

LADY WARGRAVE. It is sad—very sad.

COLONEL. More than that, Caroline—it's not respectable.

LADY WARGRAVE. That doesn't trouble *you*.

COLONEL. It shocks me. The institution of marriage is the foundation of society; and whatever tends to cast discredit on that holy "ordnance" saps the moral fibre of the community.

LADY WARGRAVE. Did you say, "ordnance?"

COLONEL. I did say, "ordnance." It was a slip of the tongue.

LADY WARGRAVE. You are not used to ordinances.

COLONEL. What do you mean, Caroline? Wasn't I baptized—wasn't I confirmed?

LADY WARGRAVE. There is another ceremony which, during a somewhat long career, you have systematically avoided.

COLONEL. A mere sin of omission, which even now it is not too late to repair. I am a young man still—

LADY WARGRAVE. Young man?

COLONEL. Comparatively. And everything in the world is comparative. What cannot be undone in the past can at least be avoided in the future.

LADY WARGRAVE. What is the matter with you, Theodore? You have suddenly become quite a moral martinet, and have developed such a severity of aspect that I scarcely know my own brother.

COLONEL [aside]. Shall I tell her? Dare I? Courage!

LADY WARGRAVE. I think I liked you better as you were. At any rate, I was used to you.

COLONEL. How peaceful it is here, Caroline—how sylvan!

LADY WARGRAVE. Yes, it's a pretty little place enough.

COLONEL. It might have been created expressly for the exchange of those sacred confidences which are never more becoming than when shared between a brother and a sister.

LADY WARGRAVE. Good gracious! you are growing quite sentimental! I have no confidences to make.

COLONEL. But *I* have.

LADY WARGRAVE. Theodore! What fresh iniquity—?

COLONEL. Caroline, I am going to be married.

[Blows his nose vigorously.]

LADY WARGRAVE [astounded]. Married!

COLONEL. To-morrow.

LADY WARGRAVE. To whom, pray?

COLONEL. Miss Bethune.

LADY WARGRAVE. Give me my smelling salts.

COLONEL [gives her them]. Enid! Pretty name, isn't it? Enid!

[Smiling to himself.]

LADY WARGRAVE. No fool like an old fool!

COLONEL. Fifty-six.

LADY WARGRAVE. Eight.

COLONEL. But don't tell Enid, will you?

LADY WARGRAVE. There are so many things I mustn't tell Enid!

COLONEL. No, Caroline; I've made a clean breast of it.

LADY WARGRAVE. *Quite* a clean breast of it?

COLONEL. Everything in the world is comparative.

LADY WARGRAVE. Then, Miss Bethune has renounced her opinions?

COLONEL. Oh, no; she's too much of a woman for that.

LADY WARGRAVE. How can she reconcile them with your enormities?

COLONEL. My peccadilloes? Oh, she doesn't believe them—or she pretends she doesn't—which is the same thing. She says we men exaggerate so; and as for the women, you simply can't believe a word they say!
[*Chuckles in his old style.*]

LADY WARGRAVE. At any rate, she means to marry you?

COLONEL. Upon the whole, she thinks I have been rather badly used.
[*Chuckles again.*]

LADY WARGRAVE. To marry! after your experience!

COLONEL. Way of the world, my dear. My poor old adjutant! went through the Mutiny unscathed, and killed in Rotten Row!

LADY WARGRAVE. Well, it was quite time that you had a nurse!
[*Rising and going R. front to meet* MARGERY.]

COLONEL. Caroline's taken it very well. Nothing like courage in these matters— courage! "Nurse" was distinctly nasty; but that's Caroline's way.

Re-enter ARMSTRONG, R., *followed by* MARGERY.

ARMSTRONG. Found her at last, my lady.

LADY WARGRAVE. Leave us together, Armstrong.
[MARGERY *drops a curtsey.*]

ARMSTRONG. Come with me, Colonel. If you'll step indoors, I'll give you a glass of ale that'll do your heart good.

COLONEL [*putting his arm through* ARMSTRONG'S]. Caroline takes it very well.
[*Quite forgetting himself.*]

ARMSTRONG. My lady's very welcome.

COLONEL [*hastily withdrawing his arm*]. No, no, no! I was talking to myself. [*Exit* ARMSTRONG, C., *roaring. Aside, glancing at* LADY WARGRAVE.] Nurse!

[Exit, C.]

LADY WARGRAVE. Margery, I've come to scold you.

MARGERY. Yes, my lady.

LADY WARGRAVE. Aunt. Come and sit down by me. [*Draws her towards seat under the tree,* L. LADY WARGRAVE *sits*—MARGERY *at her feet.*] Yes, Margery, to scold you. Why did you not confide in me? If you had only told me of your troubles, this would never have happened. It was undutiful.

MARGERY. No, aunt. There are some troubles one can confide to nobody— some griefs which are too sacred to be talked about.

LADY WARGRAVE. And is yours one of them? You are young, Margery; and youth exaggerates its sorrows as well as its joys. Nothing has happened that cannot be put right, if you will only trust me and obey me.

MARGERY. I owe my obedience elsewhere.

LADY WARGRAVE. And do you think that you have paid it?

MARGERY. Yes.

LADY WARGRAVE. Gerald *desired* you to leave him?

MARGERY. No; but I read his thoughts—just as you used to say I could read yours—and I obeyed his wishes.

LADY WARGRAVE. Then if he wished you to return, you would come back?

MARGERY. Not if he'd been talked over; not if he asked me to go back to him because he thinks it his duty, or I want him. I don't want duty; I want love.

LADY WARGRAVE. You wouldn't see him, if I sent him to you?

MARGERY. What is the use of seeing him? You can send Gerald, but not Gerald's heart. I have done all I can—I can't do any more. I've saved his honour— I've resigned his love. All I ask is, to be left alone with mine.

[Turning away.]
[LADY WARGRAVE rises, and as GERALD advances, retires into the house, C.]

GERALD. Margery!

MARGERY. Gerald!

GERALD. I am not here to ask you to come back to me. How can I say what I have come for? I have come—because I cannot keep away from you. To ask for your forgiveness—

MARGERY. You have that.

GERALD. And, if it's possible, some place in your esteem. Let me say this, and I will say no more. If, for a little space, my heart strayed from you, Margery— if, for a moment, words escaped my lips which cannot be recalled, that is my only infidelity. You understand me?

MARGERY. Yes.

GERALD. That's what I came to say—that's all!

MARGERY [*giving him her hand*]. Thank you for telling me.

GERALD [*holding her hand*]. Not all I want to say, but all I must. I am no longer a free man. My lips are sealed.

MARGERY. What seals them?

GERALD. Haven't you heard? Sylvester's left his wife—and it is all my doing.

MARGERY. No, it is his.

GERALD. His?

MARGERY. I may tell you now. He left his wife, not through your fault or hers, but to make love to me.

GERALD. He has been here?

MARGERY. But he has gone.

GERALD. Where?

MARGERY. To his wife. I sent him back to her.

GERALD. Then, I am free!

MARGERY. Yes, Gerald.

GERALD. Free to say how I love you—how I have always loved you! Yes, Margery, I loved you even then—then when I spoke those unjust, cruel words; but love's so weird a thing it sometimes turns us against those we love. But when I saw you, there upon the ground, my heart turned back to you—no, it was not my heart, only my lips that were unfaithful! My heart was always yours—not half of it, but all—yours when I married you, yours when you said good-bye, and never more yours, never as much as now, now I have lost you.

MARGERY. You have not lost me, if you love me that much!

[*Throwing her arms round him.*]

GERALD. Margery!

LADY WARGRAVE *and* COLONEL *re-enter, quietly, C., and stand, looking on, at back, amongst the trees.*

GERALD. My wife again!

MARGERY. But, Gerald, remember I am nothing more. I don't think I shall ever be a lady.

GERALD. Always in my eyes!

MARGERY. No, not even there. Only a woman.

GERALD. I want you to be nothing less or more—only a woman!

>   [*About to kiss her.* LADY WARGRAVE, *at back, bows her head, with her fan half spread before the* COLONEL's *face.* GERALD *kisses* MARGERY.]

CURTAIN.

THE NOTORIOUS MRS. EBBSMITH
A DRAMA IN FOUR ACTS

ARTHUR W. PINERO

1895

CHARACTERS

AGNES.	REV. AMOS WINTERFIELD.
LUCAS CLEEVE.	SIR GEORGE BRODRICK.
SYBIL CLEEVE.	DR. KIRKE.
SIR SANDFORD CLEEVE.	FORTUNÉ.
DUKE OP ST. OLPHERTS.	ANTONIO POPPI.
GERTRUDE THORPE.	NELLA.

HEPHZIBAH.

The Scene is laid in Venice— first at the Palazzo Arconati, a lodging-house on the Grand Canal; afterwards in an apartment in the Campo S. Bartolomeo.

It is Easter-tide, a week passing between the events of the ACT 1 and ACT 2.

THE NOTORIOUS MRS. EBBSMITH

ACT 1.   *The Scene is a room in the Palazzo Arconati, on the Grand Canal, Venice. The room itself is beautiful in its decayed grandeur, but the furniture and hangings are either tawdry and meretricious or avowedly modern. The three windows at the back open on to a narrow covered balcony, or loggia, and through them can be seen the west side of the canal. Between recessed double doors on either side of the room is a fireplace out of use and a marble mantelpiece, but a tiled stove is used for a wood fire. Breakfast things are laid on a table. The sun streams into the room.*

ANTONIO POPPI *and* NELLA, *two Venetian servants, with a touch of the picturesque in their attire, are engaged in clearing the breakfast-table.*

137

NELLA [*Turning her head*]. Ascolta! (Listen!)

ANTONIO. Una gondola allo scalo. (A gondola at our steps.) [*They open the centre window, go out on to the balcony, and look down below.*] La Signora Thorpe. (The Signora Thorpe.)

NELLA. Con suo fratello. (With her brother.)

ANTONIO [*Calling*]. Buon di, Signor Winterfield! Iddio la benedica! (Good day, Signor Winterfield! The blessing of God be upon you!)

NELLA [*Calling*]. Buon di, Signora! La Madonna l'assista! (Good day, Signora! May the "Virgin have you in her keeping!)

ANTONIO [*Returning to the room*]. Noi siamo in ritardo di tutto questa mattina. (We are behindhand with everything this morning.)

NELLA [*Following him*]. È vero. (That is true.)

ANTONIO [*Bustling about*]. La stufa! (The stove.)

NELLA [*Throwing wood into the stove*] Che tu sia benedetta per rammentarmelo! Questi Inglesi non si contentono del sole. (Bless you for remembering it. These English are not content with the sun.)

> [*Leaving only a vase of flowers upon the table, they hurry out with the breakfast things. At the same moment, Fortuné, a man servant, enters, showing in* MRS. THORPE *and the* REV. AMOS WINTERFIELD. GERTRUDE THORPE *is a pretty, frank-looking young woman of about seven-and-twenty. She is in mourning, and has sorrowful eyes and a complexion that is too delicate, but natural cheerfulness and brightness are seen through all.* AMOS *is about forty—big, burly, gruff; he is untidily dressed, and has a pipe in his hand.* FORTUNÉ *is carrying a pair of freshly-cleaned tan-coloured boots upon boot-trees.*]

GERTRUDE. Now, Fortuné, you ought to have told us downstairs that Dr. Kirke is with Mrs. Cleeve.

AMOS. Come away, Gerty. Mrs. Cleeve can't want to be bored with us just now.

FORTUNÉ. Mrs. Cleeve give 'er ordares she is always to be bored wiz Madame Thorpe and Mr. Winterfield.

AMOS. Ha, ha!

GERTRUDE [*Smiling*]. Fortuné!

FORTUNÉ. Besides, ze doctares vill go in 'alf a minute, you see.

GERTRUDE. Doctors!

AMOS. What, is there another doctor with Dr. Kirke?

FORTUNÉ. Ze great physician, Sir Brodrick.

GERTRUDE. Sir George Brodrick? Amos!

AMOS. Doesn't Mr. Cleeve feel so well?

FORTUNÉ. Oh yes. But Mrs. Cleeve 'appen to read in a newspapare zat Sir George Brodrick vas in Florence for ze Pâque—ze Eastare. Sir Brodrick vas Mr. Cleeve's doctare in London, Mrs. Cleeve tell me, so 'e is acquainted wiz Mr. Cleeve's inside.

AMOS. Ho, ho!

GERTRUDE. Mr. Cleeve's constitution, Fortuné.

FORTUNÉ. Excuse, madame. Zerefore Mrs. Cleeve she telegraph for Sir Brodrick to come to Venise.

AMOS. To consult with Dr. Kirke, I suppose.

FORTUNÉ [*Listening*]. 'Ere is ze doctares.

> DR. KIRKE *enters, followed by* SIR GEORGE BRODRICK. KIRKE *is a shabby, snuff-taking old gentleman—blunt, but kind;* SIR GEORGE, *on the contrary, is scrupulously neat in his dress, and has a suave, professional manner.* FORTUNÉ *withdraws.*

KIRKE. Good morning, Mr. Winterfield. [*To* Gertrude.] How do you do, my dear? You're getting some colour into your pretty face, I'm glad to see. [*To* Sir George.] Mr. Winterfield—Sir George Brodrick. [SIR GEORGE *and* AMOS *shake hands.*]

KIRKE. [*To* SIR GEORGE.] Mrs. Thorpe. [SIR GEORGE *shakes hands with* GERTRUDE.] Sir George and I started life together in London years ago; now he finds me here in Venice. Well, we can't all win the race—eh?

SIR GEORGE. My dear old friend! [*To* GERTRUDE.] Mr. Cleeve has been telling me, Mrs. Thorpe, how exceedingly kind you and your brother have been to him during his illness.

GERTRUDE. Oh, Mr. Cleeve exaggerates our little services.

AMOS. *I've* done nothing.

GERTRUDE. Nor I.

KIRKE. Now, my dear!

GERTRUDE. Dr. Kirke, you weren't in Florence with us; you're only a tale-bearer.

KIRKE. Well, I've excellent authority for my story of a young woman who volunteered to share the nursing of an invalid at a time when she herself stood greatly in need of being nursed.

GERTRUDE. Nonsense! [*To* SIR GEORGE.] You know, Amos—my big brother over there—Amos and I struck up an acquaintance with Mr. and Mrs. Cleeve at Florence, at the Hotel d'Italie, and occasionally one of us would give Mr. Cleeve his dose while poor Mrs. Cleeve took a little rest or a drive—but positively that's all.

KIRKE. You don't tell us—

GERTRUDE. I've nothing more to tell, except that I'm awfully fond of Mrs. Cleeve—

AMOS. Oh, if you once get my sister on the subject of Mrs. Cleeve—[*Taking up a newspaper.*]

GERTRUDE [*To* SIR GEORGE]. Yes, I always say that if I were a man searching for a wife, I should be inclined to base my ideal on Mrs. Cleeve.

SIR GEORGE [*Edging away towards Kirke, with a surprised, uncomfortable smile*]. Eh? Really?

GERTRUDE. You conceive a different ideal, Sir George?

SIR GEORGE. Oh—well—

GERTRUDE. Well, Sir George?

AMOS. Perhaps Sir George has heard that Mrs. Cleeve holds regrettable opinions on some points. If so, he may feel surprised that a parson's sister—

GERTRUDE. Oh, I don't share all Mrs. Cleeve's views, or sympathise with them, of course. But they succeed only in making me sad and sorry. Mrs. Oleeve's opinions don't stop me from loving the gentle, sweet woman; admiring her for her patient, absorbing devotion to her husband; wondering at the beautiful stillness with which she seems to glide through life—!

AMOS [*Putting down the newspaper, to* SIR GEORGE *and* KIRKE]. I told you so! [*To* GERTRUDE.] Gertrude, I'm sure Sir George and Dr. Kirke want to be left together for a few minutes.

GERTRUDE [*Going up to the window*]. I'll sun myself on the balcony.

AMOS. And I'll go and buy some tobacco. [*To* Gertrude] Don't be long, Gerty. [*Nodding to* SIR GEORGE *and* KIRKE.] Good morning.

> [*They return his nod; and he goes out.*]

GERTRUDE [*On the balcony*]. Dr. Kirke, I've heard what doctors' consultations consist of. After looking at the pictures, you talk about whist.

> [*She closes the window and sits outside.*]

KIRKE [*Producing his snuff-box*]. Ha, ha!

SIR GEORGE. Why, this lady and her brother evidently haven't the faintest suspicion of the actual truth, my dear Kirke!

KIRKE [*Taking snuff*]. Not the slightest.

SIR GEORGE. The woman made a point of being extremely explicit with you, you tell me?

KIRKE. Yes, she was plain enough with me. At our first meeting she said: " Doctor, I want you to know so-and-so, and so-and-so, and so-and-so."

SIR GEORGE. Really? Well, it certainly isn't fair of Cleeve and his—his associate to trick decent people like Mrs. Thorpe and her brother. Good gracious, the brother is a clergyman too!

KIRKE. The rector of some dull hole in the North of England.

SIR GEORGE. Really!

KIRKE. A bachelor; this Mrs. Thorpe keeps house for him. She's a widow.

SIR GEORGE. Really?

KIRKE. Widow of a captain in the army. Poor thing! She's lately lost her only child and can't get over it.

SIR GEORGE. Indeed, really, really? .... But about Cleeve, now—he had Roman fever of rather a severe type?

KIRKE. In November. And then that fool of a Bickerstaff at Rome allowed the woman to move him to Florence too soon, and there he had a relapse. However, when she brought him on here the man was practically well.

SIR GEORGE. The difficulty being to convince him of the fact, eh? A highly-strung, emotional creature?

KIRKE. You've hit him.

SIR GEORGE. I've known him from his childhood. Are you still giving him anything?

KIRKE. A little quinine, to humour him.

SIR GEORGE. Exactly. [*Looking at his watch.*] Where is she? where is she? I've promised to take my wife shopping in the Merceria this morning. By-the-bye, Kirke—I must talk scandal, I find—*this* is rather an odd circumstance. Whom do you think I got a bow from as I passed through the hall of the Danieli last night ? [KIRKE *grunts and shakes his head.*] The Duke of St. Olpherts.

KIRKE [*Taking snuff*]. Ah! I suppose you're in with a lot of swells now, Brodrick.

SIR GEORGE. No, no; you don't understand me. The Duke is this young fellow's uncle by marriage. His Grace married a sister of Lady Cleeve—of Cleeve's mother, you know.

KIRKE. Oh! This looks as if the family are trying to put a finger in the pie.

SIR GEORGE. The Duke may be here by mere chance. Still, as you say, it does look—[*Lowering his voice as* KIRKE *eyes an opening door.*] Who's that?

KIRKE. The woman.

AGNES *enters. She moves firmly, but noiselessly—a placid woman, with a sweet, low voice. Her dress is plain to the verge of coarseness; her face, which has little colour, is at the first glance almost wholly unattractive.*

AGNES [*Looking from one to the other*]. I thought you would send for me, perhaps. [*To* SIR GEORGE.] What do you say about him?

KIRKE. One moment. [*Pointing to the balcony.*] Mrs. Thorpe—

AGNES. Excuse me. [*She goes to the window and opens it.*]

GERTRUDE. Oh, Mrs. Cleeve! [*Entering the room.*] Am I in the way?

AGNES. You are never that, dear. Run along to my room; I'll call you in a minute or two. [GERTRUDE *nods, and goes to the door.*] Take off your hat and sit with me a little while.

GERTRUDE. I'll stay for a bit, but this hat doesn't take off. [*She goes out.*]

AGNES [*To* SIR GEORGE *and* KIRKE]. Yes?

SIR GEORGE. We are glad to be able to give a most favourable report. I may say that Mr. Cleeve has never appeared to be in better health.

AGNES [*Drawing a deep breath*]. He will be very much cheered by what you say.

SIR GEORGE [*Bowing stiffly*]. I'm glad—

AGNES. His illness left him with a morbid, irrational impression that he would never be quite his former self again.

SIR GEORGE. A nervous man recovering from a scare. I've helped to remove that impression, I believe.

AGNES. Thank you. We have a troublesome, perhaps a hard time before us; we both need all our health and spirits. [*Turning her head, listening.*] Lucas?

LUCAS *enters the room. He is a handsome, intellectual looking young man of about eight-and-twenty.*

LUCAS [*To* AGNES, *excitedly*]. Have you heard what they say of me?

AGNES [*Smiling*]. Yes.

LUCAS. How good of you, Sir George, to break up your little holiday for the sake of an anxious, fidgety fellow. [*To* AGNES.] Isn't it?

AGNES. Sir George has rendered us a great service.

LUCAS [*Going to* KIRKE, *brightly*]. Yes, and proved how ungrateful I've been to you, doctor.

KIRKE. Don't apologise. People who don't know when they're well are the mainstay of my profession. [*Offering snuff-box.*] Here [LUCAS *takes a pinch of snuff laughingly.*]

AGNES [*In a low voice to* SIR GEORGE]. He has been terribly hipped at times. [*Taking up the vase of flowers from the table.*] Your visit will have made him another man.

> [*She goes to a table, puts down the vase upon the tray, and commences to cut and arrange the fresh flowers she finds there.*]

LUCAS [*Seeing that* AGNES *is out of hearing*] Excuse me, Kirke—just for one moment. [*To* SIR GEORGE.] Sir George [KIRKE *joins* AGNES.] You still go frequently to Great Cumberland Place?

SIR GEORGE. Your mother's gout has been rather stubborn lately.

LUCAS. Very likely she and my brother Sandford will get to hear of your visit to me here; in that case you'll be questioned pretty closely, naturally.

SIR GEORGE. My position is certainly a little delicate.

LUCAS. Oh, you may be perfectly open with my people as to my present mode of life. Only—[*He motions* SIR GEORGE *to be seated; they sit facing each other.*] Only I want you to hear me declare again plainly [*looking towards* AGNES] that but for the care and devotion of that good woman over there, but for the solace of that woman's companionship, I should have been dead months ago—I should have died raving in my awful bedroom on the ground-floor of that foul Roman hotel. Malarial fever, of course! Doctors don't admit—do they?—that it's possible for strong men to die of miserable marriages. And yet I was dying in Borne, I truly believe, from *my* bitter, crushing disappointment, from the consciousness of my wretched, irretrievable—

> [FORTUNÉ *enters, carrying* LUCAS's *hat, gloves, overcoat, and silk wrap, and, upon a salver, a bottle of medicine and a glass.*]

LUCAS [*Sharply*]. Qu'y a-t-il, Fortuné?

FORTUNÉ. Sir, you 'ave an appointment.

LUCAS [*Rising*]. At the Danieli at eleven. Is it so late?

> [FORTUNÉ *places the things upon the table.* LUCAS *puts the wrap round his throat;* AGNES *goes to him and arranges it for him solicitously.*

SIR GEORGE [*Rising*]. I have to meet Lady Brodrick at the Piazzetta. Let me take you in my gondola.

LUCAS. Thanks—delighted.

AGNES [*To* SIR GEORGE]. I would rather Lucas went in the house gondola: I know its cushions are dry. May he take you to the Piazzetta?

SIR GEORGE [*A little stiffly*]. Certainly.

AGNES [*To* FORTUNÉ]. Mettez les coussins dans la gondole.

FORTUNÉ. Bien, madame.

> [FORTUNÉ *goes out.* AGNES *begins to measure a dose of medicine.*]

SIR GEORGE [*To* AGNES]. Er—I—ah—

LUCAS [*Putting on his gloves*]. Agnes, Sir George—

AGNES [*Turning to* SIR GEORGE, *the bottle and glass in her hands*]. Yes?

SIR GEORGE [*Constrainedly*]. We always make a point of acknowledging the importance of nursing as an aid to medical treatment. I—I am sure Mr. Cleeve owes you much in that respect.

AGNES. Thank you.

SIR GEORGE [*To* LUCAS]. I have to discharge my gondola; you'll find me at the steps, Cleeve. [AGNES *shifts the medicine-bottle from one hand to the other so that her right hand may be free, but* SIR GEORGE *simply bows in a formal way and moves towards the door.*] You are coming with us, Kirke?

KIRKE. Yes.

SIR GEORGE. Do you mind seeing that I'm not robbed by my gondolier? [*He goes out.*]

AGNES [*Giving the medicine to* LUCAS, *undisturbed*]. Here, dear.

KIRKE [*To* AGNES]. May I pop in to-night for my game of chess?

AGNES. Do, doctor; I shall be very pleased.

KIRKE [*Shaking her hand in a marked way*]. Thank you.

> [*He follows* Sir George]

AGNES [*Looking after him*]. Liberal little man.

> [*She has* LUCAS's *overcoat in her hand; a small pen-and-ink drawing of a woman's head drops from one of the pockets. They pick it up together.*]

AGNES. Isn't that the sketch you made of me in Florence?

LUCAS [*Replacing it in the coat-pocket*]. Yes.

AGNES. You are carrying it about with you?

LUCAS. I slipped it into my pocket, thinking it might interest the Duke.

AGNES [*Assisting him with his overcoat*]. Surely I am too obnoxious in the abstract for your uncle to entertain such a detail as a portrait.

LUCAS. It struck me it might serve to correct certain preconceived notices of my people's.

AGNES. Images of a beautiful temptress with peach-blossom cheeks and stained hair?

LUCAS. That's what I mean; I assume they suspect a decline of taste on my part, of that sort. Good-bye, dear.

AGNES. Is this mission of the Duke of St. Olpherts the final attempt to part us, I wonder? [*Angrily, her voice hardening.*] Why should they harass and disturb you as they do?

LUCAS [*Kissing her*]. Nothing disturbs me now that I know I am strong and well. Besides, everybody will soon tire of being shocked. Even conventional morality must grow breathless in the chase.

> [*He leaves her. She opens the other door and calls.*]

AGNES. Mrs. Thorpe! I'm alone now.

> [*She goes on to the balcony, through the centre window, and looks down below.*
> GERTRUDE *enters, and joins her on the balcony.*]

GERTRUDE. How well your husband is looking!

AGNES. Sir George Brodrick pronounces him quite recovered.

GERTRUDE. Isn't that splendid! [*Waving her hand and calling.*] Buon giorno, Signor Cleeve! Come molto meglio voi state! [*Leaving the balcony, laughing.*] Ha, ha! my Italian!

> [AGNES *waves finally to the gondola below, returns to the room, and slips her arm through* GERTRUDE's.]

AGNES. Two whole days since I've seen you.

GERTRUDE. They've been two of my bad days, dear.

AGNES [*Looking into her face*]. All right now?

GERTRUDE. Oh, "God's in His heaven" this morning! When the sun's out I feel that my little boy's bed in Ketherick Cemetery is warm and cosy.

AGNES [*Patting* GERTRUDE's *hand*]. *Ah!*

GERTRUDE. The weather's the same all over Europe, according to the papers. Do you think it's really going to settle at last? To me these chilly, showery nights are terrible. You know, I still tuck my child up at night-time; still have my last peep at him before going to my own bed; and it is awful to listen to these cold rains—drip, drip, drip upon that little green coverlet of his!

> [*She goes and stands by the window silently.*]

AGNES. This isn't strong of you, dear Mrs. Thorpe. You mustn't—you mustn't.

> [AGNES *brings the tray with the cut flowers to the nearer table; calmly and methodically she resumes trimming the stalks.*]

GERTRUDE. You're quite right. That's over. Now then, I'm going to gabble for five minutes gaily. [*Settling herself comfortably in an armchair.*] What jolly flowers you've got there! What have you been doing with yourself? Amos took me to the Caffè Quadri yesterday to late breakfast, to cheer me up. Oh, I've something to say to you! At the Caffè, at the next table to ours, there were three English people—two men and a girl—home from India, I gathered. One of the men was looking out of the window, quizzing the folks walking in the Piazza, and suddenly he caught sight of your husband. [AGNES's *hands pause in their work.*] "I do believe that's Lucas Cleeve," he said. And then the girl had a peep, and said: "Certainly it is." And the man said: "I must find out where he's stopping; if Minerva is with him, you must call." "Who's Minerva? " said the second man. "Minerva is Mrs. Lucas Cleeve," the girl said. "It's a pet name—he married a chum of mine, a daughter of Sir John Steyning's, a year or so after I went out." Excuse me, dear. Do these people really know you and your husband, or were they talking nonsense?

[AGNES *takes the vase of faded flowers, goes on to the balcony, and empties the contents of the vase into the canal. Then she stands by the window, her back towards* GERTRUDE.]

AGNES. No, they evidently know Mr. Cleeve.

GERTRUDE. Your husband never calls you by that pet-name of yours. Why is it you haven't told me you're a daughter of Admiral Steyning's?

AGNES. Mrs. Thorpe—

GERTRUDE [*Warmly*]. Oh, I must say what I mean! I have often pulled myself up short in my gossips with you, conscious of a sort of wall between us. [AGNES *comes slowly from the window.*] Somehow, I feel now that you haven't in the least made a friend of me. I'm hurt. It's stupid of me; I can't help it.

AGNES [*After a moments pause*]. I am not the lady these people were speaking of yesterday.

GERTRUDE. Not—?

AGNES. Mr. Cleeve is no longer with his wife; he has left her.

GERTRUDE. Left—his wife!

AGNES. Like yourself, I am a widow. I don't know whether you've ever heard my name—Ebbsmith. [GERTRUDE *stares at her blankly.*] I beg your pardon sincerely. I never meant to conceal my true position; such a course is opposed to every principle of mine. But I grew so attached to you in Florence and— well, it was contemptibly weak; I'll never do such a thing again.

[*She goes back to the table and commences to refill the vase with the fresh flowers.*]

GERTRUDE. When you say that Mr. Cleeve has left his wife, I suppose you mean to tell me you have taken her place?

AGNES. Yes, I mean that.

[GERTRUDE *rises and walks to the door.*]

GERTRUDE [*At the door*]. You knew that I could not speak to you again after hearing this?

AGNES. I thought it almost certain you would not.

[*After a moment's irresolution,* GERTRUDE *returns, and stands by the settee.*]

GERTRUDE. I can hardly believe you.

AGNES. I should like you to hear more than just the bare fact.

GERTRUDE [*Drumming on the back of the settee*]. Why don't you tell me more?

AGNES. You were going, you know.

GERTRUDE [*Sitting*]. I won't go quite like that. Please tell me.

AGNES [*Calmly*]. Well, did you ever read of John Thorold—" Jack Thorold, the demagogue"? [GERTRUDE *shakes her head.*] I daresay not. John Thorold, once a schoolmaster, was my father. In my time he used to write for the two or three, so-called, inflammatory journals, and hold forth in small lecture-halls, occasionally even from the top of a wooden stool in the Park, upon trade and labour questions, division of wealth, and the rest of it. He believed in nothing that people who go to church are credited with believing in, Mrs. Thorpe; his scheme for the readjustment of things was Force; his pet doctrine, the ultimate healthy healing that follows the surgery of Revolution. But to me he was the gentlest creature imaginable; and I was very fond of him, in spite of his—as I then thought—strange ideas. Strange ideas! Ha! many of 'em luckily don't sound quite so irrational to-day!

GERTRUDE [*Under her breath*]. Oh!

AGNES. My home was a wretched one. If dad was violent out of the house, mother was violent enough in it; with her it was rage, sulk, storm, from morning till night; till one day father turned a deaf ear to mother and died in his bed. That was my first intimate experience of the horrible curse that falls upon so many.

GERTRUDE. Curse?

AGNES. The curse of unhappy marriage. Though really I'd looked on at little else all my life. Most of our married friends were cursed in a like way; and I remember taking an oath, when I was a mere child, that nothing should ever push me over into the choked-up, seething pit. Fool! When I was nineteen I was gazing like a pet sheep into a man's eyes; and one morning I was married, at St. Andrew's Church in Holborn, to Mr. Ebbsmith, a barrister.

GERTRUDE. In church?

AGNES. Yes, in church—in church. In spite of father's unbelief and mother's indifference, at the time I married I was as simple—ay, in my heart as devout—as any girl in a parsonage. The other thing hadn't soaked into me. Whenever I could escape from our stifling rooms at home, and slam the front door behind me, the air blew away uncertainty and scepticism; I seemed only to have to take a long, deep breath to be full of hope and faith. And it was like this till that man married me.

GERTRUDE. Of course, I guess your marriage was an unfortunate one.

AGNES. It lasted eight years. For about twelve months he treated me like a woman in a harem, for the rest of the time like a beast of burden. Oh! when I think of it! [*Wiping her brow with her handkerchief.*] Phew!

GERTRUDE. It changed you?

AGNES. Oh yes, it changed me.

GERTRUDE. You spoke of yourself just now as a widow. He's dead?

AGNES. He died on our wedding-day—the eighth anniversary.

GERTRUDE. You were free then—free to begin again.

AGNES. Eh? [*Looking at* GERTRUDE.] Yes; but you don't begin to believe all over again. [*She gathers up the stalks of the flowers from the tray, and, kneeling, crams them into the stove.*] However, this is an old story. I'm thirty-three now.

GERTRUDE [*Hesitatingly*]. You and Mr. Cleeve?

AGNES. We've known each other since last November—no longer. Six years of my life unaccounted for, eh? Well, for a couple of years or so I was lecturing.

GERTRUDE. Lecturing.

AGNES. Ah, I'd become an out-and-out child of my father by that time— spouting, perhaps you'd call it, standing on the identical little platforms he used to speak from, lashing abuses with my tongue as he had done. Oh, and I was fond, too, of warning women.

GERTRUDE. Against what?

AGNES. Falling into the pit.

GERTRUDE. Marriage?

AGNES. The choked-up, seething pit—until I found my bones almost through my skin and my voice too weak to travel across a room.

GERTRUDE. From what cause?

AGNES. Starvation, my dear. So, after lying in a hospital for a month or two, I took up nursing for a living. Last November I was sent for by Dr. Bickerstaff to go through to Rome to look after a young man who'd broken down there, and who declined to send for his friends. My patient was Mr. Cleeve—[*taking up the tray*]—and that's where his fortunes join mine.

[*She crosses the room and puts the tray upon the cabinet.*]

GERTRUDE. And yet, judging from what that girl said yesterday, Mr. Cleeve married quite recently?

AGNES. Less than three years ago. Men don't suffer as patiently as women. In many respects his marriage story is my own, reversed—the man in place of the woman. I endured my hell, though; he broke the gates of his.

GERTRUDE. I have often seen Mr. Cleeve's name in the papers. His future promised to be brilliant, didn't it!

AGNES [*Tidying the table, folding the newspapers, &c.*]. There's a great career for him still.

GERTRUDE. In Parliament—*now?*

AGNES. No, he abandons that and devotes himself to writing. We shall write much together, urging our views on this subject of Marriage. We shall have to be poor, I expect, but we shall be content.

GERTRUDE. Content!

AGNES. Quite content. Don't judge us by my one piece of cowardly folly in keeping the truth from you, Mrs. Thorpe. Indeed, it's our great plan to live the life we have mapped out for ourselves, fearlessly, openly; faithful to each other, helpful to each other, for as long as we remain together.

GERTRUDE. But tell me—you don't know how I—how I have liked you!—tell me, if Mr. Cleeve's wife divorces him he will marry you?

AGNES. No.

GERTRUDE. No!

AGNES. No. I haven't made you quite understand—Lucas and I don't desire to marry, in your sense.

GERTRUDE. But you are devoted to each other!

AGNES. Thoroughly.

GERTRUDE. What, is that the meaning of "for as long as you are together?" You would go your different ways if ever you found that one of you was making the other unhappy?

AGNES. I do mean that. We remain together only to help, to heal, to console. Why should men and women be so eager to grant to each other the power of wasting life? That is what marriage gives—the right to destroy years and years of life. And the right, once given, it *attracts—attracts!* We have both suffered from it. So many rich years out of my life have been squandered by it. And out of his life, so much force, energy—spent in battling with the shrew, the termagant he has now fled from; strength never to be replenished, never to be repaid—all wasted, wasted!

GERTRUDE. Your legal marriage with him might not bring further miseries.

AGNES. Too late! We have done with marriage; we distrust it. We are not now among those who regard marriage as indispensable to union. We have done with it!

GERTRUDE [*Advancing to her*]. You know it would be impossible for me, if I would do so, to deceive my brother as to all this.

AGNES. Why, of course, dear.

GERTRUDE [*Looking at her watch*]. Amos must be wondering—

AGNES. Run away, then.

[GERTRUDE *crosses quickly towards the door.*]

GERTRUDE [*Retracing a step or two*]. Shall I see you—? Oh!

AGNES [*Shaking her head*]. Ah!

GERTRUDE [*Going to her, constrainedly*]. When Amos and I have talked this over, perhaps—perhaps—

AGNES. No, no, I fear not. Come, my dear friend—[*with a smile*]—give me a shake of the hand.

GERTRUDE [*Taking her hand*]. What you've told me is dreadful. [*Looking into* AGNES's *face*.] And yet you're not a wicked woman! [*Kissing* AGNES.] In case we don't meet again.

[*The women separate quickly, looking towards the door, as* LUCAS *enters.*]

LUCAS [*Shaking hands with* GERTRUDE]. How do you do, Mrs. Thorpe? I've just had a wave of the hand from your brother.

GERTRUDE. Where is he?

LUCAS. On his back in a gondola a pipe in his mouth as usual, gazing skywards. [*Going on to the balcony.*] He's within hail. [GERTRUDE *goes quickly to the door, followed by* AGNES.] There! by the Palazzo Sforza. [*He re-enters the room;* GERTRUDE *has disappeared. He is going towards the door*] Let me get hold of him, Mrs. Thorpe.

AGNES [*Standing before* LUCAS, *quietly*]. She knows, Lucas dear.

LUCAS. Does she?

AGNES. She overheard some gossip at the Caffe Quadri yesterday, and began questioning me; so I told her.

LUCAS [*Taking off his coat*]. Adieu to them, then—eh?

AGNES [*Assisting him*]. Adieu.

LUCAS. I intended to write to the brother directly they had left Venice, to explain.

AGNES. Your describing me as "Mrs. Cleeve" at the hotel in Florence helped to lead us into this; after we move from here I must always be, frankly, "Mrs. Ebbsmith."

LUCAS. These were decent people. You and she had formed quite an attachment?

AGNES. Yes.

[*She places his coat, &c., on a chair, then fetches her work-basket from the cabinet.*]

LUCAS. There's something of the man in your nature, Agnes.

AGNES. I've anathematised my womanhood often enough.

[*She sits at the table, taking out her work composedly.*]

LUCAS. Not that every man possesses the power you have acquired—the power of going through life with compressed lips.

AGNES [*Looking up, smiling*]. *A propos?*

LUCAS. These people—this woman you've been so fond of. You see them shrink away with the utmost composure.

AGNES [*Threading a needle*]. You forget, dear, that you and I have prepared ourselves for a good deal of this sort of thing.

LUCAS. Certainly, but at the moment—

AGNES. One must take care that the regret lasts no longer than a moment. Have you seen your uncle?

LUCAS. A glimpse. He hadn't long risen.

AGNES. He adds sluggishness to other vices, then?

LUCAS [*Lighting a cigarette*]. He greeted me through six inches of open door, His toilet has its mysteries.

AGNES. A stormy interview?

LUCAS. The reverse. He grasped my hand warmly, declared I looked the picture of health, and said it was evident I had been most admirably nursed.

AGNES [*Frowning*]. That's a strange utterance. But he's an eccentric, isn't he?

LUCAS. No man has ever been quite satisfied as to whether his oddities are ingrained or affected.

AGNES. No man. What about women?

LUCAS. Ho! they have had opportunities of closer observation.

AGNES. Hah! And they report?

LUCAS. Nothing. They become curiously reticent.

AGNES [*Scornfully, as she is cutting a thread*]. These noblemen!

LUCAS. [*Taking a packet of letters from his pocket*]. Finally, he presented me with these, expressed a hope that he'd see much of me during the week, and dismissed me with a fervent "God bless you!"

AGNES [*Surprised*]. He remains here, then?

LUCAS. It seems so.

AGNES. What are those, dear?

LUCAS. The Duke has made himself the bearer of some letters, from friends. I've only glanced at them: reproaches—appeals—

AGNES. Yes, I understand.

> [*He sits looking through the letters impatiently, then tearing them up and throwing the pieces upon the table.*]

LUCAS. Lord Warminster—my godfather: "My dear boy, for God's sake—!" [*Tearing up the letter and reading another.*] Sir Charles Littlecote: "Your brilliant future .... blasted ...." [*Another letter.*] Lord Froom: "Promise of a useful political career unfulfilled .... cannot an old friend ....?" [*Another letter.*] Edith Heytesbury. I didn't notice a woman had honoured me. [*In an undertone.*] Edie—! [*Slipping the letter into his pocket and opening another.*] Jack Brophy: "Your great career—" Major Leete: "Your career—" [*Destroying the rest of the letters without reading them.*] My career! my career! That's the chorus, evidently. Well, there goes my career!

> [*She lays her work aside and goes to him.*]

AGNES. Your career? [*Pointing to the destroyed letters.*] True, that one is over. But there's the other, you know—*ours*.

LUCAS [*Touching her hand*]. Yes, yes. Still, it's just a little saddening, the saying good-bye—[*disturbing the scraps of paper*]—to all this.

AGNES. Saddening, dear? Why, this political career of yours—think what it would have been at best? Accident of birth sent you to the wrong side of the House; influence of family would always have kept you there.

LUCAS [*Partly to himself*]. But I made my mark. I did make my mark.

AGNES. Supporting the Party that retards; the Party that preserves for the rich, palters with the poor. [*Pointing to the letters again.*] Oh, there's not much to mourn for there!

LUCAS. Still, it was—success.

AGNES. Success!

LUCAS. I was talked about, written about, as a Coining Man—the Coming Man!

AGNES. How many "coming men" has one known! Where on earth do they all go to?

LUCAS. Ah yes, but I allowed for the failures, and carefully set myself to discover the causes of them. And, as I put my finger upon the causes and examined them, I congratulated myself and said, "Well, I haven't that weak point in my armour, or *that*;" and, Agnes, at last I was fool enough to imagine I had no weak point, none whatever.

AGNES. It was weak enough to believe that.

LUCAS. I couldn't foresee that I was doomed to pay the price all nervous men pay for success; that the greater my success became, the more cancer-like grew the fear of never being able to continue it, to excel it; that the triumph of to-day was always to be the torture of to-morrow! O Agnes, the agony of success to a nervous, sensitive man; the dismal apprehension that fills his life and gives each victory a voice to cry out "Hear, hear! Bravo, bravo, bravo! But this is to be your last— you'll never overtop it!" Ah yes! I soon found out the weak spot in my armour— the need of constant encouragement, constant reminder of my powers; [*taking her hand*] the need of that subtle sympathy which a sacrificing, unselfish woman alone possesses the secret of. [*Rising.*] Well, my very weakness might have been a source of greatness if, three years ago, it had been to such a woman that I had bound myself—a woman of your disposition; instead of to—! Ah!
[*She lays her hand upon his arm soothingly.*]

LUCAS. Yes, yes. [*Taking her in his arms.*] I know I have such a companion now.

AGNES. Yes—now—

LUCAS. You must be everything to me, Agnes—a double faculty, as it were. When my confidence in myself is shaken, you must try to keep the consciousness of my poor powers alive in me.

AGNES. I shall not fail you in that, Lucas.

LUCAS. And yet, whenever disturbing recollections come uppermost; when I catch myself mourning for those lost opportunities of mine; it is your love that must grant me oblivion—[*kissing her upon the lips*]—your love!
[*She makes no response, and after a pause gently releases herself and retreats a step or two.*]

LUCAS [*His eyes following her*]. Agnes, you seem to be changing towards me, growing colder to me. At times you seem positively to shrink from me. I don't understand it. Yesterday I thought I saw you look at me as if I— frightened you!

AGNES. Lucas—Lucas dear, for some weeks, now, I've wanted to say this to you.

LUCAS. What?

AGNES. Don't you think that such a union as ours would be much braver, much more truly courageous, if it could but be—be—

LUCAS. If it could but be—what?

AGNES [*Averting her eyes*]. Devoid of passion, if passion had no share in it.

LUCAS. Surely this comes a little late, Agnes, between you and me.

AGNES [*Leaning upon the back of a chair, staring before her and speaking in a low, steady voice*]. What has been was inevitable, I suppose. Still, we have hardly yet set foot upon the path we've agreed to follow. It is not too late for us, in our own lives, to put the highest interpretation upon that word—Love. Think of the inner sustaining power it would give us! [*More forcibly.*] We agree to go through the world together, preaching the lessons taught us by our experiences. We cry out to all people, "Look at us! Man and woman who are in the bondage of neither law nor ritual! Linked simply by mutual trust! Man and wife, but something better than man and wife! Friends, but even something better than friends!" I say there is that which is noble, finely defiant, in the future we have mapped out for ourselves, if only—if only—

LUCAS. Yes?

AGNES [*Turning from him*]. If only it could be free from passion!

LUCAS [*In a low voice*]. Yes, but—is that possible?

AGNES [*In the same tone, watching him askance, a frightened look in her eyes*]. Why not?

LUCAS. Young man and woman .... youth and love ....? Scarcely upon this earth, my dear Agnes, such a life as you have pictured.

AGNES. I say it can be, it can be—!

FORTUNÉ *enters, carrying a letter upon a salver and a beautiful bouquet of white flowers. He hands the note to* LUCAS.

LUCAS [*Taking the note, glancing at* AGNES]. Eh! [*To* FORTUNÉ, *pointing to the bouquet.*] Qu'avez-vous là?

FORTUNÉ. Ah, excuse. [*Presenting the bouquet to* AGNES.] Wiz compliment. [AGNES *takes the bouquet wonderingly.*] Tell Madame ze Duke of St. Olphert bring it in person 'e says.

LUCAS [*Opening the note*]. Est-il parti?

FORTUNÉ. 'E did not get out of 'is gondola.

LUCAS. Bien. [FORTUNÉ *withdraws. Reading the note aloud.*] "While brushing my hair, my dear boy, I became possessed of a strong desire to meet the lady with whom you are now improving the shining hour. Why the devil shouldn't I, if I want to? Without prejudice, as my lawyer says, let me turn up this afternoon and chat pleasantly to her of Shakespeare, also the musical-glasses. Pray hand her this flag of truce—I mean my poor bunch of flowers—and believe me yours, with a touch of gout, St. Olpherts." [*Indignantly crushing the note.*] Ah!

AGNES [*Frowning at the flowers*]. A taste of the oddities, I suppose!

LUCAS. He is simply making sport of us. [*Going on to the balcony and looking out.*] There he is. Damn that smile of his!

AGNES. Where? [*She joins him.*]

LUCAS. With the two gondoliers.

AGNES. Why—that's a beautiful face! How strange!

LUCAS [*Drawing her back into the room*]. Come away. He is looking up at us.

AGNES. Are you sure he sees us?

LUCAS. He did.

AGNES. He will want an answer—
　　　　[*She deliberately flings the bouquet over the balcony into the canal, then returns to the table and picks up her work.*]

LUCAS [*Looking out again cautiously*]. He throws his head back and laughs heartily. [*Re-entering the room.*] Oh, of course, his policy is to attempt to laugh me out of my resolves. They send him here merely to laugh at me, Agnes, to laugh at me—[*coming to* Agnes *angrily*] laugh at me!

AGNES. He must be a man of small resources. [*Threading her needle.*] It is so easy to mock.

ACT 2.　　*The Scene is the same as that of the previous Act. Through the windows some mastheads and flapping sails are seen in the distance. The light is that of late afternoon.*

　　AGNES, *very plainly dressed, is sitting at the table, industriously copying from a manuscript. After a moment or two,* ANTONIO *and* NELLA *enter the room, carrying a dressmaker's box, which is corded and labelled.*

NELLA. È permesso, Signora. (Permit us, Signora.)

ANTONIO. Uno scatolone per la Signora. (An enormous box for the Signora.)

AGNES [*Turning her head*]. Eh?

NELLA. È venuto colla ferrovia—(It has come by the railway—)

ANTONIO [*Consulting the label*]. Da Firenze. (From Florence.)

AGNES. By railway, from Florence?

NELLA [*Reading from the label*]. "Emilia Bardini, Via Rondinelli."

AGNES. Bardini? That's the dressmaker. There must be some mistake. Non è per me, Nella. (It isn't for me.)

[ANTONIO *and* NELLA *carry the box to her animatedly.*]

NELLA. Ma guardi, Signora! (But look, Signora!)

ANTONIO. Alla Signora Cleeve!

NELLA. E poi abbiamo pagato il porto della ferrovia. (Besides, we have paid the railway dues upon it.)

AGNES [*Collecting her sheets of paper*]. Hush, hush! don't trouble me just now. Mettez-la n'importe où.

[*They place the box on another table.*]

NELLA. La corda intaccherebbe la forbice della Signora, Vuole che Antonio la tagli. (The cord would blunt the Signora's scissors. Shall Antonio cut the cord?)

AGNES [*Pinning her sheets of paper together*]. I'll see about it by-and-by. Laissez-moi!

NELLA [*Softly to* ANTONIO]. Taglia, taglia! (Cut, cut !)

[ANTONIO *cuts the cord, whereupon* NELLA. *utters a little scream.*]

AGNES [*Turning, startled*]. What is it?

NELLA [*Pushing* ANTONIO *away*]. Questo stupido non ha capito la Signora e ha tagliata la corda. (The stupid fellow misunderstood the Signora, and has severed the cord.)

AGNES [*Rising*]. It doesn't matter. Be quiet!

NELLA [*Removing the lid from the box angrily*]. Ed ecco la scatola aperta contro voglia della Signora! (And now here is the box open against the Signora's wish!) [*Inquisitively pushing aside the paper which covers the contents of the box.*] O Dio! Si vede tutto quel che vi é! (O God! and all the contents exposed!)

[*When the paper is removed, some beautiful material trimmed with lace, &c., is seen.*]

NELLA. Guardi, guardi, Signora! (Signora, look, look!) [AGNES *examines the contents of the box with a puzzled air.*] Oh, che bellezza! (How beautiful!)

LUCAS *enters.*

ANTONIO [*To* NELLA]. Il padrone. (The master.)

[NELLA *courtesies to* LUCAS, *then withdraws with* ANTONIO.]

AGNES. Lucas, the dressmaker in the Via Rondinelli at Florence—the woman who ran up the little gown I have on now—

Lucas [*With a smile*] What of her?

Agnes. This has just come from her. Phuh! What does she mean by sending the showy thing to me?

Lucas. It is my gift to you.

Agnes [*Producing enough of the contents of the box to reveal a very handsome dress*]. This!

Lucas. I knew Bardini had your measurements; I wrote to her, instructing her to make that. I remember Lady Heytesbury in something similar last season.

Agnes [*Examining the dress*]. A mere strap for the sleeve, and sufficiently décolletée, I should imagine.

Lucas. My dear Agnes, I can't understand your reason for trying to make yourself a plain-looking woman when nature intended you for a pretty one.

Agnes. Pretty!

Lucas [*Looking hard at her*]. You *are* pretty.

Agnes. Oh, as a pretty girl I may have been—[*disdainfully*]—pretty. What good did it do anybody? [*Fingering the dress with aversion*] And when would you have me hang this on my bones?

Lucas Oh, when we are dining, or—

Agnes. Dining in a public place?

Lucas. Why not look your best in a public place?

Agnes. Look my best! You know, I don't think of this sort of garment in connection with our companionship, Lucas.

Lucas. It is not an extraordinary garment for a lady.

Agnes. Rustle of silk, glare of arms and throat—they belong, in my mind, to such a very different order of things from that we have set up.

Lucas. Shall I appear before you in ill-made clothes, clumsy boots—

Agnes. Why? We are just as we always have been, since we've been together. I don't tell you that your appearance is beginning to offend.

Lucas. Offend! Agnes, you—you pain me. I simply fail to understand why you should allow our mode of life to condemn you to perpetual slovenliness.

Agnes. Slovenliness!

Lucas. No, no, shabbiness.

Agnes [*Looking down upon the dress she is wearing*]. Shabbiness!

Lucas [*With a laugh*]. Forgive me, dear; I'm forgetting you are wearing a comparatively new afternoon-gown.

AGNES. At any rate, I'll make this brighter to-morrow with some trimmings, willingly. [*Pointing to the dressmaker's box.*] Then you won't insist on my decking myself out in rags of that kind—eh! There's something in the idea—I needn't explain.

LUCAS [*Fretfully*]. Insist! I'll not urge you again. [*Pointing to the box.*] Get rid of it somehow. Are you copying that manuscript of mine?

AGNES. I had just finished it.

LUCAS. Already! [*Taking up her copy.*] How beautifully you write! [*Going to her eagerly.*] What do you think of my Essay?

AGNES. It bristles with truth; it is vital.

LUCAS. My method of treating it?

AGNES. Hardly a word out of place.

LUCAS [*Chilled*]. *Hardly* a word?

AGNES. Not a word, in fact.

LUCAS. No, dear, I daresay your "hardly" is nearer the mark.

AGNES. I assure you it is brilliant, Lucas.

LUCAS. What a wretch I am ever to find the smallest fault in you! Shall we dine out to-night?

AGNES. As you wish, dear

LUCAS. At the Grünwald? [*He goes to the table to pick up his manuscript; when his back is turned she looks at her watch quickly*] We'll solemnly toast this, shall we, in Montefiascone?

AGNES [*Eyeing him askance*]. You are going out for your chocolate this afternoon as usual, I suppose?

LUCAS. Yes, but I'll look through your copy first, so that I can slip it into the post at once. You are not coming out?

AGNES. Not till dinner-time.

LUCAS [*Kissing her on the forehead*]. I talked over the points of this—[*tapping the manuscript*]—with a man this morning; he praised some of the phrases warmly.

AGNES. A man? [*In an altered tone.*] The Duke?

LUCAS. Er—yes.

AGNES [*With assumed indifference, replacing the lid on the dressmaker's box*]. You have seen him again to-day, then?

LUCAS. We strolled about together for half an hour on the Piazza.

AGNES [*Replacing the cord round the box*]. You—you don't dislike him as much as you did?

LUCAS. He's somebody to chat to. I suppose one gets accustomed even to a man one dislikes.

AGNES [*Almost inaudibly*]. I suppose so.

LUCAS. As a matter of fact, he has the reputation of being rather a pleasant companion; though I—I confess—I—I don't find him very entertaining.

> [*He goes out. She stands staring at the door through which he has disappeared. There is a knock at the opposite door.*]

AGNES [*Rousing herself*]. Fortuné! [*Raising her voice.*] Fortuné!

> [*The door opens, and* GERTRUDE *enters hurriedly.*]

GERTRUDE. Fortuné is complacently smoking a cigarette in the Campo.

AGNES. Mrs. Thorpe!

GERTRUDE [*Breathlessly*]. Mr. Cleeve is out, I conclude?

AGNES. No. He is later than usual in going out this afternoon.

GERTRUDE [*Irresolutely*]. I don't think I'll wait, then.

AGNES. But do tell me: you have been crossing the streets to avoid me during the past week; what has made you come to see me now?

GERTRUDE. I *would* come. I've given poor Amos the slip; he believes I'm buying beads for the Ketherick school-children.

AGNES [*Shaking her head*]. Ah, Mrs. Thorpe!—

GERTRUDE. Of course, it's perfectly brutal to be underhanded. But we're leaving for home to-morrow; I couldn't resist it.

AGNES [*Coldly*]. Perhaps I'm very ungracious—

GERTRUDE [*Taking* AGNES's *hand*]. The fact is, Mrs. Cleeve—oh, what do you wish me to call you?

AGNES [*Withdrawing her hand*]. Well—you're off to-morrow. Agnes will do.

GERTRUDE. Thank you. The fact is, it's been a bad week with me—restless, fanciful. And I haven't been able to get you out of my head.

AGNES. I'm sorry.

GERTRUDE. Your story, your present life; you, yourself—such a contradiction to what you profess! Well, it all has a sort of fascination for me.

AGNES. My dear, you're simply not sleeping again. [*Turning away.*] You'd better go back to the ammonia Kirke prescribed for you.

GERTRUDE [*Taking a card from her purse with a little light laugh*]. You want to physic me, do you, after worrying my poor brain as you've done? [*Going to her.*] "The Rectory, Daleham, Ketherick Moor." Yorkshire, you know. There can be no great harm in your writing to me sometimes.

AGNES [*Refusing the card*]. No; under the circumstances I can't promise that.

GERTRUDE [*Wistfully*]. Very well.

AGNES [*Facing her*]. Oh, can't you understand that it can only be—disturbing to both of us for an impulsive, emotional creature like yourself to keep up acquaintanceship with a woman who takes life as I do? We'll drop each other, leave each other alone.
[*She walks away, and stands leaning upon the stove, her back towards* GERTRUDE.]

GERTRUDE [*Replacing the card in her purse*] As you please. Picture me, sometimes, in that big, hollow shell of a rectory at Ketherick, strolling about my poor dead little chap's empty room.

AGNES [*Under her breath*] Oh!

GERTRUDE [*Turning to go*] God bless you!

AGNES. Gertrude! [*With altered manner.*] You—you have the trick of making me lonely also. [*Going to* GERTRUDE *taking her hands and fondling them.*] I'm tired of talking to the walls! And your blood is warm to me! Shall I tell you, or not—or not?

GERTRUDE. Do tell me.

AGNES. There is a man here, in Venice, who is torturing—flaying me alive.

GERTRUDE. Torturing you?

AGNES. He came here about a week ago; he is trying to separate us.

GERTRUDE. You and Mr. Cleeve?

AGNES. Yes.

GERTRUDE. You are afraid he will succeed?

AGNES. Succeed! What nonsense you talk!

GERTRUDE. What upsets you, then?

AGNES. After all, it's difficult to explain--the feeling is so indefinite. It's like—something in the air. This man is influencing us both oddly. Lucas is as near illness again as possible; I can hear his nerves vibrating. And I—you know what a fish-like thing I am as a rule—just look at me now, as I'm speaking to you.

GERTRUDE. But don't you and Mr. Cleeve—talk to each other?

AGNES. As children do when the lights are put out—of everything but what's uppermost in their minds.

GERTRUDE. You have met the man?

AGNES. I intend to meet him.

GERTRUDE. Who is he?

AGNES. A relation of Lucas's—the Duke of St. Olpherts

GERTRUDE. He has right on his side, then?

AGNES. If you choose to think so.

GERTRUDE [*Deliberately*]. Supposing he *does* succeed in taking Mr. Cleeve away from you?

AGNES [*Staring at* GERTRUDE]. What, *now*, do you mean?

GERTRUDE. Yes.

> [*There is a brief pause; then* AGNES *walks across the room, wiping her brow with her handkerchief.*]

AGNES. I tell you, that idea's—preposterous.

GERTRUDE. Oh, I can't understand you!

AGNES. You'll respect my confidence?

GERTRUDE. Agnes!

AGNES [*Sitting*]. Well, I fancy this man's presence here has simply started me thinking of a time—oh, it may never come!—a time when I may cease to be—necessary to Mr. Cleeve. Do you understand?

GERTRUDE. I remember what you told me of your being prepared to grant each other freedom if—

AGNES. Yes, yes; and for the past few days this idea has filled me with a fear of the most humiliating kind.

GERTRUDE. What fear?

AGNES. The fear lest, after all my beliefs and protestations, I should eventually find myself loving Lucas in the helpless, common way of women—

GERTRUDE [*Under her breath*]. I see.

AGNES. The dread that the moment may arrive some day when, should it be required of me, *I shan't feel myself able to give him up easily.* [*Her head drooping, uttering a low moan.*] Oh!—

LUCAS, *dressed for going out, enters, carrying* AGNES's *copy of his manuscript, rolled and addressed for the post.* AGNES *rises.*

AGNES [*To* LUCAS]. Mrs. Thorpe starts for home to-morrow; she has called to say good-bye.

LUCAS [*To* GERTRUDE]. It is very kind. Is your brother quite well?

GERTRUDE [*Embarrassed*]. Thanks: quite.

LUCAS [*Smiling*]. I believe I have added to his experience of the obscure corners of Venice during the past week.

GERTRUDE. I—I don't—Why?

LUCAS. By so frequently putting him to the inconvenience of avoiding me.

GERTRUDE. Oh, Mr. Cleeve, we—I—I—

LUCAS. Please tell your brother I asked after him.

GERTRUDE. I—I can't; he—doesn't know I've—I've—

LUCAS. Ah! really? [*With a bow.*] Good-bye.

> [*He goes out,* AGNES *accompanying him to the door.*]

GERTRUDE [*To herself*]. Brute! [*To* AGNES.] Oh, I suppose Mr. Cleeve has made me look precisely as I feel.

AGNES. How?

GERTRUDE. Like people deserve to feel who do godly, mean things.

> [FORTUNÉ *appears.*]

FORTUNÉ [*To* AGNES, *significantly*]. Mr. Cleeve 'as jus' gone out.

AGNES. Vous savez, n'est-ce pas?

FORTUNÉ [*Glancing at* GERTRUDE]. But Madame is now engage.

GERTRUDE [*To* AGNES]. Oh, I am going.

AGNES [*To* GERTRUDE]. Wait. [*Softly to her.*] I want you to hear this little comedy. Fortuné shall repeat my instructions. [*To* FORTUNÉ.] Les ordres que je vous ai donnés, répétez-les.

FORTUNÉ [*Speaking in an undertone*]. On ze left 'and side of ze Campo—

AGNES. Non non—tout haut.

FORTUNÉ [*Aloud, with a slight shrug of the shoulders*]. On ze left 'and side of ze Campo—

AGNES. Yes.

FORTUNÉ. In one of ze doorways between Fiorentini's and ze leetle lamp-shop— ze—ze—h'm—ze person.

AGNES. Precisely. Dépêchez-vous. [FORTUNÉ *bows and retires.*] Fortuné flatters himself he is engaged in some horrid intrigue. You guess whom I am expecting?

GERTRUDE. The Duke?

AGNES [*Ringing a bell*]. I've written to him asking him to call upon me this afternoon while Lucas is at Florian's. [*Referring to her watch.*] He is to kick his heels about the Campo till I let him know I am alone.

GERTRUDE. Will he obey you?

AGNES. A week ago he was curious to see the sort of animal I am. If he holds off now, I'll hit upon some other plan. I will come to close quarters with him, if only for five minutes.

GERTRUDE. Good-bye. [*They embrace, then walk together to the door.*] You still refuse my address?

AGNES. You bat! Didn't you see me make a note of it?

GERTRUDE. You!

AGNES [*Her hand on her heart*]. Here.

GERTRUDE [*Gratefully*]. Ah!

[*She goes out.*]

AGNES [*At the open door*]. Gertrude!

GERTRUDE [*Outside*]. Yes?

AGNES [*In a low voice*]. Remember, in my thoughts I pace that lonely little room of yours with you. [*As if to stop* GERTRUDE *from re-entering.*] Hush! No, no.
[*She closes the door sharply.* NELLA *appears.*]

AGNES [*Pointing to the box on the table*]. Portez ce carton dans ma chambre.

NELLA. [*Trying to peep into the box as she carries it*]. Signora, se Ella si mettesse questo magnifico abito! Oh! quanto sarebbe più bella! (Signora, if you were to wear this magnificent dress, oh, how much more beautiful you would be!)

AGNES [*Listening*]. Sssh! Sssh! [NELLA *goes out.* FORTUNÉ *enters.*] Eh, bien?

FORTUNÉ *glances over his shoulder. The* DUKE OF ST. OLPHERTS *enters; the wreck of a very handsome man, with delicate features, a transparent complexion, a polished manner, and a smooth, weary voice. He limps, walking with the aid of a cane.* FORTUNÉ *retires.*

AGNES. Duke of St. Olpherts?

ST. OLPHERTS [*Bowing*]. Mrs. Ebbsmith?

AGNES. Mr. Cleeve would have opposed this rather out-of-the-way proceeding of mine. He doesn't know I have asked you to call on me to-day.

ST. OLPHERTS. So I conclude. It gives our meeting a pleasant air of adventure.

AGNES. I shall tell him directly he returns.

ST. OLPHERTS [*Gallantly*]. And destroy a cherished secret.

AGNES. You are an invalid. [*Motioning him to be seated.*] Pray don't stand. [*Sitting.*] Your Grace is a man who takes life lightly. It will relieve you to hear that I wish to keep sentiment out of any business we have together.

ST. OLPHERTS. I believe I haven't the reputation of being a sentimental man. [*Seating himself.*] You send for me, Mrs. Ebbsmith—

AGNES. To tell you I have come to regard the suggestion you were good enough to make a week ago—

ST. OLPHERTS. Suggestion?

AGNES. Shakespeare, the musical-glasses, you know—

ST. OLPHERTS. Oh yes. Ha! ha!

AGNES. I've come to think it a reasonable one. At the moment I considered it a gross impertinence.

ST. OLPHERTS. Written requests are so dependent on a sympathetic reader.

AGNES. That meeting might have saved you time and trouble.

ST. OLPHERTS. I grudge neither.

AGNES. It might perhaps have shown your Grace that your view of life is too narrow; that your method of dealing with its problems wants variety; that, in point of fact, your employment upon your present mission is distinctly inappropriate. Our meeting to-day may serve the same purpose.

ST. OLPHERTS. My view of life?

AGNES. That all men and women may safely be judged by the standards of the casino and the dancing-garden.

ST. OLPHERTS. I have found those standards not altogether untrustworthy. My method—?

AGNES. To scoff, to sneer, to ridicule.

ST. OLPHERTS. Ah! And how much is there, my dear Mrs. Ebbsmith, belonging to humanity that survives being laughed at?

AGNES. More than you credit, Duke. For example, I—I think it possible you may not succeed in grinning away the compact between Mr. Cleeve and myself.

ST. OLPHERTS. Compact?

AGNES. Between serious man and woman.

ST. OLPHERTS. Serious *woman*.

AGNES. Ah! at least you must see that—serious woman. [*Rising, facing him.*] You can't fail to realise, even from this slight personal knowledge of me, that you are not dealing just now with some poor, feeble ballet-girl.

ST. OLPHERTS. But how well you put it! [*Rising.*] And how frank of you to furnish, as it were, a plan of the fortifications to the—the—

AGNES. Why do you stick at "enemy"?

ST. OLPHERTS. It's not the word. Opponent! For the moment, perhaps, opponent. I am never an enemy, I hope, where your sex is concerned.

AGNES. No, I am aware that you are not over-nice in the bestowal of your patronage—where my sex is concerned.

ST. OLPHERTS. You regard my appearance in an affair of morals as a quaint one?

AGNES. Your Grace is beginning to know me.

ST. OLPHERTS. Dear lady, you take pride, I hear, in belonging to—The People. You would delight me amazingly by giving me an inkling of the popular notion of my career.

AGNES [*Walking away*]. Excuse me.

ST. OLPHERTS [*Following her*]. Please! It would be instructive, perhaps chastening. I entreat.

AGNES. No.

ST. OLPHERTS. You are letting sentiment intrude itself. [*Sitting, in pain.*] I challenge you.

AGNES. At Eton you were curiously precocious. The head-master, referring to your aptitude with books, prophesied a brilliant future for you; your tutor, alarmed by your attachment to a certain cottage at Ascot which was minus a host, thanked his stars to be rid of you. At Oxford you closed all books, except, of course, betting-books.

ST. OLPHERTS. I detected the tendency of the age—scholarship for the masses. I considered it my turn to be merely intuitively intelligent.

AGNES. You left Oxford a gambler and spendthrift. A year or two in town established you as an amiable, undisguised debauchee. The rest is modern history.

ST. OLPHERTS. Complete your sketch. Don't stop at the—rude outline.

AGNES. Your affairs falling into disorder, you promptly married a wealthy woman—the poor, rich lady who has for some years honoured you by being your duchess at a distance. This burlesque of marriage helped to reassure your friends, and actually obtained for you an ornamental appointment for which an over-taxed nation provides a handsome stipend. But, to sum up, you must always remain an irritating source of uneasiness to your own order, as, luckily, you will always be a sharp-edged weapon in the hands of mine.

ST. OLPHERTS [*With a polite smile*]. Yours! Ah, to that small, unruly section to which I understand you particularly attach yourself. To the—

AGNES [*With changed manner, flashing eyes, harsh voice, and violent gestures*]. The sufferers, the toilers; that great crowd of old and young—old and young stamped by excessive labour and privation all of one pattern— whose backs bend under burdens, whose bones ache and grow awry, whose skins, in youth and in age, are wrinkled and yellow. Those from whom a fair share of the earth's space and of the light of day is withheld. [*Looking down upon him fiercely.*] The half-starved who are bidden to stand with their feet in the kennel to watch gay processions in which you and your kind are borne high. Those who would strip the robes from a dummy aristocracy and cast the broken dolls into the limbo of a nation's discarded toys. Those who—mark me!—are already upon the highway, marching, marching; whose time is coming as surely as yours is going!

ST OLPHERTS [*Clapping his hands gently*]. Bravo! bravo! Really a flash of the old fire. Admirable! [*She walks away to the window with an impatient exclamation.*] Your present *affaire du cœur* does not wholly absorb you, then, Mrs. Ebbsmith. Even now the murmurings of love have not entirely superseded the thunderous denunciations of—h'm—You once bore a nickname, my dear.

AGNES [*Turning sharply*]. Ho! so you've heard *that*, have you?

ST. OLPHERTS. Oh yes.

AGNES. Mad—Agnes? [*He bows deprecatingly.*] We appear to have studied each other's history pretty closely.

ST. OLPHERTS. Dear lady, this is not the first time the same roof has covered us.

AGNES. No?

ST. OLPHERTS. Five years ago, on a broiling night in July, I joined a party of men who made an excursion from a clubhouse in St. James's Street to the unsavoury district of St. Luke's.

AGNES. Oh yes.

ST. OLPHERTS. A depressin' building; the Iron Hall, Barker Street—no—Carter Street.

AGNES. Precisely.

ST. OLPHERTS. We took our places amongst a handful of frowsy folks who cracked nuts and blasphemed. On the platform stood a gaunt, white-faced young lady resolutely engaged in making up by extravagance of gesture for the deficiencies of an exhausted voice. "There," said one of my companions, "that is the notorious Mrs. Ebbsmith." Upon which a person near us, whom I judged from his air of leaden laziness to be a British working man, blurted out, "Notorious Mrs. Ebbsmith! Mad Agnes! That's the name her sanguinary friends give her—Mad Agnes!" At that moment the eye of the panting oratress caught mine for an instant, and you and I first met.

AGNES [*Passing her hand across her brow, thoughtfully*]. Mad—Agnes .... [*To him, with a grim smile.*] We have both been criticised, in our time, pretty sharply, eh, Duke?

ST. OLPHERTS. Yes. Let that reflection make you more charitable to a poor peer.
[*A knock at the door.*]

AGNES. Entrez!

FORTUNÉ *and* ANTONIO *enter,* ANTONIO *carrying tea, &c., upon a tray.*

AGNES [*To* ST. OLPHERTS]. You drink tea—fellow-sufferer?
[*He signifies assent.* FORTUNÉ *places the tray on the table, then withdraws with* ANTONIO. AGNES *pours out tea.*

ST. OLPHERTS [*Producing a little box from his waistcoat-pocket*]. No milk, dear lady. And may I be allowed—saccharine?
[*She hands him his cup of tea; their eyes meet.*]

AGNES [*Scornfully*]. Tell me now—really—why do the Cleeves send a rip like you to do their serious work?

ST. OLPHERTS [*Laughing heartily*]. Ha, ha, ha! Rip! ha, ha! Poor solemn family! Oh, set a thief to catch a thief, you know. That, I presume, is their motive.

AGNES. [*Pausing in the act of pouring out tea, and staring at him*]. What do you mean?

ST. OLPHERTS [*Sipping his tea*]. Set a thief to catch a thief. And by deduction, set one sensualist—who, after all, doesn't take the trouble to deceive himself—to rescue another who does.

AGNES. If I understand you, that is an insinuation against Mr. Cleeve.

ST. OLPHERTS. Insinuation!—

AGNES [*Looking at him fixedly*]. Make yourself clearer.

ST. OLPHERTS. You have accused me, Mrs. Ebbsmith, of narrowness of outlook. In the present instance, dear lady, it is *your* judgment which is at fault.

AGNES. Mine?

ST. OLPHERTS. It is not I who fall into the error of confounding you with the designing *danseuse* of commerce; it is, strangely enough, you who have failed in your estimate of Mr. Lucas Cleeve.

AGNES. What is my estimate?

ST. OLPHERTS. I pay you the compliment of believing that you have looked upon my nephew as a talented young gentleman whose future was seriously threatened by domestic disorder; a young man of a certain courage and independence, with a share of the brain and spirit of those terrible human pests called "reformers"; the one young gentleman, in fact, most likely to aid you in advancing your vivacious social and political tenets. You have had such thoughts in your mind?

AGNES. I don't deny it.

ST. OLPHERTS. Ah! But what is the real, the actual Lucas Cleeve?

AGNES. Well—what is the real Lucas Cleeve?

ST. OLPHERTS. Poor dear fellow! I'll tell you. [*Going to the table to deposit his cup there; while she watches him, her hands tightly clasped, a frightened look in her eyes.*] The real Lucas Cleeve. [*Coming back to her.*] An egoist. An egoist.

AGNES. An egoist. Yes.

ST. OLPHERTS. Possessing ambition without patience, self-esteem without self-confidence.

AGNES. Well?

ST. OLPHERTS. Afflicted with a desperate craving for the opium like drug, adulation; persistently seeking the society of those whose white, pink-tipped fingers fill the pernicious pipe most deftly and delicately. Eh?

AGNES. I didn't—Pray, go on.

ST. OLPHERTS. Ha! I remember they looked to his marriage to check his dangerous fancy for the flutter of lace, the purr of pretty women. And now, here he is—loose again.

AGNES [*Suffering*]. Oh!

ST. OLPHERTS. In short, in intellect still nothing but a callow boy; in body, nervous, bloodless, hysterical; in morals—an epicure.

AGNES. Have done! Have done!

ST. OLPHERTS. "Epicure" offends you. A vain woman would find consolation in the word.

AGNES. Enough of it! Enough! enough!

> [*She turns away, beating her hands together. The light in the room has gradually become subdued; the warm tinge of sunset now colours the scene outside the windows.*]

ST. OLPHERTS [*With a shrug of his shoulders*]. The real Lucas Cleeve.

AGNES. No, no! Untrue, untrue! [LUCAS *enters. The three remain silent for a moment.*] The Duke of St. Olpherts calls in answer to a letter I wrote to him yesterday. I wanted to make his acquaintance.

> [*She goes out.*]

LUCAS [*After a brief pause*]. By a lucky accident the tables were crowded at Florian's; I might have missed the chance of welcoming you. In God's name, Duke, why must you come here?

ST. OLPHERTS [*Fumbling in his pockets for a note*]. In God's name? You bring the orthodoxy into this queer firm, then, Lucas? [*Handing the note to* LUCAS.] A peremptory summons.

LUCAS. You need not have obeyed it. [ST. OLPHERTS *takes a cigarette from his case and limps away.*] I looked about for you just now. I wanted to see you.

ST. OLPHERTS [*Lighting his cigarette*]. How fortunate!

LUCAS. To tell you that this persecution must come to an end. It has made me desperately wretched for a whole week.

ST. OLPHERTS. Persecution?

LUCAS. Temptation.

ST. OLPHERTS. Dear Lucas, the process of inducing a man to return to his wife isn't generally described as temptation.

LUCAS. Ah, I won't hear another word of that proposal. [ST. OLPHERTS *shrugs his shoulders.*] I say my people are offering me, through you, a deliberate temptation to be a traitor. To which of these two women—my wife or—[*pointing to the door*]—to her—am I really bound now? It may be regrettable, scandalous, but the common rules of right and wrong have ceased to apply here. Finally, Duke—and this is my message—I intend to keep faith with the woman who sat by my bedside in Rome, the woman to whom I shouted my miserable story in my delirium, the woman whose calm, resolute voice healed me, hardened me, renewed in me the desire to live.

ST. OLPHERTS. Ah! Oh, these modern nurses, in their greys, or browns, and snowy bibs! They have much to answer for, dear Lucas.

LUCAS. No, no! Why will you persist, all of you, in regarding this as a mere morbid infatuation, bred in the fumes of pastilles? It isn't so! Laugh, if you care to; but this is a meeting of affinities, of the solitary man and the truly sympathetic woman.

ST. OLPHERTS. And oh—oh these sympathetic women!

LUCAS. No! Oh, the unsympathetic women! There you have the cause of half the world's misery. The unsympathetic women—you should have loved one of them.

ST. OLPHERTS. I dare say I've done that in my time.

LUCAS. Love one of these women—*I* know!—worship her, yield yourself to the intoxicating day-dreams that make the grimy world sweeter than any heaven ever imagined. How your heart leaps with gratitude for your good fortune! how compassionately you regard your unblest fellow-men! What may you not accomplish with such a mate beside you; how high will be your aims, how paltry every obstacle that bars your way to them; how sweet is to be the labour, how divine the rest! Then—you marry her. Marry her, and in six months, if you've pluck enough to do it, lag behind your shooting-party and blow your brains out, by accident, at the edge of a turnip-field. You have found out by that time all that there is to look for—the daily diminishing interest in your doings, the poorly-assumed attention as you attempt to talk over some plan for the future; then the yawn, and by degrees, the covert sneer, the little sarcasm, and finally, the frank, open stare of boredom. Ah, Duke, when you all carry out your repressive legislation against women of evil lives, don't fail to include in your schedule the Unsympathetic Wives. They are the women whose victims show the sorriest scars; they are the really "bad women" of the world: all the others are snow-white in comparison!

ST. OLPHERTS. Yes, you've got a great deal of this in that capital Essay you quoted from this morning. Dear fellow, I admit your home discomforts; but to jump out of that frying-pan into this confounded—what does she call it?—compact!

LUCAS. Compact?

ST. OLPHERTS. A vague reference, as I understand, to your joint crusade against the blessed institution of Marriage.

LUCAS [*An alteration in his manner*]. Oh—ho, that idea! What—what has she been saying to you?

ST. OLPHERTS. Incidentally she pitched into me, dear Lucas; she attacked my moral character. You must have been telling tales.

LUCAS. Oh, I—I hope not. Of course, we—

St. Olpherts. Yes, yes—a little family gossip, to pass the time while she has been dressing her hair, or By-the-bye, she doesn't appear to spend much time in dressing her hair.

Lucas [*Biting his lips*]. Really?

St. Olpherts. Then she denounced the gilded aristocracy generally. Our day is over; we're broken wooden dolls, and are going to be chucked. The old tune; but I enjoyed the novelty of being so near the instrument. I assure you, dear fellow, I was within three feet of her when she deliberately Trafalgar Squared me.

Lucas [*With an uneasy laugh*]. You're the red rag, Duke. This spirit of revolt in her—it's ludicrously extravagant; but it will die out in time, when she has become used to being happy and cared for—[*partly to himself, with clenched hands*] yes, cared for.

St. Olpherts. Die out? Bred in the bone, dear Lucas.

Lucas. On some topics she's a mere echo of her father—if you mean that?

Sr. Olpherts. The father—one of these public-park vermin, eh?

Lucas. Dead years ago.

St. Olpherts. I once heard her bellowing in a dirty little shed in St. Luke's. I told you?

Lucas. Yes, you've told me.

St. Olpherts. I sat there again, it seemed, this afternoon. The orator not quite so lean perhaps—a little less witchlike; but—

Lucas. She was actually in want of food in those days! Poor girl! [*Partly to himself.*] I mean to remind myself of that constantly. Poor girl!

St. Olpherts. Girl! Let me see—you're considerably her junior?

Lucas. No, no; a few months perhaps.

St. Olpherts. Oh, come!

Lucas. Well, years—two or three.

St. Olpherts. The voice remains rather raucous.

Lucas. By God, the voice is sweet!

St. Olpherts. Well—considering the wear and tear. Really, my dear fellow, I do believe this—I do believe that if you gowned her respectably—

Lucas [*Impulsively*]. Yes, yes, I say so. I tell her that.

St. Olpherts [*With a smile*]. Do you? That's odd, now.

Lucas. What a topic! Poor Agnes's dress!

St. Olpherts. Your taste used to be rather aesthetic. Even your own wife is one of the smartest women in London.

Lucas. Ha, well! I must contrive to smother these aesthetic tastes of mine.

St. Olpherts. It's a pity that other people will retain their sense of the incongruous.

Lucas [*Snapping his fingers*]. Other people!—

St. Olpherts. The public.

Lucas. The public?

St. Olpherts. Come, you know well enough that unostentatious immodesty is no part of your partner's programme. Of course, you will find yourself by-and-by in a sort of perpetual public parade with your crack-brained visionary—

Lucas. You shall not speak of her so! You shall not.

St. Olpherts [*Unconcernedly*]. Each of you bearing a pole of the soiled banner of Free Union. Free Union for the People! Ho, my dear Lucas!

Lucas. Good heavens, Duke, do you imagine, now that I am in sound health and mind again, that I don't see the hideous absurdity of these views of hers?

St. Olpherts. Then why the deuce don't you listen a little more patiently to *my* views?

Lucas. No, no. I tell you I intend to keep faith with her, as far as I am able. She's so earnest, so pitiably earnest. If I broke faith with her entirely, it would be too damnably cowardly.

St. Olpherts. Cowardly!

Lucas [*Pacing the room agitatedly*]. Besides, we shall do well together, after all, I believe—she and I. In the end we shall make concessions to each other and settle down, somewhere abroad, peacefully.

St. Olpherts. Hah! And they called you a Coming Man at one time, didn't they?

Lucas. Oh, I—I shall make as fine a career with my pen as that other career would have been. At any rate, I ask you to leave me to it all—to leave me!

Fortuné *enters. The shades of evening have now deepened; the glow of sunset comes into the room.*

Fortuné. I beg your pardon, sir.

Lucas. Well?

Fortuné. It is pas' ze time for you to dress for dinner.

LUCAS. I'll come.

[FORTUNÉ *goes out.*]

ST. OLPHERTS. When do we next meet, dear fellow?

LUCAS. No, no—please not again.

NELLA *enters excitedly.*

NELLA [*Speaking over her shoulder*]. Si, Signora; ecco il Signore. (Yes, Signora; here is the Signor.) [*To* CLEEVE.] Scusi, Signore. Quando la vedra come é cara—! (Pardon, Signor. When you see her you'll see how sweet she looks!)

[AGNES's *voice is heard.*]

AGNES [*Outside*]. Am I keeping you waiting, Lucas?

[*She enters, handsomely gowned, her throat and arms bare, the fashion of her hair roughly altered. She stops abruptly upon seeing* ST. OLPHERTS; *a strange light comes into her eyes; her voice, manner, bearing, all express triumph. The two men stare at her blankly. She appears to be a beautiful woman.*]

AGNES [*To* NELLA]. Un petit châle noir tricot é—cher-chezle. [NELLA *withdraws.*] Ah, you are not dressed, Lucas dear.

LUCAS. What—what time is it?

[*He goes towards the door, still staring at* AGNES.]

ST. OLPHERTS [*Looking at her, and speaking in an altered tone*]. I fear my gossiping has delayed him. You—you dine out?

AGNES. At the Grünwald. Why don't you join us? [*Turning to* LUCAS, *lightly.*] Persuade him, Lucas.

[LUCAS *pauses at the door.*]

ST. OLPHERTS. Er—impossible. Some—friends of mine may arrive to-night. [LUCAS *goes out.*] I am more than sorry.

AGNES [*Mockingly*]. Really? You are sure you are not shy of being seen with a notorious woman?

ST. OLPHERTS. My dear Mrs. Ebbsmith—!

AGNES. No, I forget—that would be unlike you. *Mad* people scare you, perhaps?

ST. OLPHERTS. Ha, ha! Don't be too rough.

AGNES. Come, Duke, confess—isn't there more sanity in me than you suspected?

ST. OLPHERTS [*In a low voice, eyeing her*]. Much more. I think you are very clever.

LUCAS *quietly re-enters the room; he halts upon seeing that* ST. OLPHERTS *still lingers.*

ST. OLPHERTS [*With a wave of the hand to* LUCAS]. Just off, dear fellow. [*He offers his hand to* AGNES; *she quickly places hers behind her back.*] You—you are charming. [*He walks to the door, then looks round at the pair.*] Au'voir!

[ST. OLPHERTS *goes out.*]

AGNES. Au'voir! [*Her head drooping suddenly, her voice hard and dull.*] You had better take me to Fulici's before we dine and buy me some gloves.

LUCAS [*Coming to her, and seizing her hand*]. Agnes dear!

AGNES [*Releasing herself and sitting with a heavy, almost sullen look upon her face*]. Are you satisfied?

LUCAS [*By her side*]. You have delighted me! How sweet you look!

AGNES. Ah!—

LUCAS. You shall have twenty new gowns now; you shall see the women envying you, the men envying me. Ah, ha! fifty new gowns! You will wear them?

AGNES. Yes.

LUCAS. Why, what has brought about this change in you?

AGNES. What!

LUCAS. What?

AGNES. I know.

LUCAS. You know?

AGNES. Exactly how you regard me.

LUCAS. I don't understand you—

AGNES. Listen. Long ago, in Florence, I began to suspect that we had made a mistake, Lucas. Even there I began to suspect that your nature was not one to allow you to go through life sternly, severely, looking upon me more and more each day as a fellow-worker, and less and less as—a woman. I suspected this— oh, proved it!—but still made myself believe that this companionship of ours would gradually become, in a sense, colder—more temperate, more impassive. [*Beating her brow.*] Never! never! Oh, a few minutes ago this man, who means to part us if he can, drew your character, disposition, in a dozen words.

LUCAS. You believe *him!* You credit what *he* says of me!

AGNES. I declared it to be untrue. Oh, but—

LUCAS. But—but—!

AGNES [*Rising, seizing his arm*]. The picture he paints of you is not wholly a false one. Sssh! Lucas. Hark! attend to me! I resign myself to it all! Dear, I must resign myself to it!

LUCAS. Resign yourself? Has life with me become so distasteful?

AGNES. Has it? Think! Why, when I realised the actual conditions of our companionship—why didn't I go on my own way stoically? Why don't I go at this moment?

LUCAS. You really love me, do you mean—as simple, tender women are content to love? [*She looks at him, nods slowly, then turns away and droops over the table. He raises her, and takes her in his arms.*] My dear girl! My dear, cold, warm-hearted girl! Ha! You couldn't bear to see me packed up in one of the Duke's travelling-boxes and borne back to London—eh? [*She shakes her head; her lips form the word "No."*] No fear of that, my—my sweetheart!

AGNES [*Gently pushing him from her*]. Quick—dress—take me out.

LUCAS. You are shivering; go and get your thickest wrap.

AGNES. That heavy brown cloak of mine?

LUCAS. Yes.

AGNES. It's an old friend, but—dreadfully *shabby*. You will be ashamed of me again.

LUCAS. Ashamed!—

AGNES. I'll write to Bardini about a new one to-morrow. I won't oppose you—I won't repel you any more—

LUCAS. Repel me! I only urged you to reveal yourself as what you are—a beautiful woman.

AGNES. Ah! Am I that?

LUCAS [*Kissing her*] Beautiful—beautiful!

AGNES [*With a gesture of abandonment*]. I—I'm glad.
> [*She leaves him and goes out. He looks after her for a moment thoughtfully, then suddenly passes his hands across his brow and opens his arms widely as if casting a burden, from him.*]

LUCAS. Oh!—oh! [*Turning away alertly.*] Fortuné—

ACT 3. *The Scene is the same as before, but it is evening, and the lamps are lighted within the room, while outside is bright moonlight.*

> AGNES, *dressed as at the end of the preceding Act, is lying upon the settee propped up by pillows. A pretty silk shawl, with which she plays restlessly, is over her shoulders. Her face is pale, but her eyes glitter, and her voice has a bright ring in it.* KIRKE *is seated at a table writing.* GERTRUDE, *without hat or mantle, is standing behind the settee looking down smilingly upon* AGNES.

KIRKE [*Writing*]. H'm—[*To* AGNES.] Are you often guilty of this sort of thing?

AGNES [*Laughing*]. I've never fainted before in my life; I don't mean to do so again.

KIRKE [*Writing*]. Should you alter your mind about that, do select a suitable spot on the next occasion. What was it your head came against?

GERTRUDE. A wooden chest, Mr. Cleeve thinks.

AGNES. With beautiful, rusty, iron clamps. [*Putting her hand to her head, and addressing* GERTRUDE.] The price of vanity.

KIRKE. Vanity?

AGNES. Lucas was to take me out to dinner. While I was waiting for him to dress I must needs stand and survey my full length in a mirror.

KIRKE [*Glancing at her*]. A very excusable proceeding.

AGNES. Suddenly the room sank and left me—so the feeling was—in air.

KIRKE. Well, most women can manage to look into their pier-glasses without swooning—eh, Mrs. Thorpe?

GERTRUDE [*Smiling*]. How should I know, doctor?

KIRKE [*Blotting his writing*]. There. How goes the time?

GERTRUDE. Half-past eight.

KIRKE. I'll leave this prescription at Mantovani's myself. I can get it made up to-night.

AGNES [*Taking the prescription out of his hand playfully*]. Let me look.

KIRKE [*Protesting*]. Now, now!

AGNES [*Reading the prescription*]. Ha, ha! After all, what humbugs doctors are!

KIRKE. You've never heard me deny it.

AGNES [*Returning the prescription to him*]. But I'll swallow it—for the dignity of my old profession.

[*She reaches out her hand to take a cigarette.*]

KIRKE. Don't smoke too many of those things.

AGNES. They never harm me. It's a survival of the time in my life when the cupboard was always empty. [*Striking a match.*] Only it had to be stronger tobacco in those days, I can tell you.

[*She lights her cigarette.* GERTRUDE *is assisting* KIRKE *with his overcoat.* LUCAS *enters, in evening dress, looking younger, almost boyish.*]

LUCAS [*Brightly*]. Well?

KIRKE. She's to have a cup of good *bouillon*—Mrs. Thorpe is going to look after that—and anything else she fancies. She's all right. [*Shaking hands with* AGNES.] The excitement of putting on that pretty frock—[AGNES *gives a hard little laugh. Shaking hands with* LUCAS.] I'll look in to-morrow. [*Turning to* GERTRUDE.] Oh, just a word with you, *nurse.*

[LUCAS *has been bending over* AGNES *affectionately; he now sits by her, and they talk in undertones; he lights a cigarette from hers.*]

KIRKE [*To* GERTRUDE]. There's many a true word, *et cetera.*

GERTRUDE. Excitement?

KIRKE. Yes, and that smart gown's connected with it too.

GERTRUDE. It is extraordinary to see her like this.

KIRKE. Not the same woman.

GERTRUDE. No, nor is he quite the same man.

KIRKE. How long can you remain with her?

GERTRUDE. Till eleven—if you will let my brother know where I am.

KIRKE. What, doesn't he know?

GERTRUDE. I simply sent word, about an hour ago, that I shouldn't be back to dinner.

KIRKE. Very well.

GERTRUDE. Look here! I'll get you to tell him the truth.

KIRKE. The truth—oh?

GERTRUDE. I called here this afternoon, unknown to Amos, to bid her good-bye. Then I pottered about, rather miserably, spending money. Coming out of Naya's the photographer's, I tumbled over Mr. Cleeve, who had been looking for you, and he begged me to come round here again after I had done my shopping.

KIRKE. I understand.

GERTRUDE. Doctor, have you ever seen Amos look dreadfully stern and knit about the brows—like a bishop who is put out?

KIRKE. No.

GERTRUDE. Then you will.

KIRKE. Well, this is a pretty task!

[*He goes out.* GERTRUDE *comes to* AGNES. LUCAS *rises.*]

GERTRUDE. I am going down into the kitchen to see what these people can do in the way of strong soup.

LUCAS. You are exceedingly good to us, Mrs. Thorpe. I can't tell you how ashamed I am of my bearishness this afternoon.

GERTRUDE [*Arranging the shawl about* AGNES's *shoulders*]. Hush, please!

AGNES. Are you looking at my shawl? Lucas brought it in with him, as a reward for my coming out of that stupid faint. I—I have always refused to be—spoilt in this way, but now—now—

LUCAS [*Breaking in deliberately*]. Pretty work upon it, is there not, Mrs. Thorpe?

GERTRUDE. Charming. [*Going to the door, which* LUCAS *opens for her.*] Thank you. [*She passes out.* AGNES *rises.*]

LUCAS. Oh, my dear girl!—

AGNES [*Throwing her cigarette under the stove*]. I'm quite myself again, Lucas dear. Watch me—look!

[*Walking firmly.*]

LUCAS. No trembling?

AGNES. Not a flutter. [*Watching her open hand.*] My hand is absolutely steady. [*He takes her hand and kisses it upon the palm.*] Ah!—

LUCAS. [*Looking at her hand.*] No, it is shaking.

AGNES. Yes, when you—when you—oh, Lucas!—
[*She sinks into a chair, turning her back upon him, and covering her face with her hands; her shoulders heaving.*]

LUCAS [*Going to her*]. Agnes dear!

AGNES [*Taking out her handkerchief*]. Let me—let me—

LUCAS [*Bending over her*]. I've never seen you—

AGNES. No, I've never been a crying woman. But some great change has befallen me, I believe. What is it? That swoon—it wasn't mere faintness, giddiness; it was this change coming over me!

LUCAS. You are not unhappy?

AGNES [*Wiping her eyes*]. No, I—I don't think I am. Isn't that strange?

LUCAS. My dearest, I'm glad to hear you say that, for you've made me very happy.

AGNES. Because I—?

LUCAS. Because you love me—naturally, that's one great reason.

AGNES. I have always loved you.

LUCAS. But never so utterly, so absorbingly, as you confess you do now. Do you fully realise what your confession does? It strikes off the shackles from me, from us—sets us free. [*With a gesture of freedom.*] Oh, my dear Agnes, free!

AGNES [*Staring at him*]. Free?

LUCAS. Free from the burden of that crazy plan of ours of trumpeting our relations to the world. Forgive me—"crazy" is the only word for it. Thank heaven, we've at last admitted to each other that we're ordinary man and woman! Of course, I was ill—off my head. I didn't know what I was entering upon. And you, dear—living a pleasureless life, letting your thoughts dwell constantly on old troubles; that is how cranks are made. Now that I'm strong again body and mind, I can protect you, keep you right. Ha, ha! What were we to pose as? Examples of independence of thought and action! [*Laughing.*] Oh, my darling, we'll be independent in thought and action still; but we won't make examples of ourselves—eh—

AGNES [*Who has been watching him with wide-open eyes*]. Do you mean that all idea of our writing together, working together, defending our position, and the positions of such as ourselves, before the world, is to be abandoned?

LUCAS. Why, of course.

AGNES. *I—I* didn't quite mean that.

LUCAS. Oh, come, come! We'll furl what my uncle calls the banner of Free Union finally. [*Going to her and kissing her hair lightly.*] For the future, mere man and woman. [*Pacing the room excitedly.*] The future! I've settled everything already. The work shall fall wholly on my shoulders. My poor girl, you shall enjoy a little rest and pleasure.

AGNES [*In a low voice*]. Rest and pleasure—

LUCAS. We'll remain abroad. One can live unobserved abroad, without actually hiding. [*She rises slowly.*] We'll find an ideal retreat. No more English tourists prying round us! And there, in some beautiful spot, alone except for your company, I'll work! [*As he paces the room, she walks slowly to and fro, listening, staring before her.*] I'll work. My new career! I'll write under a *nom de plume*. My books, Agnes, shall never ride to popularity on the back of a scandal. Our life! The mornings I must spend by myself, of course, shut up in my room. In the afternoon we will walk together. After dinner you shall hear what I've written in the morning; and then a few turns round our pretty garden, a glance at the stars with my arm round your waist—[*she stops abruptly, a look of horror on her face*]—while you whisper to me words of tenderness, words of [*There is the distant sound of music from mandolin and guitar.*] Ah! [*To* AGNES.] Keep your shawl over your shoulders. [*Opening the window, and stepping out; the music, becoming louder.*] Some mandolinisti in a gondola. [*Listening at the window, his head turned from her.*] How pretty, Agnes! Now, don't those mere sounds, in such surroundings, give you a sensation of hatred for revolt and turmoil! Don't they conjure up alluringly pictures of peace and pleasure, of golden days and star-lit nights—pictures of beauty and of love?

AGNES [*Sitting on the settee, staring before her, speaking to herself*]. My marriage—the early days of my marriage—all over again!

LUCAS [*Turning to her*]. Eh? [*Closing the window and coming to her, as the music dies away.*] Tell me that those sounds thrill you.

AGNES. Lucas—

LUCAS [*Sitting beside her*]. Yes?

AGNES. For the first few months of my marriage—[*Breaking off abruptly and looking into his face wonderingly.*] Why, how young you seem to have become; you look quite boyish!

LUCAS [*Laughing*]. I believe that this return of our senses will make us both young again.

AGNES. Both? [*With a little shudder.*] You know, I'm older than you.

LUCAS. Tsch!

AGNES [*Passing her hand through his hair*] Yes, I shall feel that now. [*Stroking his brow tenderly.*] Well—so it has come to this.

LUCAS. I declare you have colour in your cheeks already.

AGNES. The return of my senses?

LUCAS. My dear Agnes, we've both been to the verge of madness, you and I—driven there by our troubles. [*Taking her hand.*] Let us agree, in so many words, that we have completely recovered. Shall we?

AGNES. Perhaps mine is a more obstinate case. My enemies called me mad years ago.

LUCAS [*With a wave of the hand*] Ah, but the future, the future. No more thoughts of reforming unequal laws from public platforms, no more shrieking in obscure magazines. No more beating of bare knuckles against stone walls. Come, say it!

AGNES [*With an effort*]. Go on.

LUCAS [*Looking before him—partly to himself, his voice hardening*]. I'll never be mad again—never. [*Throwing his head back.*] By heavens! [*To her, in an altered tone.*] You don't say it.

AGNES [*After a pause*]. I—I will never be mad again.

LUCAS [*Triumphantly*]. Hah! ha, ha! [*She deliberately removes the shawl from her shoulders, and, putting her arms round his neck, draws him to her.*] Ah, my dear girl!

AGNES [*In a whisper, with her head on his breast*]. Lucas.

LUCAS. Yes?

AGNES. Isn't *this* madness?

LUCAS. I don't think so.

AGNES. Oh! oh! oh! I believe, to be a woman is to be mad.

LUCAS. No, to be a woman trying not to be a woman—that is to be mad.
[*She draws a long, deep breath, then, sitting away from him resumes her shawl mechanically.*]

AGNES. Now, you promised me to run out to the Capello Nero to get a little food.

LUCAS. Oh, I'd rather—

AGNES [*Rising*]. Dearest, you need it.

LUCAS. [*Rising.*] Well—Fortuné shall fetch my hat and coat.

AGNES. Fortuné! Are you going to take *all* my work from me?
[*She is walking towards the door; the sound of his voice stops her.*]

LUCAS. Agnes! [*She returns.*] A thousand thoughts have rushed through my brain this last hour or two. I've been thinking—my wife—

AGNES. Yes?

LUCAS. My wife—she will soon get tired of her present position. If, by-and-by, there should be a divorce, there would be nothing to prevent our marrying.

AGNES. Our—marrying!

LUCAS [*Sitting, not looking at her, as if discussing the matter with himself*]. It might be to my advantage to settle again in London some day. After all, scandals quickly lose their keen edge. What would you say?

AGNES. Marriage—

LUCAS. Ah, remember, we're rational beings for the future. However, we needn't talk about it now.

AGNES. No.

LUCAS. Still, I assume you wouldn't oppose it. You would marry me if I wished it?

AGNES [*In a low voice*]. Yes.

LUCAS. That's a sensible girl! By Jove, I *am* hungry! [*He lights a cigarette as she walks slowly to the door, then throws himself idly back on the settee.*]

AGNES [*To herself, in a whisper*]. My old life—my old life coming all over again!
[*She goes out. He lies watching the wreaths of tobacco smoke. After a moment or two FORTUNÉ enters, closing the door behind him carefully.*]

LUCAS. Eh?

FORTUNÉ [*After a glance round, dropping his voice*]. Ze Duke of St. Olphert 'e say 'e vould like to speak a meenit alone.

> [LUCAS *rises, with a muttered exclamation of annoyance.*]

LUCAS. Priez Monsieur le Duc d'entrer.

> [FORTUNÉ *goes to the door and opens it. The* DUKE OF ST. OLPHERTS *enters; he is in evening dress.* FORTUNÉ *retires.*]

ST. OLPHERTS. Quite alone?

LUCAS. For the moment.

ST. OLPHERTS. My excuse to Mrs. Ebbsmith for not dining at the Grünwald— it was a perfectly legitimate one, dear Lucas. I was really expecting visitors.

LUCAS [*Wonderingly*]. Yes?

ST. OLPHERTS [*With a little cough and a drawn face*]. Oh, I am not so well to-night. Damn these people for troubling me! Damn 'em for keeping me hopping about! Damn 'em for every shoot I feel in my leg. Visitors from England—they've arrived.

LUCAS. But what—?

ST. OLPHERTS. I shall die of gout some day, Lucas. Er—your wife is here.

LUCAS. Sybil!

ST. OLPHERTS. She's come through with your brother. Sandford's a worse prig than ever—and I'm in shockin' pain.

LUCAS. This—this is your doing!

ST. OLPHERTS. Yes. Damn you, don't keep me standing!

> AGNES *enters with* LUCAS's *hat and coat. She stops abruptly on seeing* ST. OLPHERTS.

ST. OLPHERTS [*By the settee—playfully, through his pain*]. Ah, my dear Mrs. Ebbsmith, how can you have the heart to deceive an invalid, a poor wretch who begs you—[*sitting on the settee*]—to allow him to sit down for a moment?

> [AGNES *deposits the hat and coat.*]

AGNES. Deceive—?

ST. OLPHERTS. My friends arrive, I dine scrappily with them, and hurry to the Grünwald thinking to catch you over your Zabajone. Dear lady, you haven't been near the Grünwald.

AGNES. Your women faint sometimes, don't they?

ST. OLPHERTS. My—? [*In pain.*] Oh, what *do* you mean?

AGNES. The women in your class of life?

ST. OLPHERTS. Faint? Oh yes, when there's occasion for it.

AGNES. I'm hopelessly low-born; I fainted involuntarily.

ST. OLPHERTS [*Moving nearer to her*]. Oh, my dear, pray forgive me. You've recovered? [*She nods.*] Indisposition agrees with you, evidently. Your colouring to-night is charming. [*Coughing.*] You are—delightful—to—look at.

> GERTRUDE *enters, carrying a tray on which are a bowl of soup, a small decanter of wine, and accessories. She looks at* ST. OLPHERTS *unconcernedly, then turns away and places the tray on a table.*

ST. OLPHERTS [*Quietly to* AGNES]. Not a servant?

AGNES. Oh no.

ST. OLPHERTS [*Rising promptly*]. Good God! I beg your pardon. A friend?

AGNES. Yes.

ST. OLPHERTS [*Looking at* GERTRUDE *critically*]. Very nice. [*Still looking at* GERTRUDE, *but speaking to* AGNES *in undertones.*] Married or—? [*Turning to* AGNES.] Married or—?

> [AGNES *has walked away.*]

GERTRUDE [*To* LUCAS, *looking round*]. It is draughty at this table.

LUCAS [*Going to the table near the settee, and collecting the writing materials*]. Here—

> [AGNES *joins* GERTRUDE.]

ST. OLPHERTS [*Quietly to* LUCAS]. Lucas—[LUCAS *goes to him.*] Who's that gal?

LUCAS [*To* ST. OLPHERTS]. An hotel acquaintance we made in Florence—Mrs. Thorpe.

ST. OLPHERTS. Where's the husband?

LUCAS. A widow.

ST. OLPHERTS. You might—

> [GERTRUDE *advances with the tray.*]

LUCAS. Mrs. Thorpe, the Duke of St. Olpherts wishes to be introduced to you.
> [GERTRUDE *inclines her head to the* DUKE. LUCAS *places the writing materials on another table.*]

ST. OLPHERTS [*Limping up to* GERTRUDE *and handling the tray*]. I beg to be allowed to help you. [*At the table.*] The tray here?

GERTRUDE. Thank you.

ST. OLPHERTS. Ha, how clumsy I am! We think it is so gracious of you to look after our poor friend here who is not quite herself to-day. [*To* AGNES.] Come along, dear lady—everything is prepared for you. [*To* GERTRUDE.] You are here with—with your mother, I understand.

GERTRUDE. My brother.

ST. OLPHERTS. Brother. Now do tell me whether you find your—your little hotel comfortable.

GERTRUDE [*Looking at him steadily*]. We don't stay at one.

ST. OLPHERTS. Apartments?

GERTRUDE. Yes.

ST. OLPHERTS. Do you know, dear Mrs. Thorpe, I have always had the very strongest desire to live in lodgings in Venice?

GERTRUDE. You should gratify it. Our quarters are rather humble; we are in the Campo San Bartolomeo.

ST. OLPHERTS. But how delightful!

GERTRUDE. Why not come and see our rooms?

ST. OLPHERTS [*Bowing*]. My dear young lady! [*Producing a pencil and writing upon his shirt-cuff.*] Campo San Bartolomeo—

GERTRUDE. Five—four—nought—two.

ST. OLPHERTS [*Writing*]. Five—four—nought—two. To-morrow afternoon? [*She inclines her head.*] Four o'clock?

GERTRUDE. Yes; that would give the people ample time to tidy and clear up after us.

ST. OLPHERTS. After you—?

GERTRUDE. After our departure. My brother and I leave early to-morrow morning.

ST. OLPHERTS [*After a brief pause, imperturbably*]. A thousand thanks. May I impose myself so far upon you as to ask you to tell your landlord to expect me? [*Taking up his hat and stick.*] We are allowing this soup to get cold. [*Joining* LUCAS.] Dear Lucas, you have something to say to me—?

LUCAS [*Opening the door*] Come into my room.
                    [*They go out. The two women look at each other significantly.*]

AGNES. You're a splendid woman.

GERTRUDE. That's rather a bad man, I think. Now, dear—
        [*She places* AGNES *on the settee, and sets the soup, &c., before her.* AGNES *eats.*]

GERTRUDE [*Watching her closely*]. So you have succeeded in coming to close quarters, as you expressed it, with him.

AGNES [*Taciturnly.*] Yes.

GERTRUDE. His second visit here to-day, I gather.

AGNES. Yes.

GERTRUDE. His attitude towards you—his presence here under any circumstances—it's all rather queer.

AGNES. His code of behaviour is peculiarly his own.

GERTRUDE. However, are you easier in your mind?

AGNES [*Quietly, but with intensity*]. I shall defeat him. I shall defeat him.

GERTRUDE. Defeat him? You will succeed in holding Mr. Cleeve, you mean?

AGNES. Oh, if you put it in that way—

GERTRUDE. Oh, come, I remember all you told me this afternoon. [*With disdain.*] So it has already arrived, then, at a simple struggle to hold Mr. Cleeve?
[*There is a pause.* AGNES, *without answering, stretches out her hand to the wine. Her hand shakes—she withdraws it helplessly.*]

GERTRUDE. What do you want—wine?
[AGNES *nods.* GERTRUDE *pours out wine and gives her the glass.* AGNES *drains it eagerly and replaces it.*]

GERTRUDE. Agnes—

AGNES. Yes?

GERTRUDE. You are dressed very beautifully.

AGNES. Do you think so?

GERTRUDE. Don't you know it? Who made you that gown?

AGNES. Bardini.

GERTRUDE. I shouldn't have credited the little woman with such excellent ideas.

AGNES. Oh, Lucas gave her the idea when he—when he—

GERTRUDE. When he ordered it?

AGNES. Yes.

GERTRUDE. Oh, the whole thing came as a surprise to you?

AGNES. Er—quite.

GERTRUDE. I noticed the box this afternoon, when I called.

AGNES. Mr. Cleeve wishes me to appear more like—more like—

GERTRUDE. An ordinary smart woman. [*Contemptuously.*] Well, you ought to find
no difficulty in managing that. You can make yourself very charming, it appears.
[AGNES *again reaches out a hand towards the wine.* GERTRUDE *pours a
very little wine into the wine-glass and takes up the glass;* AGNES *holds out
her hand to receive it.*]

GERTRUDE. Do you mind my drinking from your glass?

AGNES [*Staring at her*]. No.
[GERTRUDE *empties the glass and then places it, in a marked way, on the
side of the table farthest from* AGNES.]

GERTRUDE [*With a little shudder*]. Ugh! Ugh! [AGNES *moves away from*
GERTRUDE, *to the end of the settee, her head bowed, her hands clenched.*] I
have something to propose. Come home with me to-morrow.

AGNES [*After a pause, raising her head*]. Home—?

GERTRUDE. Ketherick. The very spot for a woman who wants to shut out
things. Miles and miles of wild moorland! For company, purple heath
and moss covered granite, in summer; in winter, the moor-fowl and the
snow glistening on top of the crags. Oh, and for open-air music, our little
church owns the sweetest little peal of old bells! [Agnes *rises, disturbed.*] Ah,
I can't promise you their silence! Indeed, I'm very much afraid that on a
still Sunday you can even hear the sound of the organ quite a long distance
off. I am the organist when I'm at home. That's Ketherick. Will you come?
[*The distant tinkling of mandolin and guitar is again heard.*]

AGNES. Listen to that. The mandolinisti! You talk of the sound of your church
organ, and I hear his music.

GERTRUDE. His music?

AGNES. The music he is fond of; the music that gives him the thoughts that I
lease him, soothe him.

GERTRUDE [*Listening—humming the words of the air, contemptuously:*
"Bell' amore deh! porgi l'orecchio,
Ad un canto che parte dal cuore. . . ."] *Love*-music!

AGNES [*In a low voice, staring upon the ground*]. Yes, love-music.

[*The door leading from* LUCAS's *room opens, and* ST. OLPHERTS *and*
LUCAS *are heard talking.* GERTRUDE *hastily goes out.* LUCAS *enters; the
boyishness of manner has left him—he is pale and excited.*]

AGNES [*Apprehensively*]. What is the matter?

LUCAS. My wife is revealing quite a novel phase of character.

AGNES. Your wife—?

LUCAS. The submissive mood. It's right that you should be told, Agnes. She is here, at the Danieli, with my brother Sandford. [St. Olpherts *enters slowly*.] Yes, positively! It appears that she has lent herself to a scheme of Sandford's—[*glancing at* St. Olpherts]—and of—and—

ST. OLPHERTS. Of Sandford's.

LUCAS [*To* AGNES]. A plan of reconciliation. [*To* ST. OLPHERTS.] Tell Sybil that the submissive mood comes too late, by a year or so!

[*He paces to and fro.* AGNES *sits with an expressionless face.*]

AGNES [*Quietly, to* ST. OLPHERTS]. The "friends" you were expecting, Duke?

ST. OLPHERTS [*Meekly*]. Yes.

[*She smiles at him scornfully.*]

LUCAS. Agnes dear, you and I leave here early to-morrow.

AGNES. Very well, Lucas.

LUCAS [*To* ST. OLPHERTS]. Duke, will you be the bearer of a note from me to Sandford?

ST. OLPHERTS. Certainly.

LUCAS [*Going to the door of his room*]. I'll write it at once.

ST. OLPHERTS [*Raising his voice*]. You won't see Sandford, then, dear Lucas, for a moment or two?

LUCAS. No, no; pray excuse me.

[*He goes out.* ST. OLPHERTS *advances to* AGNES. *The sound of the music dies away.*]

ST. OLPHERTS [*Slipping his coat off and throwing it upon the head of the settee*]. Upon my soul, I think you've routed us!

AGNES. Yes.

ST. OLPHERTS [*Sitting, breaking into a laugh*]. Ha, ha! he, he, he! Sir Sandford and Mrs. Cleeve will be so angry. Such a devil of a journey for nothing! Ho! [*Coughing.*] Ho, ho, ho!

AGNES. This was to be your grand coup.

ST. OLPHERTS. I admit it—I have been keeping this in reserve.

AGNES. I see. A further term of cat-and dog life for Lucas and this lady—but it would have served to dispose of me, you fondly imagined. I see.

ST. OLPHERTS. I knew your hold on him was weakening. [*She looks at him.*] You knew it too. [*She looks away.*] He was beginning to find out that a dowdy demagogue is not the cheeriest person to live with. I repeat, you're a dooced clever woman, my dear. [*She rises, with an impatient shake of her body, and walks past him, he following her with his eyes.*] And a handsome one, into the bargain.

AGNES. Tsch!

ST. OLPHERTS. Tell me, when did you make up your mind to transform yourself?

AGNES. Suddenly, after our interview this afternoon; after what you said—

ST. OLPHERTS. Oh—!

AGNES [*With a little shiver*] An impulse.

ST. OLPHERTS. Impulse doesn't account for the possession of those gorgeous trappings.

AGNES. These rags? A surprise gift from Lucas, to-day.

ST. OLPHERTS. Really, my dear, I believe I've helped to bring about my own defeat. [*Laughing softly.*] Ho, ho, ho! How disgusted the Cleeve family will be! Ha, ha! [*Testily.*] Come, why don't you smile—laugh? You can afford to do so! Show your pretty white teeth! Laugh!

AGNES [*Hysterically*]. Ha, ha, ha! Ha!

ST. OLPHERTS [*Grinning*]. That's better!
> [*Pushing the cigarette-box towards him, she takes a cigarette and places it between her lips. He also takes a cigarette gaily. They smoke—she standing, with an elbow resting upon the top of the stove, looking down upon him.*]

ST. OLPHERTS [*As he lights his cigarette*] This isn't explosive, I hope? No nitric and sulphuric acid, with glycerine—eh? [*Eyeing her wonderingly and admiringly.*] By Jove! Which is you—the shabby, shapeless rebel who entertained me this afternoon or—[*kissing the tips of his fingers to her*]—or that?

AGNES. This—this. [*Seating herself, slowly and thoughtfully, facing the stove, her book turned to him.*] My sex has found me out.

ST. OLPHERTS. Ha! tsch! [*Between his teeth.*] Damn it, for your sake I almost wish Lucas was a different sort of feller!

AGNES [*Partly to herself, with intensity*] Nothing matters now—not even that. He's mine. He would have died but for me. I gave him life. He is my child, my husband, my lover, my bread, my daylight—all—everything. Mine! Mine!

ST. OLPHERTS [*Rising and limping over to her*] Good luck, my girl!

AGNES. Thanks.

ST. OLPHERTS. I'm rather sorry for you. This sort of triumph is short-lived, you know.

AGNES [*Turning to him*]. I know. But I shall fight for every moment that prolongs it. This is my hour.

ST. OLPHERTS. Your hour—?

AGNES. There's only one hour in a woman's life.

ST. OLPHERTS. One—?

AGNES. One supreme hour. Her poor life is like the arch of a crescent; so many years lead up to that hour, so many weary years decline from it. No matter what she may strive for, there is a moment when Circumstance taps her upon the shoulder and says, "Woman, this hour is the best that Earth has to spare you." It may come to her in calm or in tempest, lighted by a steady radiance or by the glitter of evil stars; but however it comes, be it good or evil, *it is her hour*—let her dwell upon every second of it!

ST. OLPHERTS. And this little victory of yours—the possession of this man; you think this is the best that Earth can spare you? [*She nods slowly and deliberately, with fixed eyes.*] Dear me, how amusing you women are! And in your dowdy days you had ambitions? [*She looks at him suddenly.*] They were of a queer, gunpowder-and-faggot sort—but they were ambitions.

AGNES [*Starting up*]. Oh! [*Putting her hands to her brows.*] Oh! [*Facing him.*] Ambitions! Yes, yes! You're right! Once, long ago, I hoped that my hour would be very different from this. Ambitions! I have seen myself, standing, humbly clad looking down upon a dense, swaying crowd—a scarlet flag for my background. I have seen the responsive look upon thousands of white, eager, hungry faces, and I've heard the great hoarse shout of welcome as I have seized my flag and hurried down amongst the people—to be given a place with their leaders! I with the leaders, the leaders! Yes, that is what I once hoped would be my hour! [*Her voice sinking.*] But this is my hour.

ST. OLPHERTS. Well, my dear, when it's over, you'll have the satisfaction of counting the departing footsteps of a ruined man.

AGNES. Ruined—!

ST. OLPHERTS. Yes, there's great compensation in that—for women.

AGNES [*Sitting*]. Why do you suggest he'll be ruined through me? [*Uneasily.*] At any rate, he'd ended his old career before we met.

ST. OLPHERTS. Pardon me; it's not too late now for him to resume that career. The threads are not quite broken yet.

AGNES. Oh, the scandal in London—

ST. OLPHERTS. Would be dispelled by this sham reconciliation with his wife.

AGNES [*Looking at him*]. Sham—?

St. Olpherts. Why, of course. All we desired to arrange was that for the future their household should be conducted strictly *à la mode*.

Agnes. *À la mode?*

St. Olpherts [*Behind the settee, looking down upon her*] Mr. Cleeve in one quarter of the house, Mrs. Cleeve in another.

Agnes. Oh yes.

St. Olpherts. A proper aspect to the world, combined with freedom on both sides. It's a more decorous system than the aggressive Free Union you once advocated; and it's much in vogue at my end of the town.

Agnes. Tour plan was a little more subtle than I gave you credit for. This was to be your method of getting rid of me!

St. Olpherts. No, no. Don't you understand? With regard to yourself, we could have arrived at a compromise.

Agnes. A compromise?

St. Olpherts. It would have made us quite happy to see you placed upon a— upon a somewhat different footing.

Agnes. What kind of—footing?

St. Olpherts. The suburban villa, the little garden, a couple of discreet servants—everything *à la mode*.
[*There is a brief pause. Then she rises and walks across the room, outwardly calm but twisting her hands.*]

Agnes. Well, you've had Mr. Cleeve's answer to *that*.

St. Olpherts. Yes.

Agnes. Which finally disposes of the whole matter—disposes of it—

St. Olpherts. Completely. [*Struck by an idea.*] Unless *you*—

Agnes [*Turning to him*]. Unless *I*—

St. Olpherts. Unless you—

Agnes [*After a moment's pause*]. What did Lucas say to you when you—?

St. Olpherts. He said he knew you'd never make that sacrifice for him. [*She pulls herself up rigidly.*] So he declined to pain you by asking you to do it.

Agnes [*Crossing swiftly to the settee, and speaking straight into his face*]. That's a lie!

St. Olpherts. Keep your temper, my dear.

Agnes [*Passionately*]. His love may not last—it won't!—but at this moment he loves me better than that! He wouldn't make a mere light thing of me!

ST. OLPHERTS. Wouldn't he? You try him!

AGNES. What!

ST. OLPHERTS. You put him to the test!

AGNES [*With her hands to her brows*]. Oh—!

ST. OLPHERTS. No, no—don't!

AGNES [*Faintly*]. Why?

ST. OLPHERTS. I like you. Damn *him*—you deserve to live your hour!

    LUCAS *enters with a letter in his hand.* AGNES *sits.*

LUCAS [*Giving* ST. OLPHERTS *the letter*]. Thanks.
  [ST. OLPHERTS *pockets the letter and picks up his cloak,* LUCAS *assisting him.*]

AGNES [*Outwardly calm*]. Oh—Lucas—

LUCAS. Yes?

AGNES. The Duke has been—has been—telling me—

LUCAS. What, dear?

AGNES. The sort of arrangement proposed for your going back to London.

LUCAS. Oh, my brother's brilliant idea!

AGNES. Acquiesced in by your wife.

    [ST. OLPHERTS *strolls away from them.*]

LUCAS. Certainly; as I anticipated, she has become intensely dissatisfied with her position.

AGNES. And it would be quite possible, it seems, for you to resume your old career?

LUCAS. Just barely possible—well, for the moment, quite possible.

AGNES. Quite possible.

LUCAS. I haven't, formally, made a sign to my political friends yet. It's a task one leaves to the last. I shall do so now—at once. My people have been busying themselves, it appears, in reporting that I shall return to London directly my health is fully re-established.

AGNES. In the hope—? Oh yes.

LUCAS. Hoping they'd be able to separate us before it was too—too late.

AGNES. Which hope they've now relinquished?

LUCAS. Apparently.

AGNES. They're prepared to accept a—a compromise, I hear?

LUCAS. Ha!—yes.

AGNES. A compromise in my favour?

LUCAS [*Hesitatingly*]. They suggest—

AGNES. Yes, yes, I know [*Looking at him searchingly.*] After all, your old career was—a success. You made your mark, as you were saying the other day. You did make your mark. [*He walks up and down restlessly, abstractedly, her eyes following him.*] You were generally spoken of, accepted, as a Coming Man. The Coming Man, often, wasn't it?

LUCAS [*With an impatient wave of the hand*]. That doesn't matter!

AGNES. And now you are giving it up—giving it all up.
[*He sits on the settee, resting his elbow on his knee, pushing his hand through his hair.*]

LUCAS. But—but you believe I shall succeed equally well in this new career of mine?

AGNES [*Stonily*]. There's the risk, you must remember.

LUCAS. Obviously, there's the risk. Why do you say all this to me now?

AGNES. Because *now* is the opportunity to—to go back.

LUCAS [*Scornfully*]. Opportunity—?

AGNES. An excellent one. You're so strong and well now.

LUCAS. Thanks to you.

AGNES [*Staring before her*]. Well—I did nurse you carefully, didn't I?

LUCAS. But I don't understand you. You are surely not proposing to—to—break with, me?

AGNES. No—I—I—I was only thinking that you—you might see something in this suggestion of a compromise.
[LUCAS *glances at* ST. OLPHERTS, *whose back is turned to them.* ST. OLPHERTS *instinctively looks round, then goes and sits by the window.*]

LUCAS [*Looking at her searchingly*]. Well, but—*you*—?

AGNES [*With assumed indifference*]. Oh, I—

LUCAS. *You?*

AGNES. Lucas, don't—don't make *me* paramount.
[*He moves to the end of the settee, showing by a look that he desires her to sit by him. After a moment's hesitation she takes her place beside him.*]

LUCAS [*In an undertone*]. I do make you paramount. I do. My dear girl, under any circumstances you would still be everything to me—always. [*She nods with a vacant look.*] There would have to be this pretence of an establishment of mine—that would have to be faced; the whited sepulchre, the mockery of dinners and receptions and so on. But it would be to you I should fly for sympathy, encouragement, rest.

AGNES. Even if you were ill again—

LUCAS. Even then, if it were practicable—if it could be—if it—

AGNES [*Looking him in the face*]. Well—?

LUCAS [*Avoiding her gaze*]. Yes, dear?

AGNES. What do you say, then, to asking the Duke to give you back that letter to your brother?

LUCAS. It wouldn't settle matters, simply destroying that letter. Sandford begs me to go round to the Danieli to-night, to—to—

AGNES. To see him? [LUCAS *nods*.] And her? [*He shrugs his shoulders.*] At what time? Was any time specified?

LUCAS. Half-past nine.

AGNES. I—I haven't my watch on.

LUCAS [*Referring to his watch*]. Nine twenty-five.

AGNES. You can almost manage it—if you'd like to go.

LUCAS. Oh, let them wait a few minutes for me; that won't hurt them.

AGNES [*Dazed*]. Let me see—I did fetch your hat and coat—
[*She rises and walks mechanically, stumbling against a chair.* LUCAS *looks up, alarmed;* ST. OLPHERTS *rises.*]

AGNES [*Replacing the chair*]. It's all right; I didn't notice this. [*Bringing* LUCAS'S *hat and coat, and assisting him with the latter.*] How long will you be?

LUCAS. Not more than half an hour. An hour at the outside.

AGNES [*Arranging his neckhandkerchief*]. Keep this so.

LUCAS. Er—if—if I—if we—

AGNES. The Duke is waiting.
[LUCAS *turns away and joins* ST. OLPHERTS.]

LUCAS [*To him, in a low voice*]. I am going back to the hotel with you.

ST. OLPHERTS. Oh, are you?
[*The door opens* and FORTUNÉ *enters, followed by* AMOS WINTERFIELD. FORTUNÉ *retires.*]

AMOS [*To* LUCAS, *sternly*]. Is my sister still here, may I ask?
[LUCAS *looks to* AGNES *interrogatively. She inclines her head.*]

AMOS. I should like her to know that I am waiting for her.

[AGNES *goes out.*]

LUCAS [*To* AMOS]. Pray excuse me.

[AMOS *draws back.* ST. OLPHERTS *passes out. At the door,* LUCAS *pauses, and bows slightly to* AMOS, *who returns his bow in the same fashion; then* LUCAS *follows* ST. OLPHERTS. GERTRUDE *enters, wearing her hat and mantle.* AGNES *follows; her movements are unsteady, and there is a wild look in her eyes.*]

GERTRUDE. You've come to fetch me, Amos?

[*He assents with a nod.*]

AMOS [*To* AGNES]. I'm sorry to learn from Dr. Kirke that you've been ill. I hope you're better.

AGNES [*Turning away,* GERTRUDE *watching her*]. Thank you, I am quite well.

AMOS [*Gruffly*]. Are you ready, Gertrude?

GERTRUDE. No, dear, not yet. I want you to help me.

AMOS. In what way?

GERTRUDE. I want you to join me in persuading Mrs. Ebbsmith—*my friend,* Mrs. Ebbsmith—to come to Ketherick with me.

AMOS. My dear sister—!

GERTRUDE [*Firmly*]. Please, Amos!

AGNES. Stop a moment! Mr. Winterfield, your sister doesn't in the least understand how matters are with me. I am returning to England, but with Mr. Cleeve. [*Recklessly.*] Oh, you'd hear of it eventually! He is reconciled to his wife.

GERTRUDE. Oh—! Then, surely, you—!

AGNES. No. The reconciliation goes no further than mere outward appearances. He relies upon me as much as ever. [*Beating her hands together passionately.*] He can't spare me—can't spare me!

AMOS [*In a low voice to* GERTRUDE]. Are you satisfied?

GERTRUDE. I suspected something of the kind. [*Going to* AGNES, *gripping her wrist tightly.*] Pull yourself out of the mud! Get up out of the mud!

AGNES. I have no will to—no desire to!

GERTRUDE. You mad thing!

AGNES [*Releasing herself, facing* GERTRUDE *and* AMOS]. You are only breaking in upon my hour.

GERTRUDE. Your hour—?

AGNES [*Waving them away*]. I ask you to go—to go!

[GERTRUDE *returns to* AMOS.]

AMOS. My dear Gertrude, you see what our position is here. If Mrs. Ebbsmith asks for our help it is our duty to give it.

GERTRUDE. It is especially *my* duty, Amos.

AMOS. And I should have thought it especially mine. However, Mrs. Ebbsmith appears to firmly decline our help. And at this point, I confess, I would rather you left it—*you*, at least.

GERTRUDE. You would rather *I* left it—I, the virtuous, unsoiled woman! Yes, I am a virtuous woman, Amos; and it strikes you as odd, I suppose, my insisting upon friendship with her. But look here, both of you. I'll tell you a secret. You never knew it, Amos, my dear. I never allowed anybody to suspect it—

AMOS. Never knew what?

GERTRUDE. The sort of married life mine was. It didn't last long, but it was dreadful, almost intolerable.

AMOS. Gertrude!

GERTRUDE. After the first few weeks—weeks, not months!—after the first few weeks of it, my husband treated me as cruelly—[*turning to* AGNES]—just as cruelly, I do believe, as your husband treated *you*. [AMOS *makes a movement, showing astonishment.*] Wait! Now, then! There was another man—one I loved—one I couldn't help loving! I could have found release with him, perhaps happiness of a kind. I resisted, came through it. They're dead—the two are dead! And here I am, a virtuous, reputable woman; saved by the blessed mercy of Heaven! There, you are not surprised any longer, Amos! [*Pointing to* AGNES.] "My friend, Mrs. Ebbsmith!" [*Bursting into tears.*] Oh! Oh, if my little boy had been spared to me, he should have grown up tender to women—tender to women! he should, he should—!

[*She sits upon the settee, weeping. There is a short silence.*]

AMOS. Mrs. Ebbsmith, when I came here to-night I was angry with Gertrude—not altogether, I hope, for being in your company. But I was certainly angry with her for visiting you without my knowledge. I think I sometimes forget that she is eight-and-twenty, not eighteen. Well, now I offer to delay our journey home for a few days, if you hold out the faintest hope that her companionship is likely to aid you in any way.

[AGNES, *standing motionless, makes no response.* AMOS *crosses to her, and as he passes* GERTRUDE, *he lets his hand drop over her shoulder; she clasps it, then rises and moves to a chair, where she sits, crying silently.*]

AMOS [*By* AGNES's *side—in a low voice*]. You heard what she said. Saved by the mercy of Heaven.

AGNES. Yes, but she can feel that.

AMOS. You felt so once.

AGNES. Once—!

AMOS. You have, in years gone by, asked for help upon your knees.

AGNES. It never came.

AMOS. Repeat your cry!

AGNES. There would be no answer.

AMOS. Repeat it!

AGNES [*Turning upon him*]. If miracles *could* happen! If "help," as you term it, *did* come! Do you know what "help" would mean to *me*?

AMOS. What—?

AGNES. It would take the last crumb from me!

AMOS. This man's—protection?

AGNES [*Defiantly*]. Yes!

AMOS. Oh, Mrs. Ebbsmith—!

AGNES [*Pointing to the door*] Well, I've asked you both to leave me, haven't I? [*Pointing at* GERTRUDE, *who has risen.*] The man she loves is dead and gone! She can moralise—! [*Sitting, beating upon the settee with her hands.*] Leave me!

[AMOS *joins* GERTRUDE.]

GERTRUDE. We'll go, Amos.

[*He takes from his pocket a small leather bound book; the cover is well-worn and shabby.*]

AMOS [*Writing upon the fly-leaf of the book with a pencil*]. I am writing our address here, Mrs. Ebbsmith.

AGNES [*In a hard voice*]. I already have it.

[GERTRUDE *glances at the book over* AMOS's *shoulder and looks at him wonderingly.*]

AMOS [*Laying the book on the settee by* AGNES's *side*]. You might forget it.

[*She stares at the book, with knitted brows, for a moment, then stretches out her hand and opens it.*]

AGNES [*Withdrawing her hand sharply*]. No—I don't accept your gift.

AMOS. The address of two friends is upon the fly-leaf.

AGNES. I thank both of you; but you shall never be troubled again by me. [*Rising, pointing to the book.*] Take that away! [*Sitting facing the stove, the door of which she opens, replenishing the fire—excitedly.*] Mr. Cleeve may be back soon; it would be disagreeable to you all to meet again.

[GERTRUDE *gently pushes* AMOS *aside, and picking up the book from the settee, plates it upon the table.*]

GERTRUDE [*To* AGNES, *pointing to the book*]. This frightens you. Simple print and paper, so you pretend to regard it; but it frightens you. [*With a quick movement,* AGNES *twists her chair round and faces* GERTRUDE *fiercely.*] I called you a mad thing just now. A week ago I did think you half-mad—a poor, ill-used creature, a visionary, a moral woman living immorally; yet, in spite of all, a woman to be loved and pitied. But now I'm beginning to think that you're only frail—wanton. Oh, you're not so mad as not to know you're wicked! [*Tapping the book forcibly.*] And so this frightens you.

AGNES. You're right! Wanton! That's what I've become! And I'm in my right senses, as you say. I suppose I was mad once for a little time, years ago. And do you know what drove me so? [*Striking the book with her fist.*] It was *that—that*!

GERTRUDE. That!

AGNES. I'd trusted in it, clung to it, and it failed me. Never once did it stop my ears to the sounds of a curse; when I was beaten it didn't make the blows a whit the lighter; it never healed my bruised flesh, my bruised spirit! Yes, that drove me distracted for a while; but I'm sane now—now it is you that are mad, mad to believe! You foolish people, not to know—[*beating her breast and forehead*]—that Hell or Heaven is here and here I [*Pointing to the book.*] Take it!

[GERTRUDE *turns away and joins* AMOS, *and they walk quickly to the door.*]

AGNES [*Frantically*]. I'll not endure the sight of it—!

[*As they reach the door,* GERTRUDE *looks back and sees* AGNES *hurl the book into the fire. They go out.* AGNES *starts to her feet and stands motionless for a moment, her head bent, her fingers twisted in her hair. Then she raises her head; the expression of her face has changed to a look of fright and horror. Uttering a loud cry, she hastens to the stove, and, thrusting her arm into the fire, drags out the book.* GERTRUDE *and* AMOS *re-enter quickly in alarm.*]

GERTRUDE. Agnes—!

[*They stand looking at* AGNES, *who is kneeling upon the ground, clutching the charred book.*]

ACT 4.   *The Scene is an apartment in the Campo San Bartolomeo. The walls are of plaster; the ceiling is frescoed in cheap modern Italian fashion. At the end of the room is a door leading to* AGNES's *bedroom; to the left is an exit on to a landing, while a nearer door, on the same side, opens into another room. The furniture and the few objects attached to the walls are characteristic of a moderate-priced Venetian lodging. Placed about the room, however, are photographs in frames and pretty knickknacks personal to* GERTRUDE, *and a travelling-trunk and bag are also to be seen. The shutters of the two nearer windows are closed; a broad stream of moonlight, coming through the further window, floods the upper part of the room.*

HEPHZIBAH, *a grey-haired north-country woman dressed as a lady's maid, is collecting the knickknacks and placing them in the travelling-bag.*

After a moment or two, GERTRUDE *enters by the farther door.*

GERTRUDE [*At the partly-closed door, speaking into the farther room*]. I'll come back to you in a little while, Agnes. [*Closing the door and addressing* HEPHZIBAH.] How are you getting on, Heppy?

HEPHZIBAH. A' reet, Miss Gerty. I'm puttin' together a' the sma' knick-knacks, to lay them wi' the claes i' th' trunks.

GERTRUDE [*Taking some photographs from the table and bringing them to* HEPHZIBAH]. We leave here at a quarter to eight in the morning; not a minute later.

HEPHZIBAH. Aye. Will there be much to pack for Mistress Cleeve?

GERTRUDE. Nothing at all. Besides her hand-bag, she has only the one box.

HEPHZIBAH [*Pointing to the trunk*]. Nay, nobbut that thing!

GERTRUDE. Yes, nobbut that. I packed that for her at the Palazzo.

HEPHZIBAH. Eh, it won't gi' us ower much trouble to maid Mistress Cleeve when we get her hame.

GERTRUDE. Heppy, we are not going to call—my—my friend—"Mrs. Cleeve."

HEPHZIBAH. Nay! what will thee call her?

GERTRUDE. I'll tell you—by-and-by. Remember, she must never, never be reminded of the name.

HEPHZIBAH. Aye, I'll be maist carefu'. Poor leddy! After the way she tended that husband o' hers in Florence neet and day, neet and day.

GERTRUDE. The world's full of unhappiness, Heppy.

HEPHZIBAH. The world's full o' husbands. I canna' bide 'em. They're true enough when they're ailin'—but a lass can't keep her Jo always sick. Hey, Miss Gerty, do forgi'e your auld Heppy!

GERTRUDE. For what?

HEPHZIBAH. Why, your own man, so I've heered, ne'er had as much as a bit headache till he caught his fever and died o't.

GERTRUDE. No, I never knew Captain Thorpe to complain of an ache or a pain.

HEPHZIBAH. And *he* was a rare, bonny husband to thee, if a' tales be true.

GERTRUDE. Yes, Heppy. [*Listening, startled.*] Who's this?

HEPHZIBAH [*Going and looking*]. Maister Amos.

[AMOS *enters briskly.*]

AMOS [*To* GERTRUDE]. How is she?

GERTRUDE [*Assisting him to remove his overcoat*]. More as she used to be—so still, so gentle. She's reading.

AMOS [*Looking at her significantly*]. Reading?

GERTRUDE. Reading.

[*He sits, humming a tune, while* HEPPY *takes off his shoes and gives him his slippers.*]

HEPHZIBAH. Eh, Maister Amos, it's good to see thee sae gladsome.

AMOS. Home, Heppy, home!

HEPHZIBAH. Aye, hame!

AMOS. With our savings!

HEPHZIBAH. Thy savings—!

AMOS. Tsch! get on with your packing.

[HEPHZIBAH *goes out, carrying the travelling-bag and* AMOS's *shoes. He exchanges the coat he is wearing for a shabby little black jacket which* GERTRUDE *brings him.*]

GERTRUDE [*Filling* AMOS's *pipe*]. Well, dear! Go on!

AMOS. Well, I've seen them.

GERTRUDE. Them—

AMOS. The Duke and Sir Sandford Cleeve.

GERTRUDE. At the hotel?

AMOS. I found them sitting together in the hall, smoking, listening to some music.

GERTRUDE. Quite contented with the arrangement they believed they had brought about.

AMOS. Apparently so. Especially the Baronet—a poor, cadaverous creature.

GERTRUDE. Where was Mr. Cleeve?

AMOS. He had been there, had an interview with his wife, and departed.

GERTRUDE. Then by this time he has discovered that Mrs. Ebbsmith has left him?

AMOS. I suppose so.

GERTRUDE. Well, well! the Duke and the cadaverous Baronet?

AMOS. Oh, I told them I considered it my duty to let them know that the position of affairs had suddenly become altered—[*she puts his pipe in his mouth, and strikes a match*]—that, in point of fact, Mrs. Ebbsmith had ceased to be an element in their scheme for re-establishing Mr. Cleeve's household.

GERTRUDE [*Holding a light to his pipe*]. Did they inquire as to her movements?

AMOS. The Duke did—guessed we had taken her.

GERTRUDE. What did they say to that?

AMOS. The Baronet asked me whether I was the chaplain of a Home for—[*angrily*]—ah!

GERTRUDE. Brute! And then?

AMOS. Then they suggested that I ought hardly to leave *them* to make the necessary explanation to their relative, Mr. Lucas Cleeve.

GERTRUDE. Yes—well?

AMOS. I replied that I fervently hoped I should never set eyes on their relative again.

GERTRUDE [*Gleefully*]. Ha!

AMOS. But that Mrs. Ebbsmith had left a letter behind her at the Palazzo Arconati, addressed to that gentleman, which I presumed contained as full an explanation as he could desire.

GERTRUDE. Oh, Amos—!

AMOS. Eh?

GERTRUDE. You're mistaken there, dear; it was no letter.

AMOS. No letter—?

GERTRUDE. Simply four shakily-written words.

AMOS. Only four words!

GERTRUDE. "My—hour—is—over."

HEPHZIBAH *enters with a card on a little tray.* GERTRUDE *reads the card and utters an exclamation.*

GERTRUDE [*Taking the card and speaking under her breath*]. Amos!

> [*He goes to her; they stare at the card together.*]

AMOS [*To* HEPHZIBAH]. Certainly.

> [HEPHZIBAH *goes out, then returns with the* DUKE OF ST. OLPHERTS, *and retires.* ST. OLPHERTS *bows graciously to* GERTRUDE *and more formally to* AMOS.]

AMOS. Pray, sit down.

> [ST. OLPHERTS *seats himself on the settee.*]

ST. OLPHERTS. Oh, my dear sir!—if I may use such an expression in your presence—here is the devil to pay!

AMOS [*To* ST. OLPHERTS]. You don't mind my pipe? [ST. OLPHERTS *waves a hand pleasantly.*] And I don't mind your expression [*sitting by the table.*] The devil to pay?

ST. OLPHERTS. This, I daresay well-intentioned, interference of yours has brought about some very unpleasant results. Mr. Cleeve returns to the Palazzo Arconati and finds that Mrs. Ebbsmith has flown.

AMOS. That result, at least, was inevitable.

ST. OLPHERTS. Whereupon he hurries back to the Danieli and denounces us all for a set of conspirators.

AMOS. Your Grace doesn't complain of the injustice of that charge?

ST. OLPHERTS [*Smilingly*]. No, no, *I* don't complain. But the brother—the wife! Just when they imagined they had bagged the truant—there's the sting!

GERTRUDE. Oh, then Mr. Cleeve now refuses to carry out his part of the shameful arrangement?

ST. OLPHERTS. Absolutely. [*Rising, taking a chair, and placing it by the settee.*] Come into this, dear Mrs. Thorn—!

AMOS. Thorpe.

ST. OLPHERTS. Come into this! [*Sitting again.*] You understand the sort of man we have to deal with in Mr. Cleeve.

GERTRUDE [*Sitting*]. A man who prizes a woman when he has lost her.

ST. OLPHERTS. Precisely.

GERTRUDE. Men don't relish, I suppose, being cast off by women.

ST. OLPHERTS. It's an inversion of the picturesque; the male abandoned is not a pathetic figure. At any rate, our poor Lucas is now raving fidelity to Mrs. Ebbsmith.

GERTRUDE [*Indignantly*]. Ah—!

ST. OLPHERTS. If you please, he cannot, will not, exist without her. Reputation, fame, fortune are nothing when weighed against—Mrs. Ebbsmith. And we may go to perdition, so that he recovers—Mrs. Ebbsmith.

AMOS. Well—to be plain—you're not asking us to sympathise with Mrs. Cleeve and her brother-in-law over their defeat?

ST. OLPHERTS. Certainly not. All I ask, Mr. Winterfield, is that you will raise no obstacle to a meeting between Mrs. Cleeve and—and—

GERTRUDE. No!

[ST. OLPHERTS *signifies assent*; GERTRUDE *makes a movement.*]

ST. OLPHERTS [*To her*]. Don't go.

AMOS. The object of such a meeting?

ST. OLPHERTS. Mrs. Cleeve desires to make a direct, personal appeal to Mrs. Ebbsmith.

GERTRUDE. Oh, what kind of woman can this Mrs. Cleeve be?

ST. OLPHERTS. A woman of character, who sets herself to accomplish a certain task—

GERTRUDE. Character!

AMOS. Hush, Gerty!

ST. OLPHERTS. And who gathers her skirts tightly round her and gently tip-toes into the mire.

AMOS. To put it clearly: in order to get her unfaithful husband back to London, Mrs. Cleeve would deliberately employ this weak, unhappy woman as a lure.

ST. OLPHERTS. Perhaps Mrs. Cleeve is an unhappy woman.

GERTRUDE. What work for a wife!

ST. OLPHERTS. Wife—nonsense! She is only married to Cleeve.

AMOS [*Walking up and down*]. It is proposed that this meeting should take place—when?

ST. OLPHERTS. I have brought Sir Sandford and Mrs. Cleeve with me. [*Pointing towards the outer door.*] They are—

AMOS. If I decline?

ST. OLPHERTS. It's known you leave for Milan at a quarter to nine in the morning; there might be some sort of foolish inconvenient scene at the station.

AMOS. Surely your Grace—?

St. Olpherts. Oh no, *I* shall be in bed at that hour. I mean, between the women, perhaps—and Mr. Cleeve. Come, come, sir, you can't abduct Mrs. Ebbsmith—nor can we. Nor must you gag her. [Amos *appears angry and perplexed*.] Pray be reasonable. Let her speak out for herself—here, finally—and settle the business. Come, sir, come!

Amos [*Going to* Gertrude *and speaking in a low voice*]. Ask her. [Gertrude *goes out*.] Cleeve! Where is he while this poor creature's body and soul are being played for? You have told him that she is with us?

St. Olpherts. No, *I* haven't.

Amos. He must suspect it.

St. Olpherts. Well, candidly, Mr. Winterfield, Mr. Cleeve is just now employed in looking for Mrs. Ebbsmith elsewhere.

Amos. Elsewhere?

St. Olpherts. Sir Sandford recognised that, in his brother's present mood, the young man's presence might be prejudicial to the success of these delicate negotiations.

Amos. So some lie has been told him, to keep him out of the way?

St. Olpherts. Now, Mr. Winterfield—!

Amos. Good heavens, Duke—forgive me for my roughness—you appear to be fouling your hands, all of you, with some relish!

St. Olpherts. I must trouble you to address remarks of that nature to Sir Sandford Cleeve. I am no longer a prime mover in the affair. I am simply standing by.

Amos. But how can you "stand by"?

St. Olpherts. Confound it, sir, if you will trouble yourself to rescue people, there is a man to be rescued here as well as a woman; a man, by the way, who is a—a sort of relative of mine.

Amos. The woman first!

St. Olpherts. Not always. You can rescue this woman in a few weeks' time; it can make no difference.

Amos [*Indignantly*]. Ah—!

St. Olpherts. Oh, you are angry!

Amos. I beg your pardon. One word. I assure your Grace that I truly believe this wretched woman is at a fatal crisis in her life. I believe that if I lose her now there is every chance of her slipping back into a misery and despair out of which it will be impossible to drag her. Oh, I'll be perfectly open with you. At this moment we—my sister and I—are not sure of her. Her affection for this man may still induce her to sacrifice herself utterly for him; she is still in danger of falling to the lowest depth a woman can attain. Come, Duke, don't help these people! And don't "standby!" Help me and my sister! For God's sake!

ST. OLPHERTS. My good Mr. Winterfield, believe me or not, I—I positively like this woman.

AMOS [*Gladly*]. Ah!

ST. OLPHERTS. She attracts me curiously. And if she wanted assistance—

AMOS. Doesn't she?

ST. OLPHERTS. Money—

AMOS. No, no.

ST. OLPHERTS. She should have it. But as for the rest—well—

AMOS. Well?

ST. OLPHERTS. Well, sir, you must understand me. It is a failing of mine; I can't approach women—I never could—in the missionary spirit.

> GERTRUDE *re-enters; the men turn to face her.*

AMOS [*To* GERTRUDE] Will she—?

GERTRUDE. Yes. [ST. OLPHERTS *limps out of the room, bowing to* GERTRUDE *as he passes.*] Oh, Amos!

AMOS. Are we to lose the poor soul after all, Gerty?

GERTRUDE. I—I can't think so. Oh, but I'm afraid!

> ST. OLPHERTS *returns, and* SIR SANDFORD CLEEVE *enters with* SYBIL CLEEVE. SANDFORD *is a long, lean, old-young man with a pinched face.* SYBIL *is a stately, handsome young woman, beautifully gowned and thickly veiled.*

ST. OLPHERTS. Mrs. Thorpe—Mr. Winterfield.

> [SANDFORD *and* SYBIL *bow distantly to* GERTRUDE *and* AMOS.]

AMOS [*To* SANDFORD *and* SYBIL, *indicating the settee*]. Will you? [SYBIL *sits on settee;* SANDFORD *takes the chair beside her.*] Gertrude—

> [GERTRUDE *goes out.*]

SIR SANDFORD [*Pompously*]. Mr. Winterfield, I find myself engaged upon a peculiarly distasteful task.

AMOS. I have no hope, Sir Sandford, that you will not have strength to discharge it.

SIR SANDFORD. We shall object to loftiness of attitude on your part, sir. You would do well to reflect that we are seeking to restore a young man to a useful and honourable career.

AMOS. You are using very honourable means, Sir Sandford.

SIR SANDFORD. I shall protest against any perversion of words, Mr. Winterfield—

The door of the further room opens, and GERTRUDE *comes in, then* AGNES. *The latter is in a rusty, ill-fitting, black stuff dress; her hair is tightly drawn from her brows; her face is haggard, her eyes are red and sunken. A strip of linen binds her right hand.*

ST. OLPHERTS [*Speaking into* SYBIL's *ear*]. The lean witch again! The witch of the Iron Hall at St. Luke's.

SYBIL [*In a whisper*]. Is *that* the woman?

ST. OLPHERTS. You see only one of 'em—there are two there.

[SANDFORD *rises as* AGNES *comes slowly forward accompanied by* GERTRUDE. AMOS *joins* GERTRUDE; *and they go together into the adjoining room,* GERTRUDE *giving* AGNES *an appealing look.*]

SIR SANDFORD [*To* AGNES]. I—I am Mr. Lucas Cleeve's brother—[*with a motion of the hand towards* SYBIL] this is—this is—

[*He swallows the rest of the announcement and retires to the back of the room, where he stands before the stove.* ST. OLPHERTS *strolls away and disappears.*]

SYBIL [*To* AGNES, *in a hard, dry, disdainful voice*]. I beg that you will sit down. [AGNES *sits mechanically, with an expressionless face.*] I—I don't need to be told that this is a very—a very unwomanly proceeding on my part.

SIR SANDFORD. I can't regard it in that light, under the peculiar circumstances.

SYBIL. I'd rather you wouldn't interrupt me, Sandford. [*To* AGNES.] But the peculiar circumstances, to borrow my brother-in-law's phrase, are not such as develop sweetness and modesty, I suppose.

SIR SANDFORD. Again I say you wrong yourself there, Sybil—

SYBIL [*Impatiently*]. Oh, please let me wrong myself, for a change. [*To* AGNES.] When my husband left me, and I heard of his association with you, I felt sure that his vanity would soon make an openly irregular life intolerable to him. Vanity is the cause of a great deal of virtue in men; the vainest are those who like to be thought respectable.

SIR SANDFORD. Really, I must protest—

SYBIL. But Lady Cleeve—the mother—and the rest of the family have not had the patience to wait for the fulfilment of my prophecy. And so I have been forced to undertake this journey.

SIR SANDFORD. I demur to the expression "forced," Sybil—

SYBIL. Cannot we be left alone? Surely! [SANDFORD *lows stiffly and moves away, following* ST. OLPHERTS.] However—there's this to be said for them, poor people—whatever is done to save my husband's prospects in life must be done now. It is no longer possible to play fast and loose with friends and supporters—to say nothing of enemies. His future now rests upon a matter of days—hours almost. [*Rising and walking about agitatedly.*] That is why I am sent here—well, why I *am* here.

AGNES [*In a low, quavering voice*]. What is it you are all asking me to do now?

SYBIL. We are asking you to continue to—to exert your influence over him for a little while longer.

AGNES [*Rising unsteadily*]. Ah—! [*She makes a movement to go, falters, and irresolutely sits again.*] My influence—mine!

SYBIL [*With a stamp of the foot*]. You wouldn't underrate your power if you had seen him, heard him, about an hour ago—[*mockingly*] after he had discovered his bereavement.

AGNES. He will soon forget *me*.

SYBIL. Yes—if you don't forsake him.

AGNES. I am going to England, into Yorkshire; according to your showing, that should draw him back.

SYBIL. Oh, I've no doubt we shall hear of him—in Yorkshire! You'll find him dangling about your skirts in Yorkshire!

AGNES. And he will find that I am determined—strong.

SYBIL. Ultimately he will tire, of course. But when? And what assurance have we that he returns to us when he has wearied of pursuing you? Besides, don't I tell you that we must make sure of him *now*? It's of no use his begging us, in a month's time, to patch up home and reputation. It must be now—and you can end our suspense. Come, hideous as it sounds, this is not much to ask.

AGNES [*Shrinking from her*]. Oh—!

SYBIL. Oh, don't regard me as the wife! That's an unnecessary sentiment, I pledge you my word. It's a little late in the day, too, for such considerations. So, come, help us!

AGNES. I will not.

SYBIL. He has an old mother—

AGNES. Poor woman!

SYBIL. And remember, *you* took him away—!

AGNES. I!

SYBIL. Practically you did—with your tender nursing and sweet compassion. Isn't it straining a point—to shirk bringing him back?

AGNES [*Rising*]. I did not take him from you. You—you sent him to me.

SYBIL. Oh yes! that tale has been dinned into your ears often enough, I can quite believe. *I* sent him to you—my coldness, heartlessness, selfishness sent him to you. The unsympathetic wife—eh? Yes, but you didn't put yourself to the trouble of asking for *my* version of the story before you mingled your woes with his. [AGNES *faces her suddenly*.] You know him now. Have I been altogether to blame, do you still think? Unsympathetic! Because I've so often had to tighten my lips, and stare blankly over his shoulder, to stop myself from crying out in weariness of his vanity and pettiness? Cruel! Because, occasionally, patience became exhausted at the mere contemplation of a man so thoroughly, greedily self-absorbed? Why, *you* married miserably, the Duke of St. Olpherts tells us! Before you made yourself my husband's champion and protector, why didn't you let your experience speak a word for *me*? [AGNES *quickly turns away and sits upon the settee, her hands to her brow*.] However, I didn't come here to revile you. [*Standing by her*.] They say that you're a strange woman—not the sort of woman one generally finds doing such things as you have done; a woman with odd ideas. I hear—oh, I'm willing to believe it!—that there's good in you.

[AGNES *breaks into a low peal of hysterical laughter*.]

AGNES. Who tells you—that?

SYBIL. The Duke.

AGNES. Ha, ha, ha! A character—from him! ha, ha, ha!

SYBIL [*Her voice and manner softening*]. Well, if there *is* pity in you, help us to get my husband back to London, to his friends, to his old ambitions.

AGNES. Ha, ha, ha, ha! your husband!

SYBIL. The word slips out. I swear to you that he and I can never be more to each other than companion figures in a masquerade. The same roof may cover us; but between two wings of a house, as you may know, there often stretches a wide desert. I despise him; he hates me. [*Walking away, her voice breaking*.] Only—I did love him once .... I don't want to see him utterly thrown away—wasted .... I don't quite want to see that ....

[AGNES *rises and approaches* SYBIL, *fearfully*.]

AGNES. [*In a whisper.*] Lift your veil for a moment. [SYBIL *raises her veil.*] Tears—tears—[*with a deep groan*]—Oh—! [SYBIL *turns away.*] I—I'll do it .... I'll go back to the Palazzo .... at once. . . . [SYBIL *draws herself up suddenly.*] I've wronged you! wronged you! O God! O God!

> [*She totters away and goes into her bedroom. For a moment or two* SYBIL *stands still, a look of horror and repulsion upon her face. Then she turns and goes towards the outer door.*]

SYBIL [*Galling*]. Sandford! Sandford!

> [SIR SANDFORD, CLEEVE *and the* DUKE OF ST. OLPHERTS *enter.*]

SIR SANDFORD [*To* SYBIL]. Well—?

SYBIL. She is going back to the Palazzo.

SIR SANDFORD. You mean that she consents to—?

SYBIL. [*Stamping her foot*]. I mean that she will go back to the Palazzo. [*Sitting and leaning her head upon her hands.*] Oh! oh!

SIR SANDFORD. Need we wait longer, then?

SYBIL. These people—these people who are befriending her! Tell them.

SIR SANDFORD. Really, it can hardly be necessary to consult—

SYBIL [*Fiercely*]. I will have them told! I will have them told!

> [SANDFORD *goes to the door of the adjoining room and knocks, returning to* SYBIL *as* GERTRUDE *and* AMOS *enter.* SYBIL *draws down her veil.*]

GERTRUDE [*Looking round*]. Mrs. Ebbsmith—? Mrs. Ebbsmith—!

SIR SANDFORD. Er—many matters have been discussed with Mrs. Ebbsmith. Undoubtedly she has, for the moment, considerable influence over my brother. She has consented to exert it, to induce him to return at once to London.

AMOS. I think I understand you!

> [AGNES *appears at the door of her room dressed in bonnet and cloak.*]

GERTRUDE. Agnes—!

> [AGNES *comes forward, stretches out her hand to* GERTRUDE, *and throws herself upon the settee.*]

SYBIL [*To* SANDFORD, *clutching his arm*]. Take me away.

> [*They turn to go.*]

GERTRUDE [*To* SYBIL]. Mrs. Cleeve—! [*Looking down upon* AGNES.] Mrs. Cleeve, we—my brother and I hoped to save this woman. She was worth saving. You have utterly destroyed her.

> [SYBIL *makes no answer, but walks slowly away with* SANDFORD, *then stops and turns abruptly.*]

SYBIL [*With a gasp*]. Oh—! No—I will not accept the service of this wretched woman. I loathe myself for doing what I have done. [*Coming to* AGNES.] Look up! Look at me! [*Proudly—lifting her veil.*] I decline your help—I decline it. [*To* GERTRUDE *and* AMOS.] You hear me—you—and you? I unsay all that I've said to her. It's too degrading; I will not have such an act upon my conscience. [*To* AGNES.] Understand me! If you rejoin this man I shall consider it a fresh outrage upon me. I hope you will keep with your friends.

[GERTRUDE *holds out her hand to* SYBIL; SYBIL *touches it distantly.*]

AGNES [*Clutching at* SYBIL'*s skirts*]. Forgive me! forgive—!

SYBIL [*Retreating*]. Ah, please—! [*Turning and confronting* SANDFORD.] Tell your mother I have failed. I am not going back to England.

LUCAS *enters quickly; he and* SYBIL *come face to face. They stand looking at each other for a moment, then she sweeps past him and goes out.* SANDFORD *follows her.*

LUCAS [*Coming to* AGNES]. Agnes—[*To* AGNES, *in rapid, earnest undertones.*] They sent me to the railway station; my brother told me you were likely to leave for Milan to-night. I ought to have guessed sooner that you were in the hands of this meddling parson and his sister. Why has my wife been here—?

AGNES [*In a low voice, rocking herself gently to and fro*]. Your wife—your wife—?

LUCAS. And the others? What scheme is afoot now? Why have you left me? Why didn't you tell me outright that I was putting you to too severe a test? You tempted me, you led me on, to propose that I should patch up my life in that way. [*She rises with an expressionless face.*] But it has had one good result. I know now how much I depend upon you. Oh, I have had it all out with myself, pacing up and down that cursed railway station. [*Laying his hand upon her arm and speaking into her ea*r.] I don't deceive myself any longer. Agnes, *this* is the great cause of the unhappiness I've experienced of late years—I'm not fit for the fight and press of life. I wear no armour; I am too horribly sensitive. My skin bleeds at a touch; even flattery wounds me. Oh, the wretchedness of it! But you can be strong—at your weakest, there is a certain strength in you. With you, in time, I feel *I* shall grow stronger. Only I must withdraw from the struggle for a while; you must take me out of it and let me rest—recover breath, as it were. Come! Forgive me for having treated you ungratefully, almost treacherously. To-morrow we will begin our search for our new home. Agnes!

AGNES. I have already found a home.

LUCAS. Apart from me, you mean?

AGNES. Apart from you.

LUCAS. No, no. You'll not do that!

AGNES. Lucas, this evening, two or three hours ago, you planned out the life we were to lead in the future. We had done with "madness," if you remember; henceforth we were to be "mere man and woman."

LUCAS. You agreed—

AGNES. Then. But we hadn't looked at each other clearly then, as mere man and woman. You, the man—what are you? You've confessed—

LUCAS. I lack strength; I shall gain it.

AGNES. Never from me—never from me. For what am I? Untrue to myself, as you are untrue to yourself; false to others, as you are false to others; passionate, unstable, like yourself; like yourself, a coward. A coward. I—*I* was to lead women! *I* was to show them, in your company, how laws—laws made and laws that are natural—may be set aside or slighted; how men and women may live independent and noble lives without rule, or guidance, or sacrament. *I* was to be the example—the figure set up for others to observe and imitate. But the figure was made of wax—it fell awry at the first hot breath that touched it! You and I! What a partnership it has been! How base, and gross, and wicked, almost from the very beginning! We know each other now thoroughly—how base and wicked it would remain! No, go your way, Lucas, and let me go mine.

LUCAS. Where—where are you going?

AGNES. To Ketherick—to think. [*Wringing her hands.*] Ah! I have to think too, now, of the woman I have wronged.

LUCAS. Wronged?

AGNES. Your wife; the woman I have wronged, who came here to-night, and— spared me. Oh, go!

LUCAS. Not like this, Agnes! not like this!

AGNES [*Appealingly*]. Gertrude! [LUCAS *looks round—first at* GERTRUDE *then at* AMOS—*and, with a hard smile upon his face, turns to go. Suddenly* AGNES *touches his sleeve.*] Lucas, when I have learnt to pray again, I will remember you, every day of my life.

LUCAS [*Staring at her*]. Pray!. . . . you! . . . .

> [*She inclines her head twice, slowly; without another word he walks away and goes out.* AGNES *sinks upon the settee;* AMOS *and* GERTRUDE *remain, stiffly and silently, in the attitude of people who are waiting for the departure of a disagreeable person.*]

St. Olpherts [*After watching* Lucas's *departure*]. Now I wonder whether, if he hurried to his wife at this moment, repentant, and begged her to relent—I wonder whether—whether she would—whether—[*looking at* Amos *and* Gertrude, *a little disconcerted*]—I beg your pardon—you're not interested?

Amos. Frankly, we are not.

St. Olpherts. No; other people's affairs are tedious. [*Producing his gloves.*] Well! A week in Venice—and the weather has been delightful. [*Shaking hands with* Gertrude, *whose expression remains unchanged.*] A pleasant journey! [*Going to* Agnes, *offering his hand.*] Mrs. Ebbsmith—? [*She lifts her maimed hand.*] Ah! An accident? [*She nods wearily.*] I'm sorry .... I ....

[*He turns away and goes out, bowing to* Amos *as he passes.*]

THE END.

NEW WOMAN FICTION

Eugenia

Sarah Grand

From "Our Manifold Nature" 1894

I. I AM A humble artist, studying always in the life-school of the world, blinking nothing that goes to the making or marring of life, more especially to the marring of it, for if we would make it lovely, we must know exactly the nature of the diseases that disfigure it, and experiment upon them until we discover the great specific which, when properly applied, shall remedy all that. And it so happened that, in order to be accurate in every detail of a work upon which I was then engaged, I required to study human nature, as it appears behind the scenes, at the time of night when that part of a theatre is most characteristically crowded with the company in costume, and such visitors as are admitted. A brother of mine made the necessary arrangements for me, and was so good as to escort me himself, the leading managers, to whom he had explained my difficulty, having most courteously allowed me free access for my purpose. I have only to mention here one of the numerous little items of interest I noted at the time. It happened at the beginning of the enterprise when everything was new and strange, and while the incident itself, although trivial, remains distinctly impressed upon my mind, the surrounding details, doubtless because of their number and novelty, escape me for the most part, as in a well-balanced picture when all is unobtrusive, save the main idea; but I remember that we were wedged in a crowd of theatrical characters variously and even fantastically attired as if for a fancy-dress ball, and that the clatter of tongues was bewildering. Rank odours of a variety of scents saluted one's afflicted nostrils on all sides. This way white rose flowed from a fan, which a much-bedizened, vulgarly handsome daughter of the people was waving over a repulsively dissipated-looking young man in evening dress who was sprawling disrespectfully on a couch. On the other side patchouly polluted the air, and wood violet on a nymph in front of us was waging war with the whisky and *eau de Cologne* which were being wafted abroad by an old unvenerable man who was essaying to ogle with dim watery eyes, and to simper with loose lips that were too tremulous to respond simultaneously to the weak-willed intention.

Every affectation of society was apparent about us, but coarsened into caricature. Flirtations were more evident, and grosser in the conduct of them, than in Belgravia, and powder, paint, and paste-diamonds were flaunted more conspicuously. Tight lacing was also carried to a more painful extent. Women's voices shrilled loudly, the cockney accent predominating. Most of the things said struck me as being disagreeably personal and flippant, when not actually coarse and rude. The laughter was noisy and incessant, but mirthless, and although there was plenty of excitement in the assembly, there was obviously little if any genuine pleasure, and as to happiness, I could detect no line, even on the youngest face, to indicate it. The predominant expression was one of anxiety, only relieved in the more callous by moments of sensual apathy. As a whole the scene remains impressed upon my mind as an unlovely travesty of much to which one becomes accustomed in society, but it possessed the attraction of repulsion for me, and I could have stood there studying all night.

My brother knew many of the people present, but I only saw one man with whom I was personally acquainted, and it so happened that I knew him well, for it was Brinkhampton, the eldest son of a near neighbour of ours in my childhood. The two families had always been intimate.

He was standing talking to some woman just behind me, and I recognised his voice before I saw him.

"I'm sure your waist's smaller than Kitty Green's," he was saying quite earnestly.

"Aow, nao, you flatter me," the lady responded nasally. "Only I daown't tight laice."

There was a little pause, then Brinkhampton asked: "What are you looking for?"

"My fan. I laid it on the taible."

"Here it is. Let me have the pleasure of fanning you."

"Pleasure, indeed! Aow, I saiy! What do you want, I'd like to knaw? With those sheep's eyes! I'm up to you—" And so on all up the gamut of the cheapest inanity, silly, sillier, and silliest.

I turned to look at the lady, expecting to see something so satisfying to the eye of man that no other sense asked for anything, but she struck me as being a joyless antique, largely proportioned, well-preserved, and still able to affect a sprightliness she must have been far from feeling spontaneously at that time of life. "That was the celebrated Sylvia," my brother told me as we came away.

"Wherein lieth the charm of her fatal fascination?" I asked.

"In *prestige*, which lasts longer than anything," he answered.

Out of the crowd and heat into the open air was an intoxicating transition, so great was the relief of it. I stood for some minutes on the pavement inhaling deep draughts of the freshness, and feeling as if I could never rid myself of the fever and fumes of that tawdry place.

II. THE NEXT NIGHT, driving home late from some entertainment, I was forced by a block in the traffic to sit for some time at the entrance to a popular "Theatre of Varieties." The lights blazed brilliantly, streaming across the pavement and into the carriage so that I could have read a book had I had one, and any of my friends seeing me there must have recognised me. The thought was amusing, particularly as I happened to be alone, but it was also a trifle embarrassing, because the carriage I was in belonged to friends with whom I was staying for the moment, austere people, whose livery was somewhat conspicuous, and as they were well-known to the public, there was always a chance of some enterprising reporter giving my friends the credit in the next day's news of having spent their evening at this garish resort. There was a fiendish racket going on all about me. In the road, men, women and policemen, cabs, carts and carriages, seemed to be in extricably mixed, as if they had been performing some mystical rite with which they were imperfectly acquainted, the consequence of the confusion being great differences of opinion, and eager, angry, incessant, loud disputes. I was busy looking out on that side, improving my knowledge of the vulgar tongue by making notes in my own mind of any peculiar expressions used, when I heard myself addressed by name through the window on the "Theatre of Varieties" side of me, and at the same moment recognised Brinkhampton.

"I thought I could not be mistaken," he was saying, "however much I may be surprised by your choice of a place of amusement."

"From whence come you?" I answered tranquilly.

"From these same halls of light," he replied, indicating the gaudy place behind him; "and to tell you the truth," he added, in a worn-out, weary, satiated way—"I am sick of all that. I'm utterly used up. I think it's time for me to reform and marry. Can you recommend me to somebody who would make a nice wife? I suppose it wouldn't do for me to ask you for a seat in your carriage at this time of night?" This was said tentatively, but I crushed the aspiration with a decided shake of my head. Men have to have reputations nowadays, and I should have been sorry to have been seen alone with Brinkhampton under any circumstances—poor fellow—although I had known him all my life. "I know you are mighty particular," he went on, disconsolately, "but I assure you I'm thoroughly in earnest this time. Let me come and tell you all about it."

As he blocked up the whole of the window, the fact that he was reeking of tobacco and stimulants could not fail to impress me unpleasantly, and his somewhat bloated features, inflamed eyes, and dissipated appearance generally rendered him still more unattractive to my fastidious mind; so, to get rid of him, I told him that I should be "at home" next day, and if he came early enough, he might find me alone for a few minutes. I quite expected he would have no recollection of the engagement, but to my surprise he arrived, and rather sooner too than was altogether convenient.

It was evident from the way he was dressed, that the matter had cost him some thought; but no care could conceal the "used-up" look about his eyes, nor produce a deceptive tinge of health on the opaque sallow of his cheeks. The effort had not been wanting, his valet having obviously done his best, but it is only fresh and healthy skin that really takes paint and powder well; the transparency once lost, artificial attempts to restore it show on the surface like a light layer of dust on standing water. But he was a young man still, and a good-looking one too, of the big coarse-moustached type, a typical guardsman, broad shouldered, and so apparently strong that a casual acquaintance would never have suspected flabby muscular tissue discounted by alcohol. He had a pleasant voice, and his manners were easy and unaffected, if a trifle too candidly self-complacent. With the old-fashioned sort of society-woman he was a favourite, and I confess I liked him well enough in a way myself, but then I had acquired the habit of liking him when we were children together.

"Well, and so you are inclined to marry and settle?" I said, as soon as we were seated.

"Not merely inclined," he answered, " I am quite determined. I've had a good time, don't you know, rather too much of a good time if anything, and now I feel it would be better for me to settle; and I want something nice and young and fresh, with money, for a wife, so that I may repair all my errors at once; some one who has lived all her life at the back of beyond, never been any where nor seen anyone to speak of, and is refreshingly unsophisticated enough to mistake the first man who proposes to her for an unsullied hero of romance. And I mean to be that man, don't you see."

"But where do I come into this delightfully delicate, original plan?" I drily inquired.

"Well, you go a good deal to country houses," he answered, with what might have been either a dash of diffidence or a shade of anxiety in his manner. "You must have met the kind of girl I want—good-looking, you know, with an ivory skin and—and money. Don't jeer at me. I'm in earnest."

I composed my countenance, and took time to reflect. How to decline to help him without hurting his feelings was the difficulty. There used to be a superstition in society, that a man could at any time repair the errors of his youth by making a good match, and there are women still who will introduce "used-up" brothers and so on to their girl friends as eligible husbands; but I belong to the party of progress myself, and would not under any circumstances have done such a thing. I had not the courage of my opinions, however, at that time to the extent of saying so bluntly, and therefore I "smiling passed the question by;" but as I had not absolutely refused, he chose to take it that I would help him if I could, and thereupon he thanked me with effusion, and I could see that he was more than satisfied, for it was as if a load of care had been lifted from his mind and left him lighter-hearted.

III. THAT SUMMER SAW me seated one afternoon in a shady nook on a cliff in the north, overlooking the sea. Behind me there was a lovely stretch of country, hill and dale, field and forest, with the gold of ripening grain, the scarlet glint of intrusive poppies, and the manifold tints of green, shooting to gray, and even to yellow and brown in the woods, where the earlier trees were already assuming a dash of their autumn bravery. Before me was the mildly murmurous unrest of rippling wavelets, bursting with incessant merriment as they feigned to fly from the pursuit of the incoming tide, which flowed on always swiftly over the long level reaches of the sandy shore. It was a scene to soothe and enlighten, for such solitudes people the mind with goodly companies of glad ideas, and just and vigorous thoughts. My meditations were not long uninterrupted that day, however, for in the most absorbing midst of them I was aroused by the surprised enunciation of my own name, and, on looking up, I discovered Brinkhampton staring at me.

"Well!" I ejaculated. "What are you doing here?"

"Potting rabbits," he answered, sententiously. "I have taken the shooting."

"You mean to be in time for it, apparently."

"Oh, I thought I'd come and amuse myself with the rabbits. It's the fresh air I want really, you see. My nerves have all gone to pieces. I want to be out of sinner's ways for awhile, and I knew fellows wouldn't come bothering much before September. I've taken the shooting with leave to live about here for six months if it suits me. In the absence of a lord, the lady of the manor lets the right, I understand."

"Do you know her?" I asked.

"No," he replied, "I have not that pleasure. Do you?"

"I am staying with her now."

Then there was a pause, during which Brinkhampton carefully examined his gun, lock, stock, and barrel. "It's a nice place," he remarked at last, glancing about him comprehensively. "Is the lady as goodly as her acres?"

"Has she 'an ivory skin' do you mean? You may judge for yourself, for behold her approach down yonder forest glade, hatless, gloveless, robed in white, with a purple parasol shielding the burnished brightness of her lovely tresses from the too ardent kisses of the sun."

Brinkhampton stared with interest.

"She's quite young!" he exclaimed.

"Twenty-one exactly," I replied.

He was about to say something else, but Eugenia had come up to us by this time, and I hastened to present them to each other.

"It is you who have taken my shooting off my hands this year, I suppose," Eugenia said, glancing at his gun.

"So I have just learnt," he answered, looking into her sweet grave face with undisguised interest and admiration.

"I hope you will find it worth your while," she said.

"The coverts are pretty well stocked this year, I believe. Where have you put up?"

"At the village inn," he answered with a grimace.

"Oh!" she exclaimed, "then you must be uncomfortable. When I heard you were coming alone, I hoped you had friends in the neighbourhood with whom you would stay."

"It so happens that I know nobody here as yet," he replied. "But I really must get some decenter accommodation."

"Why not come to the hall?" Eugenia asked easily.

"It would be a kindness to help us to occupy a little more of it. The house has suffered from having been so long shut up."

The frank assurance of her manner seemed to surprise him. He glanced at her gloveless left hand to see if perchance she was married, and he confessed to me afterwards he could not quite class her when he found she wore no wedding-ring, being "puzzled to make out whether she was Americanized, unsophisticated, or not quite the right form, don't you know." But at any rate the offer was a good one.

"I should be afraid of intruding," he feebly deprecated.

"No fear of that," she answered smiling; then

appealing to me, she added: "I am sure I may say we shall both be glad to see you. We dine at half-past seven."

We smartened ourselves up that evening somewhat in honour of the young man, and I noticed that he and Eugenia were studying each other with a certain pleased intentness which augured well for their future friendliness. Certainly his coming had enlivened Eugenia as the coming of an eligible should enliven a girl, and I waited with interest to hear what she had to say about him. He had been looking his best when they met in the afternoon, the rough tweed shooting suit he wore being just of the cut and colour best adapted to conceal his defects, but his evening dress was altogether too calculated for effect, too evidently the outcome of serious attention to be manly. There was more than a suspicion of some horrid expensive scent about him, and his cheeks had a velvety texture which was cruelly suggestive of powder—*apropos* of all of which Eugenia remarked to me afterwards in a mysterious whisper laughingly: "I suspect stays." But that was all she said about him, somewhat to my surprise, for I should have expected that the advent of a man of that kind would have caused a flutter of curiosity at least in the heart of a country girl. However in such a case not asking questions is no proof of an absence of interest.

IV. EUGENIA AND I breakfasted at half-past eight next morning, but Brinkhampton did not appear until after ten. It was Sunday, and we were in the breakfast-room ready dressed for church when he entered.

"What will you have?" Eugenia, as hostess, asked him, thinking of tea, coffee or chocolate.

"Aw," he answered, looking round to the sideboard, "claret or hock, I really don't care which."

Eugenia ordered both to be brought, and then we hurried away to church.

In the middle of the Litany Brinkhampton entered, and, lounging down the aisle with conspicuous deliberation, took a side seat from which he could survey us all at his ease. He was dressed, as usual, with extreme attention to detail, in the manner most approved for the occasion, and it was certainly not his fault if the latest thing in frock coats, as worn by himself, appeared to be ridiculously singular to the rest of the congregation in contrast to the archaic cut to which their eyes were accustomed. He looked hard at Eugenia from the moment he took his seat, but she was deep in her devotions, and took not the slightest notice of him.

It was a quaint, old-fashioned little church, only attended as a rule by tenants on the estates and the household at the hall, close to which it was so situated as to seem more of a private chapel than a public place of worship. All about us, in the midst of the quiet people, Eugenia's ancestors were taking their long rest. Knight and dame, lord and lady, soldier, sailor, and priest, good and bad, looked down upon us or appeared prone in effigies of stone upon old tombs, while tablets of brass or marble recorded the brave deeds of one, the learning of another, the statesmanship of a third, and so on, ascribing every available virtue to each. I have often seen Eugenia beguiling the tedious sermon-time by studying these tablets, and always imagined her ignorant of the true characters of her notorious ancestors, idealizing them all, and being elevated by the deep interest, the natural affection, and the innate reverence she must feel for those to whom she attributed all that was best about her.

She was peculiarly situated, being one of a long line of dominant women, the estates having descended from mother to daughter in regular succession, in accordance with a curse which had been laid upon all heirs male of the family forever—so it was said—or, at all events, until such time as an heiress should contrive to expiate the crime for which the sons of her house were (somewhat unfairly, as it seems to our modern ideas of justice) doomed to suffer. Eugenia had been left an orphan at an early age, and brought up in the midst of a people who still clung fervently to all the old-world superstitions. I did not know how much of these she accepted literally, but I always attributed a certain dignity and general air as of one who is not to be trifled with, which settled upon her early, to the romantic associations of the place, and her faith in those who had gone before. They, her people, having been noble, it was proper that she also should be self-respecting and noble too—so, at least, I read her reflections when I watched her weighing the worth of those epitaphs in her own mind Sunday after Sunday as she grew to girlhood, and I fancied that the gentle gravity, which gradually became the habitual expression of her countenance in repose, was due to thoughts like these.

This morning, however, she was not thinking of her ancestors in the pauses of the service. When her eyes wandered at all it was to the green graves in the churchyard, and the old trees that sheltered them. The day was warm and bright, and through the open windows the scented summer air streamed in upon her, and also there came an incessant twittering of birds, the coo of a woodpigeon now and then, and the hoarse caws of rooks—not as interruptions to the service, however, but rather as an accustomed addition to it, the whole, with the rural people, sober in dress, and solemnly attentive in their demeanour, producing an impression of remoteness from the world and proportionate nearness to nature, which was inexpressibly soothing. Even Brinkhampton's starved soul expanded for the moment just enough to let him feel some joy in life—something sufficiently worth having to make him forget for once to measure time with a view to shortening it, or "passing" it, as is the insane fashion of those who have not learnt to live.

When the service was over he walked on with me to the house, Eugenia having lingered in the porch talking to the people.

"I have found my ideal!" he exclaimed fervently, as soon as we were alone.

"Ivory skin and all?"

"Don't be malicious," he answered. "I'm in earnest. But I've a bone to pick with you. You seem to have forgotten your promise to me. Why did you not tell me of this lovely lady hidden away here in the hills?"

"For the reason you mention," I answered coolly. "I had forgotten your request."

"How could you; when she is so exactly what I asked you to find for me too! But tell me about her. How does she come to be so situated—here, you know, like this?"

"She is in a somewhat unusual position," I answered. "She has no relation in the whole world but an old uncle—who was once in your regiment, by the way. All her own people died in her infancy, and she has been brought up here principally by a very charming and excellent woman who came to be her governess, and has remained to be a mother to her. She is away just now, and I am here on duty partly, looking after Eugenia, you know, during her absence. The property's nice, is it not? It was a good deal encumbered by debts, but has been well nursed during Eugenia's long minority, and she is bent upon economy herself until it is cleared."

"Then she really is sole heiress?" he observed, looking about him with an air of complete satisfaction, as if he already had a proprietary right to the place.

"Sole inheritress, I should say. Half the neighbourhood is hers."

"But why should she be buried here still?" he asked, then added: "But I am glad she has been. I should like to see her wonder when she enters the great world! her delight when she finds what it really is to be mistress of means, with jewels and lace, a centre of attraction! She can't know what her wealth is worth a bit until she comes into competition with other women and finds herself able to eclipse them."

This noble thought seemed to enchant him, and I could see he was hugging himself already on the prospect of her brilliant social success, and the glory which it would reflect upon himself.

I made him no answer because I had determined to be neutral. Here were the conventional elements of most romances, youth, beauty, rank, wealth, experienced man, inexperienced girl—but not a commonplace girl either. There was no knowing exactly how she would act under the circumstances, and the uncertainty was great enough to relieve the story from insipidity. I thought it would be interesting to watch the plot unfold, and I was anxious to see for myself how this *Ouidaesque* hero would really strike a modern maiden with ideas of her own.

That kind of man is accustomed to the Sylvias in and out of society, who will sell their immortal souls for gewgaws, and his mind had probably continued to divert him with promises of the irresistible attraction of such things when used with women as an argument to influence their feelings, for at our early Sunday dinner he said a good deal about diamonds, to which Eugenia listened with evident interest. She was highly intelligent, and at an age when the opposite point of view is always surprising. She was not in the habit of saying much, however. Brinkhampton was voluble, and she heard him out, then answered with a smile and in a casual tone: "You seem to be fond of diamonds. I have a lot upstairs somewhere if you would like to see them. I used to delight in them myself for their glitter when I was a child, but now of course I only value them for the sake of any little family history that attaches to them."

Brinkhampton stared at her, not at all perceiving that the art of being agreeable to a Sylvia is not always effectual with other girls, and divided between the pleasing thought that Eugenia would appreciate her advantages better by-and-by, when she came into competition with other women, and had opportunities of testing the value of diamonds as an aid to eclipsing them, and an uncomfortable though vague perception of the unpleasant possibility of a peculiar personal equation "that might by some mischance be swaying her taste eccentrically in the matter."

Out in the grounds later he began to fear that there was not much to amuse her, that she must often find it very dull in this benighted country place, whereupon she made big eyes of astonishment at him, and ejaculating "dull!" glanced comprehensively at the surrounding wonders of sky, and sea, and shore, then added, "where can dulness come into a life like mine?"

The question nonplussed him for the moment. To be so unsophisticated as not even to have the slightest conception of the better life which includes shopping in London and the full swing of everything there in the season, was a little too much. "But," as he remarked to me afterwards, "all this enhances the charm, don't you know; it's so fresh, and it will be fun to see how her views change as her mind is enlarged by intercourse with the world, and to hear what she thinks by-and-by of this rural retreat."

"But do you suppose she has any mind?" I ventured.

"Oh, dear, yes," he answered. "Quite enough for a woman, especially if she's to be one's wife. A clever woman is apt to have 'views' and that sort of thing, and lead a man a dance generally. What one wants in a wife is something nice to look at and agreeable to caress when one's in the mood, with average intelligence of course, but conventional ideas."

"Are you going to have anybody down for the shooting?"

"Well, I don't know," he answered. "That was my idea at first. But my primary motive was to get away from everybody and recruit. I told you in town. I've had too good a time, and I'm quite used up. My nerve's gone to that extent that I'm afraid to fire my own gun if I think about it. It would certainly be better for me to settle, and the more I see of the place the more I like it. The air's delicious, and suits me too. I'm beginning to revive already."

He had just come in from "potting" rabbits, and we were sitting on a seat in the garden, he nursing his gun, when he said this, and after he had spoken he reflected a little, then added: "It would suit me down to the ground to have this quiet retreat and Eugenia to come to whenever I felt played out, as I am now."

"Then you've abandoned the idea of making a society woman of her?"

"Oh, not at all. But I should require her to be here when I'm otherwise engaged, and can't look after her, don't you know."

I admired his foresight, it being evident that he was preparing, with playful toleration of his own weakness, to be tempted back now and then to gloat on Sylvia's super abundant flesh, and at the same time was thinking how refreshing it would be, when that kind of thing palled upon him, to return to the rarefied atmosphere which surrounded the lily of love whom he was also anxious to secure.

V. Their acquaintance rapidly ripened into intimacy, and very soon I perceived that they had adopted that tone of light banter which enables young people to say so much to each other. The playful controversy turned for the most part on the relative merits of town and country, and the brilliancy and wit of society compared with the petty concerns which Brinkhampton held to be all there was to discuss in a neighbourhood like this.

"I am sure," he maintained, "you would like to hear people talk cleverly."

"I would much rather hear them talk kindly," she answered.

She was always ready with some such response, but he soon nattered himself that her perversity was a coquettish assumption to pique him, and would try to provoke her in return by assuring her that she would know better when she was older.

The brightness which I had noticed on the first evening of the coming of the young man into Eugenia's quiet life did not diminish, but on the contrary increased if anything with the ripening of their acquaintance. Her nature was naturally joyous, and under Brinkhampton's influence her manner, while losing none of its dignified simplicity, became more girlishly playful, which was a distinct improvement, for until now she had been apt to display a too great earnestness for her age. Nothing in her attitude, however, gave me the slightest clue to her feelings for him. I did not know in the least whether she had ever thought of him as a possible lover or not.

With him it was quite different. He talked of her incessantly, and of what he called his "love" for her. He even got so far as to consider the settlements, and if there would be ready money enough in hand at the time of the marriage to pay off his innumerable debts and start them clear, because it would be a pity to have to sell out anything, don't you know. The "love" and the lucre longings mixed in his conversation in curiously exact proportions, but still the frank boyishness of it all was taking.

It was hot harvest weather; radiant mornings turning to turquoise and pearl-grey noons, and always exquisite amethyst seas—an ideal love-time, and it would have been strange if it had failed altogether of its effect upon two young people so thrown together. The first positive sign of serious feeling I detected in Brinkhampton was an improvement in his habits. On Sunday morning he had breakfasted between ten and eleven, on Wednesday he was up at seven o'clock. Eugenia and I were just starting for the meadows with baskets to gather mushrooms for breakfast when he appeared. He volunteered to accompany us, and wanted to carry our baskets, but Eugenia said that would only be robbing us of our occupation, and suggested that he should have one of his own.

We straggled down the road after each other. The morning was deliciously fresh, and so was Eugenia. Brinkhampton could not take his eyes off her, and, although she never glanced at him, I knew by the smile that constantly hovered about her mouth, the brightness of her eyes, the slightly heightened colour on her delicate cheeks, and the buoyancy of her step, that she was aware of his earnest gaze, and animated by his admiration. They chatted incessantly, disagreeing generally, but it was impossible to tell whether they were pulling apart or only arriving at a better understanding. There was sufficient difference of opinion to read both ways, but owing to the cheerful playfulness of the tone in which it was all expressed, it was hard to determine how much either of them really meant.

Cock pheasants crowed in the coverts as we passed, rabbits ran nimbly out of the way. We crossed a limpid trout stream in a little wood, and, coming out into the open ground again, found ourselves on the edge of the cliff in full view of the sun-smitten sea. The many-murmurous voice of ocean was in our ears, the vital breath of it upon our cheeks. Eugenia, standing on the brink with longing eyes, looked out first over the moving waters into the morning mist where the sea-birds revel, then turned to Brinkhampton brightly, and asked: "Did you ever see anything like this in Bond Street?"

Brinkhampton sighed sentimentally, but wisely held his peace.

It was a high cliff upon which we were standing, and there was a narrow precipitous winding path, cut out of the chalk and very dangerous-looking, running down to the beach.

"Let us go back by the sands," Eugenia exclaimed, our baskets being full by this time, and away she went, nimbly as a goat, I following without a thought. At the bottom we looked back, and discovered Brinkhampton at one of the bends about half-way down leaning against the cliff—I had almost said clinging to it.

"Anything the matter?" Eugenia cried.

"I'm stuck," he answered.

"How thoughtless of me," I exclaimed, and ran back to help him. He was pale, and clutched my hand eagerly when I offered it to him.

"You see I have not exaggerated," he said, dejectedly.

"I've no nerve left for anything. I'm used up. It's high time I settled."

My hand, however, and also perhaps the now familiar formula, helped to restore his confidence, and we got down together pretty creditably. I could see that Brinkhampton expected some sympathy for his giddiness, but Eugenia was throwing stones into the water unconcernedly when we rejoined her, and went on without a word as if nothing had happened. Near the house a tall good-looking young man of distinguished appearance met us.

"There's Saxon," Eugenia exclaimed when he came in sight, and greeted him familiarly, but did not introduce him to Brinkhampton.

I knew him of old, and asked him why he had not been to see me.

"We have had to make the most of this harvest weather," he answered. "But I shall be able to call soon now, I hope, if I may."

"Yes, do come, Saxon," Eugenia exclaimed. "There are ever so many things I want to consult you about."

"Who was that?" Brinkhampton asked afterwards.

"Saxon Wake, a friend of my youth," Eugenia answered lightly. "His people have been here as long as we have. They were Yeoman farmers, but now they own a part of what were our estates."

"The yokel has passable manners," Brinkhampton said, patronisingly. "I suppose he picks up a little veneer at race-meetings and hunt-breakfasts."

"The yokel was a wrangler of his year," Eugenia answered icily.

Brinkhampton said no more. He had not taken any degree himself.

VI. WE HAD A private letter-bag at the hall which was brought in for Eugenia to unlock every morning, and she usually distributed the letters herself. That day she took out one among others that instantly filled the room with some strong scent of which it was reeking. "Ugh!" she exclaimed; "after the open air, how coarse this is. Who can it be for? You,"—to Brinkhampton. "It savours of 'Society' to me,—'the thick of life,'—'excitement!' but my rustic nose is unequal to the demands of such an assault. Please take it!"

Brinkhampton glanced at the superscription as she handed him the note, and his countenance expressed "Faugh!" as clearly as a countenance can speak. He was about to put the note in his pocket, but changed his mind, and laid it beside his plate. It had occurred to him that he might draw suggestions of the mysterious "fuller" life of a man from it with which to enhance his *prestige* with this little country girl.

"It is from Sylvia," he observed.

"The burlesque actress?" Eugenia asked. "I suppose you know numbers of people of that kind."

He smiled complacently.

"You must find it very different being here with us," she remarked.

"Of course it is a change," he confessed.

"Yes," she answered, thoughtfully. "But I wonder you can endure it, even for a change."

"Oh, one would endure a good deal for the sake of some people," he blundered.

I noticed that the shooting claimed less and less of his attention. He did not even make a pretence of going out to-day, and Eugenia herself had scarcely paid a visit, or had anyone at the house since his arrival. The young man, set in sunshine with an accompaniment of lovely languid autumn weather, had sufficed so far for an absorbing interest, but now at last as we loitered in the dining-room after lunch she raised that question of What shall we do? which usually implies the palling of an old pleasure and a desire for something new.

She was sitting on the sill of one of the wide-open windows with her feet on the deep-cushioned window-seat, and as she spoke there was a sound of horse's feet spattering through the gravel below.

"Here's Saxon!" she exclaimed with animation. "Saxon, I'm delighted to see you. We want something to do this afternoon. Come and consult."

"Why not have out the coach, drive to Greenwood Sound, send the saddle-horses by the short cut across the fields to wait for you there, and race the tide home round Towindard Head," Saxon rejoined from below. "The tide will be just right for the ride if you get off in half an hour."

"Excellent!" Eugenia exclaimed. "But you must come with us, Saxon. One gentleman is not enough for two ladies, and Lord Brinkhampton does not know the coast. Do ride round to the stables and order the coach and despatch Gould with the horses while we are putting on our habits. Come, boot and spur, my lord," she called to Brinkhampton as she dragged me from the room.

"He doesn't look very gracious about it," she said, as we ran upstairs together, "and I expect he'll take an hour to adorn himself. I suppose I shall be obliged to let him drive. Saxon won't, I know. But I do wonder what kind of a whip he is. If he can't drive, however, he shan't pretend to, for I don't believe true womanliness consists in letting a man do badly what a woman can do well, simply because men generally are more accustomed to perform that particular exercise than women are. But let us hope he has forgotten to provide himself with the last thing in driving gloves. He would never use anything already out of date by a season."

This last little sarcasm, although playfully uttered, sounded significant, but if Brinkhampton had gone down in her estimation for any reason, he rose again when it came to offering him the reins, by the frank way in which he acknowledged he was no whip, and had never been able to handle a team in his life.

Contrary to our expectation, he was waiting for us in the porch when we went down, and was also, wonderful to relate, amicably discussing the points of the horses with Saxon. It was a smart turn-out, and doubtless the possession of it, by adding an important item to other evidences of Eugenia's many material attractions, had improved his humour.

VII. BRINKHAMPTON SAT BESIDE Eugenia on the front seat, Saxon and I were behind them, and at the back were Baldwin, the old family coachman, and a groom with the coach-horn. The horses, dark glossy bays with black points, were mettlesome beasts. They danced down the drive as if unaware of the slight encumbrance of the coach and its load behind them. It was a wonderful thing to see Eugenia, a slender girl, almost standing against her high seat with her feet planted firmly in front of her, controlling the four great prancing creatures without apparent effort. One could not help calculating what the nerve-power must be behind such ease, and what the strength of the sinews which were masked by her "ivory skin." She never looked better than on that occasion. Her riding habit, clinging close, showed the perfection of her figure. The sun was still hot, and she wore, slightly tilted back, a low-crowned white sailor hat, the roundness of which set off the delicate oval of her cheeks. Her ripe red lips were slightly parted in a smile showing the white teeth between, her eyes danced in liquid light; one could trace the course of the blue veins beneath the transparent skin, and the fresh air and exertion had brought a brilliant colour to her cheeks. But for those with the inner eyes that see beneath the surface, there was more about her to attract than mere good looks and the ineffable charm of youth. There shone in her face the happy spirit that makes much of the smallest joy in life, and sees in the most obvious admiration of her friends only an evidence of their own good dispositions. There is more beauty than character as a rule in the delicate curves and lineless smoothness of a young girl's face; but still, in studying Eugenia, one felt that, for all her soft voice and gentle courteous bearing, she was not a person to be trifled with. There are natures which may be taught but must not be dictated to, and hers was one of those.

She was, in fact, essentially a modern maiden, richly endowed with all womanly attributes, whose value is further enhanced by the strength. Which comes of the liberty to think, and of the education out of which is made the material for thought. With such women for the mothers of men, the English-speaking races should rule the world.

As he watched her, Brinkhampton's petty disdain of Saxon the yeoman sank into the background of his consciousness. One could see his countenance expand until he looked superlatively happy, as his delight in her loveliness gained upon him.

And Saxon, sitting beside me with his arms folded, thoughtfully watched her too, but there was a somewhat sad expression on his handsome face. They had been playfellows, but still he saw in Brinkhampton only what was appropriate to her station in the way of a suitor, and there was no bitterness in him. It was what he had all along prepared himself to be resigned to eventually. Brinkhampton himself was not so proudly conscious of the difference of position as Saxon was; but Brinkhampton was accustomed to consider only his own interests in regard to women, and naturally assumed that Saxon was equally inferior.

It was ten miles from Towindard Hall to Greenwood Sound, but the horses seemed to have covered the ground in no time, for it was still early in the afternoon when we halted in a shady lane between the river on our left, seen through a frame of foliage, and a high bank on our right, a green bank dotted with clumps of fern, and crowned with trees, beneath which sheep were quietly browsing. No one would have suspected that we were in the near neighbourhood of the treacherous ocean and a dangerous shore. There was a deep glow as of approaching sunset upon the placid river, a babble of birds in the trees above us, and somewhere unseen, a cock crowed cheerily at intervals. The horses, only refreshed apparently by their ten miles' scamper, pawed the ground impatiently, tossed their heads till the harness jingled, and recognising their stable companions who were already awaiting us under the trees with their saddles on, saluted them with loud neighs joyously.

"We must make tea here, there is plenty of time," said Saxon, as he clambered down.

"Oh, how delightful!" Eugenia exclaimed. "I forgot all about tea. You always remember everything, Saxon." She threw down the reins.

"Come," she said to Brinkhampton, "come and collect sticks."

Brinkhampton went of necessity, but he was not one of those men who readily adapt themselves to any position, and as he picked up the sticks his whole attitude was awkwardly condescending, and he evidently did not agree when Eugenia contended that it was half the fun on these expeditions to do all that kind of thing for one's self. I saw that she observed how he picked up the sticks by their dryest ends, and held them away from him daintily; but her countenance remained unruffled, and I could not tell if she saw anything ludicrous in such extreme fastidiousness. Stooping made Brinkhampton red in the face, and giddy, and he had to stop frequently to recover himself, and always when he did so, he looked about him haughtily as if he were asking nature to be so good as to observe that a Peer of the Realm was picking up sticks.

We soon had a big fire blazing in the shade, and while we were waiting for the kettle to boil, we lolled about on cushions taken from the coach, and by degrees were gained upon by the enchanting day, the heavenly quiet, and the associations of the place, so that insensibly our modern mood slipped from us, the charm of ancient days was on us, and we found ourselves a prey to thoughts of that which is not seen or known, but only felt.

"Is this Greenwood Sound?" Brinkhampton said suddenly.

"Yes," Eugenia answered, "and when I am here I am always overpowered with a strange feeling of remoteness. It is as if my kindred claimed me—not as if they came to me here, but as if they took me to themselves—to their own times. This is a spot which has been specially sanctified by the sins of my ancestors."

Brinkhampton asked her if she were superstitious.

"I don't know," she answered, in a surprised tone. "I never thought about it." Then she reflected a little. "But certainly," she added, "no son of the house has ever succeeded."

"Are these church lands then?" Brinkhampton asked.

"No, the tradition is older than that," she said. " By the way, isn't it evident they worshipped the Evil One of old? Their cursings were so effectual, while their blessings were of such small avail. But, Saxon, tell the tale. You know it best."

"The country folks hereabouts preserve it in ballads," he answered unaffectedly. "They give the vague date of hundreds of years ago, when Towindard Hall was a castle owned by a miserly old earl. He was a direct ancestor of yours, as you know, and he had an only daughter whom he meant to barter for gold to the highest bidder when she should be old enough to marry. She was a girl of magnificent physique, with a spirit as fine as her form and features, and moreover she was dowered, says the legend, with caution, and the gift of silence, so that, when at last her father ordered her to prepare to marry a man she had hardly seen, and was not prepossessed by, she held her peace instead of raising useless objections, and waited until she should know more of him. It does not say that she ever really disliked him, but at that time a man had to have as much physical courage as he has nowadays to have moral courage to recommend him to a girl—"

"A man must have both," Eugenia put in, decidedly.

"Well, at any rate," Saxon pursued, "from what your ancestress saw of Lord Willoughby, her suitor, before they were married, she shrewdly suspected that he was a coward, 'unmeet with me to wed,' as the ballad says; but there was no getting out of the match, she being her father's chattel and entirely at his disposal. She determined, however, that before she settled down for life with the man, she would test his courage just to see who should be master; so she stipulated that on their wedding-day, he should let her drive him from Greenwood Sound (where we are now), to Willoughby Chase (his place), by Towindard Head. He refused her nothing, the ballad says:

> "The day broke cloudy, the wind was high,
> The storm-clouds fought in a murky sky,
> The wild waves whitened the sands with scud,
> The sunset brightened the sky with blood.
> O wild! O wild! Ah, well-a-day!
> Does the bridegroom note that the bride is gay?
> "The chariot stood at the castle door,
> The hinds were holding the horses four,
> The storm wind tosses the horses' manes,
> The bride has gathered the fluttering reins.
> O wild! O wild! Ah, well-a-day!
> Does the bridegroom note that the bride is gay?
>
> "From Greenwood Sound to Willoughby Chase,
> By Towindard Head in a chariot race,
> Four horses racing the rising tide,
> A white-faced bridegroom, a desp'rate bride.
> O wild! O wild! Ah, well-a-day!
> For the gale blows fierce in Towindard Bay.
>
> "'Now, good, my lord, though art pledged to race,
> From Greenwood Sound to Willoughby Chase,
> To race the tide round Towindard Head,
> But methinks thou art frighted, my lord,' she said.
> O wild! O wild! Ah, well-a-day!
> 'Crouch down on your knees at my feet and pray.'

"At Willoughby Chase there was dole that night,
The bride has arrived all scared and white.
And the four black steeds have reached the shore,
But the bridegroom cometh again no more.
O wild! O wild! Ah, well-a-day!
Lord Willoughby sleeps in Towindard Bay."

"She had drowned him then," Brinkhampton exclaimed.

"So it was eventually supposed," Eugenia answered easily. It is customary to assume a modest tone with regard to the crimes committed by our remote ancestors, and not to boast about them on account of their misdeeds, however narrowly they may have escaped hanging, and Eugenia always alluded to this one in the most becomingly casual manner. "She was not suspected of having done so at first, however," she pursued. "It was believed to have been an accident, and so it may have been, for my greatest great-grandmother was evidently one of those people of strongly marked character and independent habits, around whose names all kinds of stories collect by degrees, until at last there are so many that they must have done something notable on every day of their lives in order to accomplish such an amount. By Lord Willoughby's death she became mistress of Willoughby Chase, and as she inherited Towindard also, she was in a powerful position for the times. She married again and became my ancestress, but of her second husband, my ancestor, nothing is known except that there was such a person. He was apparently one of those people who don't count."

"And is that all?" said Brinkhampton.

"No," Eugenia answered, "the most important part is yet to come. According to the story, everything succeeded with my remarkable ancestress during her life, but on her death-bed she was seen to be in sore distress of mind, and at last she sent for a priest, but exactly what she confessed to him was never revealed, only it was observed that, when he left her, his eyes were wild and his cheeks were pale. And it is known that he had laid what he thought to be a curse on one daughter of the family in every generation. A celibate priest naturally did not understand women; he thought property and power would be a bane to us, so he condemned one of us to inherit the estates always, until such time as we should discover how to remove the curse!"

"And you have not done so yet?" Brinkhampton said.

"Nobody has ever tried that I know of," Eugenia answered naively. "It's rather hard on the boys, but if it had not been for the curse, there probably would not have been any property by this time."

"Churchman's justice is peculiar," I interjected. "I can't see upon what principle the unoffending innocents were condemned to death."

"But there was some sense in the penance which the priest prescribed for your ancestress," Saxon pursued. "He condemned her to drive her wild black horses against the rising tide with her cowering bridegroom crouching at her feet forever, or until such time as her troubled spirit should be released by one of her descendants—

> "And so for evermore
> Along the shore
> She hears the swift wild surges roar,
> For evermore she urges
> Hot headstrong steeds to brave the roaring surges.
> With tightened traces
> Pull speed she races—
> And those who ride
> Shall hear their thund'ring rush against the rising tide."

"But has anyone ever heard them?" Brinkhampton objected.

"We all have," I answered, whereupon he looked mystified, because he did not consider me superstitious—nor was he, oh dear no, not a bit!

This broke the spell. The tea was ready, and tea with cream and cakes and ravenous appetites brought us back incontinently to the most sceptical mood of our own day.

"But what exactly are we going to do?" Brinkhampton asked.

"Oh, just race the tide round Towindard Head," Eugenia answered casually. "If we are there first we shall get round easily, and find ourselves near home, but if the sea is before us, it complicates matters. What about the weather, Baldwin? Here in the hollow it seems to be perfectly stagnant."

The old man looked up at the sky, and then out over the river through the gap in the greenery which formed a frame for the shining sluggish water.

"There'll be no sea on to-day, missie," he answered deliberately.

"You're coming with us?" said Eugenia.

"Ah'm certainly comin' wi' you, missie," he answered decidedly.

The servants had had their tea by this time, and were preparing to take back the coach.

We mounted our horses.

"I suppose you can calculate the state of the tide pretty accurately," Brinkhampton remarked as he settled Eugenia in her saddle. I might have been mistaken, but I thought I detected a shade of anxiety in his voice.

"No, that is the difficulty," Eugenia replied. "The weather affects it. Sometimes it is a rushing race-horse, white-crested and impetuous, and sometimes it is a crawling snake, equally swift, you know, but insidious. You are caught before you suspect there is danger."

"I suppose you love the sea," he rejoined, in a tone which affected to be as casual as her own.

"Yes," she answered, "and I also loathe it. I look upon it as a treacherous enemy to be outwitted, and dote upon its changeful beauty all the same."

We were off now, down the winding lane. The green bank was behind us, grey sand-dunes were on either side, ahead was the desolate wide waste of shore, and far out, under a low and leaden sky, little bright sapphire wavelets, scarcely flecked with foam, crisped and broke with baby impotence upon the sand. The scene was solemn in its dreariness, but not depressing. Some suggestions of boundless space are more elevating than the mountains. Away to our right the flat shore shot up suddenly into precipitous cliffs, and these, curving out with a fine sweep seawards, resulted abruptly in the towering promontory which it was our object to ride round. But between us and it there were miles of desolation.

Our horses were now being tried by the ruts of the heavy cart track which formed the only road across the sand-dunes.

"This is slow going," said Eugenia, "but I warn you they will pull like mad the moment we are on firm sand; so sit tight."

The warning was not unnecessary. A few more struggles, then suddenly their feet were free of the heaviness, and, feeling the resistance of the firm sand, they plunged about excitedly, and then set off in a frantic gallop—pitapat, pitapat, pitapat, the hoofs beat rhythmically. We were well away now, with the sea on our left, the land on our right, and on in front, looming gigantic through the haze, Towindard Head—

> "Onward and northward fierce and fleet,
> As if life and death were in it!
> 'Tis a glorious race, a race against time,
> A thousand to one we win it."

The sea-sweet air was wildly exhilarating. Even the horses seemed seized upon by the gladness there is in rapid motion and in windswept spaces. Every face was eager now. I felt I should shout aloud upon the slightest provocation—

> "This ride was ray delight. I love all waste
> And solitary places; where we taste
> The pleasure of believing what we see
> Is boundless, as we wish our souls to be:
> And such was this wild ocean, and this shore
> More barren than its billows."

Our gallop was checked by a sudden wild commotion. I was aware of old Baldwin shouting something, of Saxon spurring on ahead of me, of Brinkhampton's horse floundering, of a scared look on his face, of Eugenia catching his reins, giving her own horse its head, and swinging her heavy whip with sounding slashes. The horses responded gallantly, plunging and straining. I don't know if we all shouted encouragement, but it seemed only an instant till the incident was over, and we were off again, tearing along in a body, having swerved inland considerably. When the pace relaxed, Brinkhampton wiped his forehead. "What was it?" he asked.

"The outer edge of the quicksand," Eugenia answered. "It shifts. The last time it was here where we are now, and I thought we were giving it a wide berth to-day. Forgive me for touching your reins. There was such a racket, I despaired of making you hear, and you were pulling right into it. Look at the horses, poor brutes, how terrified they are? It would be humane to pull them up for a breathing space—" she looked on ahead, then added significantly, "*if there were time.*"

So far we had been keeping a middle course between the sea and shore, but now we began to bear down towards the water. The horses glanced suspiciously this way and that, ready to shy or swerve on the least occasion. They kept their ears pricked too, or laid them back in a nervous way, and were foaming at their mouths; and every now and then they broke out of the steady canter at which we were endeavouring to keep them in order to save them for a big spurt, if necessary, towards the end of the race, into a gallop which would soon have become a wild stampede had we not held them well in hand. But in the midst of these efforts, whilst I was altogether intent upon them, and without the slightest warning, my horse made an awkward stumble, which sent me gracefully circling from my saddle to a safer seat on the sand. Old Baldwin, seeing what was coming, had roared: "Look out!" but not in time to save me.

Brinkhampton, being on in front, did not see what had happened, and his shattered nerves, shaken already by horror of the quicksand, betrayed him. The moment he heard the shout, without waiting to see what was wrong, he let his horse go, and galloped on some distance, leaving us to our fate.

"'is ludship 'e doan't like yer wickstands an' yer ghosteses," old Baldwin chuckled, as he picked me up.

But Brinkhampton had discovered his mistake by this time, and was cantering back to us with a deprecating look on his face like that of a diffident schoolboy who finds he has done the wrong thing and is covered with confusion. The expression suited him, and, being a splendid horseman, he looked so handsome as he approached Eugenia, that I thought with a qualm: "She will pity him."

"My horse is very nervous," he said, apologetically.

She glanced down at the horse's feet, and then looked straight before her without a word, her air of calm indifference being exactly the same as she had worn when Brinkhampton and I joined her after he had been stuck on the cliff, and found her watching the stones she was throwing make ducks and drakes on the water. On this occasion her demeanour so disconcerted Brinkhampton that he lost his head, and contradicted himself as soon as he had spoken.

"I thought it was a signal to double," he said to me.

"No; it was not a signal," I answered, "but a stone which my horse apparently mistook for a bit of seaweed."

We had moved on again, and were close to the water's edge by this time. The monstrous sea, oily and waveless, crawled up in great irregular curves over the shining sand. The horses kept their eyes fixed on the incoming stream in frightened anticipation, and leaned away from it, as if ready to swerve if the horrid thing should touch them. Now and then, so insidious and imperceptible was its oncoming, we found ourselves surrounded, and our startled steeds strained away for the shore, prancing and splashing till they churned the flint-coloured shallows white with foam. A few more minutes would bring us abreast of the great overhanging cliffs, and the space between the sea and shore was narrowing always, so that presently we should be forced up under them. A certain gravity had settled upon us, there was a look of expectation on our faces, and we pulled up abreast of each other involuntarily, Baldwin and all.

"I confess I always feel awed," I said, with an uneasy little cough, but Eugenia did not appear to hear me. She was sitting straight, with her head held high, and her eyes wide open, listening intently.

"Why awed?" Brinkhampton asked.

"The ghosts, my lud," old Baldwin ejaculated.

Brinkhampton looked about him with a superior smile, and certainly anything more unlike a suitable setting as a preparation for ghosts than this slumberous autumn afternoon, with its stagnant tranquillity of sky and sea and shore, could not have been arranged; but the inappropriate is often as astounding as the unexpected.

And now suddenly in the distance, coming apparently from under the cliffs, there arose a dull, muffled, thudding sound. The horses noticed it as soon as we did, and pricked their ears enquiringly. They had been going at an easy canter, but in order to gratify their curiosity they relaxed their pace, and instantly the sound ceased. The sudden silence startled them as a noise might have done, and with one accord they bounded forward, Brinkhampton being nearly unseated by the unexpected move, and instantly the thudding recommenced, drew nearer, and swelled into the unmistakable throb of galloping hoofs on sand. It was as if a troop of cavalry had charged us in the rear and was just upon us to ride us down. The horses broke into a frantic gallop, and Brinkhampton rising to it, turned his head and looked back with straining eyes, first over one shoulder and then over the other; but there was nothing to be seen even when the sound was just upon us, deafening us. It came with a rush, touching us as it were, and that instant it was over. The horses stared right and left, at the same time slackening their pace, and we realised a strange blank as of an empty space in that region of consciousness upon which the thundering hoofs had sounded.

Brinkhampton was the first to speak, after gazing up at the tall cliffs critically: "I suppose it is an echo," he said, looking hard at us each in turn as if he expected us to deny it. "And the legend was probably invented to account for the echo," he added.

"But the echo does not account for the failure of heirs male in my family," Eugenia objected drily.

From this point on, however, there was no time for talk.

"If we're to get round Towindard 'ead we mun ride, missie," old Baldwin decided.

"And if we don't get round?" Brinkhampton asked.

"We must climb the cliff or take our chance with the horses," Eugenia answered quietly. "Baldwin, we lead," she said, and the old man rode on with her on the offside, beaming. Eugenia on the alert, with flushed cheeks and sparkling eyes, her excitement well-contained beneath a steady calm exterior, was lovely to behold in her youth and strength as she passed on in front, and set the pace. It was racing speed now, going against the tide full-tilt. We could measure the rate at which we were going by the lumbering look of the sea-bird's flight above us—

"'Tis a glorious race, a race against time,
    A thousand to one we win it?"

The keen salt air through which we were rushing, meeting us full in the face, had freshened us at first, but now all at once I became aware of a change in it, and quite suddenly, as it seemed to me, the sea-voice sounded muffled. The change in the air was from dry to damp. The gauze veil on my hat was dripping. I looked up to see how far we were from the headland. The headland had disappeared—no, though, that must be it up in the air yonder, up above us in the clouds—no, again. I could see now. I understood. As the tide flowed in, moisture rose to the surface of the sand, making the whole wide expanse into a mirror, and it had seemed at the first glance as if the sky had come down to look at its own reflection in this; but what had deceived me was a light white curtain of mist, drawn up by the heat till it was caught in a cold current of air which condensed it into a fog that was rapidly gathering density and would presently envelop us. I was behind Eugenia, but could see by her attitude that she also was peering into the distance intently, and she raised her heavy whip and held it suspended over her horse's flank.

Baldwin was standing up in his stirrups and keeping his sharp old eyes about him. "Stick to the sea, missie," he commanded in his hoarse voice, "stick to the sea for your life."

We met the mist and plunged into it. There was no fancy work about the horses' paces now. They had buckled-to in sober earnest, with ears laid back and heads stretched out, and anxious eyes that no longer glanced askance at the treacherous water but strained on into the mist as intelligently as our own. It was the snake-sea to-day, swift but deceptive. The fog had gained on the headland by this time; the nearer we approached the less we saw of it.

"For your life, missie, for your life," old Baldwin kept muttering mechanically, and the hoarse growl mingled with the mighty murmur of ocean appropriately: "For your life, missie, for your life."

We were well-mounted, but it had been a long spin and some of it was heavy going, and now the horses began to flag perceptibly. Eugenia swung her whip round her head and brought it down swish relentlessly. The horse responded with a bound, and the others, animated by the effort, followed his example.

"Surely that is the head?" Eugenia cried. We looked up simultaneously. Something certainly loomed black above us.

"Stick to the sea, missie, stick to the sea-side for your life," old Baldwin roared. There were ridges of rock all about here under the cliffs that would have cost us many precious minutes had we come upon them.

Eugenia went boldly on, but we were late. Splash—helter-skelter—the horses were scattering he shallow water now and inclined to baulk; but down came that relentless whip again, right and left, we following the example, and once more the mettlesome brutes responded gallantly. And now there was less helter-skelter and less splash. The leaders were up to their knees. Were we silent? Were we shouting? That last wave washed up to our girths. That last wave was a seventh wave. Count six more slowly. Supposing they are taken off their feet by the next, could they swim with us? Brinkhampton's horse staggered on the slippery bottom which was stony here, mine slipped too—ugh! what a sickening sensation! now he went down, and the water came up cold about me. Ugh, again—splutter! what a ducking!

Silence had settled upon us—the panting silence of suspense. It was touch and go whether the horses would be washed away or not. All at once, however, I noticed a change in the tenseness of Eugenia's attitude. Surely she is bearing away to the right—she is out of the water—we are following—we are splashing through shallows again—are ceasing to splash. The horses find firm footing and start away of their own accord for a final spurt of relief. We are out of the fog, and there is the coach waiting for us. Eugenia pulled up, threw her reins on her horse's neck, dismounted, and stood, smiling and satisfied, but wet through.

"We shall catch our death of cold if we have far to go in these clothes," Brinkhampton exclaimed, impatient of this discomfort.

"Pooh! salt water will do you no harm," Eugenia rejoined.

"That was a near un, missie," old Baldwin observed. "Ah thowt it were all oop wi' us twicest."

"It was one of our best, I think," Eugenia answered, "and I was agreeably surprised, for I was afraid it was going to be tame." She was all animation, and when we had taken our seats on the coach in the same order as before, she addressed Brinkhampton in the bantering tone they used to each other as a rule: "Now tell me," she said, "after this, do you still pretend to offer me in exchange the vitiated air of your great wicked city, and the modest pleasure of a ride in the Row, or of being driven on a coach by way of squalid Hammersmith and pretentious Chiswick to eat without appetite at a tawdry hotel in Richmond?"

VIII. THE NEXT MORNING, early, I was writing in my room upstairs with the windows wide open, when I suddenly became aware of an altercation between Eugenia and Brinkhampton on the lawn below.

They went off together, however, with every evidence of cordial agreement between them; so much so, indeed, that I sat on the window-sill long after they had crossed the lawn and disappeared among the trees, once more weighing the probabilities, and wondering if she would accept him.

When they returned together to lunch, I could see that something had happened, but as they were both flushed and both looked discomfited, I fancied there had only been a rather more serious dispute than usual.

Directly lunch was over, however, Brinkhampton announced that he was going to order his man to pack.

"Are you off then?" I asked.

"Yes, I'm off," he answered doggedly.

"Now why should you go?" Eugenia exclaimed.

"I can only stay here on one condition," he said with severity.

"Well, that is the only condition on which I can't ask you to stay," she answered instantly. "But I do think you are stupid to give up your shooting on that account."

"You don't appreciate my feelings," he said with a hurt air.

"I hope I do," she answered. She rose from the table as she spoke, brushed a crumb from the front of her dress, and quietly left the room.

Then Brinkhampton looked hard and inquiringly at me. "I can't think you have prejudiced her against me," he said.

"I should hope not," was my dry response.

"But have you said anything about me to her?"

"As much as I have said about her to you?"

"Next to nothing, that is—then how does she know?"

"If she does know anything about you, she must have arrived at it by some process of induction," I answered, not able to imagine what she could know.

"Well, I think you might have warned me," he exclaimed, and then began to pace the room with agitated steps.

"I am afraid I have been to blame," I retorted ironically. "It would doubtless have pleased you better if I had told you all I know about her opinions and character, while carefully concealing from her all that I know about yours."

"A girl has no business to have opinions of any kind, she should adopt her husband's when she marries," Brinkhampton ejaculated. "Nothing but mischief comes of women thinking for themselves. She would have accepted me but for her opinions." He reflected a little upon this, frowning portentously, and then broke out again: "I've been regularly taken in! I gave her the credit of being a nice little English country girl, quite uninformed, and here I find her old in ideas already; and, worst of all, advanced. She didn't tell me coarsely in so many words to my face that I'm not good enough for her, but, by Jove! that is what she meant. She says she always thinks of me as a sort of man out of a novel by Ouida. What on earth have you all been doing to let her read such books?"

"It was an old uncle of hers, an ex-guardsman of your own corps, by the way," I rejoined, "who first introduced her to that kind of literature. He used to give Eugenia Ouida's books as they came out, with the emphatic comment, 'She shows 'em up! She shows 'em up!' and Eugenia, after careful study of them, has drawn her own conclusions."

He pondered upon this also for a little, and then resumed: "By Jove! I was astounded! What do you think she said to me, right out plump? 'I have no taste for nursing,' she said, 'and you are so delicate.' 'Delicate!' I exclaimed in astonishment. 'Well, you require to begin your day on wine, you know,' she said. 'I don't require it, I take it because I like it,' I said. 'Oh, then you are self-indulgent,' she rejoined, as quick as thought, 'and if you are so much so now, the weakness will grow upon you to a quite dangerous extent by-and-by, and gout and bad temper will be the order of the day.' She said it lightly, but, by Jove! she meant it."

"Then she has rejected you?"

"Emphatically! Yet she doesn't see why I shouldn't stay and finish the shooting!"

"And why not if it amuses her to have you here?"

He looked at me in tragic disgust. "Would you have me stay here simply for her amusement?" he thundered.

"Certainly," I said. "It is merely a turning of the tables. You came here simply for your own benefit, and in return the least you can do is to stay if it pleases her to ask you."

"You have a nice consideration, both of you, for my feelings!" he exclaimed.

"Your what, Brinkhampton?" I asked, laughing.

He stood before me a moment, trying to annihilate me with a look, and then stalked straight out of the room.

IX. "So you have rejected him," I said when next I saw Eugenia.

She was taken aback at first.

"So he has told you," she ejaculated. "Well, I wonder if he thought I should be mean enough to betray him! I asked him to stay on simply because I didn't want you to suspect that I had had to humiliate him by refusing him. It is hateful to hurt people's feelings. Besides, as a guest, I like him, and, further, it is good for that kind of man to be with ladies."

"Then you are by way of elevating his tastes if possible?"

"Oh, by all means. My principle is to do anything honourable for that kind of man but marry him."

I was silent, and she reflected for a little, then broke out again: "He said I did not appreciate his feelings, but indeed I think I do—debts, difficulties, debilitated nerves, and everything else that went to make up his motive for marrying me. Why, when I engage a servant, he has to have a character."

"Nevertheless, I think he cares for you in his own way. He told me he had found his ideal in you."

"Very likely," she answered. "But before one can feel flattered by such an assertion, it is necessary to know what his ideal is—a nice quiet little thing, I fancy, with lots of money, and no inconvenient intellectual capacity."

I could not help smiling, she had gauged him so exactly.

"But he is not my ideal at all," she pursued. "I want Sir Galahad, and Society provides me with Gawain, or Lancelot at the best, when all my longing is for 'the blameless king.'"

"I wonder where you will find your ideal."

"In Saxon Wake," she answered instantly. "Bit by bit his family have been developing every quality in which my own was deficient. For hundreds of years the two have been living here side by side, ours slowly deteriorating, losing by degrees much of what they possessed, his, by their virtues, as gradually acquiring what we lost. Compare Saxon's father with Uncle Paul, for instance! and Saxon's career with Lord Brinkhampton's! not to mention their respective abilities. Give me him for a husband!"

"Whom?" said Saxon himself, coming round the corner.

"You," she blurted out, turning crimson. "Why don't you care for me, Saxon?" she went on desperately—on the in-for-a-penny-in-for-a-pound principle, I suppose. " Why won't you ask me to marry you? But I know. You will leave me lonely and miserable for all my life just because I am richer than you are." She wrung her hands as she spoke, and the young man, who had stopped short, flushed and turned pale, looking from her to me in confusion.

"I hope he has more sense," I cried, flinging the words at him as I fled.

X. WHEN I RETURNED to the house, there was a carriage at the door, and I found Brinkhampton ready to depart.

"I suppose there is really no chance for me?" he said, in the dubious tone of one who is still venturing to hope.

"No, none," I answered. "Eugenia has just proposed to Saxon Wake, and I left her trying to persuade him to accept her. It seems that he has some scruples on account of the difference of wealth and position."

"Good Lord!" Brinkhampton ejaculated, quite for getting himself. "If this is your modern maiden, then give me a good old-fashioned womanly woman, who knows nothing and cares less so long as you put her in a good position and let her have lots of money. But "—he looked hard at me—"you are joking, surely."

"No, I am not," I said.

"And you approve. I can see you do."

"Yes, I do," I answered, "under the circumstances."

The roar of the rolling spheres, astronomers say, is so tremendous as to be beyond the hearing of our mortal ears; and so the sudden upward impulse of the human race in this our day, as shown in the attitude of women, is beyond the earthbound comprehension of most men. Brinkhampton could conceive of nothing more eligible for a husband than a man of good manners with a fine position. He stood for some seconds looking down at his boots after I had spoken as if considering, but nothing came of it except another withering glance, the last token with which he favoured me—poor fellow, as Eugenia said.

We were standing beside a table in the hall on which his covert coat lay, and now he picked it up, put on his hat, took one last look round as if bidding farewell to the comfortable possessions he had been so confident of making his own, then walked straight out, got into the carriage without another word, and was driven away.

And now I hear he says the most unpleasant things about myself and Mrs. Saxon Wake, but happily Eugenia's maternal duties are too all-engrossing to allow her to trouble herself about idle gossip from that section of society which, as her Uncle Paul maintains, "Ouida shows up."

Knowing the curious fatality which had befallen the sons of her family ever since that legendary curse was pronounced upon them, I had a horrid qualm one day as I sat watching her playing with her baby-boy.

"He looks strong enough," slipped from me inadvertently.

Eugenia smiled.

"You are thinking about the curse," she said. "I have thought a great deal about it myself since this young gentleman arrived, and I believe I see the mistake we women have all made in the choice of our husbands. It is a universal mistake. We admired mere animal courage in a man which is only one form of courage, instead of requiring moral courage, which includes every other kind—until I came. But I chose my husband for his moral qualities."

"Then perhaps you have—"

"I am sure I have," she concluded. "I have removed the curse unawares."

The Yellow Leaf

Sarah Grand

From "Our Manifold Nature" 1894

Part I.

> "For if they do these things in a green
> tree, what shall be done in the dry?"

I. "There will be no one to see you off to-day, as I cannot go myself," my mother said; "but I suppose if I send you to the station in the carriage you will be able to manage; and, now that you are out, the sooner you learn to look after yourself the better."

"All right," I replied confidently, under the impression that I had very little to learn. And so it happened that, on this particular occasion in my early girlhood, I found myself, with the most delightful sense of importance, travelling from London seawards, alone. The sensation was more than agreeable—it was ecstatic. On the way to the station I felt as if I had never been in a carriage before. I was looking at life from a new point of view, and the people in the streets seemed to see me as I saw myself—at least I fancied that their eyes expressed a different feeling for me from any that had ever shone on me before; but I did not try to translate it. Being pleased and happy myself, it seemed only natural that a pleased and happy expression should come into every face that was turned towards me.

Having arrived at the station, found my train, and secured a seat, I began to loiter up and down the long platform, ostensibly watching the people, but really, with the happy conceit of youth, absorbed in myself, as it appears to me now; yet it was not altogether conceit, but rather the blissful absence of that sense of comparison which comes later on with chastening effect to show us our own unimportance. The sudden sense of freedom had revealed me to myself all out of focus, as it were, and magnified, as objects appear at first to one who has just recovered his sight; and I believe if I had done a portrait of myself at that moment I should have made myself seven feet high.

But pride goeth before a fall, and I was brought up out of this happy state with a jerk which effectually upset the dignity of my demeanour. I had perceived that the train was in motion, and it flashed through my mind that it was being inconsiderate enough to depart without me. As it was the last one in the day that would suit my purpose, I made a desperate dash for a carriage door, and scrambled in, regardless of the howling officials on the platform who would have hindered me. In doing so I became aware of exactly the same performance taking place at the farther end of the compartment; it was as if I had caught a flying glimpse of myself in a mirror as I jumped on to the footboard, opened the door, and swung myself in, after the deliberate manner peculiar to guards on the Underground. But, as often happens, although I had seen the thing done, the fact did not rise from my sub-consciousness to the surface of my thoughts, in order to present itself for my consideration, for some time after I had taken my seat.

The train slid out of the dingy station, and now everything was of interest. I even strained my eyes to read the advertisements paraded on blank brick walls, corners of squalid houses, parapets and arches of railway bridges, any- and everywhere, till my brain reeled.

But then came a glimpse of the river. The unpolluted summer air streamed in upon me. The summer sunshine, unthinned by smoke, lit up the landscape, sparkled on the water, brightened the blue of the sky, whitened the clouds, reddened the roofs, intensified the green, and flooded my whole soul with another kind of joy in life, very different from that which I had just been experiencing. There had been excitement in the crowd, but here alone there was supreme content.

It was a torrid day; but Fate had befriended me, for it was a cushionless third-class compartment I had stormed, all open and airy, and also empty, as I at first supposed; but in this I was mistaken. There had been nobody visible to begin with, but, on looking across after a while, I was surprised to see a pair of bright dark eyes just appearing above the backs of the seats, at the farther end of the compartment. These eyes were fixed upon me in a confident way; and involuntarily I felt, the moment they met mine, that a flash of intelligence had passed between us. The immediate consequence was, that the owner of the eyes, a lanky, dark girl, got up, fixed a struggling bull pup under her arm, where she held it firmly in spite of its kicks and yelps and snaps, clambered clumsily over the backs of the seats from her end of the compartment to mine, regardless of any display she might make of lean legs by the way, and sat down opposite to me.

"Two's company," she remarked oracularly.

"Quite so; but you were two to begin with," I answered.

"Counting the bull pup," she said, drawing the creature from under her arm as she spoke. "Isn't he a beauty?" She held him up by the forelegs, and shook him playfully, addressing him the while in tender tones: "Look at um's chin, and um's legs how um bows; and look at um's werry magnificent nose!"

But the puppy, evidently not appreciating these compliments, began again to kick and growl and snap impatiently, exercises which drew from his delighted mistress assurances that "he *was* a game un, den!" as she settled him comfortably upon her lap. He was already a formidable-looking creature, a brindle of exceptional beauty, judged, of course, by his own standard of excellence.

"I bought him," the young lady proceeded, "to draw Aunt Marsh. I want to make her believe that the outcome of Woman's Eights is bull pups. But now I'm beginning to love him—a beauty, den!—for his own sake. What a nuisance it is metaphors will mix! I was just going to remark that Aunt Marsh is the kind of bull you must take by the horns if you would get on with her; and that's what I mean, only it isn't quite right, somehow. Now, my mother is sixty thousand times cleverer than Aunt Marsh, yet she gives in to her—they're sisters-in-law, you know—but I'm a generation in advance of my mother, thank goodness!"

"I ought to tell you," I observed, "that I believe I know your Aunt: Lady Marsh, is she not?"

She looked at me with a pitying smile. "Yes, that's the person," she answered. "But, now, do you suppose that I'm quite such an idiot as to express myself so freely to a stranger of whom I know nothing?"

"Well, then, you have the advantage of me, for I am quite sure I have never seen you before, nor have I ever heard of anything like you."

"Anything like me! Now, that's delicious. But you mean who am I? I can't abide that roundabout way of asking who a body is. But I'll tell you who I am, just because you're not egotistical."

"How have you discovered that I'm not egotistical?" I asked.

"Because you thought first of me rather than of what concerned yourself. Most people would have wanted to find out what I knew about them, and until I told them they wouldn't have taken any interest in me."

"But you haven't told me—"

"Oh, I'm Adalesa Shutt," she interrupted offhand. "Adalesa Shutt-up is the form it generally takes with the impolite. I may mention that my parents are responsible for the name. They still survive."

There was a pause after this, during which she hugged her brindle bull dog absently, with her dark eyes fixed on a far-away point of the horizon.

While under the influence of her bright, sharp, slangy manner as she talked, I had supposed her to be about fifteen. She wore her dress short, and her hair hanging down her back in a thick plait, as girls of that age generally do; but now, as she sat silently contemplative, she looked older.

"But why should you 'draw' your aunt, as you call it?" burst from me involuntarily, as I watched her.

She turned upon me with her infectious smile. "It is the only possible attitude for me in her abode," she said—"a don't-care-came-to-be-hanged kind of attitude. I daren't be docile or affectionate, because I have to keep her at a distance, otherwise she would give me good advice. She did make me suffer the first time I stayed with her!"

"But—"

"Oh, yes, I know all that," she put in impatiently. "She's the kindest woman in the world, you were going to say. Everybody says so. But just you observe! I would rather have a termagant to fight. One wouldn't be afraid of hurting her. But these soft, sweet women bruise so easily, they make you suffer all round. There are your nerves and your better nature both on the alert, while your good sense is being outraged, and your worst self is fighting to be up in opposition. Heaven help me from having to encounter a feather-bed woman!"

"But how did she make you suffer?"

"Oh—I'll show you when we arrive."

"How do you know I am going there?" I asked in surprise.

Again she looked at me and laughed, but only repeated: "I'll show you when we get there. Mind you, I don't suffer now."

The train pulled up at a little country station as she spoke, and we both alighted. An open carriage was waiting outside for us.

"Ah, there is my friend Barkins," Adalesa exclaimed, meaning the coachman. "*I'm* going to drive, Barkins—Barkins bein' willin'," she added aside to me.

"You and John must go inside," she further insisted, "because Mademoiselle here only sits on the box. She always travels third class, and sits on the box. Those are her ladyship's orders. I have them here in my pocket"—and she slapped that receptacle.

The coachman hesitated, and looked at me as if for confirmation, but I preserved my gravity. The misstatement Adalesa had made with regard to my usual mode of travelling led me to infer that the rest of the story was rather more facetious than accurate; but I would not have betrayed her for the world. I wanted to see what next.

The coachman slowly descended from his box, keeping a wary eye on Adalesa all the time, as if he were seeking a sign for his guidance, or suspected firearms. As he descended on the one side, however, she scrambled up on the other, and when she had seated herself he handed her the reins. I had followed her on to the box, so that there was nothing now but for him and the footman to get into the carriage.

"You'd better put the luggage in too," Adalesa suggested; and it was with a look of relief that the men complied. "Otherwise," she whispered to me, "any one meeting the carriage, and seeing you and me on the box, driving the servants, might have mistaken us for a travelling lunatic asylum."

"Not such a very great mistake, perhaps, after all," I ventured.

"Oh, my dear, speak for yourself," she promptly rejoined; "as for me, there's a method, you know."

She put the bull pup between her feet as she spoke, and tightened the reins; and then we were off—not at a wild gallop, as I quite expected, but at that rapid, exhilarating trot at which only a good whip can keep a good pair of horses. I understood the coachman's easy acquiescence better now. It was evident that the girl was accustomed to drive. She had that negligent look and attitude, and apparently careless way of holding the reins, which betoken mastery of the art. The road itself she scarcely seemed to see. Her eyes wandered away from it on all sides, and at that moment one would have said they were dreamy eyes, seeking sharp contrasts of sunshine and shadow less than mystical effects of dimness and distance.

The drive left impressions in my mind of a dusty road with heavy frondage of ferns by the wayside, all drooping, as though wearied and reposing from the ardent summer heat. Then there came a fertile land well wooded; the sheen of a copper beech; low hills lifting a belt of sombre pines up to the azure of the sky; the grey-white wool of sheep against the green of grass; the reflection of indolent cattle standing ankle-deep in a pool; the heavy foliage on overhanging boughs; bracken on the banks, and wild flowers everywhere. Adalesa pointed out two objects of interest with her whip: "Those chimneys there in the wood—you can see the smoke above the trees—that is the house. And there, beyond, don't you see? that shining line, that is the sea—the sea!" She drew in her breath as if the very word were a joy to her. But presently she burst out again in her usual way:

"I should think you feel like a figure in a farce," she said, on seeing me glance behind at the servants sitting solemnly with folded arms and their backs to the horses, opposite our trunks, which arrogantly occupied the other seat.

Then we entered the Chase, and began to catch glimpses of a great house among the trees. Some places have an aspect of self-denial impressed upon every feature; as you approach they seem to insist that you shall observe the economies they have had to practise; but here it was just the opposite. There was a self-indulgent, spick-and-span, affluent air about everything.

"Oh!" Adalesa exclaimed, "I begin to feel feather bedding about, don't you? Nasty unwholesome stuffy thing, feather bedding. Aunt Marsh is by way of softening me, rubbing off the rough edges, don't you know. Just you watch!"

II. Lady Marsh must have heard the crunch of carriage wheels as we drew up at the door, for she came hurrying down to meet us; but the men-servants had hopped out alertly, and we ourselves had descended from the box before she appeared, so that I doubt if she ever knew how we had come.

"Do come in, dears!" she exclaimed. "Come to the drawing-room and have some tea. Evangeline is out. She will be so sorry. She had to go for a ride, but of course she expected to be back in time, only one can't always calculate. Dear children! I am so glad to see you. Why, you seem to have grown, Adalesa. You are certainly taller and—and slimmer."

"Longer and lankier," Adalesa translated cheerfully.

"But isn't your dress just a little short, dearest, for your age?" Lady Marsh ventured in the gentlest way, when we were seated. She was known as "a *sweet* woman," "one of those whom it is restful to recall"; and I was not at all pleased to find that that seed of corruption, the trick of absurdly associating her with feather beds, had taken root in my mind; but it had, and there it remains.

"Long dresses!" Adalesa ejaculated: "no, thank you! I know what is expected of long dresses."

"Dignity, is it not, dear?" her aunt ventured, with a deprecating smile.

"Yes," Adalesa groaned; "and dignity, they say, is a mysterious carriage of the body to cover defects of the mind."

Lady Marsh sat down at the tea-table, and began to pour out tea. "But, you see, dear, men say such things," she replied, in her gentle way.

"Ah—men!" Adalesa drawled. "You see, I haven't made up my mind to like men yet—*a* man, perhaps, eventually—but *men!* too conceited, you know."

"Dear child! what do *you* know about men?"

"Absolutely nothing," was the candid rejoinder; "and that's why I wear short dresses. I want to study man, and he only shows himself to short frocks. He's off guard with them. But I'll find him out! My angles fit me for the task. Thank heaven for my angles! No man who looks at me will think of me as a young lady, that most awful of human weaknesses."

"I don't like to hear you speak in that flippant way, dear," her aunt deprecated. "The man is the head of the woman, you know."

"Yes, sometimes," said Adalesa, judicially; "and sometimes he isn't, because the woman is a long way ahead of him. But the rule is much of a muchness, I believe."

"Well, then, it would be a case of two heads are better than one in a household," her aunt answered, good-humouredly.

"Or too many cooks spoil the broth—you never know," came the ready response. "But where's my pup?" she broke off; then rushed from the room, exclaiming that she'd forgotten him.

"That child's cleverness is quite phenomenal," Lady Marsh remarked when she had disappeared. "But, oh dear, it is all so terrible—so very wrong-headed, you know! And"—stooping over to speak in an undertone, as if the matter were not quite delicate—"I am afraid it is all my poor sister's fault. She is so sadly what they call 'advanced'—woman's rights, the suffrage, short hair, and all that, you know."

Lady Marsh spoke in a confidential tone, very flattering to a young girl from a woman of her age and station, and also flattering in that it was natural to infer from it that she thought I had been brought up in a superior manner.

Adalesa returned with the bull pup under her arm.

"Isn't he *sweet*?" she demanded, putting him down, and making him run towards her aunt.

"No!" Lady Marsh exclaimed, drawing her skirts together lest he should touch her—"anything but sweet. Oh!—do take him away! How could you bring such a dreadful creature here?"

"Dreadful creature!" Adalesa repeated in an injured tone; then picking up her grotesque pet she hugged him like a mother whose babe has just been insulted. "And I *thought*—Well, if it is *womanly* to be so hard-hearted, I'd rather *not* be womanly." She tossed her head haughtily when she had spoken, and managed to look both hurt and offended.

"My dear child," Lady Marsh cried in consternation, "what have I done? You don't expect me to like that dreadful creature? I should be ashamed to have it seen about the house. Who ever heard of a gentlewoman petting such a—"

Adalesa uttered a little scream. "Don't—don't say nasty things about him. I shall hate—*any one*—who doesn't appreciate him." She drew herself up, glanced at me, and walked with dignity out of the room.

"Well!" Lady Marsh exclaimed for the second time. "Now, you see, my dear, what comes of this nonsense—taking women out of their proper sphere and all that!"

"Do you mean," I began, "that you think a fondness for bull pups—" But here I checked myself, for I perceived that I was inadvertently playing into the hands of the wicked Adalesa.

On my way upstairs to dress for dinner, I discovered that young person's dark head inserted in a doorway, round which she was peering. "Come in and kiss my pup," she said, persuasively, looking at me with languishing eyes.

"Tell me," I said, ignoring this last impertinence, "Tell me how much of your late misconduct was by way of 'drawing' your aunt, and how much was—"

"Innate cussedness?" she suggested.

"Innate cussedness," I gravely repeated.

"Oh—you pays your money, *et cætera*," she answered easily. "But I'm dressed and you're not," she proceeded; "and you're late. Let me go to your room and help you."

I led the way, smiling a little to myself as I pictured the sort of help I thought I might expect from her; but I soon found I was utterly mistaken in my surmise. I had imagined her awkward and inefficient, but found her deftness itself, and, what is more, she was kind. It was loving service that she did me when she laughed at some inartistic arrangement of ornaments I had devised for my hair, threw the artificial things aside, and cleverly replaced them with fresh and fragrant flowers. She certainly did her best to make the most of me, but all the time how she talked!

"When I first saw you to-day I thought you were older than I am," she said, "but it seems you are younger. You say such wise things, though, and look so grave, it's easy to be mistaken. But now I see you are only a babe with a big head, and you want a lot of attention. You'll have to go through a period of feather-bedasia, and you'll suffer; but don't be disheartened. Just do as I do. Be vulgar, buy a bull pup, and chatter."

"I don't in the least see what I'm to suffer from," I protested. "Your aunt is charming."

"Yes," she rejoined with a groan; "didn't I warn you that she was?"

"And as for your cousin Evangeline—"

"Now, stop," she interrupted. "I won't let you commit yourself to *that* stupid fallacy. Evangeline isn't charming. I am the reaction from feather-bedasia; she is the consequence of it; and she's a pig."

"I don't agree with you at all," I answered decidedly; "and I should think I know as much about her as you do, for we were at school together; and she was most popular with all the girls."

"Oh, yes," Adalesa answered, imitating her aunt. "She has such pretty manners, as Aunt Marsh says, 'so gentle, so refined, so unaffected'—a whole string of adjectives, a set formula that has been flung at me—no, I should say, *gently insisted upon* for my benefit so often that I am not likely to forget it. And then she always promised to be a beauty, I suppose, which must have added greatly to her *prestige* with girls at school. But all the same, she's a pig. Why wasn't she here to receive us to-day?"

"Her mother said she had had to ride—"

"Her mother ought to know better than to excuse her. It was a fine day, and Evangeline thought it would be more amusing to go for a ride than to come in the carriage to meet us; so she went, and she has not yet returned; and that is Evangeline all over. Oh, I know her! And so would you if you'd ever been here before. Have you, by the way?"

"I thought you knew all about me! You seemed to say so in the train to-day."

"I knew your name and address, for I read them on the luggage you were looking after when you came into the station," she answered, with charming candour. "I saw you peacocking about as if you were somebody, and, as your belongings were deposited under my eyes, I had the curiosity to look and see. If I hadn't known that you were coming here you wouldn't have had the honour of making my acquaintance so early in the day, for, although free with my friends, I am not in the habit of picking up any goodness-knows-who for a travelling companion."

"Aren't you?" I said in surprise. "I should have thought—"

"You would have thought!" she exclaimed. "You innocent babe! You haven't learnt to think yet. But you are very entertaining. I nearly missed my train watching you. You were so smily and pleased with yourself and everybody else, anybody could see it was the first time you'd ever been on your own hook. My, what a blush! It's running all down your back. Well, forgive me! I didn't mean to wound your pride. But you're too sensitive, my dear—as sensitive as you're simple, and as transparent. Those who run might read your every emotion; and that would be rapid reading too, for you suffer from a singular variety of emotions in a short time."

"You seem to be a singularly acute young person," I observed, bridling.

"Well, yes," she rejoined, with unvarying cheerfulness, "I am sharp, very." She stood off as she spoke to see the effect of a big bow she had pinned on my dress; adding, as she looked, with her head on one side, "So you have never been here before?"

"No," I answered. "Your aunt was a friend of my mother's, long ago, before either of them was married; but they hadn't met for years until last season, when Evangeline and I left school, and came out; and then they renewed their acquaintance. They agreed that Evangeline and I mustn't consider our education finished simply because we had left school; and as Evangeline is an only child, Lady Marsh entreated my mother to let me come here for awhile to work with her. My mother is great on the question of education. She says she has suffered all her life long from having had hers curtailed, and she is determined therefore that her daughters shall have every advantage that her sons have. If we are not clever enough to profit there will be no harm done; and if we are, she expects us to be thankful that we were allowed to experiment and see what we could do, instead of being kept ignorant in deference to a mere theory that we have no mental capacity. But of course we are not coerced. Since I left school I have been allowed to follow my own inclinations, and I have chosen to be taught the same things that my brothers are studying."

"Gracious, how clever the child talks!" Adalesa exclaimed in her irrepressible way. "It's just like a book.

Perhaps you learnt it by heart. I begin to suspect you have a mind. What a terrible thing! But, anyway, what a blessing it is you met me! A few years more, and you would have been unendurable." She stood off again, with her arms akimbo, and contemplated me from this new point of view, derisively at first, but by degrees her face softened. "And so you have come here to work with Evangeline, you innocent babe!" she said humorously. "You must be clever. Only a very clever person would have done such a stupid thing—a book-clever person I mean, not a world-clever person. It isn't human to be up to everything, and your world-clever people are all out of it in literature, but your book-clever people fail in their knowledge of life. Now, do you really suppose that Evangeline will keep up anything but showy accomplishments? And even those she will only do superficially,—a little music, a little drawing, rather more French because of the naughty books, which she reads regularly, but never leaves lying about, for

Evangeline is wise in her generation—though not wise enough to conquer her amateurishness, that curse of our sex—an amateur, that's what she is, a cunning amateur imperfect in everything, one of those, admired for their beauty and despised for their folly, who bring ridicule upon us all. Yet you believe in her! Yah, Simple Sincerity! Child of Light! Hot water, that's what's in store for you here—perpetual hot water. You'll always be putting your foot in it."

"You encourage me," I said.

"Don't mention it," she answered.

III. HAVING DRESSED ME to her satisfaction, much as a nurse does a child without consulting it, Adalesa made me a deep reverence, offered me her arm, and conducted me downstairs in the most gentlemanly manner. She had quite taken me under her wing by this time, and was prepared to pet and patronise me; but somehow I did not resent her assumption of superiority, for her mind was more mature than mine was, and I had to yield of necessity to her force of character, having no strength of my own at that time to oppose to it.

"What a lovely old house!" I exclaimed, on our way to the drawing-room.

"Yes, it is like Uncle Henry," she answered—"big, solid, comfortable, strong, warm, and good. He's early English himself, and splendid. You'll see!"

He was alone in the drawing-room when we entered, in appearance a typical English country gentleman of the best kind, standing on the hearthrug with his back to the fireplace in the typical attitude. He received us both most kindly, but with few words, contenting himself with looking from one to the other with a benign smile on his face, as if he were sorting our separate attractions, comparing and approving of us.

"That pig, Evangeline, has not been near us yet," Adalesa grumbled. "It's pretty bad manners to me, but it's downright rude to—"

The door opened as she spoke, and Evangeline- herself, all in white tulle, floated towards us, exclaiming: "*So* sorry. I was afraid you would think me rude "—she clasped her hands towards me with a little entreating gesture—"but, oh, pray don't. I really *have* an excuse."

"Let's hear what it is, then," Adalesa answered bluntly.

"My horse—I rode too far," she commenced, stammering.

"That's no excuse," Adalesa interrupted.

"Dear, do excuse me," Evangeline said to me; and when I found her so sweetly apologetic I did excuse her at once, and, moreover, felt angry with Adalesa for making such a scene, although the moment before, while under her exclusive influence, I had agreed that Evangeline was rude. Now, however, with Evangeline there to delight my eyes and soothe my senses with her gentleness and grace, I could not believe anything of her that was not altogether lovely and adorable.

"You may say what you like," Adalesa added; "but you have committed a breach of hospitality, and for the honour of the family I take upon myself to reprove you."

"Thanks," Evangeline said, smiling with unruffled sweetness.

Sir Henry sat down in an easy chair, fixed his eyes on some ferns in the grate, and looked as if he had not heard; but when Adalesa went presently and lounged on the arm of his chair, with her elbow on his shoulder, he took her hand and caressed it gently.

Lady Marsh came into the room just then, smiling amiably as usual, and dressed in an opulent manner.

"Adalesa, *dear*" she said: "do move away. You will make your uncle quite hot."

Adalesa languidly complied, and Sir Henry leant back in his chair and looked up at the ceiling. His silence struck me as significant. He seemed to be, either by way of acquiescing in, or of utterly ignoring the sayings and doings of the ladies of his family, a singularly indifferent or singularly neutral person; and I wondered if he always let Lady Marsh decide whether he was too hot or not, and that sort of thing.

There were a few good pictures in the dining-room, and after dinner he showed them to me, and told me anecdotes, also, about some family portraits that hung in the hall, and some ancient armour. The house was several centuries old, with a long, unbroken family history, which was illustrated by most of its contents. The old carved cabinets, and everything else in the way of ornament, had their associations, and even the furniture, some of it, had a history attached to it, to which I listened with an honest interest that satisfied Sir Henry. Lady Marsh and Evangeline had remained at table discussing the details of a dinner-dress they had seen somewhere; but Adalesa went with us, clinging to her uncle's arm with both hands.

"I would have you observe that there are no meaningless feminine fripperies here," she cried. "This has been the cradle of a sturdy race; and it looks like it. I'm one of the race," she added, laughing up at her uncle.

"Dear child!" Lady Marsh exclaimed, coming out of the dining-room at that moment, "don't hang on your uncle so; you will tire him." Then to me, in her amiable way: "This is but a bare old place at present, but now that Evangeline is old enough to take an interest in it, we must see what can be done."

"Oh, dear!" Adalesa groaned; "if Aunt Marsh and Evangeline are to desecrate it, the good old oak and ebony will be disguised in down cushions and dimity in no time."

"Dear, is that quite respectful?" Lady Marsh exclaimed.

"No; nor would it be respectful for an alien to alter anything here," Adalesa rejoined doggedly.

"I am afraid, dear, your uncle spoils you," Lady Marsh said in her gentlest way, and then swept on to the drawing-room, arm-in-arm with Evangeline. At the door she looked back over her shoulder, and said to Sir Henry: "Don't make that child do too much, dearest. She has had a journey, you know."

"Which child?" he asked in an undertone, looking from one to the other, as soon as the drawing-room door was shut.

"Neither," Adalesa said, scornfully.

"Then take an arm each, my dears," he rejoined, almost in a whisper, "and we'll see what there is to be seen."

From which I perceived that this benign-looking gentleman, seemingly so yielding, was in reality a bold, bad man, capable of opposition, who had put himself in my power; and I slipped my hand through his arm, and smiled up at him confidently, just as Adalesa, on the other side, was doing. He beamed down upon us both, and led us away to the library, where he lived as a rule when he was not out of doors; and there he showed us miniatures, arms, and ancient gems of his ancestors, who seemed to fill the great comfortable room as he talked about them, and to be nearer to him than the wife and daughter, with their marvellous charms of manner, whose tastes and interests were all so modern, of the Society kind, so far removed, if not so utterly opposed, to everything he cherished.

IV. EVANGELINE HAD A sitting-room of her own, a sunny south room, and here we girls were to work. We settled down to it next day, and during the morning Lady Marsh looked in, "just to see how you are getting on, dears! And what are you doing?" meaning me.

"Mathematics," I answered.

"Oh, dear!" she exclaimed. "You must excuse me, dear child, but is it nice for a young lady to study such a very masculine subject? A girl's manner, you know, should be so very different. The woman's sphere is to refine and elevate man."

"But do mathematics make one's manners masculine?" I asked in alarm. I was diffident in those days, as became my age, and the least shade of disapproval made me unhappy.

"Well, they have not done so as yet in your case, dear child," Lady Marsh answered, with infinite tact. "But still, you know, dear, they are not womanly pursuits. You will not be fit for the duties of wife and mother by-and-by if you injure your constitution now. I know your mother's idea, but I cannot agree with her, and I often tell her I am sure she would not now be the dear, sweet, *womanly* woman she is, if she had been taught these new-fangled notions as a girl. I cannot think it is right for young ladies to be educated like their brothers, and go to the university and all that nonsense, getting such ideas! I don't believe that a woman's mind is inferior to a man's, you know—far from it; and, in fact, in some things"—she looked round and lowered her voice—"there can be no doubt as to which is the superior sex, only it doesn't do to say so, men make such remarks. But, as to professions for women, and that sort of thing, why, fancy *me* a professional woman! Evangeline, *dearest*, put your French away, that's a good child, and get a story book. I am sure you have done enough for to-day."

When she had spoken she patted my shoulder kindly, smiled on us all, and left the room.

"Now see what you have brought on yourself, with your mathematics!" Adalesa exclaimed, her dark eyes dancing mischievously. "Aunt Marsh knew your mother's idea, and I believe she's got you down here to cure you of it. That's the sort of kind thing she's celebrated for. She suspected mathematics this morning, and came in prepared."

Evangeline, who had risen with cheerful alacrity to put her books away, in obedience to her mother's suggestion, turned now from the bookshelf at which she was standing dipping into a novel, and looked at Adalesa indignantly. "I don't think it is nice of you," she said, "to speak like that about my mother. She must know better than either you or I. Why, just think! You will own that we were intended to be healthy and happy—that we require to be so in order to be equal to such duties as we have to perform—and how can we be so if we go and injure ourselves with work we are not fit for? It's only common-sense, if you will think. Men were clearly intended to do all the hard work, and keep us in comfort, and screen us from anything objectionable. *My* ambition is to be a *womanly* woman. I think mamma is quite right."

By this time I was feeling very uncomfortable. To be thought unwomanly seemed to me as dreadful as to be thought wicked; but yet I felt there was something wrong somewhere, for I could not see sex in a subject of study. Why should one be masculine and another feminine? Surely there is no sex in mind? The question of what we shall be taught should be answered by finding out for us what we have the ability to learn. If a boy has a genius for cooking and a girl the faculty for medicine, he must be a sorry educator who takes pains to pervert either of them from their natural bent, with the inevitable result that the girl becomes a bad cook and the boy an indifferent doctor. Happily this time-honoured idiotcy is dying out, but, like all conventions based on prejudice, it will linger long in secluded minds—where the fact that *he* as a man and *she* as a woman is indication enough for both general and special purposes of education, and will be until preceptors are made to suffer at the hands of the bad cooks, indifferent doctors, and other mistakes they have helped to produce—commonplaces, by the way, known well to all of us, but by how few applied!

Evangeline had departed, and Adalesa was watching me with a grin on her intelligent countenance. "There is no resisting a feather bed, is there?" she asked. "Aunt Marsh is on the war path, I think, this morning. She'll go and order Uncle Henry's day till she's feather-bedded all the comfort out of it. Let's go and see!"

She jumped up, seized me by the arm, and dragged me away to the library, where we found Sir Henry slowly pacing up and down, deep in thought. He looked from one to the other of us almost sadly when we entered, but smiled indulgently at Adalesa when she dropped my arm and, seizing his in her energetic way, squeezed it between both hands, and then worked it up and down like a pump handle, as if she could get what she wanted out of him so.

"Tell us about education," she demanded.

"Ah—education," he answered. "Your aunt has just been talking to me about education. She thinks you have been foolishly over-educated, and that has made you rough; and she fears for this little lady here"—meaning me— "she is anxious about you, my dear. She has a great loving heart, and every girl is her daughter. She wants you all to *have a good time*." He used this last expression apologetically.

"And so do you," Adalesa exclaimed, on the defensive. She had dropped his arm, and stood frowning intently, and biting one of her fingers between her words. "But, isn't it nonsense? Of course I'm rough. I'm rough on purpose. I'm rougher here than anywhere. If I lived like Evangeline, in cotton wool, I should grow flabby; and she says it's education! When she sees, too, that it hasn't had that effect in this other most notable case"—looking at me. "Tell me all over again about education, Uncle Henry. I'm all ruffled. I want to know."

Sir Henry began to walk up and down the room with his hands behind him. "What we learn is but a small part of education," he said, and it sounded as if he were reflecting aloud. "It is what we think of things, not what we know of them—our opinions—that affect our conduct. If you learn the multiplication table by heart, and merely remember that you know it, the knowledge will have no consequence one way or the other; but if you are taught to think that because you know the multiplication table you ought to be a very high-principled person, you'll find yourself insensibly seeking to live up to that idea. If, however, on the other hand, you hear continually that a knowledge of the multiplication table must be lowering in effect upon the character—if it is insinuated that your taste will be corrupted by it and your manners coarsened, until the notion that such. a consequence is inevitable takes possession of your mind in spite of yourself—then it is only too probable that that will be the case."

"Now, that is true!" Adalesa exclaimed, "and here are we two in evidence of the fact."

Sir Henry stopped a moment to look at us, and then resumed his walk. "There's a great deal of cant rife just now on the subject of women and their education," he observed, "most of which, being summed up, amounts to a firm conviction that a half-educated girl, a creature who has learnt to live for the pleasure of the moment, to love for the joy of loving, and to marry in order to secure as many of the good things of this world as she can, is in every way a suitable and congenial companion for an educated man, and an admirable specimen of the 'woman's-sphere-is-home' woman. A toy—that's what the creature is, an unreasonable and illogical toy, neither reason nor logic having entered into the curriculum of that kind of 'womanly woman,' it having been supposed that a large establishment is most admirably managed by a mistress whose reasoning powers have never been cultivated, and a young family best brought up on the superstitious practices solemnly confided in mysterious whispers by Mrs. Gamp—"

The windows stood wide open, and Lady Marsh looked in at one of them. "Dearest children!" she cried, "don't you see how fine it is? You ought to be out. Adalesa, what are you worrying your uncle about? I am sure he doesn't want you here at this time of day."

V. IN THE AFTERNOON I went out for a ride with Adalesa. Evangeline would not accompany us. She had a packet of sweets in her pocket, and was deep in an entrancing novel by that time, from which she could not be induced to separate herself for the rest of the day, and on the next she had a bad headache. "Which just shows," her mother protested, with gentle emphasis, "how very necessary it is to supervise a young girl's studies, and what it would be if the dear child were being brought up, as too many young ladies are nowadays, alas! learning quite *masculine* matters: it is really dreadful!"

Adalesa looked older and better in her riding dress than I had yet seen her, and perhaps some consciousness of this had its effect upon her manner. So far, while looking like a child, she had talked like a cynical worldly woman; but now, as she took her horse skilfully down a difficult rutty lane, her face fanned by the balmy country air, heavy with odours of full-blown flowers, and at the same time freshened by the near neighbourhood of the sea, there came a far-away look into the girl's eyes, an expression of yearning tenderness which culminated, as seemed most natural, in a long-drawn sigh.

The lane we rode in was a steep by-way—a short cut to the shore, she said—only just wide enough for our two horses abreast, and so uneven that we had to look well to their going. On either hand green banks, bedecked with foxglove and harebell, rose high above us and before us, making the winding way look like a *cul de sac*, and shutting out all view save that of the sky above us, a radiant strip of sky, intensely blue—blue like a dark sapphire, and full of colour, which contrasted well with the opaque blue-green of a belt of firs that crowned the summit of the bank and held their heavy plumes up motionless against the brightness. The air was so still that inanimate nature scarcely seemed to breathe; but all about us a myriad atoms of life buzzed, and chirped, and fluttered, rejoicing to be, making the most of their moment, and claiming a kinship with us in inarticulate murmurs, quite untranslatable, and yet becoming curiously comprehensible to some sense the longer we lingered to listen to them. The horses glanced hither and thither with big sagacious eyes, flipping a long ear swiftly towards each separate sound—now to the croak of a yellow frog in the grass, and now to the cheep of a nestling up on a branch, the bleat of an unseen sheep in the meadow above to its lamb, the low of a cow to her calf; seemingly anxious to understand, nervously glad to know; gathering the import of everything with an intelligence beyond ours, perhaps, that made them more one with the teeming beings about us than we were.

But after that sigh Adalesa burst into the midst of my meditation abruptly.

"Did you ever feel a glow in your chest, and have little warm shivers run down your backbone, and all the time keep smiling?" she demanded.

"No, never," I answered decidedly.

"Ah! then you have never been in love," she observed in a disappointed tone. "I thought, perhaps, with those eyes,—and you're not so plump either."

"I don't see the connection."

"Why—don't you know? Oh, I think when girls are plump, like Evangeline, it is because they haven't felt much. Now, I'm skinny because I have a burning fiery furnace within that consumes me. So many things—interests, passions, affections,—I don't know what all! are fuel to my fire; it never goes out."

"But love—?" I said, shy of the subject, yet aglow on a sudden with natural girlish curiosity about it, newly inspired; for the moment she mentioned love I knew what was in the air.

She laughed, whipped up her horse, and rode on ahead recklessly.

When I overtook her we were in the open country, on a hard high road, with a long level of fields on either hand, and not a glimpse of the sea.

"Where are we?" I asked.

"Oh, I had forgotten," she answered apologetically. "I was leading you away in the wrong direction. I'm sorry—I was thinking. I was thinking of him!" and she flipped at the hedge with her whip, and laughed in a shamefaced way.

"Of whom?" I asked.

"Of my man," she replied. "Oh, you're obtuse! Don't you gather? I'm in love. Sometimes I'm sick with love—love-sick. But you don't know what that is, and you're a little shocked!" She looked at me keenly. "You think I am committing a breach of decorum. So it would be, perhaps, for most girls; but, don't you see—with me—oh, you must let it be different with me!"

The high road was taking us towards a belt of wood now, above which the chimneys of the great house appeared, smoking cheerfully.

"Why, we're going back!" I exclaimed.

"Yes, a little way," she answered. "I'm sorry. I took the wrong turn. We should have gone to the left through the wood, instead of to the right, down that lane. But here we are. I'd better lead the way. Look out for your hat under the branches!"

The high road ran through the wood at this point, and was bordered on either side by trees, which looked like a forest of slender masts, canopied and curtained with greenery, through which the sunlight filtered in shining shafts, making mystical pathways of dazzling brightness, beyond which the tender gloom beneath the branches deepened perceptibly. Adalesa had turned off under the trees, taking a diagonal course confidently, although there was no track that I could see; but I followed her, now in sunshine and now in shadow, winding in and out about the tree-stems, watchfully, like a princess in a land of weird enchantment, who goes, with wide-open, wistful eyes, seeking to see deep into the verdant shadows, in timidly glad anticipation of something to come that would satisfy the hunger at her heart, that strange importunate ache.

Branches broken by last year's storms crackled beneath our horses' feet, or their hoofs sank deep in delicious moss. Rabbits ran at our approach, and the shrill cry or clumsy flight of a startled pheasant sounded oddly insulting, as if uttered to injure the charmed silence. And here again there was life— superabundant, palpitating, generous—a joyous riot, in which we were asked to join by every little living thing that spoke. At first, in the wood, the soothing *susurrus* of leaves, stirred by light airs, sounded incessantly, a sort of softly whispering sound, all-pervading yet unobtrusive, not the main melody, but a manifold accompaniment. Presently, however, we were seized upon by a mightier voice, muffled at first and murmurous, but growing in distinctness and volume as we advanced; and at the same time we ceased to see sunshafts and shadows through the wood; the green depths disappeared; and now between the trees there sparkled into view the yellow sands and the sea. We had come out upon the shore, and both involuntarily drew rein.

"Yes," Adalesa resumed, as if there had been no break, "you must let it be different with me. I take everything so severely—measles, whooping cough, mumps, scarlatina—all infantile diseases. Each in its turn has threatened to kill me, and now comes this new fever—love. I had to tell Evangeline even. I should have died if I hadn't said something to some one. But now I am sorry. I wish you had come sooner, Simple Sincerity: you are another sort. If only I hadn't told Evangeline that we are engaged!"

"Engaged!" I exclaimed. "*Secretly?*"

"Yes: isn't it dreadful?" she answered, laughing at my horror. "But it happened in this way. I was staying with his people, and he and I were always together because we were the only young pair on the premises; and at last— oh, the usual thing, you know! And I wanted to tell Uncle Henry, but he seemed to dislike the idea. My father and mother are in India, you know— that is why I am here; and Percy said, weren't they the proper people to be first informed? They are on their way home by this time, I believe, round the Cape—oh, the weary time of waiting! months! And I hate to keep Uncle Henry in the dark. I always tell him everything. But then of course there is Aunt Marsh. If I told him he would make me tell her, and then we should have the affair confided to the whole county in solemn confidence. At least," she corrected herself emphatically, "*I* don't believe he would tell her; he's too good altogether; and besides, I've told him lots of other things, but I can't make Percy understand, and he says, too, that his knowing would put the affair on quite a different footing—whatever he may mean by that. I hate concealment myself; but perhaps he has finer feelings than I have, for he says something about this being altogether sacred to ourselves—not an ordinary concealment. It sounds all right as he puts it; but I am sadly afraid I don't feel about it quite what he does, because I want to tell. I must talk. My joy bubbles up and bursts out so that I cannot contain it. There's a singing at my heart I can't quite smother; if only Uncle Henry suspected, he would hear it and question me, and then I should be glad in deed—satisfied. Now at times it is only a kind of half glad. However, are you relieved? I am not so sly as you suspected, perhaps."

"I should never have thought you sly," I declared.

"Well, reckless then," she replied, "as when I told Evangeline. That was an instance of a bubbling up and a bursting out. If I had had Uncle Henry to talk to—but there! Yet I know Evangeline is not to be trusted, for all her promises."

"Oh, surely she will not betray you if she promised!" I exclaimed, shocked by the accusation.

For a moment the cynical expression returned to Adalesa's face.

"It just depends upon what will suit her own convenience," she answered, with her usual downright directness.

The horses, tired of standing, sniffed the salt air, tossed their heads, and pawed impatiently.

"We'll let them go for a gallop in a minute," she said; "but first, just look at the sea, and listen to it. That inarticulate murmur is full of meaning to me now; and so it is with the sough of the breeze in the branches and the rustle of leaves. Since *he* came into my life I have awakened to full consciousness of a curious kinship with all things animate and inanimate. The gladness in me, the singing in my heart, is all a part of some great whole, some universal plan, something I know, but can't express. But wait!—wait till you know it too!"

She had looked down at the sand as she spoke, frowning intently in the effort to put what she felt into human speech; and her horse, as if waiting upon her words, ceased for the moment to be restive; the very sea-voice seemed suspended, and the scene itself—sandhills, and shore, and grey-white, green-crowned cliffs, curving arm like about the bay, passed from my consciousness. I saw and heard her alone till she stopped; then the waves rang out their merry murmur, the cliffs whitened into view in the sunshine, the breeze sang in my ears, the open space invited, and our horses, with one accord, as though they felt our own fine impulse to fly, to be free, plunged out from amongst the heavy, dry drifts, on to the smooth, hard sand, and carried us off at a gallop into another world.

VI. EVANGELINE CAME TO my room late that night. We had not had an hour's talk together since my arrival. The moon was near the full, and she found me with my window wide open, luxuriating in the sense of stillness, which is peculiar to the exquisite, shadowy, silent night.

"Oh!" she exclaimed, with a little shiver. "Won't you take cold? Isn't that mist down there on the meadows? and aren't the trees black? It is all so comfortless—"

I shut the window.

"Ah, that's better!" Evangeline pursued, as she curled herself up in an easy chair. "I love lays of the moon, and the ecstatic solitudes one reads about; but the real thing falls far short of the description. I believe those rhapsodies are written in bed at night, with the curtains drawn, and a big fire blazing. At all events, that's the best way to read them. One forgets then, as the poet seems to have forgotten, all the unpleasant details—that it is chilly out in the merry moonlight; fatiguing to linger or loiter long, though it sounds so nice; and too damp to sit, couch, or recline on anything growing or blowing. I love poetry, but preserve me from having to live it! Cushions and comfort are my delight, ease is my ambition, and all things ordered to please me by some competent person as long as I live, my one desire!"

She cooed all this so prettily that I began to draw an invidious comparison between the sound of her words and of Adalesa's. The sense did not impress me. The gentleness of her manner, the sweetness of her voice, and the charm of her appearance disarmed criticism. One felt at rest in her presence; one did not think.

She left the easy chair, and came and sat down beside me. "Pet me," she said, putting her arms around me. "I don't seem to have seen you at all since you came; and oh, I have such lots of things I want to talk to you about. How pretty your neck is!—just like a baby's. I must kiss it! I could *eat* you, I think, you're so sweet! But you're not very responsive, I must say! I believe you like Adalesa best. Tell me, do you? I should be so miserable if I thought you did. But what do you think of her?"

"I think her delightful."

"So she is," Evangeline answered, returning to her chair. "But isn't it rather a pity, when she's so nice, that she shouldn't be perfect? She does say and do such outrageous things. She has gone and engaged herself secretly." This breach of confidence slipped out so easily and so naturally that I should have hesitated at the moment to apply any harsh epithet to it. "Yes," she pursued; " I met the man in London afterwards, and now he has become quite an ally of mine. When he found I knew all about the affair, he said he was glad, and would like to discuss it with me. You do believe, don't you, that men and women can have Platonic friendships? I think it so cynical for people not to believe in disinterestedness. He says he loves to talk to me; and of course there can be no harm when it is all about another girl. What do you think?"

"I think I'm inclined to be sorry for the other girl."

"Oh, now that is not nice of you!" she said reproachfully.

"Well, the things that are said about the kind of man who spends all his time with one girl in order to talk about another, are not nice either."

"Oh, but I'm sure *you* would never judge a man by the unkind things people say!" She said this so earnestly, so caressingly, she made me feel mean. "And, besides," she went on gravely, "I don't think he is quite satisfied, somehow. It is not that he says anything, you know, only he makes me fancy—and I think it just as well that the engagement was not announced. If there is any change—if nothing comes of it, you know, nothing can be said. I only tell you about it in confidence, because I know you are safe, and I did so want to consult some one. You see, he confided in me, and asked my advice, and I feel it is such a responsibility. But perhaps Adalesa told you herself. I thought she might, as you get on so well—" She stopped here, and looked at me expectantly, but as I only replied with a steady stare, she demanded, pointblank: "Did she?"

"How can you ask?" I answered without emphasis, so as not to betray my friend; and I saw that she was baffled, but she did not like to repeat the question.

VII. EVANGELINE HAD BEEN complaining of some mysterious pain in her arm, and the next day a famous physician who was staying in the neighbourhood came to see her. He was brought to our sitting-room, and I helped Evangeline, at her mother's request, to take off her bodice, to enable him to see what was the matter with the pretty limb. It was evident that the old gentleman was interested in his charming patient, his manners, which were naturally suave, took on such an obviously extra shade of delicate, courtly consideration. Standing a little apart with Adalesa, I became deeply interested in his method of inquiring into the cause of the trouble; but he talked about "the long bone of the arm," until at last, bored by the repetition, I ventured to vary the monotony for him by suggesting the word *humerus* aside to her.

The doctor overheard me, however. "Oh—hem—ha—yes," he observed deliberately, giving me to understand at the same time, with a look, that I had sunk low in his estimation; after which he took no further notice of me.

"I am afraid you offended the doctor, dear," Lady Marsh said afterwards. "You really must be careful by what names you call things. You see, any indelicacy in a young lady shocks a refined and cultivated man."

"But humerus is the proper name of the bone," I ventured, with a faint flicker of spirit, in spite of the softly smothery effect of her manner.

"We do not call things by their proper names," she answered with gentle dignity.

"But is it really more delicate to call it the long bone of the arm?" I exclaimed. "Do forgive me for pestering you, dear Lady Marsh," I added, seeing a shade of disapproval on her face;" but I am always being met with queer contradictions and singular gradations of right and wrong, and the effort to understand them wearies my brain."

"Of course!" she exclaimed, triumphantly. "That is what I and any sensible person would have foreseen. A young girl's brain must suffer if she studies subjects only fit for men."

When we were alone, Adalesa asked me what I thought now of her sweet Aunt Marsh.

"I am trying to allow for opposite points of view," I answered, laughing.

But in my heart I acknowledged that Adalesa had not exaggerated; for the mental agonies that perfectly delightful woman caused me to suffer, on account of the difference between her point of view and that from which I had been brought up, no one who has not been a girl under similar circumstances can possibly conceive. I began to wonder at last, when I got up in the morning, what I should blunder about that day; and from the easy absence of self-consciousness which comes of living among people who encourage discussion and allow the most extreme differences of opinion as a matter of course, I became so nervous that I shrank from speaking at all, or if by chance I did commit myself, I would have recanted every syllable in my extreme timidity rather than suffer the disapproval I detected in the attitude of those about me. Lady Marsh laboured incessantly to repair the errors of my education; and often she talked for an hour without provoking me to say anything offensive, but the moment she interested me, the moment she roused me to think for myself, I was lost. The duty of being a social success was one of her favourite themes; and she considered it the beginning of wisdom for a woman to make herself attractive. So did my mother; but when it came to ways and means, their principles were diametrically opposed to each other. Lady Marsh often talked to us girls earnestly on the subject, her teaching, as I now perceive, having been a fair mixture of worldly wisdom and amiable foolishness. So far as our conversation was concerned, it might be summed up in the advice: never to dispute; never utter an emphatic word; talk principally about little things that have happened; to recount and to listen well is the great thing; men like to be listened to; but as we valued our reputations for womanliness we were never to express opinions. It was really better not to have any. Men do not care about women who have opinions. But it was upon the subject of personal appearance that she was greatest. A girl who was good-looking was a matter of grave importance to her, and she would appraise the marriage-market value of us all quite seriously, but never would have allowed the calculation to be defined by any such expression. She would have called it "considering our prospects of happiness." She expected Evangeline, whom she considered a poem in appearance, to make a brilliant match; and she was graciously pleased to express some hope for me too: "Only you *must* be careful, dear. Don't let a man imagine for a moment that you have ever thought about anything." But for Adalesa she had little hope. "She might marry a Radical Member, or something of that sort," she said to me confidentially one day, but she spoke dubiously. "She is so thin, you see," she added.

We were waiting with Evangeline for tea in the drawing-room, and Adalesa herself came in at that moment with her bull pup under her arm.

"I'm the thin party, I expect," she said, her dark eyes dancing mischievously.

"*Party*, dear child!" Lady Marsh ejaculated. "What an expression for a young lady!"

"Diddums, den!" Adalesa said to the bull pup. "Just look at him, auntie, how he wrinkles his forehead."

"I wish, dear, you would not bring that creature into the drawing-room; he is not a proper pet for a young lady."

"But, Aunt Marsh, men love sporting dogs," Adalesa remonstrated, with an injured air. "And he'll be what I never shall, and that's a beauty of his kind."

"You make a great mistake," Lady Marsh answered. "Any girl not absolutely ugly may be good-looking if she will, and you might be most elegant with that slender figure if you chose. And then also *manner* goes a good way. A girl with a very gentle, rather timid manner is irresistible to most men. Men like women to be dependent and clinging. And further, I know, for a fact, that, if you bring up a girl to be a beauty she will develop into one."

"It's odd that you should say that," Adalesa answered ambiguously, "for I was just thinking something of the same sort. I was thinking if you bring up a girl to be wise she will be wise; but the custom is to bring up a girl to be a fool."

"Your mother used to be a lovely girl," Lady Marsh said to me, pointedly ignoring Adalesa. "I suppose she wishes her daughters to be beautiful."

"My mother does not despise beauty, but she considers it a charming incident, that cannot last, rather than a serious object in life," I blundered.

A solemn silence followed upon this, which Lady Marsh broke at last by remarking to Evangeline, with significant sweetness,—

"There is something wrong about that dress at the waist, dearest. It drags."

"I'll tighten my stays, mamma," Evangeline answered amiably.

"You'll make your nose red if you do—or *bust*!" Adalesa observed, with her mouth full of cake.

"Adalesa, how *can* you!" her aunt remonstrated.

It was interesting to see Evangeline expand sympathetically under her mother's teaching. Her mind imbibed it with reverence as well as with relish, but to what it would be transformed when it was thoroughly assimilated, girls like ourselves could not foresee. From a chance remark of Sir Henry's, however, I gathered that he had his doubts about its being a soul-making substance.

VIII. LADY MARSH WAS by way of doing her best for us, as the society mothers delicately express it, and one of the delights of that visit was to be a ball. The joy of that ball began for us from the first moment it was discussed. In a matter of that kind Lady Marsh knew how to make girls happy, and she let us arrange it all ourselves and choose our own dresses. We sent to town for specimen programmes, and drew up a formal invitation, which we had printed; and when the cards arrived we spent a long delicious morning in our sitting-room addressing them. There were no improving books about on that occasion. The table was covered with invitations and envelopes, and we all three talked nineteen to the dozen as we addressed the latter, making many mistakes in our eagerness and glee, and giving ourselves much unnecessary trouble; but it was all a part of the pleasure.

Lady Marsh came in during the morning, and found the floor strewed with evidences of these mistakes; but she only smiled indulgently.

Then came the discussion about the dresses. We decided upon red, white, and blue. Adalesa's was to be red, with coral ornaments, because of her dark eyes and hair, and olive skin. Pale passion colour, she chose, and it looked like an expression of herself. Evangeline's was to be white—white satin with tulle and pearls, the kind of conventional thing a young lady looks her loveliest in; and also, perhaps, in that it was conventional, an exact expression of herself. Mine was to be pale blue; "Because of your white skin, my dear," Adalesa said. "And also because simple sincerity should be in true blue. Your ornaments must be turquoise and pearls and diamonds. Do you happen to have any?"

I laughed, as at an absurdity, for I was not an heiress.

The discussion about the dresses took place at luncheon one day, and Sir Henry paid much amused attention to our chatter.

"But where are you to get these fine gowns?" he asked.

"Where are we to get the money for them, you mean?" said Adalesa.

Sir Henry looked at Lady Marsh expressively, and then Lady Marsh beamed round upon us: "My dears, *I* am going to give you your dresses," she said.

The next excitement was the coming of the answers to the invitations. Adalesa slipped up to me shyly one morning, with very bright eyes and very pale cheeks. "He has accepted," she said, in a breathless whisper. "He is coming." The words were gasped between two sighs, heavy with heart-beats. From that time the tiresome child in her slumbered and slept. She never "drew" Aunt Marsh now, and she had rolled up her elf-locks and left off short petticoats. She was feverishly flushed for the most part, but she was very quiet, and would steal away alone for a ramble through the woods or a ride by the sea: "To listen to the voices," as she said; "to be one with Nature, which *knows*—"

Evangeline also knew that "he" was coming, and mentioned the matter with a self-satisfied smile: "O dear! I suppose I shall be called upon again to resolve doubts and difficulties," she observed.

"You don't mean that he will take you into his confidence when she is here!" I exclaimed.

She smiled again enigmatically. "Well, really—one never knows," she said. "I can't think how it could ever have happened. But, there! you know Adalesa. Wait till you see him, and then judge if she is suitable. It is so lucky, I think, the engagement was never announced." She smiled complacently when she had spoken, then blushed at nothing, and finally ran away laughing. I could not make her out.

Our lovely dresses arrived some days before the event, and were duly doted upon. It seemed as if our delight had culminated in them, and could rise no higher; but when we went to dress for dinner on the eventful day itself, three cries of joy, uttered simultaneously in our three respective rooms, announced yet another item added to our ecstasy, for there, on our dressing-tables, a present from Sir Henry, were the very jewels Adalesa had described as essential to complete our happiness.

When we were dressed we ran down to the drawing-room together, with our arms round each other, red, white, and blue, all silk, satin, and tulle, to be inspected, only expecting to see the old people; but there, on the hearth-rug, stook a romantic-looking young man, tall, with deep dark eyes, a stranger to me, but I knew in a moment who it was. I had met him in many books, and dreamt about him too. I knew him first by the way Evangeline started and Adalesa hung back. My own heart beat to suffocation when his eyes met mine; but what with dresses and jewels and joyful anticipations, it was a highly emotional moment with all three of us—this last element, a young man to admire us, having completed the circle.

Evangeline was the first to recover herself and greet him, and then she introduced him to me; and Adalesa, at last, summoning her courage, shyly held out a seemingly reluctant hand, the damask rose on her cheeks deepening the while; but the magnetism of her dark eyes was absent from her greeting, as she never raised them from the ground.

The young man looked from one to the other of us with a kind of pleased surprise.

"Three Graces, by Jove!" Sir Henry exclaimed, as he received our thanks. "Impossible to choose between them. I'd turn Mohammedan if I were a young man."

"Then you wouldn't marry me," Adalesa flashed out at him.

"That's right, my dear," answered he good-humouredly. "I like your spirit and the way you show it. None of your pet pussy-cat girls for me, concealing their claws till they're married. You stick to that—the whole man, body, soul, and spirit, or nothing."

Several more guests arrived for dinner. Evangeline whispered to her mother. It is strange how one sometimes sees the significance of things one cannot hear on occasions of excitement, when all our faculties are on the alert. Until Evangeline spoke to her mother I had not thought of whom Mr. Perceval would take in to dinner, but both question and answer occurred to me on the instant. Evangeline had suggested, and Lady Marsh, not knowing, had acquiesced: he was to take Evangeline in, and, as he offered his arm to her, he looked into her eyes ardently. He looked at me, however, in just the same way a moment later, and I thought, perhaps, that that was his habitual expression; but all the same I began to feel sore and sorry for Adalesa.

They sat opposite to me at table, and talked together in undertones confidentially, Evangeline cooing softly and looking lovely all the time, while Adalesa, poor child, a little lower down, out of some growing feeling of dissatisfaction, uttered small aggressive raileries in high-pitched tones, doing more damage to her own cause thereby than any one else could have done. I intercepted a glance of disapproval from the other side of the table, and felt that comparisons were inevitable. Lady Marsh, who was not far from Adalesa, put in an amiable remonstrance at last:—"Now, dearest," she began, smiling, "do not rail, it is such a bad habit, and people are so apt to think you mean it—ill-natured people, of course," she hastened to add generally, beaming round on us all as if begging us to observe that she considered it impossible to include us in such a category.

But the remonstrance was unfortunate from Lady Marsh's point of view, as its immediate effect was to stimulate Adalesa to one of those flashes of mature opinion which her aunt considered so undesirable in a girl:—

"Ah, you don't know the value of raillery, Aunt Marsh," she burst out. "I believe myself that it is the railers who do all the good in the world. They are the first cause of a change for the better, because when they don't like things, they have a way of expressing themselves which is so exceedingly disagreeable to those who only want to be content and not think, that the latter are only too glad to accept their suggestions in order to silence them. It is really the heathen railers who keep a spark of religion alight in the land; they show up the difference between precept and practice, and make the professors ashamed of their own inconsistencies."

Lady Marsh shook her head solemnly:—"Dear child, what have you been reading now?" she exclaimed, and then she meandered off in an undertone to her next neighbour on the necessity of supervising a girl's education.

"Poor Adalesa!" Evangeline murmured, with a deprecating sigh. "But she is *such* a child! And of course she will get over all these exaggerated ideas when she is older and has more sense."

"With such gentle womanly surroundings she should," he answered, gazing again at Evangeline, whose white bosom heaved with another little sigh.

"But is it not strange that the sense should be so long in coming," she said, "considering that Adalesa has had exactly the same opportunities—?" She stopped, blushing alluringly, as if modestly afraid of even having indicated herself.

After dinner she singled me out for a confidence. "Hasn't he exquisite Oriental eyes?" she said. "And don't you think I succeeded?"

"I hope not: how do you mean?" I stammered.

"Succeeded in preventing any suspicion," she answered. "I was so afraid mamma might see something."

"Oh, I don't think you need have alarmed yourself," I dryly rejoined.

"But, now, *do* you think they are suited?" she asked, in a tenderly anxious tone.

"I think that is altogether their business," I replied.

She looked at me reproachfully, and then left me.

Mr. Perceval danced with me several times during the evening, and towards the end of the ball we were engaged for another dance; but when the time came I was tired, so we decided to sit it out. His manner the whole evening had shocked and offended me, as the manner of a married man who wanted to flirt would have done. He was Adalesa's property, and yet I felt that upon the slightest encouragement he would have made love to me; and I had an uncomfortable doubt as to how far he might not actually have gone with Evangeline, which proved that my faith in her was shaken. I judged him harshly then—I think I could have called him a villain—but now all I feel is a sort of amused contempt for him for acting after his kind, an ordinary animal kind. He was a common-place young man in the mood for marriage, and would have made any one of us three that had chanced to accept him a good and agreeable husband—or rather his wife would have made him pretty much what she pleased.

Because of my suspicion of him I chose to sit in the ball-room so as not to give him a chance; and, finding I would not flirt, he sat beside me quietly, and turned his attention to Evangeline and Adalesa, who were dancing, observing them closely and comparing them, as I suspected—a comparison which was far from fair to Adalesa at that age; for she was one of those girls who, in appearance, mature late. Her active mind gave her slender body no leisure to cushion itself with redundant plumpness. Evangeline might, as her mother maintained, be a poem in appearance, but Adalesa was one in fact in spite of her angles. This ordinary young man, however, with only an ideal of fleshly perfection in his mind and before his eyes, was not likely to suspect it; and, even if he had, what pleasure would it have been to him, or profit, seeing that he had no capacity to appreciate a poem?

Judged, too, merely upon that kind of observation, there was another point against Adalesa. She did not waltz well, but Evangeline floated like thistledown above the boards. Adalesa soon wearied of waltzing; she thought it monotonous, and only went on to the end of the ball to make herself useful. She excelled, however, in a higher branch of the art, to her aunt's horror. We should call it skirt-dancing now, and be applauded for the accomplishment; but at that time it was a nameless enormity for a young lady to indulge in. Adalesa, nevertheless, would take her castanets sometimes, and give us an entrancing benefit of "woven paces and of waving arms"; but Lady Marsh regularly put down this exhibition when she caught her at it; and it was hardly likely the young man knew of the accomplishment, nor could one expect him to appreciate the self-sacrifice Adalesa was making when she accepted one eligible partner after another the whole evening, "boring herself to one, two, three, turn, for the good of the house," as she elegantly expressed it.

There came to me a curious fancy as I watched those girls. I seemed to see the soul of each through the casing of finery and flesh that enveloped them.

"One of the two is as good as gold without alloy," I said to Perceval; "but the other is—"

"An inferior compound?" he suggested; "and I know which it is."

But he looked at the wrong one; and I let him, for I did not think him worth pure gold, for all his "exquisite Oriental eyes."

When the dance was over he left me, and Adalesa took his place. It had been pathetic to watch her during the evening. Her eyes had been eloquent at first of shy expectation, half joyful, half frightened; but then came surprise and inquiry; then an interregnum of blankness, no explanation occurring to her; and now the expression was altogether pained.

"My heart is heavy within me," she said, in a whispering way she had, which made me think of the soft sighing of summer air through the leaves. "He seems to have forgotten."

From where we sat I particularly noticed one of the decorations of the ball-room—a great palm, standing in a corner between a window and a door, and all in shadow with the exception of one long leaf, which it held to the light, one glossy dark green leaf, that shone and quivered like a sentient thing in the fitful airs set in motion by the whirl of the dancers. It seemed to be taking its part in the revel with delight. It had its moments of excitement when the music went mad towards the end of a dance, and the pace became frantic. Then it would flutter fan-like with pennants streaming in time to the tune, and only gradually cease to wave as the room emptied, after the crash of the final chords. I was fascinated by the emotions of that leaf, or rather its demonstrations of emotion, and found myself gauging the success of the entertainment by it. When the spirit of the ball was at its highest, there seemed to be an extra shine on its glossy surface, but as the night waned and exhaustion began to sap the energy of the dancers, the dust settled and the leaf grew dim. It quivered still as the rooms thinned, but no longer waved; and when the last carriage had driven away I found it drooping in the vitiated air. There was a lounge beneath it, and on this Evangeline, who was also drooping by this time, had thrown herself. I had seen her, during the evening, sitting there with Perceval, laughing and looking into his eyes. The arm of the plant was held out over her then, but whether menacingly or whether to protect her, I could not tell. It might have had an evil spirit in it encouraging her to her destruction, or a good one warning her back; and my imagination busied itself with both possibilities. I longed to be allowed to look into the future for a moment, so that I might see enough to interpret the sign; but my soul yearned and ached on in that direction vainly: it was all impenetrably dark. From that moment, however, the great glossy plume of the palm seemed somehow to be specially associated with Evangeline, and before I saw them drooping together I had felt that I should find her there.

Lady Marsh had retired by that time, the men were in the smoking-room, and only we three girls were left of the brilliant crowd that had flaunted there so short a time before. Scraps of ribbon and lace and tulle, torn gloves and faded flowers, bedraggled flotsam and jetsam of the ball, strewed the floor. At the farther end of the room a servant was putting out the lights.

"I am tired to death," Evangeline said, with a yawn.

"Tired, but happy, I hope?" Adalesa answered, with peculiar gentleness.

Evangeline looked sharply at her, doubtless to see if she meant it, before she replied with effusion: "Oh, yes, darling, thank you. I *have* enjoyed myself! I hope we all have! But I'm dying of hunger."

I went with Adalesa to fetch something to eat from the supper-room, and at the same time I brought a jug of water for the palm.

IX. PERCEVAL HAD COME down for the dance, and was to stay a few days. He was in every way an eligible, and Lady Marsh was exceedingly gracious to him; but I could see that Sir Henry was inspecting him critically, as if he were not sure of him, and our attitude towards the young man also came in for a share of Sir Henry's attention. Mine was morose, I confess; in Adalesa's eyes was perpetual pained inquiry; only Evangeline was natural and happy. She was extra gentle, and gracious too, as if amiably disposed to atone for what must have looked like our shortcomings.

The morning after the great event we did nothing but discuss the ball. At luncheon, however, Sir Henry suggested that we should go out: "Rest is the right thing after a dance," he said, "and then exercise in the open air. You four young people should go for a ride."

Evangeline put on a pretty little pout. "I am afraid *I* can't," she said, in a heigh-ho tone. "My horse has gone to be shod."

"I wondered why you insisted on sending him this morning," Adalesa muttered.

"But why shouldn't you three go without me?" Evangeline said sweetly.

"Why shouldn't you ride some other horse?" Sir Henry asked, rather sternly.

"Nothing would induce me to," she answered with her set smile, looking him full in the face; after which she rose with an easy, unconstrained air, carefully brushed a crumb from the front of her dress, and left the room, humming a little tune.

Adalesa had also risen from the table.

"What are we going to do?" I asked, following her into the hall.

"Nothing," she answered, sombrely. "Evangeline is going to carry out some manœuvre of her own."

"Adalesa!" Lady Marsh called.

We returned to the dining-room. The two old people were still at table, but Perceval was standing at one of the open windows, looking out into the garden.

"Just run upstairs, dear child," Lady Marsh added, "and see if you can find my yellow-and-black sunshade. It's somewhere, I'm sure."

Adalesa complied without a word, but she sauntered off slowly, as if reluctant to go.

"That child is *so* ungracious at times," Lady Marsh observed to Sir Henry in a stage aside. "She compares unfavourably with Evangeline, I am afraid. Evangeline is *always* so sweetly unselfish and good."

Sir Henry pursed up his mouth, and toyed with a glass on the table. Perceval's back was turned to us, but I fancied I saw him stiffen to attention when Lady Marsh mentioned Evangeline, and I believed the young man had heard and marked, for all the air of indifference with which he affected to look out over the lawn.

It was one of those radiant days when one seems to see the heat throbbing in the crystal atmosphere. The garden borders were a blaze of colour. The odour of mignonette streamed in through the open windows. Perceval looked out sleepily a little longer; then suddenly the dreamy look in his eyes gave way to a flash of interest. He said something about fetching a hat, and left the room as if with a purpose. Evangeline had appeared on the other side of the lawn, lingering among the roses, with a pair of scissors in her hand; but, judging by the way she lifted a heavy bud here, touching it tenderly, or stooped to inhale the fragrance of a full-blown flower there, she was reluctant to gather them. Perhaps she thought it cruel to shorten their pretty lives! At all events she hesitated, and in that attitude she made a charming picture; and I am sure Perceval must have thought so as he crossed the lawn. She had apparently not heard him approach, for she started and blushed when he accosted her, then looked up and said something in her winning way, to which he responded smiling. Then they turned off down a shady alley together, and disappeared from sight.

Adalesa returned without the parasol, but Lady Marsh did not seem disturbed because she had failed to find it.

The whole day passed, looking like other days on the surface, and the night with its heavy shadows settled down silently. When we went to bed I hoped Adalesa would come to my room and talk the trouble out, and I waited awhile, but as she did not come I went to her. She had taken off her dress, and was standing at her window looking out. Her bull dog sat beside her on the floor, leaning against her and looking up at her sympathetically. I was oppressed by a horrid sense of things gone wrong, and he seemed to be suffering from the same.

"I thought I had said good-night to you," Adalesa muttered, turning on me as I entered.

"I hoped you would come to my room," I replied.

She looked at me intently from under her dark eyebrows; but I doubt if she saw me.

"He has not spoken," she said at last. "He treats me as if we had never met before. That is all there is to tell you. Now go: excuse me, but I am better alone. I want to think."

The dog whined and nestled up closer, and the sound of a great, deep, human sigh, almost a moan, accompanied me down the dark corridor as I returned to my room.

But my nerves were strained by that time. My own breath came in a succession of sighs; and, in order to tranquillise myself, I went and sat by the open window, and leant out, looking at the misty margins of the moon lit spaces, and listening to the inarticulate murmurs of the night. Very soon the sense of silence settled upon my spirit soothingly, and I was beginning to feel as if I could lie down and rest, when all at once my attention was quickened by a sharp sound from below—the sound of gravel crunched by a springy footstep. I knew who it was before I saw her. What was she going to do? And oh, what a waste of good emotion upon a worthless object all this seemed!

I had taken off my evening dress when I came upstairs, and now had only to slip on a cap and a pair of walking shoes, which I did not wait to lace, and snatch a long cloak from my wardrobe, and I was ready to follow her. I had to put the cloak on and button it as I went, but I was in time to see which road she took. It was the road through the wood to the sea. She had on her shortest gown again, with her elf-locks hanging, and nothing on her head. Her faithful brindle, rubbing up against her still, endeavoured to keep pace with her, snuffling as he went. I could hear him. But she took no notice of him. She was looking on ahead with the same kind of look, I imagined, as that with which she had greeted me when I went to her room; yet her gait was not at all agitated, but rather lingering, as if she were taking the air in a leisurely way. Had I not known she was in trouble I should have supposed that she was enjoying the novelty of being out alone at that hour. It was dark in the wood, but she seemed sure of the way, and walked on confidently until she passed out from under the trees on to the sand-dunes. Here she paused a moment, looking up to where, on the left, the tall cliffs rose bold and black against the night sky. On in front the moonlight silvered the sea. It was a desolate scene. The tide was a long way out. For a moment I thought she was going to turn back, but she was merely looking about her before she went a little farther on and sat herself down on the shore. Her dog nestled closer, and uttered a piteous "Whuff!" and then she looked at him for the first time, and put her arm round him, and rested her cheek on his big broad forehead, which seemed to satisfy him.

I made a little *détour* to the right among the sandhills, and stole up closer, so as to see her without being seen. She was gazing at the broad path of light made by the moon on the water. She was passionately fond of her father, and that was the way he would come. Did she remember?

The wind soughed among the sandhills, rustling the rank grass. The eternal sea-song sounded afar off, muffled, monotonous, yet mighty in that it was eternal. It made me wonder once more if the sufferings of such ephemeral specks in the great universe as we are could possibly signify. We seemed so unimportant, out there on the barren sands, that, for the first time for twenty-four hours, I ceased to care what became of us. I lay my length upon the dry, white sand, pillowing my head upon my folded arms in front of me, inhaling deep draughts of the sea-sweet air and rejoicing in its healthy fragrance. Then for awhile I watched the gem-like stars shine out in the radiant blue dark above me, and saw the shadows shift upon the cliffs, and the sea approaching. By that light the wavelets showed black-grey, like shining flints, with chalk-white rims for crests. When Adalesa sat down they were too far off to be distinguished except as a dark, moving mass, relieved by burnished sparks and flashes of moonlight; but before she rose they were close upon her; the moon had set, the stars were extinguished, and low down in the east the grey dawn shone primrose and green and white shot with flame in opaline splendour.

X. I BELIEVE IN my heart that Sir Henry, in his quiet way, had more real sympathy with us girls, and more comprehension of us, than Lady Marsh, for all her demonstrations. It was to him I should have gone in any trouble rather than to her, I know; and I suppose Adalesa felt the same; for when she crawled down next morning, very late, she encountered me in the hall, and asked me where he was, and then, slipping her hand through my arm, drew me along with her to look for him. He was sitting alone in the dining-room in an easy-chair, reading a newspaper, which he put down when we entered. Adalesa went up to him and kissed him, and then sat herself down on the arm of his chair. She moved listlessly, as if there were no life left in her, and looked ill, and I could see that her uncle observed her with particular attention as she approached.

"You did not come down to breakfast," he said tentatively.

"No," she answered. Then she put her arm round his neck, and rested her cheek on his head. "I don't want to come down again," she added, with an effort. "I want to go away from here—at once."

Sir Henry seemed to reflect. "What is the matter, little girl?" he said at last. "Any thing mentionable?"

"No," she answered. "I want to go and meet my father. If you will telegraph to Aunt Morris she will be glad to have me. I want to wait for him there, in town."

Again Sir Henry took time to reflect. "Well," he said at last, slowly, "you shall go, and at once too, if you like."

He looked at me when she left us. "You know what is wrong, I suppose?" he said.

"Nothing mentionable," I answered.

He smiled at the retort, and then shook his head.

"Not mentionable," he repeated—"no, nor visible. One scents it, though, without seeing it. One feels it in the air. It is knowable without being nameable. But if one could name it one would call it—" He gave me one of his shrewd glances.

"Treachery," I blurted out. "Robbery with violence—and you will be sanctioning it with a blessing by-and-by."

He seemed amused at my vehemence. "It is contrary to the law to condemn without proof," he said. "I am here to administer the law, and if I am not furnished with any proof of guilt, I must acquit."

And so it seemed, for my tongue was tied.

I should have expected fight rather than flight from Adalesa; but perhaps some sense of the unworthiness of such a contest restrained her, for the girl was self-respecting.

She left us early that afternoon, "to await her father's arrival in town"— which was great nonsense, Lady Marsh said, since it was so uncertain when he would come; but Adalesa could do what she liked with her uncle, and when he ordered there was nothing for it but to obey.

Late that night Evangeline came to my room in a flutter. "It is just as I suspected," she burst out. "He has told me all about it. He never really loved her. But he did not know his own mind until—"

"Until you stepped in?"

"Until she went off in that heartless way to-day. He was afraid she might care for him, but you see for yourself now! So he has written to tell her he understands by her going that she wishes to be released, and therefore he offers to release her. He didn't utter a word of reproach, I know, for he showed me the letter."

"Noble creature!" I ejaculated.

"Is he not!" she exclaimed with enthusiasm. "And—oh, don't be cold and horrid!" She caught my arm and fairly shook me in her wild excitement. "*Do* congratulate me!"

"What, so soon?" I cried aghast.

"Oh, you won't understand," she rejoined, wringing her hands. "Yet you know, you *must* know, that a young man may make a mistake. They were utterly unsuited. It is all for the best. They would only have made each other miserable."

"Well, perhaps you are right," I said, upon reflection. "Adalesa is certainly difficult. And she is far above the average too. But I shall wait for the second part of the piece before I offer any of you my congratulations."

"You *are* horrid!" Evangeline exclaimed, with tears of mortification in her eyes. "And now I know why some of the girls at school said nasty things about you."

PART II.

"I have lived long enough: my way of life
Is fallen into the sere, the yellow leaf."

XI. It arrived to me, as the French phrase it, to wait once more for a midday train at that same station from which I journeyed on the occasion when Adalesa and I had first encountered each other, and to lose myself—and my train again, very nearly—in the contemplation of the crowd about me. Pullman cars had come into existence by this time; and instead of coming to in a third-class compartment, as on that first occasion, I awoke in my rightful place in one of these; and, on looking out of the window on my left, saw something familiar in the shifting scene that recalled the bygone time with a flash. Involuntarily I glanced to the opposite end of the carriage; and there, on the same side as myself, facing me, sat a slender, elegant woman, whose dark eyes met mine with a look of inquiry, which resulted in a sudden mutual recognition of each other. We rose simultaneously, and meeting halfway, embraced, there being no spectator, happily, whose presence might have checked the impulse. Adalesa returned with me to my corner and sank into the opposite seat.

"History repeats itself," she said.

"Only the framework: the details are different," I replied, recalling the tall, gaunt girl, who had thrown herself so recklessly across the intervening space, and comparing her with this richly-dressed woman, whose every move was marked with a slow, deliberate grace, as captivating as it was dignified. "When we first met we had everything to look forward to, but now we must both look back."

"True," she said. "Yet our destination is the same, I imagine. I am again going to my Aunt Marsh."

"So am I," I answered, "to welcome Evangeline back from Brazil. I haven't seen her since her marriage. Her husband is something out there, isn't he?"

"Yes—silver, or diamonds, or something. Dear Perceval! Do you remember him? But of course you remember him!" she concluded, in the old downright way, laughing a little as she spoke. Then she said, with a sigh, seriously, "But if you have not met any of them since the marriage, I am afraid you will see great changes."

"Changes are what one always seems to be seeing from the moment one has lived long enough to compare this with that," I answered. "Just now I am conscious of a great change in myself. You didn't notice me 'peacocking' about the station this time, and wonder if I were anybody because of the airs I gave myself."

Adalesa smiled.

"And I don't want to read the advertisements any more. Just look at the hideous procession! I vow I never will use anything that is advertised to death like that"

"It would be no pleasure to you now to be recognised?" Adalesa asked.

"Oh, none," I answered. "I caught my train to-day because I heard my name mentioned, and slunk into the carriage for fear my face should also be known. Yet I remember what the joy would have been—"

"Had it come earlier? But you anticipated it. I remember so many sayings of yours that show you must have felt you would be known."

"Tell me about yourself," I put in.

"Oh, I am distinguished too in my own way," she answered, in the old vein. "I lounge about the world, loving my husband, and longing for the babes that never come; and it is such an extraordinary thing for a duchess to do that I get a kind of credit for it, which I enjoy. You always said I should end by being something eccentric."

"What became of Brindle?" I asked.

"Poor dear old boy!" she ejaculated. "He attained to an honourable old age, and only lately—left me."

"Do you remember that night on the shore?" slipped from me unawares.

She raised her eyebrows, and looked at me interrogatively; and then I was obliged to confess that I had followed her. "I thought you had some desperate intent," I explained, apologetically.

"Such an idiotic idea would never have occurred to me," she answered bluntly. "It is your old-fashioned people who do that. I knew even then that there are more emotions than one worth living for, if I did not suspect that even that one, when abortive, might repeat itself perfectly. The barren sands, with the sea, and the night sky arching over all, invited me, that was all. I stole out to secure the sense of immensity which is sustaining and ennobling as well as being restful. I thought I should find there what would enable me to renounce— and I succeeded. I am most devoutly thankful to say that I succeeded." She had clasped her hands as she uttered these words, and was silent for a little afterwards. Then her countenance cleared, and she turned to me with the air of one who has put something serious aside, and means to be brighter. "Tell me about yourself," she said. "Why did you never answer my letters?"

"For fear of having to do so again!" I replied.

"Try another," she said, smiling.

"Because I had nothing to say."

"That's no better. Once more."

"Well, because I had too much to say."

"I should think so!" she ejaculated.

"And after all," I protested, "I am only an onlooker. I am always an onlooker, with no claim to a personality of my own which would interest my friends. I see and foresee. I have seen the setting of several old ideas, and the dawn of divers new ones. The electric light has come to extinguish the gas, and London is bursting out into flats, huge caravansaries, admirably arranged for the cremation of the dead in case of fire. Eternal punishment no longer holds up its head; and the commercial part of the church enterprise will soon be in a bad way if the priests don't discover that we shall all reappear rich and beautiful on earth if we are good. That is all I can think of at this moment."

Adalesa's eyes twinkled, but she said nothing; and we both looked out of the window in silence for awhile, the truth being that we were suffering from the pressure of too much to say, so that our words only came out in jerks like water glug-glugging from full bottles. We had not met because I had been abroad so much; but of course we had received all the important heads of intelligence concerning each other; and I confess that I crowed when the news came that Adalesa had proved to have been her Aunt Marsh's ugly duckling by marrying a duke.

At the station we found carriages waiting for us and our servants; Barkins, now a very old man, being on the box of one of them.

"Ah, Barkins, my friend, how are you?" Adalesa exclaimed, reaching up to shake hands with him. "So you've come to drive me yourself? I call that kind; for I know you don't often drive anybody but her ladyship now."

"Eh," he rejoined, touching his hat, "I'd be main bad when I didn't come to fetch your grace. You'll not be driving madam there to-day, perhaps?" he added, grinning.

"Barkins will never forget our first arrival together," Adalesa said, when we were seated. "But, oh, the like in unlikeness to-day! Look round: the station—the trees—the fields—the very dust on the road is exactly the same; but look at us! My heart contracts; yet I don't know why, for I am happier now—"

She did not finish the sentence; but I knew what she meant, for I felt very much the same. There was a certain solemn satisfaction in the feeling, though I cannot explain it; but I would not have had the day that was dead back for all "the tender grace" of it. One change in myself I noticed with interest. The first time I had driven along that road I was all anticipation, but now I found in myself nothing but reflection. The principal events in life lay behind me; I could think of but little more that there might be to come.

As we approached the house, I was again struck with the air of affluence about the place. It looked like a toy territory, all spick and span, and there was such an affectation of defence about it in the crenelated walls that bounded the chase, and the castellation of every building, from lodge to coach-house, that one almost expected to see ornamental soldiers at regular intervals, ordering arms mechanically.

Lady Marsh did not come out to meet us this time—another note of change. She found it necessary to save herself as much as possible now. But she rose and came forward to receive us with the stiff haste of age, when we were shown into the drawing-room, embraced us both tenderly, then held us off from her, each by a hand, looked at us, shook her head, sighed, and looked again, especially at me, whom she had not seen in the interval. While we were greeting each other, Sir Henry came pottering in—oh, so shrunken in appearance, but more benign than ever. Adalesa seized upon him, hugged him, wheeled up a big easy chair for him, and then sat herself down on a stool at his feet, with her arm on his knee. The old man's hand wandered over her head, and rested on her neck, and she took it in hers and held it, after which they both seemed satisfied.

"Adalesa, darling, it is so sweet to see you again," Lady Marsh exclaimed, turning round upon her just as she had settled herself; "but wouldn't you be more comfortable in a proper chair?"

"We're all right, thank you, dear Aunt Marsh," Adalesa said; and I saw her signal to her uncle by squeezing his hand, upon which he leant back in his chair and looked up at the ceiling abstractedly. But the little scene was reassuring, showing as it did that in point of character there was no disheartening difference here.

There were three other ladies present—Lady Parkinson and Miss Creamer Patterson, both women of property living in the neighbourhood, who had come to call; and a Mrs. Crowther, who was staying in the house, a somewhat simpering, excessively-dressed, youngish person, the kind of pretty thing who lights up when men are present, but languishes if there are only ladies in the room.

Before we had well settled ourselves, yet another lady, of much the same age and type as Mrs. Crowther, but looking more animated for the moment, hurried across the lawn, entered by one of the open windows, and proceeded to embrace Adalesa with effusion. Then she turned to me with the same intention, but I was so surprised that I hung back, and it was some seconds before it dawned upon me that this must be Evangeline.

"I believe you don't know me!" she ejaculated; and I could see that this was a shock to her. Patches of red appeared on her somewhat sunken, sallow cheeks, and the look in her eyes quite startled me, it was so scared. She had evidently had no notion of the change in herself until I failed to recognise her, and had perhaps been cherishing the fond delusion that, however much others might alter, time had only touched her charms to round and ripen them. "I should have known you anywhere," she added reproachfully.

"And I you—by your voice." I blundered again, in my anxiety to be truthful as well as to atone. I felt angry with Adalesa. She should have prepared me. Changes, indeed! Evangeline was a wreck.

"I know I am looking washed out," she continued, glancing anxiously from one to the other of us. "The hot climate, you know. But one always recovers one's complexion at home."

The manner was much the same, at all events, showing that here again in her case the change had been incomplete, which was a pity; for the simplicity which had been winsome at eighteen seemed silliness now, and the little *moues* and attitudes she still affected sat incongruously upon her altered looks. She was girlishly dressed, in a white frock and a large hat, much as she might have been when first we met. Her unconcealed sensitiveness about her appearance had made us all feel awkward for a moment; but Lady Marsh diverted the rest of the party by directing their attention to me.

"So now you write books?" she said, shaking her head involuntarily.

Miss Creamer Patterson changed countenance, and edged her chair away from me a little, and then edged it back again, as if, on second thoughts, she regretted the impulse. Old Lady Parkinson peered at me, with undisguised interest, through a single eyeglass. She was prepared to relish any impropriety there might be in my occupation.

"Do tell me how you do it," she said, in an undertone, looking about her mysteriously, and then leaning forward as if she were about to hear something one only mentions in a whisper. "I am curious to know how things are written. I've often thought I should like to do something of that kind myself—*on the sly, you know*. It must be so pleasant to write things. But," she added quickly, "I shouldn't like to do anything to interfere with my night's rest."

Miss Creamer Patterson, having overcome her first instinctive shrinking, and being kindly anxious to atone if she had hurt my feelings, now decided to countenance me, while, of course, carefully avoiding any allusion to my lapse.

"It has been a very *dull* day," she said.

But before I could do more than glance at her in response, Lady Parkinson began again.

"And when you write a book do you put in the stops yourself? Stops and everything! Oh, no! not the stops, of course! All that must be done for you."

This was added as if she feared I should think she had been expecting too much of me.

"It is really most enjoyable weather—" Miss Creamer Patterson recommended.

"But, now, do tell me," Lady Parkinson interposed. "Do you *really* only write on one side of the paper? I've been told so, but one *never* knows. People spread such reports about, you know. Then, I suppose, you make your notes on the other side?"

"This is most enjoyable weather for the country," Miss Creamer Patterson again essayed, with exaggerated mildness—as an example, doubtless, to Lady Parkinson, who spoke out authoritatively; but the correction was lost upon the latter.

"You must write very legibly, of course," she broke in once more.

"They say I don't," I had time to reply. "But it doesn't much matter now, as we can have our things type-written."

"Ah! type-written," Lady Parkinson repeated knowingly. "I know what that is—that long, thin kind of writing. They put it on cards of invitation. But it must spoil your night's rest. *Surely* it does!"

"No," I answered; "I only write in the morning. Large entertainments do that when I go to them; but I seldom go. People are never at their best in a crowd, and I like to see my friends at their best. Numbers take the individuality out of them, somehow; and the man or woman who is excellent good company by one's own fire-side, feet on fender, can only cackle in a crowd like everybody else. That which makes us kin only comes out at quiet times. When there is silence, we say an angel is passing."

She stared at me vacantly, as though not comprehending in the least, and then her eyes wandered over the floor as if she were looking for something.

"I should have thought it would interfere with your night's rest," she said at last. "And of course it must prevent your going into society as much as you ought."

"Society would interfere with my writing if I would let it," I answered. "But I never let it. I hate society."

She gave a sort of little jump. "Hate society!" she echoed under her breath. "Oh!"

If I had blasphemed she could not have been more horrified.

Mrs. Crowther and Evangeline were talking about some lady-milliner.

"I don't like lady-milliners, because you can't beat them down in their prices," Mrs. Crowther declared languidly.

"That is so like you, dear child," Lady Marsh ejaculated.

"What I object to about her is that she has taken to selling cheap things," Evangeline remarked. "She offered me a bonnet for two guineas the other day."

"Ridiculous!" said Mrs. Crowther.

Miss Creamer Patterson had had a little confidential chat with Evangeline since she last addressed me; and now she turned and beamed upon me cordially. "I hear you are a cousin by marriage of the dear duchess's," she said.

"I am distantly related to her husband," I answered stiffly, seeing that she meant to wait until I spoke.

"I hope you'll come and see me," she rejoined. "It has been nice bright weather to-day, hasn't it? But the country is always fresh, don't you think so? I was three months in London this year. I am going to give an at-home. I hope you will come. It is so nice to have interesting people at one's parties, you know. People always like to meet writers and that kind of thing, don't you know—when they are of good family. Of course that is the difficulty. But there *are* some undoubtedly—eccentric, don't you know; only that is amusing, and people like to meet them. Now, you will come, won't you? Do promise me."

On the way upstairs I asked Adalesa if she thought women were ready for the suffrage.

"Oh, I don't know," she answered carelessly. "Female fools are not worse than male fools; and if you tested the sexes for folly by examination you would find them much of a muchness. You can't make flour without corn, my dear. When people have nothing to think about they don't think."

XII. IN GOING THROUGH the old house I became aware of a change in it also, as sorrowful in its way as that which I had observed in the old people. I remembered it as spacious above everything, a place where one's lungs rejoiced in pure air always, and body and soul could expand healthily and be at ease. It had been Sir Henry's house at that time; but as the years rolled on, that trick of not troubling had grown upon him, and he had retreated further into himself, and oftener into his library, leaving his wife and daughter to have their way, even to the blotting out of every sign of his own personality if they chose, so long as they never meddled with his own sanctum and private place of abode, the big library. There he and the things he loved grew old together in gentle fellowship, built up of interest and early association; and there he had preserved the space he had been born to move in, and kept the memory of his people and the traditions of his ancient house alive. I went to see him in the library next morning, and found him with a little book in his hand, looking idly out of one of the windows; and, coming upon him unawares, surprised a look of patient resignation on his face that saddened me. It was a grand old age, upright and uncomplaining, but terribly pathetic in its loneliness. Adalesa was the one creature upon earth, I believe, with whom his soul found fellowship, and she did what she could for him with joy, her great grief being that they could not meet except under the sombre shadow of an approaching parting: "If only you were a pauper, Uncle Henry," she used to exclaim in her quaint way, "I could have you with me always."

Outside that room the house was crowded now to suffocation with curtains, cushions, couches, ottomans, and easy chairs, upholstered in the modern manner with mere trivialities of a costly fashion, devoid of association with the past, and not likely or even intended to last into any distant future. It was decorated, too, in excess with pictures, statues, china, arms and ornaments of every sort, stuck any-and everywhere till the eye was satiated; and it would have been a relief to it to have found a square yard of old oak panelling to repose upon, and a stimulant to the mind had there been any story connected with the panel to arouse reflection. It was a house furnished to death, to the great discomfort of people like myself, who crave for light to luxuriate in, air to breathe, and space in which to move freely. The excessive air of affluence out of doors had been bad enough in its suggestion of a little toy territory, but indoors it was worse, being oppressive. Every appointment was too luxurious, and it seemed impossible for human beings to live long in such surroundings and not become enervated, both from want of thought and in consequence of habitual self-indulgence. Lotus eaters they were bound to be, growing flabbier from day to day, morally and physically, through having had everything excluded from their lives that might have served to stimulate them to the wholesome exercise of their minds and muscles. It was impossible to think of such a place as belonging to a man, or at all events as the outcome of a vigorous character. Everything about it now was womanish, to such a degree as to create a prejudice in advance, in the mind of one who likes men to be manly, against any man who lingered there. It seemed unlikely that he could be anything but of the tame cat kind, a domestic animal kept about the place by the ladies, like their other pets, for his usefulness, or to delight their eyes, and serve at odd times as an excuse for something to lavish their love upon.

Evangeline, being an only child and not very fond of the tropics, had naturally lived much of her married life at home. Our old schoolroom was now her boudoir. She had made it stuffily effeminate in the fashionable manner, with tambourines and ribbons, painted plaques, and things of all kinds converted from their honest use to serve as ornaments absurdly—as, for instance, a salad-oil bottle with a pink ribbon tied round its neck, filled with grasses and hung upon the wall—dusty fripperies! "Just like a beastly bazaar," as Adalesa remarked. "Don't I know them, for my sins? I'm always having to open them. And I always buy these kind of things, and then give a children's party, so that some one may get some pleasure out of them, if it's only the pleasure of demolishing them. I should so like to see Evangeline the Second throw billiard balls at that oil bottle."

It was the day after our arrival, and we had looked in there for a moment on our way to the drawing-room for afternoon tea. This meal was quite a function when Adalesa was in the house. People dropped in for it from all parts of the county, and one could see that none of them ever forgot that she was a duchess.

We found the room full on this occasion, and Evangeline, very much in her element, flitting about from one to another, all little airs and graces, gesticulating with her pretty hands to help her words out, and altogether very youthful indeed. Two lovely little children, a boy and a girl, dreadfully over-dressed, were brought in presently.

"My babies!" she exclaimed, fluttering off to meet them, and then flopping down on her knees and holding out her arms, into which the little girl sprang confidently. The boy hung back.

"Ah, this is my child, this is *my* darling!" Evangeline cried, covering the girl with kisses. "You go away," she said to the other; "you're not *my* boy at all."

If this were meant for playfulness the little fellow did not see it, for he shrank off sensitively, and seemed too preoccupied to respond when Adalesa took him upon her knee and began to lavish attentions upon him. He sat with his eyes fixed on his mother and sister, watching them with a countenance so blank, one wondered at it, but could not understand it. I discovered afterwards, however, that he was utterly neglected, if not absolutely ill-treated, by his mother, because a dark drop that there was in his father's family had come out in him. Evangeline had been sentimental, as a girl, on the subject of Perceval's "exquisite Oriental eyes," but during her sojourn in the tropics she had acquired some further information on the subject of such eyes, and now associated them with other than romantic ideas. The little girl was as fair as herself, but abroad the boy had been stigmatised as "coloured." He was a charming child, but almost morbidly sensitive, and one could see that his mother's continual jibes, although always delivered with an affectation of playfulness, never failed to cut him to the quick. Adalesa and I both begged hard to be allowed to keep him.

"You can halve him between you if you like," his mother rejoined. "I only want my girl—my beauty!"

"You *are* a brute, Evangeline!" was Adalesa's gentle comment.

"Ah, my dear," said Evangeline airily, "it is fortunate for the family that you became a duchess. In a less exalted position people might have tried you by your language, and found you wanting in refinement."

"Good, by way of t*u quoque,*" said Adalesa appreciatively.

They had an encounter of this kind almost every time they met, and it was strange to find these two mature women jarring still, without ever quarrelling exactly, just as they used to do in their early girlhood.

XIII. Mrs. Crowther was Evangeline's bosom friend at this time; but they had two other bosom friends, Mr. Regy Vincent and Mr. Paul Marks, who came continually to the house to pay them that kind of court which very young men are apt to lavish on dressy young women, a good deal older than themselves, if they are encouraged; and it was evident to me, so far as Evangeline was concerned, that what she lived on now was the adoration of these

> "Things whose place 'tis over ladies
> To lean and flirt and stare and simper,
> Till all that is divine in woman
> Grows cruel, courteous, smooth, inhuman;
> Crucified 'twixt a smile and a whimper."

She took either or both about with her impartially, according to circumstances, or as they might become available for purposes of escort. She shared them fairly with Mrs. Crowther, but would show signs of dissatisfaction if they ventured to pay any but the most unavoidable attention to other ladies. Beyond these young men, however, and the constant care and thought she bestowed upon her dress and appearance, she did not seem to have any special interest in life. It was a continual case of "What shall we do next?" with her—an inveterate running from one trivial amusement to another in order to pass the time—to get it over with as little consciousness of its flight as possible. The only moments she really lived were those which brought her some petty personal social triumph, emphasised by a tribute of admiration or of envy, no matter which, since either proved that she was still a success.

"One would think it was something glorious you were hurrying to arrive at," Adalesa said to her one day, "instead of old age, which will be upon you soon enough, I should think, without going to meet it half-way as you do, seeing that you dread it so."

Mr. Regy Vincent and Mr. Paul Marks lounged in after dinner on the evening of our arrival. They were stiff and neglectful in their attentions to Lady Marsh on account of her age, familiar with Evangeline and Mrs. Crowther, deferential to "the duchess," and suspicious of me. Sir Henry they would have treated as an equal had he not overlooked them altogether.

"Awful fun at the cricket match this afternoon," Mr. Vincent remarked to the ceiling. He was sprawling in an armchair beside Mrs. Crowther, with his hands in his trousers pockets and his legs spread out before him.

"Oh, did you hear that girl?" said Mr. Marks, who stood near with an eyeglass in his right eye, looking down on the ladies in every sense of the word. "I can't remember exactly what she said, but I know it was awfully good. Some one had been caught out, or something of that kind, don't you know, and so she thought that side had lost!"

"Yet women want the suffrage!" Mr. Vincent said softly to the ceiling.

Mr. Marks very much appreciated this good thing; and the three ladies also smiled, as though to show their perfect agreement with the conclusion that, because one woman, not having learnt the ins and out of such an important thing as a game of cricket, makes a mistake, therefore the pretensions of all women to be considered reasonable beings are absurd.

"Take care!" Lady Marsh said to Mr. Vincent playfully. "That dear child there"—meaning Adalesa—"claims equality with you."

"Oh, for heaven's sake—pardon me," Adalesa cried, with more than necessary emphasis, after a horrified glance at the young man's sloping skull—"not equality! I could never come to that!"

Mr. Vincent frowned thoughtfully, and even Mr. Marks seemed to think there might be more than he perceived in this reply; but Lady Marsh smiled on serenely. There was a little pause, however, and some remarks made in undertones before the chatter recommenced; then somebody began about hands and feet.

"I know who has the smallest feet I ever saw," Mr. Vincent declared, looking significantly at Evangeline, who assumed a simpering air of unconsciousness.

"Well, I know whose feet are the best shaped," Mr. Paul Marks declared, with a companion glance at Mrs. Crowther.

"I'll bet you ten to one Mrs. Perceval has the smallest foot in the room," Mr. Vincent cried.

"Done with you," said Mr. Marks. "Ladies, a slipper each, please, to measure."

"I beg to be excused," Adalesa said, with dignity.

"How horrid of you!" Evangeline exclaimed. "How is the bet to be decided? It is only fun."

"I fail to see the fun," said Adalesa.

Others were not so fastidious, however, and the vulgar competition went on without her, one inanity leading to another until it was time to retire.

"Isn't it delightful to see Evangeline so young and fresh?" Lady Marsh whispered to me as I wished her good-night. "She is quite a girl. Every little thing amuses her."

I smiled as well as I could, thinking the while that it might have been better had she been less "a girl" and more fastidious.

"Oh, by the way," Mr. Vincent exclaimed, "will you come out for a row to-morrow? We can carry four ladies in the back of the boat."

"Where?" I asked.

"Mr. Vincent means the stern," Adalesa explained; "but he didn't think a lady would understand." We were leaving the room together at the moment; and she continued laughingly, when we were out of earshot, "I always think it so kind and considerate of those dear boys to talk down to our ladylike level."

Adalesa laughed; then asked if I felt sleepy, because she did not, and proposed that we should go to Evangeline's room and cackle.

We surprised Evangeline dabbing some cosmetic on her faded cheeks.

"Don't you do anything to *your* face?" she asked Adalesa, in a sort of gently reproachful tone, as if it were not honourable to neglect cosmetics.

"I wash it," said Adalesa.

Evangeline had left her husband in Brazil, but he was expected home next day.

"How delighted you will be to see him!" I said innocently.

Evangeline failed in an attempt to look so.

"You haven't seen him since Evangeline took him off my hands for his good, have you?" Adalesa remarked, in her flippant way.

I had been nervously toying with some bottles on the dressing-table when she spoke, and now I knocked one over.

"My drops!" Evangeline exclaimed. "I am obliged to take something. The doctor prescribed them for my nerves: I can't trust my nerves; I can't keep up without something."

This was said almost defiantly, as if she thought we should object; but Adalesa recommended her to have some drops.

"Judging by your appearance, I should say you will never want them more than you do at this moment," she said.

When I was alone with Adalesa, I could not help remarking on the change in Evangeline.

"It amazes me," I said.

"Do you mean the change in her appearance or in her character?" she asked. "Or the further development of her character rather, I should say, for essentially she is the same."

"Both," I answered.

"Well, neither need," she said; "for those soft, plump, pink-and-white girls, who mature early, and have no muscular training to strengthen and develop their physique, go off early as a rule; and if you will remember how she was taught to believe that a woman's great aim in life is to be attractive, particularly in appearance, to men, you won't wonder that she begins to be embittered by the suspicion that she is less so than she was."

"What is Perceval like now?"

"Stoutish—the last time I saw him; and I expect by now he will have quite lost his girlish figure. But in one respect he has not altered. He is still much as he was when he thought he preferred Evangeline to me—the sort of man, that is to say, who hasn't the brains to know what a fool he is."

XIV. It was Adalesa, as it happened, who welcomed the traveller back next day, Evangeline having gone out early, with Mrs. Crowther and the two young men, on some expedition, from which she did not return in time to meet her husband.

He looked to me now a somewhat irritable, elderly, careworn man, more altered for the worse, I thought, in appearance and manner than she was even. But he won my heart by his devotion to his dark little boy. The way the two clung to each other was significant. When the father was reading his paper in the morning, the child would steal in stealthily, glancing about, as if afraid of being captured and ordered off, and would climb up on his father's knee, and nestle there happily so long as he was left in peace, his father fondling him half-unconsciously with his disengaged hand. And they would talk to each other, too, when nobody seemed to be noticing them; but if Evangeline came and caught them, she would gently insist upon sending the boy off to the nursery, or out for a walk, arranging and ordering for them according to her own mood of the moment, after her mother's manner; and neither he nor his father ever had the courage to disobey her.

These episodes were painfully significant. They made one heartsore and sorrowful, and all the more so because there was such a falsification in it all of the unvarying sweetness of manner and womanly graces Evangeline cultivated. She was enough to make one distrust all simple-seeming, apparently amiable women; and one felt one would rather have had downright roughness with some affection, than that silken selfishness which had spoilt the only chance a man ever had to become better than his natural self, was crushing his son, and bringing his daughter up to be detestable.

One of Evangeline's ideas was to have a ball while we were all together, "just like the one we had when we were girls," she said, clapping her hands youthfully. It did not seem to me to be a very happy idea, considering what Adalesa had suffered on that occasion; but the latter was too healthy minded, even if she had not been too happily situated, to be troubled by inconvenient reminiscences.

Lady Marsh aided and abetted Evangeline. We should arrange it all ourselves, she said, just as we did before, in the same sitting-room, and all be girls again. But, oh, the pathetic absurdity of the attempt! three married women at the meridian expected to ape themselves as they were in the morning of life. Only Evangeline could seriously think of such a thing. She insisted that our costumes for the ball should be red, white, and blue again; and that we should wear the jewels Sir Henry had given us for the first event; and she sorrowed because the very same dresses were not in existence to be worn again.

"What *should* we look like!" Adalesa exclaimed, with her frank laugh. She was sitting beside her uncle, and now proceeded to make merry with him over the disappearance of her angles, and the apparition of a wrinkle:—"I was so surprised when I first caught a glimpse of one at the corner of my eye," she said. "I thought there was something the matter with the glass. It had never occurred to me that *I* should become wrinkled."

Evangeline was shocked at such levity. She thought any allusion to altered looks very bad taste; and besides, she was treating the whole thing like a sacred function, which, if solemnly performed in the right spirit, would rejuvenate us all. "You always had those wrinkles," she said severely. "It is the way you laugh. You pucker up your eyes."

One of Evangeline's wearing tricks was to exact a lover-like devotion from her husband; but only by fits and starts, when others failed or their attentions palled upon her, or when she suspected him of having looked admiringly at some one else. The poor man always did his best to respond to these exactions; but it was pitiful to witness what the effort cost him, and ridiculous to see him attach himself to her train, and feign again to be a passionate young lover. At such times he made me think of a performing dog in a state of trepidation, doing his best with one eye on his master's whip, in dread anticipation of what will follow if he fails to satisfy him.

I was standing beside her when the ball began.

"How delightful to renew all the old associations!" she exclaimed. "I feel quite as excited as I did—then, you know."

I could see, however, that it was an anxious kind of excitement, more painful than pleasurable. This ball was to be decisive in some way. She kept glancing at herself in a mirror near. She had always loved the good points of her own anatomy; it had been a positive pleasure to her to consider them; but now there was no pleasure in her eyes, only incessant inquiry.

"I think we look pretty much the same," she said at last, airily, but tentatively also.

"The same considerably older," I answered, but instantly regretted the careless speech when I saw its effect upon her. She. was not so much offended as frightened, I thought, and I was glad to see her husband approaching to make a diversion.

"We will have the first waltz together for old sake's sake," he began, with a kindly smile.

"I am engaged for it. You should have come sooner," she answered shortly.

"Well, never mind, dear," he rejoined. "Keep me one during the evening."

"If you really care about it, I think you might particularise the one," she answered.

He took her programme, and looked at it quietly; but there was no longer any of the animation in his face with which he had approached her. She had banished the light of other days effectually; and in its place there reappeared the lines which had been deeply graven there by the friction of such scenes as these.

Evangeline's partner carried her off, and then her husband turned to Adalesa, who was also standing by. I had noticed that it was always to her he turned in times of trial. "You see I never do the right thing," he said, dejectedly.

"I should have said that you did so just then," she answered.

"Ah! well, then," he rejoined, "I suppose I did not do it in the right way."

He sighed as he spoke, and at that moment Evangeline glided by with Mr. Vincent, to whom she whispered and simpered as they waltzed.

There was a bevy of girls at the ball, charming, fresh, merry girls, whom it was a pleasure just to sit and watch, their enjoyment of everything was so hearty. It was a joy to us elder women to have them come and cosy up to us with frank, affectionate confidence, sure of our sympathy and discretion. There was a double delight in it for us, the pleasure of entering into all their feelings, and the hope of being able to help them to realize some of their anticipations.

Adalesa and I busied ourselves in finding partners for them. Evangeline had fought against having so many girls asked, but we ultimately overruled her objection. A ball without plenty of girls would be intolerable. In my leisure moments—that is, to say when a dance was in progress—I saw her several times sitting out; and towards the end of the evening an unmistakable air of deep dissatisfaction settled upon her. She had determined to dance till daylight, but only her husband, Mr. Vincent and Mr. Marks had asked her; by all the other men she had been overlooked.

Once during the night I saw her hurriedly leave the ball-room alone, and followed her, fearing she might be ill. I found her in her own room, having recourse to those fatal "drops," without which she professed to be so seldom equal to anything now. They seemed to raise her spirits for the moment; but, later on, during a dance, she came to where Adalesa and I were sitting out together, and sank on to the ottoman beside us with such a weary, dejected air that I felt sorry for her, and tried to think of something to say that would solace her. The effort brought back a vivid recollection of the day that we were commemorating. I recognised the very spot where I had sat looking on at the ball and wondering at her conduct; and recalled with a rush the yearning to peep into the future—and the palm. I looked across to the corner where it had stood, and there, by a natural coincidence, was again a palm. Probably one had been placed on that same spot for every ball given in the house. But this palm looked so exactly like the other, even to the position of that particular leaf on which the light had shone as it waved to the whirl of the dancers, or bent, in quiet moments, above those who sat under it, that it might have been the same plant, especially as time had touched it, so that the leaf was no longer fresh and green, but dry and brown, with frayed edges much in need of the gardener's shears.

I had confided my fancy of long ago about it to Adalesa, and now she remarked upon it.

"Does it speak of spirits still?" she asked.

"Alas! no," I answered. "It has 'fallen into the sere, the yellow leaf' and is altogether prosaic. I should have it cut off; it only disfigures the plant."

Evangeline looked up at it absently; then suddenly her eyes gleamed.

"Do I look like a horrid, wizened old woman?" she demanded.

"No," I answered sincerely.

"And what would it matter if one did?" Adalesa asked.

"What would it matter!" she groaned. "It would mean an end of everything that makes life endurable."

"Nonsense!" said Adalesa. "Every age has its pleasures; and how a woman can care to be a day younger than she is—can crave for the admiration paid to twenty when she should be enjoying the homage due to forty, I cannot conceive. The buds are beautiful in the spring, and there is beauty also in the full-blown foliage of summer; but are either more admirable in their day than the exquisite autumn leaf?"

"But men say such things about old women," Evangeline wailed.

"Ah—men!" Adalesa laughed. "Well, *my* man is sound on the subject. But why be for ever thinking about men, Evangeline? Why don't you go in for something sensible now? Look at Mrs. Crowther! It is for men, I suppose, that *she* makes up so abominably. And what does she gain by it? Nothing but ridicule; for if there is one thing men despise more than another, it is an artificial woman. Are you ill?"

This was said with concern, on seeing Evangeline's face contract, as if with a spasm of pain.

"No, thank you," she answered faintly. Then, after a little, she exclaimed, "But what is there to live for, if you cease to be attractive?"

"Oh, if we are careful, we need never cease to be attractive," Adalesa answered easily, and then abruptly changed the subject.

XV. WHEN THE GUESTS had gone, and we had got into our dressing-gowns, Adalesa came to my room, and found me sitting by the open window looking out at the lingering night. She drew up a chair, and sat beside me silently for some time.

There was no moon, and only a few stars appeared low down on the horizon; but still it was possible to see the shadowy outlines of trees and shrubs; and the scent of summer flowers was wafted up to us, the chirrup of a bird disturbed, the mournful cry of some creature far away—bird of night or beast in distress, it was impossible to say which at so great a distance—and even the round clear warble of a nightingale arose now and then, though it was late in the season for these; occasionally, too, one of the dogs would set up a dismal howl, which would arouse the others in the neighbourhood, one by one, till a whole pack had joined in vigorous chorus, which subsided again into single barks, as it had begun, making room for the silence proper to the hour—that silence, never empty or distasteful to the healthy mind, which is as an atmosphere wrapped about us, through which we are conscious of the throbbing of continuous soft sounds. There came to us now from far away the solemn, deep-toned tolling of a bell; while the constant gurgle and drip of water near at hand and the voices of whispering leaves filled up every pause with lingering *crescendo* murmur and rustle, inexpressibly soothing.

"What an exquisite hour!" Adalesa said at last softly; "a night like that other night long ago ; but, oh, the difference! the like in unlikeness! I *did* suffer. And now I have everything—by which I mean that in myself which is everything; while Evangeline I do pity her; and I am anxious about her too. I never dreamt any sane woman could be so seriously affected by the suspicion that she has gone off. She has everything in the world but the charm of youth and the tribute paid to it, and that, it seems, is the only thing she cares for."

"Oh, well, it is natural to mourn when a sudden sense of loss comes upon us," I answered temperately. "I don't believe, until to-night, she ever even suspected that she could go off. It must have been a blow to find herself set aside all at once. But let us hope she is sleeping now, and will awake with her mind strengthened."

"Yes, let us hope it," Adalesa answered. "Let us hope she will reconcile herself to the loss of her beauty, and begin to look about for more lasting interests. And let us slip out, you and I, just to mark the good time we are having, and the great change let us slip out and sit on the shore, and watch the sun rise over the sea. Come and invoke 'tender morning visions of beauteous souls,' and be glad. You can be glad now?" she said, with sudden sympathy, recollecting.

"Oh yes," I answered quickly; "I enjoy every hour of my life now."

"That's right. That is how it should be as we get older," she replied. "Here, let me help you into a walking-dress. Don't you appreciate things better now than you did?—at the moment, I mean. When one is young, one is never so satisfied. One looks back and lives those delights over again; but at the time we did not understand, and so lost the full flavour. Later one has realised how precious it is just to be alive; and then, I think, it is that one begins to live."

We were ready by this time, and, having slipped out by a side-door, we took our way through the murmuring pine wood to the beach. It was so dusky under the trees that we could see no path; and now our feet sank deep in moss, and now dry branches crackled beneath them, making what seemed, by contrast, to be a terrific noise in the stillness. In the thicker part of the wood great shadows rushed out upon and then engulfed us; and filmy forms that hovered above the path flitted aside to make way for us; while the pine-needles falling kept up a continuous patter, as of lively little feet; and the fragrant pine-plumes, answering to a touch, bent above us caressingly.

Presently, however, we raised our heads again out in the open. It was a very different scene. The breezy sandhills lay about us, desolate as deserted streets, which they somewhat resembled in their irregular outlines, by that light—streets that the dust of ages has settled upon, making mounds, beneath which all outward semblance of human habitation is blotted out. The coarse grass, through which the wind swished, and the heavy sand hindered our feet as we stumbled on; but presently we came out upon the beach, close beside the sea, for the tide was up. And there we sat us, and together saw the sapphire dark melt out of the sky, and the first faint grey streaks of dawn shoot up in the east, shaft-like, from horizon to zenith, then slowly take on a faint flush of pink, scarcely a shadow at first, but growing momentarily deeper, and spreading till the whole east shone crimson, and the sea responded to the glory of it. Then the rim of the sun arose from the waters, and the wavelets welcomed it with merry murmurs as they broke upon the sandy shore. We saw in silence, there being no word of human speech to express the emotions of such a moment. The sea-voice sang in our ears; we scented the exquisite iodine freshness of the air, the joy of nature filled and encompassed us. No hour of earthly triumph can exceed in ecstasy the gladness of such a time. The holy calm of it settled upon us, and when at last we rose and returned arm in arm, our souls were satisfied, and our hearts were strengthened as by a solemn service.

XVI. Next morning, at a late hour, I was dressing in a leisurely manner for a late breakfast; and as I dressed I sang to myself, until the saying "Sing before breakfast cry before night" flashed through my mind, bringing with it a hundred memories of happy mornings when the songs would out in spite of the saying.

Now, however, somehow it silenced me, and I was just thinking, when without warning, Adalesa burst in upon me and stood on the threshold gasping, with scared, white face.

"Come!" she tried to articulate, but her voice failed her.

I understood, however, and followed her from the room without a word.

Outside in the corridor we encountered Sir Henry and Lady Marsh. He, with a blank, stunned look on his fine old countenance, was tenderly supporting her as he led her to her room. Poor old people, fast failing both of them,—it was a terrible sight. She was all dishevelled in appearance, as if she had rushed out from her bed, with white hair streaming, and the pleased, perpetual smile banished at last and for ever from her distorted features. When she saw us she sent up a shriek, like one distraught.

"What horror has happened?" I tried to say, but my voice was strangled in my throat.

Adalesa, clasping her hand round my arm, hurried me on to Evangeline's room. The door was open, and several servants, with awestruck countenances, stood outside craning their necks to peep in over each other's heads and satisfy their curiosity. As we approached they silently made way for us, and we entered. The blinds were up, and the summer sun exposed the scene, touching with tawdriness what the moon would have enriched, and making merely revolting that which night would have divested of all but romantic interest. Was it only a few hours since we had seen that same sun rise resplendent, and felt we could cling to every hour of life only to see and salute him again and again? We had flattered ourselves then that Evangeline was sleeping off her childish pique; and now, at the first glance, she seemed to be sleeping; but at the second we stood transfixed, seeing but not believing, knowing but not acknowledging.

There was a large luxurious couch near the window; and there, still in her ball dress and her jewels, lit by the full blaze of day, she lay prone, with eyes half-shut and lips drawn back in a dreadful grin. She had many more jewels on than she had worn at the ball the night before; and I was seized with the horrid suspicion that the ball dress had been kept on for effect, and the extra diamonds added to complete the picture. But oh! if she could have seen the effect! I wish—I wish *I* never had, for I cannot forget it. Patches of rouge stood out on her sallow, shrunken cheeks, making her whole face look like old ill-coloured wax, the rigidity being further emphasised by a fly, which buzzed about, lighting now here, now there, with impunity. It was horrible not even to expect her to feel it, and flip it away.

Her husband stood beside her; looking down at her, but there was neither love nor grief in his face—only a kind of wonder mingled with repulsion. It is dreadful to see death and not weep; but all who stood by, her lovers and her friends, were dry-eyed; and the fact that there was not one tearful face to relieve the tension with a touch of pathos made the tragedy more hideous.

Mr. Regy Vincent outside said audibly to Mrs. Crowther: "She looks too horrid; you mustn't go in."

Could she have heard him, had she had imagination enough even to have anticipated such a thing, she might have been saved!

Suddenly a child set up a shrill cry. It was her little boy, who had slipped in unnoticed, and now clung, shrieking and terrified, to his father. A servant, shrinking from the task, hastily tore the coverlet from the bed; and, with lips compressed, as if nerving herself, covered the couch and its ghastly burden, and then, snatching up the child, hurriedly made her escape.

Outside, Mrs. Crowther was asking Mr. Vincent if there would be an inquest.

"Oh yes! and we shall be asked to give evidence," he answered.

"What—*me?*" she cried. "How horrid! I was never mixed up in anything so dreadful in my life. Can't I get away?"

"Well, *I'm* going," he rejoined; "I'll see you safely to town if you like."

Now that there was nothing to be seen but the dim suggestion of a figure beneath the coverlet, we were able to speak to each other.

Perceval was the first to find words.

"She seemed dreadfully depressed after the ball," he whispered. "I could not understand why exactly. She said several times she had nothing left to live for. Then she begged me to leave her for the night. She wanted to be alone. She said she thought she should sleep if I left her alone. So I went into the next room, and was soon asleep myself, never dreaming—"

He looked absently at a little bottle he held in his hand, and muttered something about a dangerous medicine.

Adalesa slipped her hand through my arm, and whispering "I want to speak to you," led me away to her room. "Look," she said, drawing a paper from her pocket when she had shut the door and looked round carefully to make sure that we were alone, "I found this, but no one else has seen it. It is not addressed to any one, and there is no signature, you see. What shall I do with it? She had it in her hand. I was the first to find her. I went in early, because I was anxious. I thought I could cheer her. She seemed to be holding it out to me, as I entered; and I took it, and kissed her, and asked her pardon if I had hurt her—before I saw. I ran in, you know, and flopped down on my knees beside her, giving myself no time either to see or think; so that it did not strike me as strange that she should be lying there in her ball dress and jewels, with the sun streaming in upon her. It was the cold of her cheek—"

She finished by crushing the crumpled sheet into my hand with a shudder; and I shuddered too, as I opened it. One does not shrink from anything that the honoured dead have touched; but this was different—this firmly written, cool, cynical, heartless expression of a selfish determination.

When I had read it I looked at Adalesa, and made as if I would have torn it up.

"Yes, yes," she said eagerly; "or burn it—for the sake of an honoured name—for the old people—for the children's sake—burn it. No one need ever know. Thank Heaven we were here!"

Accordingly, a large and sorrowing circle of shocked and sympathetic friends were informed eventually by the verdict that the sad occurrence had been the result of misadventure, in the shape of an overdose of morphia "taken to relieve pain."

From THE STORY OF A MODERN WOMAN

ELLA HEPWORTH DIXON

1894

CHAPTER I. AN END AND A BEGINNING

GLARING SPRING SUNSHINE and a piercing east wind rioted out of doors, and here and there overflowing flower baskets made startling patches of colour against the vague blue-grey of the streets, but indoors, in the tall London house, there was only a sickly, yellow twilight, for the orange-toned blinds were scrupulously drawn down. There was awe in the passages, and hushed tones even in the kitchen, as if the dead could hear! Some wreaths and crosses of wax-like exotic flowers lay on the hall table, filling the passage with their sensuous odour. Friends calling to inquire had left them there, but they had not yet been taken up—up to that awful room where a marble figure, a figure which was strangely unlike Professor Erle—lay stretched, in an enduring silence, on the bed.

Downstairs, in the little study giving on a meagre London yard, a girl was bending over a desk. *"You will, I know, be grieved to hear that my dear father passed suddenly away the night before last,"* she wrote, while a great nerve in her forehead went tick, tick, tick. The visitors who came all day long, leaving bits of pasteboard, spoke in low, inquisitive tones. When the bell rang, there were veiled whispers at the hall-door. "So terrible—so sudden!" Mary could hear them inquire how she was keeping up? And Elizabeth's answer: "Miss Erle is as well as could be expected." The trite, worn-out, foolish sentence almost made her laugh. All the stock phrases of condolence, all the mental trappings of woe, seemed. to be ready-made for the "sad occasion," like the crape skirts and cloaks which had been forwarded immediately from the mourning establishment in Regent Street. "Yes, I am as well as could be expected," she thought, "and father is dead. Father is dead."

And all the long afternoon she went mechanically on writing, *"I am sure you will be sorry when I tell you that my dear father—"* on paper bordered with black an inch deep. How he would have disliked that foolish ostentation of mourning; it was contrary to the spirit of his life. "To-morrow," she said to herself, "I must send for some note paper with a narrower edge." These letters were to be sent abroad. The English newspapers had sufficiently announced the death, for Professor Erle was perhaps the best-known man of science of the day.

In the little back-room they had to light the lamp early, there was so much to do, so many details to arrange. The ceremony was to be as simple as might be; above all, no paid priest would stand at the grave to give hearty thanks that the great thinker had been delivered out of the miseries of the sinful world. The sinful world would have as its spokesman another famous professor, who had asked to be allowed to say a few words.

Then there were the newspapers. There was the brisk, smartly dressed young gentleman who came to do a leader for a daily paper, who had a wandering, observant eye and a leather note-book, and who proceeded to make a number of notes in short-hand, asking innumerable questions as his omnivorous glance travelled rapidly round the study. Another reporter—a small, apologetic man with greyish hair and a timid cough, who asked to see the house for the *Evening Planet*. He begged of Elizabeth on the hall steps to tell him if the professor had said anything—anything particular, which would work up as a leader, just at the last? "Oh! sir," said Elizabeth, " didn't you know? Master didn't say anything. He just died in his sleep."

The daughter went about her tasks with a sense of detachment, of intense aloofness. "I wonder if I really feel it?" she thought, "and why I have never cried? I should like to, but it is impossible; I shall never, never cry again." It was as if Death, with his cruel, searing wings had cauterised her very soul. Sometimes she pictured herself in her long crape veil at the funeral, and heard in imagination her friends' murmuring, pitying words, as they all followed the coffin up the Highgate slope. Alison Ives, of course, would be with her. She would stay by her, perhaps, and hold her hand. And probably Vincent Hemming would be near. Yes, he, too, would be there.

At dinner-time she had to sit down to table alone. She was hungry, and she ate hardly knowing what was on her plate. Nothing happened as it does in tales and romances. In innumerable novels she had read how the heroine, in a house of mourning, lies on the bed for days and steadily refuses to eat. As for Mary, a demon of unrest possessed her during that horrible week, and it was as if she could not eat nourishing food enough. She never stopped arranging, writing, adding-up accounts. It was useless to try and read. Did she but take a book, that dominant image in her mind—the image of a dear face turned to marble, with the cold, triumphant smile of eternity on its lips—shut out the sense of the words as her eyes travelled down the page.

And the strange, unmistakable odour of death, mixed with the scent of waxen hot house flowers, hung, night and day, about the staircase.

Toward the end of the week, there was more noise and bustle, and at last had come the morning when the house swarmed with undertaker's men, and Mary and her young brother Jim, who had arrived from Winchester, sat with a few old friends in the dining-room, waiting for the signal to go. There was the shuffling of men's feet, as they staggered down the narrow London staircase with their heavy burden, and then someone had made the girl swallow some sal volatile, and she was pushed gently into the first mourning carriage, along with Jim. They had made the boy drink some of the sal volatile too, and they both felt strangely elated and highly strung. There were only those two now, and Mary felt warmly drawn to Jimmie, as they sat side by side in their new black clothes, the two chief personages in the ceremony of to-day. She even pretended not to hear when, some gutter urchins making complicated cartwheels as their contribution to the imposing procession, Jim, boy-like, gave way to a furtive giggle.

The drive to Highgate seemed interminable, but at last, when the long procession crept slowly up the hill, it was in a kind of stupor that the girl saw and heard what happened. There was, she remembered afterward, a long line of people, habited in black, awaiting them in silence inside the cemetery gate; a tolling bell, neighing horses, and a penetrating scent of early lilac. Sunlight on the paths, on the shining marble tombs, on the humble little mounds covered with plush like grass; then a moving mass of black, a yawning hole, the creaking of ropes, and the mellifluous voice of the eminent professor, speaking his oration over the upturned clay.

"England, I may say the world, is mourning to-day for her illustrious son"—how the people pressed round the yawning gap, and pushed against the guelder rose-tree overhead, so that the flowers fell in a minute white shower on to the oaken coffin below—"England is mourning for her illustrious son. Not that her tears will flow in vain, for those tears will moisten and fructify the precious tree of Truth; a tree which is evermore putting forth fresh branches and new fruits which are indispensable to the physical and moral evolution of humanity."

In a neighbouring laburnum-bush, a thrush was swelling its brown throat with a joyous morning song. Athwart the pale sky dappled with fleecy clouds, the lilac bushes were burgeoning with waxen pinkish blossoms. The very air throbbed with coming life.

"Nature," continued the orator, in his measured, lecture-room tones, "Nature, who works in inexorable ways, has taken to herself a life full of arduous toil, of epoch-making achievement, of immeasurable possibilities, but to what end, and for what purpose, it is not given to us, who stand to-day with full hearts and yearning eyes around his last resting place, to know."

The sun was warm overhead, the scent of the pink may was strong in the nostrils; a joyous twittering in an adjacent bush told of mating birds, of new life in the nests, of Nature rioting in an insolent triumph.

The orator paused for an instant, coughed, and felt in his breast pocket for his notes. He was anxious, above all things, that the reporters should not print a garbled version of his speech. Round the open grave pressed the devotees of science, the followers of the religion of humanity; grey-skinned, anxious-looking men and women, with lined foreheads, and hair prematurely tinged with grey; large heads with bulging foreheads, thin throats and sloping shoulders; the women with nervous, over-worked faces, the men with the pathetic, unrestful features of those who are sustained in a life of self-denial by their ethical sense alone. The ceremony of to-day was a great moral demonstration. All classes who think were represented. Side by side stood a white-haired Radical countess in simple half-mourning and the spare form of a Socialist working woman, with red, ungloved wrists and an inspired look on her worn face. There, with her mother, Lady Jane, was Alison Ives. Lady Jane, who was impressionable, was already exhibiting a pocket-handkerchief, and not far off, Mary caught for one instant the brown, wistful eyes of Vincent Hemming.

The sun grew hotter and hotter overhead. One or two of the mourners began putting up umbrellas. The perfume of pink hawthorn became almost oppressive; an early butterfly lighted on a baby's grave planted with sweet-smelling flowers. A light breeze fluttered through a laburnum-bush which hung over a neighbouring marble tomb, a large, opulent marble tomb, on which was cut in glittering gilt letters: "of such is the kingdom of heaven." And everywhere there was the whiteness of graves. In ridges, in waves, in mounds, they stuck, tooth-like, from the fecund earth. They shone, in gleaming, distant lines, up to the ridge of the hill; they crowded in serried battalions, down to the cemetery gates.

The speaker was concluding his speech. "For though to isolated men," he said, raising his voice so that all who were on the edge of the crowd should hear, "it may be given here and there to scale the loftiest heights—aye, and ever new peaks rising upon peaks in the great undiscovered country which we call the realm of science; there, too, the finite touches the infinite, and must recognise what of tentativeness, what of inconclusiveness belongs to mere human effort. Here, on a sudden, the dark impenetrable curtain, which none may draw aside, envelopes us; here we know not whether all ends with this our last prison house, or if to us may be opened out yet further cycles of aspiring activity."

In the silence which followed there was heard one long, sweet, penetrating bird-call.

One of the chief mourners, the boy Jimmie, was sobbing loudly when the professor's voice stopped, and with something gripping at her throat, the sister led him away. She reproached herself with having brought him; the young, she thought, should not know what sorrow is. The two spare, black-clad figures stepped aside up the hill.

Out yonder, at their feet, the dun colour of the buildings lost in the murkiness of the horizon line, London was spread out. Here and there a dome, a spire loomed out of the dim bluish-grey panorama. A warm haze hung over the great city; here and there a faint fringe of tree-tops told of a placid park; now and again the shrill whistle of an engine, blown northward by the wind, spoke of the bustle of journeys, of the turmoil of railway stations, of partings, of arrivals, of the change and travail of human life, of the strangers who come, of the failures who must go.

"Jim," said the girl suddenly, taking the boy by the arm, "there's London! We're going to make it listen to us, you and I. We're not going to be afraid of it—just because it's big, and brutal, and strong."

"N—no, dearest," said the boy, turning up a pretty, sensitive face, and a pink nose all smeared with tears. "Of course not."

The black cloud yonder was swaying, separating, and disintegrating itself into separate sable dots, which were now seen descending the paths to the cemetery gate. And slowly, they, too, stepped down the grand path.

They came home to a house that was empty and orderly again; a house in which *his* door stood open, the pale light of a spring afternoon filling the desolate room. The blinds were pulled up, and downstairs, in the kitchen, the servants had begun to talk and laugh.

Toward dusk Jimmie got engrossed in a new book of adventures, but the girl, restless still, wandered about the house in her black gown, looking at everything with strange eyes. Something terrible, unforeseen, had happened which altered her whole life. Toward the boy poring over the picture-book she felt much of a mother's feeling; it behooved her to look after him now that his father was gone. How long the time seemed—would the interminable day never end? There must be lots for her to do. And casting about in her mind, she remembered that this was the day on which she always gave out the groceries from her store cupboard; there was the seamstress to pay, too, who was altering a black dress for her upstairs. So Mary dragged herself down to the kitchens, and presently to the top of the house. It would be nice of her, she thought, to go in and speak to the woman who was sewing alone. It was sad for a young woman to be alone.

The pale, pinkish light of a spring evening fell on a drab-complexioned girl, whose fat hand moved, as she sewed, with the regularity of a machine. Now the needle was thrust in the folded black stuff, and the light fell on her ill-cut nails; now the hand was aloft, in the semi-obscurity; it was all tame, monotonous, and regular as a clock. She was a docile, humble, uncomplaining creature, who suggested inevitably some patient domestic animal. Her features, rubbed out and effaced with generations of servility, spoke of the small mendacities of the women of the lower classes, of the women who live on ministering to the caprices of the well-to-do. To-day it would seem she had assumed an appropriately dolorous expression.

It sometimes soothed Mary to stitch. Taking up a strip of black merino, she began to hem. The 'seamstress' hand continued to move with docile regularity, and, as Mary looked at her, she was curiously reminded of many women she had seen: ladies, mothers of large families, who sat and sewed with just such an expression of unquestioning resignation. The clicking sound of the needle, the swish of the drawn-out thread, the heavy breathing of the workwoman, all added to the impression. Yes, they too were content to exist subserviently, depending always on someone else, using the old feminine stratagems, the well-worn feminine subterfuges, to gain their end. The woman who sews is eternally the same.

The light began to fail now; very soon it would be dark. Mary threw down her work with an impatient gesture, and, in the grey twilight, an immense pity seized her for the patient figure bending, near the window, over her foolish strips of flounces.

It was not so much a woman, but The Woman at her monotonous toil.

Chapter II. A Child.

THE LIFE OF Mary Erle, like that of many another woman in the end of the nineteenth century, had been more or less in the nature of an experiment. Born too late for the simple days of the fifties, when all it behooved a young woman to do was to mind her account-book, read her Tennyson, show a proper enthusiasm for fancy-work stitches, and finally, with many blushes accept the hand of the first young man who desired to pay taxes and to fulfil the duties of a loyal British subject (and the young man, it must be remembered, in the middle of this century, actually did both), Mary was yet too soon for the time when parents begin to take their responsibilities seriously, and when the girl is sometimes as carefully prepared, as thoroughly equipped, as her brother for the fight of life. A garden full of flowers, a house full of books, scraps of travel: these things were her education. Out of the years she could pick scenes and figures which typified her bringing-up.

There was the plain, self-contained, and not too clean baby. A child who was always grubbing in a garden, for it lived then in a house in St. John's Wood; a child who was devoted to animals and insects, who was on intimate terms with the many-legged wood-lice, which curled themselves up with all haste into complete balls when she touched them; a child for whom snails and black-beetles had no terrors, and who had much to say to the fat, hairy caterpillars which hung about the pear-tree.

There was a huge, fluffy black cat, too, which represented, perhaps, the child's primitive idea of a deity; for, though she adored it, the adoration was leavened with a wholesome awe, a feeling which was not unconnected with certain unmerited chastisements in the shape of scratches on her fat, bare legs. More often, to be sure, the black cat was amiable, and even allowed itself to be carried up to bed, with its hind legs straying out helplessly from under the child's arm, to be presently concealed with all haste and caution under the white sheets and blankets, from whence its sharp-pointed ears and fat black cheeks arose with the most exquisitely mirth-provoking effect. With what inscrutable amber eyes did the black cat gaze for hours into hers: how it imposed on her babyish imagination with its self-contained, majestic manners, its air of detachment from the vain shows of the world! The man with the kind smile, whom the child called "father," used to laugh at her adoration, tell her she was a little Egyptian, and called the cat "Pasht." She thought it a funny name, and not being altogether sure the black cat would approve of it, she generally addressed it as "you." And the cat would sit on long summer afternoons on the grass under the pear-tree, or on foggy autumn days on a stool by the fireside, with paws neatly tucked away, its neck-ruff fluffed out, purring benignly in response to her confidences. Indeed, in looking back, the first tragedy of the child's life was the death of the black cat. It lay, one sultry July day, under a laurel bush in the garden, with glazed eyes which gave no signs of life. All morning and all afternoon the child sat there and fanned the flies away, until her idol was stiff, and then a hole was hastily dug, and the black cat was thrust out of sight. And never any more, in the warm summer afternoons, did a soft, furry thing go sailing, tail in air, over the close-cropped lawn; nor, on winter evenings, was a rhythmical purring to be heard hard by the tall fender which guarded the nursery fire. It was the first great void; the first heart-ache had come.

A strange, indolent, not too clean child, whose little hands were usually thrust beneath her pinafore when anyone spoke to her; for surely she could not be always washing herself, and to be on really intimate terms with insects and things, one cannot, like grown-up people, be always thinking of one's nails. She usually, too, concealed a small piece of putty about her person—an unpardonable sin, this, in the eyes of mother and nurse—for putty is useful in a thousand ways, and is, besides, so thrillingly delicious to feel surreptitiously in the recesses of one's pocket. At this time the child held the whole race of dolls in high scorn. They were a foolish, over-dressed, uninteresting tribe, with manifestly absurd cheeks and eyelashes, and with a simper which was as artificial as that of the ladies in chignons and flounces who came to call at the house in St. John's Wood. She, on her part, was all for the violent delights of miniature guns and real gunpowder, the toilsome construction of fleets of wooden boats with the aid of a blunt knife and a plank of wood: fleets which were set a-sail, with flying penants, on the cistern hard by the kitchen. There were boy neighbors who aided and abetted her in these delights, and great naval battles would come off between the Dutch and English fleets in the kitchen cistern, in which sometimes Van Tromp and sometimes Blake emerged victorious. The child, perhaps, did not take her patriotism seriously, as the boys did; she was content to be Van Tromp, since they insisted on being Blake and Monk. All that was of vital importance was that a fight of some sort should come off.

The mother sank early out of ken. First they said that she was poorly, and had gone to Italy, and then they said that she was very ill, and afterward that she was in heaven; so that for a long time the child used to think vaguely, as she sat in the summerhouse with pursed-up lips and knitted brows, notching and slicing at her ships, that Italy and heaven were perhaps the same place. Nurse said that her mummy was an angel now; but in all the picture-books angels had long, smooth hair, wore a kind of nightgown, and had enormous, folding wings. The child could not picture her mother looking like that; she always remembered her in many flounces, with a head-ache; and certainly, no certainly, mummy never had any wings out of her back.

The child could recollect that, some little time before her mother went to Italy, they took her upstairs one day and showed her a baby, with a red, crinkled face, lying in an over-trimmed cradle. She did not care for babies, she would rather have had a nice, new, fluffy kitten to replace the old black cat; but when they told her it was a little brother, of course that altered matters. She was sorry her brother should be so small, so fretful, and so red in the face; she would rather have had him the same size as herself, so that he could have been Van Tromp for once, and she the victorious Blake; but still, any sort or size of brother was better than none. Although, in a year or so, the baby developed into something suspiciously like a doll, with his fat, pink cheeks, his round, china-blue eyes, his dump of a nose, and his entire absence of chin, still, he was far more entertaining than that simpering and foolish tribe. Baby Jim's pink toes could kick; his little fist, with the creases of fat at the wrist, could hit out; there were warlike possibilities in him. In a word, Baby Jim was alive.

At ten years old the girl began to have strange fits of vanity. There were little shoes and frocks which she held in high favour, and others which nothing would induce her to put on. To wear a pinafore, now, was a bitter humiliation, and about this period she had the most definite theories about the dressing of hair. The discussion on coiffures usually took place in her bath, when a small, slippery person covered in soap-suds was to be heard arguing with her nurse—an argument which was not unusually enforced by physical violence—on the superior attractions of crimped to curled locks. At ten years old she was of opinion a person was grown up, or at least as old as anyone should be. Why, big, tall men, with long beards and spectacles, who came to see her father, would bend down and ask her gravely if she would be their little wife? The child had been to more than one wedding, and she was aware that a wife was a person who began by wearing a beautiful white satin train, with white flowers and a veil; a person who was as imposing as that angel which nurse said her mother had become, although she had not, of course, any wings. The child was not sure whether she would best like to be a bride or an angel. The latter, it was true, had the additional attraction of a golden halo; but she thought, probably, that matters might be compromised, and that she could be a wife and have a halo too.

The scene shifts now, for they had moved to another quarter of London, and the change made a vast difference in the child's tastes and habits. There was no cropped lawn, where the pear-tree made long shadows on summer afternoons, where she had a personal interest in a plot of ground of her own, and at least a bowing acquaintance with a whole host of fussy bumble-bees, gay yellow butterflies, furry caterpillars, and lazy snails. There was no summerhouse in which ship building could be carried on, and no convenient cistern in which to sail one's fleet. The firing off of toy guns was erased from the list of possible amusements. The house was a tall one, in a street in town, and rural delights were represented by a square yard at the back, which was haunted by stray, attenuated cats, and in which grew a solitary, stunted sycamore. But, on the other hand, there was the new fascination of bookshelves, which ran all over the new house, so that the child had but to mount a chair and reach out a small hand, and lo! romance and battles, laughter and tears, were all to be enjoyed at her will. She had only to pick out her volume. It was a revelation in the possibilities of life.

Looking back now, it must be owned that she led an odd life. The man with the kind smile was fond of his little daughter, but he was always at work, either at experiments in his laboratory or bending over his desk in the study. Nothing happened in the way of experience as it does to other children. One night her father took her to the theatre for the first time. A famous actress, an old friend, was giving *Antony* and *Cleopatra*, and they went first behind the scenes. They walked across a bare, lofty, cavern-like place, with dusty wooden boards which sloped upward, and the child was lifted up to peep through a little hole in a red velvet curtain, and through it she saw a large horseshoe with quantities of people chattering as they waited. There was a great deal of tawdry gilt, and many gas chandeliers, and the people, especially at the top of the horseshoe, stamped with their feet and whistled. She did not care much for the play, when they presently took their places in a box close to the stage. There was a stout lady in long amber draperies, who kept throwing her arms round a tired-looking man with a brown face and a suit of gilt armour. The child was more amused when, between the acts, they went behind the scenes again to see the famous actress in her dressing-room. Unfortunately, the stout lady looked fatter than ever when seen close, but there were so many amusing things about—a wig with long plaits, several serpent bracelets, a diadem, and a beautiful golden girdle set with emeralds as big as pheasants' eggs. There was a middle-aged gentleman, too, who sat at his ease in a shabby armchair, and drank some pinkish, sparkling wine out of a low, round glass. Someone said that he was the editor of a great paper. The child had never seen an editor; she was glad to see one, because she had always thought they were quite different from other people. She liked to see him laugh, and whisper in a familiar, condescending way to the stout lady, and yet keep on drinking the pink wine out of the round glass.

The child was incorrigibly idle. A mild, nondescript, unimaginative governess and a fat, bald Frenchman who came once a week to instruct her in the Gallic tongue did nothing to take away the inherent unattractiveness of "lessons." She could read, and that was enough. The child read all day long. She lay concealed among the footstools under the long dining-room table, poring over "The Ancient Mariner"—her favourite poem—or thrilled with the lurid emotion of "Wuthering Heights." A little later, "Villette" became her cherished book; a well-thumbed copy, long ago bereft of its cover, stands on the girl's shelf to-day. Poor drab, patient, self-contained Miss Snow! How the child's heart ached for you in your bare, dismal, Belgian schoolroom, when Dr. John grew fickle; how she rejoiced when you found your ugly, be-spectacled Fate; how choky she felt at the throat when she read those last pessimistic, despairing words—words full of the sound and fury of angry seas and moaning winds. Why, poor patient hypochondriacal soul, were you destined never to be happy? And all these people were real to the child, much more real than the people she saw when she went out to tea-parties in her best frock and sash. They were as real as the little Tin Soldier and the little Sea-maiden of Hans Christian Andersen, types of humanity which will last as long as there are tender little human hearts to be touched.

And, later on, there is the rather plain girl of fourteen, with somewhat inscrutable eyes, and a seriousness which would have been portentous were it not laughable. Gone, for the time being, were her fits of high spirits and her wild gaiety; lost, the love of battle, and even the love of books about battles. The girl had much to occupy her mind. She began to understand something of life now. It was no longer a kind of coloured picturebook, made to catch the eye and amuse an idle half-hour. The pictures meant a great deal more than that. There were dreadful things, sad things, horrible things behind. Things that the girl could only guess at, but which were there, she was sure, all the same. The world, she could see from her books and newspapers, was full of injustice.

There was the great wrong which had been done some eighteen hundred years ago, when the most beautiful life that was ever lived had come to a shameful end, when the pale Socialist of Nazareth was thrown to the howling populace just as a bone is thrown to a pack of snarling dogs. The girl was always reading that moving, touching story; the Old Testament, with its revengeful, ferocious Deity, did not appeal to her at all. The poignant tragedy enacted at Jerusalem ate into her heart, and this child of fourteen felt herself burdened with the reproach which that senseless crime had left on humanity for well-nigh two thousand years.

Yes, those were serious days. At fourteen, one has to make up one's mind on a great many subjects. There are the questions of marriage, of maternity, of education. The girl had learned French by now, and the chance fingering of a small, last century volume—under the somewhat fantastic and insecure guidance of Jean Jacques Rousseau, made her approach those supremely feminine subjects. She imbibed, indeed, the Swiss philosopher's diatribes on virtue before she had comprehended what civilised mankind stigmatises as vice. "Émile; ou, de l'Education" was wearily, conscientiously toiled through for the sake of posterity. "Le Contrat Social " was a work which it behooved a person of fourteen, who wished to understand the scheme of civilisation, to know.

Strange, anxious days, passed in the twilight of ignorance, groping among the vain shadows with which man in his wisdom has elected to surround the future mothers of the race. It was not, of course, till years afterward, that Mary became conscious of the fine irony of the fact that man, the superior intelligence, should take his future companion, shut her within four walls, fill that dimly lighted interior with images of facts and emotions which do not exist, and then, pushing her suddenly into the blinding glare of real life, should be amazed when he finds that his exquisite care of her ethical sense has stultified her brain.

The little girl was reading "David Copperfield" when she descended one day, with knitted brows, to the room where her governess was laboriously copying in watercolours a lithographed bunch of roses.

"What is a fallen woman really, Miss Brown?" demanded the child, with her tense look. "Dickens says that Little Em'ly is a fallen woman, because she goes to Italy with that Mr. Steerforth. Was Mr. Steerforth a fallen man, too?"

The little girl, it was evident, with all her reading, had yet a great deal to learn. She had yet to apprehend the hard-and-fast rules by which civilised man sets to work to cast stones at his neighbour—and more especially at his female neighbour.

When, at sixteen, the girl—still burdened with doubts—had to pack her trunks for a sojourn in Germany, she packed among the books which she was to take, her New Testament, and the "Men and Women" of Robert Browning. When she returned, a year later, she had some difficulty to find room for her Testament, for her favourite volumes of Darwin and Renan took up so much space, and from the virile optimism of Browning she could not now afford to part.

CHAPTER III. WONDERINGS.

THE SCENE SHIFTS now to a garden in a German town. Over yonder, across the swirling, rushing river, lie the bare, barrack-like university buildings, the narrow streets vandyked with gables, the noisy drinking-shops and the green-canopied anlage; while over the mediaeval bridge come and go, all day long, a procession of students, dogs, school-children, market-women and burghers of all sorts and conditions, sweltering under the fierce summer sun.

But here, in the professor's garden, it is placid enough; in the vine-trellised *laubgang* it is always cool and shady. There is the arbour to sit in, after the twelve o'clock dinner, where the sultry afternoon can be dreamed away till coffee-time with an open book on one's knee. The rest of the household have probably gone to bed again, for in Germany, where one rises at six, the weakness of the flesh is apt to manifest itself after a Teutonic midday meal, and sleep becomes imperative unless one has secured the "Buch der Lieder" from off the top book-shelf in the study, and Heine's "cynical smile" is illuminating the placid German landscape for the first time. Other days it would be the "Wahlverwandtschaften" or, "Wilhelm Meister," or the red-hot, palpitating *novellen* of Paul Heyse. Was the worthy Frau Professorin asleep, or looking after the *sauerkraut* fermenting in tubs in the cellar, or seeing to the pressing of the little white wine, which grew primarily in small bunches of green grapes, overhead in the *laubgang*? The Frau Professorin led a busy life. So long as the English professor's daughter was reading German, what did it matter much what she read? The good little woman had a nice eye for the baking of a cake or the stewing of cherries to be served with tomorrow's roast veal, but with all that poring over books she had no patience. When one had secured a distinguished husband like the Herr Professor—she always alluded to him by this title—and produced several boys and girls who all wore spectacles, and gave promise of the highest intellectual attainments, a German female citizen had surely fulfilled her mission?

In her own opinion, she, the Frau Professorin, had every intellectual attainment. When she was a young girl, she had learned by heart portions of Schiller's plays, and could have recited to you, had you suffered it, the whole of "Hermann und Dorothea." Goethe's domestically didactic idyl embodied all the virtues as well as all the emotions which were permissible to the German girl of the mid-century. When the Frau Professorin was formally betrothed, on that well-remembered-and-never-to-be-forgotten night when she wore a wreath of real myrtle on her smooth blond hair, together with a comfortable gown of brown linsey-woolsey, and sat, with her plump hand clasped by her betrothed, on the state sofa in the drawing-room at home, where the stove had been lighted expressly for the occasion and wax candles were actually placed on the piano—on that never-to-be-forgotten-and-dearly-cherished evening, her father had presented her with a framed line-engraving of the famous pair of

German lovers. And the English professor's daughter might see them now, for they hung on one side of the tall white porcelain stove, in the best drawing-room upstairs. Hermann, with luxuriant locks, and tenderly solicitous of his beloved's safety; Dorothea, with her amazingly solid ankles, forever descending those steps with that docile, cow-like expression of subserviency. This picture the Frau Professorin intended to hand on to Ottilie, her eldest, when that damsel should have been fortunate enough to secure the hand of one of the many hard working *privat-docenten*, over yonder in the town.

But Ottilie, who was rising eighteen, and extremely short-sighted, would have none of it. Fräulein Ottilie insisted not only on smoking cigarettes, but on reading Strauss and Schopenhauer. She announced herself a determined agnostic, and, indeed, a succession of South German cook-maids had summarily "given notice," because the fräulein, when she went to the kitchen to make the pastry, persisted in stating her views on the apostolic legend of the Annunciation. These heated arguments, it must be owned, had a disastrous effect on Fräulein Ottilie's pies, while they wholly failed in the desired effect of convincing the round-cheeked Bavarian peasant girls. But if the young lady's cates left something to be desired, there was no fault to be found with her logic; a faculty which she probably inherited from her father, a not undistinguished German scientist. He has long since slipped away into the brumous Teutonic Walhalla, but the recollection of his personality is strangely clear. Tall, spare, and pale, with keen grey eyes shining behind ample spectacles, he was the kindest, the most lovable of men. Of guile he had not a trace. Year out, year in, he toiled at his laboratory, at his books, at his university lectures, keeping up a close and uninterrupted correspondence with Professor Erle, whose cult like his own was a simple and an all-embracing one—to wit, worship of Truth.

The simple, German home life pleased the motherless English girl. It was like returning to primeval Saxon ways. The thrift, the frugality, the delight in simple little pleasures—a luncheon of black bread and coarse cheese in some tiny inn among the mountains, when she had walked in the pine-scented air since early morning, singing *volkslieder* in chorus, or arguing on the old, old problems as they stepped along—all delighted the girl who had been accustomed to a far more elaborate scheme of life. On dark, velvety summer nights, when the very air caressed them like a beloved hand, they would sit out on the terrace overhanging the river and watch the students slip down stream in their torch-laden boats, singing sturdily in unison:

"Bleib du in ewigen Leben
Mein guter Kamarad!"

Over yonder, across the black river, twinkled the lights of the town. There were the lecture-rooms where young Germany toiled and moiled; the taverns where they hiccoughed eternal friendship over their endless mugs of beer; the mysterious holes and corners where they fought their duels and slashed at each other's cheek-bones and foreheads, or made boisterous love to stout, frowsy damsels of equivocal renown. It was the first decade after the great war. Young Germany was full of the lust of life, of the bravado of a supreme victory. Hence forward the Teuton, armed to the teeth, was to regenerate an effete Europe; nay, even to become the great coloniser.

And at home at the villa, Fräulein Ottilie, who was addicted to the surreptitious perusal of the romances of Georges Sand (MM. Zola and de Goncourt had not been invented as yet, so far as the "young person" was concerned), was also given to discoursing on love as she puffed at her cigarettes in the nightingale-haunted woods at the back of the garden. Love, she said, was like certain diseases, such as scarlatina, the measles, chicken-pox: one might escape it in one's youth, but so much the worse for you if you caught it when you were middle-aged. One caught it, and once infected, one sometimes gave it to the object of one's affection; more often one did not. Then came unhappiness, an aggravation of the malady, and in cases of weak will, even death. On the other hand, the best treatment was something like that since practiced by M. Pasteur. To be dosed with the beloved object was an almost certain means of cure, and marriage was, in nine cases out of ten, the only infallible remedy. The English girl, listening with pricked ears to the words that fell between Fräulein Ottilie's neat rings of smoke, said little, but marvelled exceedingly. She never talked of love. It was an almost sacred subject, something intangible, far-off, priceless; a thing which she might grasp some day, or which she might never see or hold within her hands in her long journey from the cradle to the grave.

At the end of the year, in the burning, stiffling summer-heat, there came a strange listlessness over the young girl. She crept about the garden, looking at the familiar potato plots and the green grapes in the *laubgang* with leaden eyes. One day, she was too tired to get up, and later on, when Fräulein Ottilie insisted on reading aloud a burning love-scene from "Indiana," she thanked her with a smile. She had suddenly become deaf. The doctor who was called in looked grave. At night, grinning skeletons gibbered in the four corners of the room, while it was an absolute certainty that a thing which made a noise was concealed in a roomy cupboard where her dresses hung. It was an eternity till the next morning, when the doctor came again, and then all at once, everyone seemed much concerned, and late in the evening a nurse in cap and apron appeared, and the girl, lying prone on the bed with her leaden head and aloofness from all that were up and stirring, caught the words of the doctor:

"Yes, typhoid fever. And rather a ticklish case."

Then came æons of tossing nights and restless days, the burning nights of mid-Europe, where no fresh breeze from the sea ever penetrates, and where the mosquitoes whizz, and the open window lets in the sultry air and the sound of a tolling church bell. Days of fierce, sultry heat which could not be kept out, and when a students' *fête*, with its firing cannon, gave exquisite torture to the fever patient. But the cannon were only fired through one endless day, while there were other forms of torture which went; on and on. There came a dreadful hour when double bags of ice were laid on her head and chest, and when she laid on her back, struggling heroically for each breath that seemed likely to be her last. The girl was perfectly conscious now; she could see the anxious eyes of Herr Professor behind his gleaming spectacles, the set mouths and the searching glances of the two doctors who were bending over the bed.

"Is father there?" asked the girl suddenly.

"No, dear child. Shall we send for him?" said the Herr Professor.

The girl nodded. And so it was all over! She must be very, very ill, or in that thrifty German household they would never dream of telegraphing to London to insist on the hurried journey. It was all over, and somehow it did not matter. The bed was so uncomfortable, and how that swarm of mosquitoes buzzed round her head! All day, all night, the *schnarken* went on buzzing. And there were flies, too. Ugh, how she hated flies! Years ago, when the black cat lay ill under the laurel bush in the garden, she herself had sat there all day and fanned away the flies. And so it was all over? Well, she was not afraid. One could die even if one were only a girl, and, now, at any rate, it was impossible to rest. Life—Death? They were perhaps only phrases. The main thing was that the bed on which she lay was like a newly ploughed turnip field; she ached all over, and there were tons of lead on her forehead. Too weak to turn over, she lay on her back, until a new nurse came, who touched her gently and turned her on one side. Ah, that was better, to be with one's face to the wall.

"Perhaps, if I am lucky," she thought, "father's dear head will come round that door before—" The girl lay a long time, gazing with dull eyes at the foolish pattern of the wall paper—little bunches of pink roses on stiff diamonds of an ugly grey.

And then, one morning, a dear, kind, well-remembered face did come round the door, and in another minute a pair of strong arms was lifting her up in bed. The traveller had arrived from London.

After that, all went well. The worst was over, and now the healing process was to begin. Ten days later, the invalid was carried down, wrapped in shawls, and placed in a basket chair in the *laubgang*, where the warm summer sunshine only filtered through a canopy of vine-leaves. As often happens in cases of typhoid fever, the girl, as she recovered, found herself, mentally, a child again. She was hungry, ravenously hungry; she whimpered when the doctor came and forbade her anything more solid than broth or jelly. She wanted so much to get well and strong!

Out yonder, over the whirling, hurrying river, lay the busy little town, with its university buildings, its green *anlage*, its shops. Across the old bridge, with its quaint spans, she could watch once more that ever-moving procession of townsfolk hurrying to and fro. How good to breathe the pure, open air, to hear the young voices on the river, to watch the grapes ripening in the *laubgang* overhead. It was Life, glorious, sunshiny, palpitating Life. She wanted to know it, to seize it, to make sure that she had lived. Hence forward, she was sure she would never care much for books. Why, they were but the vain reflections of someone else's life—that one desirable thing which one must make haste to seize, before the dark curtain falls which shuts us out for ever from the beautiful things we see and touch and hear.

CHAPTER IV. A YOUNG GIRL.

LOOKING BACK, ACROSS the vague, misty years, the egotism, the ferocious egotism, of the young girl appears well-nigh incredible. At eighteen, she, with her fluffy hair and her white shoulders, is the most important thing in her little world. There is the day she first discovers she has a throat with fine lines; the secret delight with which she hears an artist tell her that the movements of her body are graceful. Does black, or blue, or white become her best? It is never too late, and she is never too tired when she comes back from a ball, to light all the candles again in her bedroom and examine herself critically, anxiously, in the glass. There is a little pink spot of excitement on each cheek; her hair is ruffled. She looks pretty, she has been happy to-night. Someone—no matter who—has told her she looks charming.

There is the desire of the young girl to coquet, to play with, to torture, when she first learns the all-powerful influence which she possesses by the primitive fact of her sex. With all the arrogance which belongs to personal purity, she stands on her little pedestal and looks down on mankind with a somewhat condescending smile. She is—and she feels it instinctively—a thing apart, a kind of forced plant, a product of civilisation. At present, the ball-room, with its artificial atmosphere, its fleeting devotions, its graceful mockery of real life, is the scene of her little triumphs. The eyes of all men—young and old alike—follow the girl approvingly, wistfully, as she ascends the staircase, her full heart beating against her slim satin bodice, the clear, peachlike cheeks pink with excitement, her swimming eyes raised invitingly to some favourite partner, or dropped as she passes a man she wishes to avoid. At the door her slender white arms and shoulders disappear in a circle of black coats; the programme is scrawled all over; she notes exultingly that one or two men are scowling at each other, and that she has no dance to give someone who has joined the group too late. It is the woman's first taste of power.

There is, too, the *joie de vivre*, the delight of the young animal at play, the imperious will-to-live of a being in perfect health. The girl must dance till her feet ache horribly, the room swings round, and the pink dawn comes creeping in behind the drawn blinds; but still she must go on till that music stops, the swaying, voluptuous, heartrending music which draws her feet round and round. The violins with their *navrant* tones, the human, dolorous strains of the cornets, the brilliant, metallic, artificial sounds of the piano, all act powerfully on the young girl's nervous system. Then comes the stifling crowded supper-room, with its indigestible food and sweet champagne; the young men who move nearer and look at her with strange eyes, after they have eaten and drunk. It is all new and intoxicating, and a little frightening; but it is life, or the nearest approach to it that a young girl, gently nurtured and carefully looked after, can know.

Admiration, at this period, is the very breath of her nostrils. No matter from whom, no matter when or where. A smile, seen like a flash, on a face in a passing hansom; the ill-bred pertinacity of a raised lorgnette at a theatre; the dubious gaze of men about town, leaning against ball-room doors—nothing offends her. It is simply incense burnt at the feet of her youth.

But at last, out of the vague crowd of black coats and wistful eyes, the first lover emerges. It is a little difficult to recall his face, after all these years. Looking back dispassionately, he seems to have been very like all the others, only that he made her suffer, while the others, perhaps, suffered a little for her sake. There were the horrible half-hours of torture when she waited, in some crowded party, for his sleek head and somewhat foolish smile to appear in the doorway; the blank, empty days when there was no letter; the shamefully sweet, the incredible surrender to the first tentative embrace, a surrender which tortured her night and day, and then the joy, the supreme joy of knowing, for certain, that he cared.

It is all a little remote, now, but the beautiful secret was hugged like a very treasure. He was young, he was poor, there were difficulties of every sort to contend with, and finally there was a parting one warm, windy night in November. It was a Sunday, about seven o'clock, and through the window, which was ajar in the drawing-room where they stood, came the sound of a tolling bell. It was only a neighbouring church summoning pious folk to evening service, but it sounded like a knell. It was a well-nigh hopeless affair, and all that they could do was to promise to write to each other. For some weeks the girl watched in the column of the shipping intelligence, the eastward progress of a Peninsular and Oriental steamer on its way to Australia, and after that, on Monday mornings, when the mail comes in, she would stand, with her heart in her mouth, and her hand on the knob of the dining-room door, afraid to go in and find that no foreign envelope lay beside her plate. For some months, to be sure, the letters pretty nearly always lay there, but gradually they got rarer and rarer, and one day she told herself finally that she need not expect any more. Torture is not made more bearable by being slowly applied. During the months in which those letters from Australia grew rarer, the girl understood for the first time the helplessness, the intolerable burden which society has laid on her sex. All things must be endured with a polite smile. Had she been a boy, she was aware that she might have made an effort to break the maddening silence; have stifled her sorrow with dissipation, with travel, or hard work. As it was, the trivial round of civilised feminine existence made her, in those days, almost an automaton. One looks back, with wonder, at the courage of the girl. To find a smile with which to face her father at the dinner table; to take a sisterly interest in Jim's exploits at school; to show clue surprise each time her brother announced the arrival of a new batch of rabbits; and a partisan's joy in the licking which Smith minor had administered to Jones major—these were the immediate duties which lay before her.

Not feeling strong just now, the girl gave up going to balls; they reminded her too much of that episode which she wished to forget; and now the prospect that opened out before her was a vista of years full of scientific soirées, where one walked down long sparsely peopled rooms and looked through microscopes at things which wriggled and squirmed. Sometimes the girl felt strangely like one of those much-observed bacilli; the daughter of a scientist, she knew well enough that her little troubles had about as much importance as theirs in relation to the vast universe. Yet there she was, fixed down under her little glass case, while the world kept a coldly observant eye upon her. Ah, the torture of the young—the young who are always unhappy, and whose little lives are continually coming to a full stop, with chapters that cease bluntly, brutally, without reason and without explanation!

That she was thrown aside, dropped overboard, as it were, in the terrific battle for existence mattered nothing to the young girl. Having no self-pity, she never questioned the justice of the blow that had been dealt her. Afterward, in the years to come, she might wonder why she should have been made to suffer so. But not then. One's first sorrow is a very precious thing. In those far-off days, she would gladly have sacrificed everything—even life itself—for the young man who forgot to write, and whose face, with its rather foolish smile, it is so difficult to recall exactly as it was.

About this time, when she began to work at the Central London School of Art, father and daughter became great friends. On the days when he went to lecture at the London University, she would either walk with him, or go to fetch him on those afternoons when he was coming straight home to tea instead of making his way to the Athenaeum Club. With her chin in the air, looking straight before her, she stepped along, in the half-dark, with a royal scorn for the well-dressed loafers who find their pleasure in accosting ladies in the street. She was twenty-one, and a woman now; it behooved her to be able to take care of herself. And, after all, they were perhaps more easily disposed of than some of the men who took her in to dinner, men who had tired eyes and a dubious smile, and who were fond of starting doubtful topics with a sidelong tentative glance.

They went out a great deal to dinner, father and daughter, so that she early learnt the ways of the world, or at least the ways of the world which gives and goes to dinner parties. There were always nice men, famous men, interesting men, at the parties at home in Harley Street. The girl smiled again a good deal in those days, scrupulously hiding what she thought was a dried-up little heart. How well she always remembered the last time they had gone out together. She could recollect driving with her father in a hansom, and their talk on the way to the Foreign Office. His last book but one had but lately appeared, and was now being scratched and bespluttered assiduously by clerical pens, while it was received with rapture by the large class which like their advanced thinking done for them and turned out in fat print with ample margins once in every third year. All the way up the crowded staircase there is a great display of teeth, of tiaras, of stars and orders, and shining bald heads. The wife of the Foreign Secretary is delighted to see the professor, though no one in that eminently aristocratic gathering "insists" on anything, and most people are content to exchange two fingers, two words, and two smiles, one at greeting and one at passing on. His Excellency the German Ambassador detains the father and daughter, for he has just heard that the Emperor intends to bestow on the English professor the Order of the Crown, for his distinguished services to the progress of modern thought. The two move on, and are caught up in other small circles, where they hear agreeable commonplaces, in an atmosphere where everything is taken for granted, and in which smooth phrases and smooth faces abound—faces which have inherited, for hundreds of years, the art of expressing nothing in a polite way. It is all suave and artificial and decorous. No epigrams make themselves conspicuous in the well-bred chatter, and one great lady, exhibiting a superfluity of bare flesh, raises a tortoise-shell lorgnette when someone—who can it be?—is heard to laugh outright. A famous guardsman has several charming things to say, and the girl finds her chatter received with flattering attention by the handsome man with the garter, who is at once a viceroy and the most suave of diplomats. Surely, when one looks back, the girl's eyes are bright again that night; her blond hair is full of electricity; she has regained, though with a curious little composed manner, something of the roundness, the joyousness, of nineteen. Life is a compromise, and must not be taken too seriously. It is absurd to be much in earnest, and it bores people. So much the girl has learned. She works now regularly with her father, acting as his amanuensis when his eyes are tired, or verifying facts in the library. It is better, far better, more satisfactory in every way, than leading an ordinary "young lady's" existence. Jimmie, the little brother, has grown into a boy with charming, insinuating manners, who is curiously un-British in his demonstrativeness. His sister, he says, is the most charming of girls. He announces that he is always going to live with her. Nothing shall separate them. His whole life, he declares, with his arms round her neck, is to be devoted to his dearest Mary.

Yes, the pictures which rise up of the home life are pleasant; those are happy, but entirely irresponsible years. There is plenty of travel, and the practical kind of culture that comes of travel. And more and more father and daughter are drawn together.

And then came that spring when the father was hard at work. The two rarely left the study now, except for a short walk after dinner, for the professor's book absorbed him. Not feeling quite himself, he was anxious—terribly anxious—to get it done. After this they would go abroad and get quite a long holiday. He wanted to go to Zermatt. At the Riffel Alp he would get the air and exercise he craved. No, he was not quite himself; he felt overstrained, nervous; he had a continual headache. It was, perhaps, he said, a touch of bile.

But one evening, just before dinner, the book was actually done. He bent over the girl at the desk, kissed her crisp hair, and wrote at the bottom of the page, in his own cramped hand, these words: "The End."

And so it was, indeed.

The next morning, when the servant went up to call him, the professor had been dead some hours. The doctors spoke of a clot of blood in the brain, of overwork, and overstrain.

And in the tall, darkened house in Harley Street, the child who had played, the girl who had danced, died too.

Chapter V. Alison.

As sometimes happens with busy people in London, the Erles had hundreds of acquaintances and but few intimate friends. A friendship is costly, in point of time, and Mary found, when one chapter of her life was done that spring morning, that there were two people only that she must imperatively see. A man and a woman—Vincent Hemming and Alison Ives. How their features stood out among the crowd of vague faces, which belonged to that other life. Alison Ives especially, with her handsome, clever face, looking like a Reynolds, with her superb air, and her huge hat tied under the chin. With that grave sweetness which endears to us the Siddons in the National Gallery, she yet had the look of a thinker—modernised by a slightly bored expression—and a little distinguished way which at once made other women in her vicinity look dowdy or vulgar. Her clothes always seemed to suit her as its feathers do a bird. There are women who look like an *édition de luxe* of a poor book; Alison Ives suggested that of a classic.

It had been her habit for a couple of years past to sit at the feet of Professor Erle; she constantly announced, laughing, that he was the only man she ever wanted to marry, only that he was firm, and would not permit it. Besides, it was no good trying to compete with her mother, Lady Jane, who was sixty-five and irresistible. Widows of sixty-five, she said, were nowadays the only people who inspired a great passion. She supposed her turn would come—a quarter of a century hence. But all the same, the daughter was much admired in "the world;" but "the world" as understood by her mother, Lady Jane, by no means entirely satisfied this eminently modern young woman. It was whispered that she had serious views, though it was certain that she was pretty enough to please a Prime Minister and clever enough to entertain a guardsman, if she found herself next to either at dinner. Alison did not mind which, she said; in fact, after a long day in the East End, when she was tired, she rather preferred the guardsman, who would be content to talk of polo ponies, whereas when a young woman is put next to a Premier, it behooves her to look, at any rate, very brilliant indeed. Though she never smoked, was ignorant of billiard-cues and guns, and hated playing the man, Mary had heard Alison murmur something like an oath—but only when they were alone. It was a habit which she had picked up in Paris, when she was working in a sculptor's studio; and she always declared that "*dame*" and "*sapristi*," being in a foreign tongue, were notoriously less efficacious and by inference more pardonable, than swearing in the vernacular. For the rest, with the best heart in the world, she had a somewhat caustic tongue, could interpret Chopin like an artist, and always had her hair exquisitely dressed.

What attracted people at once was her intense womanliness, her utter absence of snobbery, her real desire to be in sympathy with her own sex. Like all exceptional people, she had her moods, and sometimes, for months together, she was heard of only as forming one of a party in this or that great country house, while at other times she would come to town and study fitfully, or devote herself to the task of helping young girls. Once, in the middle of the season, she took a lodging in a by-street in the Mile End Road, but she only stayed seven weeks, and when she appeared again, the expression on her face was sadder than before. "Of course one ought to *know* what it is like," she said, when Mary asked her why she had left so soon. "It's an experience—but a terrible one. It's not only the drunkenness, the down-at-heel vice, the astounding absence of any thrift or forethought, and the incredible repetition of one solitary adjective; but it seems to me that when one or two of us go and live down there we absolutely do no permanent good at all. The thing will be to bring the East End here. One by one, of course, just as we go there."

Alison kept her word. This spring had found her ensconced in a workman's flat in the Mayfair district, with one small servant whom she had rescued in Whitechapel. "But it's as much for myself as her," explained Alison, laughing. She hated to be thought philanthropic. "All we women are so incredibly dependent on other people. It's absurd that we do not know how to do anything useful. I shall keep my flat, and go to it now and again, when I am tired of shooting parties. It will be a little home for my East End girls, whom I intend to train. I daresay I shall be disappointed in them, but that's inevitable with all experiments. Anyway, it will probably do me more good than it will them. The only real slavery nowadays is the slavery of luxury. We are all getting so pampered that we can't exist without it. People do the most incredible things. I have known a woman stay with a husband whom she loathed, and whom it was an outrage to live with, simply because she couldn't do her own hair. I'm going to get our cook at Ives Court to teach me how to broil a mutton chop, though I daresay she's too grand for that; and I shall go and watch the laundry-maid at her work."

"And your hands, you lunatic?" Mary had exclaimed. "I think I see you with red knuckles!"

"Oh," said Alison, laughing, "I shall tell that little manicure just out of Bond Street to come twice a week. There's that new stuff, 'Eau des Orchidées'; it's wonderful. Don't imagine I'm going to give up the only old-fashioned quality we modern women have got—our vanity. It's the only thing that makes us still bearable."

This was the young woman who was shown into the study by Elizabeth one morning a few days after the funeral at Highgate. Mary was bending over a desk, busy with her father's proofs, when she came in. The elder girl's beautiful brown eyes were suspiciously shiny; it had evidently cost her an effort to come into the study which she knew so well. The two girls wrung each other's hands silently. But after the first kiss, in which she said everything that she dared not put in words, Alison, with her ready tact, began talking business at once.

The younger girl announced her plans frankly. There was just enough money for her to live meagrely, quietly for the next few years, while she tried her luck at art. Mary had always meant to paint some day, when her whole time should be at her own disposal. Why, she had always drawn ever since she was a child, and the sense of colour was almost an emotion to her. Yes, to paint was a long-cherished ambition, mused over on long, drowsy afternoons in the reading-room of the British Museum, nursed during the days when she had remained bending over a desk in her father's study, patiently inscribing what the professor dictated as he walked up and down the little room. As for Jimmie, he was to remain at Winchester, and, if he could succeed in winning a scholarship, was to go to Oxford as the father had wished. By living very carefully this could be managed.

"No woman ever made a great artist yet," said Alison, shrugging her shoulders, "but if you don't mind being third-rate, of course go in and try. I suppose it'll mean South Kensington, the Royal Academy, and then—portraits of babies in pastel or cottage gardens for the rest of your life."

"Oh, don't."

"Never mind, my dear girl. You must work at something. Try the British Art School. Has Vincent Hemming been?" she added, rather inconsequently.

"Yes, he has called. Two or three times, Elizabeth says, but I haven't seen anyone," said Mary, remembering with a little shudder the inquisitive voices at the door.

"I don't see why," said Alison thoughtfully, "you shouldn't take a flat in the same building with me. Of course there are little drawbacks. The ladies use a limited, if somewhat virulent, vocabulary, and now and again one has to step over an elderly gentleman who lives just below, and who comes home tired, and sometimes goes to sleep on the stairs. But one gets accustomed to that."

"I think, on the whole," said Mary, smiling, "I'll take some rooms near, and furnish them. There's Jimmie, you see."

"Where is the boy, by the bye?"

"Oh, the poor boy, I let him go—the day—the day after. He was very good; he said that nothing would induce him to leave me, and sat, poor child, for at least an hour with his arms round my neck, crying. Then another note came from Smith minor—the boy who keeps so many lop-eared rabbits, you remember—asking him to go and spend a week with them in the country."

"And then," said Allison quietly, "ah! I can see Jimmie saying he shouldn't dream of going, and then, when that was settled, wandering round the room, asking if you were not perhaps going out of town yourself? 'It would look rather rude if he refused, as they—the Smiths—knew he wouldn't have any other engagement,' I can hear Jimmie urging. And about seven o'clock an epistle was indited to say that he would be very pleased to go, and the next morning Jimmie went off in a four-wheel cab, looking quite cheerful."

Mary smiled in spite of herself.

"Poor boy," she said softly, in an extenuating voice, "he can't bear anything sad!"

"So much," said Alison after a pause, "for brothers."

"We've got," answered the other, "fortunately or unfortunately, to depend upon ourselves in all the crises of life. I've got lots to do: lawyers to see, these proofs to correct, and to make arrangements for my own future."

"Only that? She refuses herself nothing," said Alison. "I am modestly contented with arranging for Evelina's future. Evelina is my last girl. As for my own, I leave it to Providence."

"You can afford to," replied Mary, "but we have it on the authority of a proverb that Heaven is not above taking assistance from mortals in this respect."

"Mary, you're trying to be cynical, and it doesn't suit you. I want to tell you about Evelina," she went on feverishly, afraid every minute that one or other of them might break down. "That is my new girl,' she continued, settling down on the fender-stool. "Her name is actually Evelina—isn't it preposterous? I should like to call her Polly, only I don't believe in changing poor people's names to suit your own fancy, as if they were cats or canaries. Well, Evelina's baby—"

"Oh, there is a baby?"

"Why, of course. A poor waxen little thing that screams all day long. I've put it out to nurse in a *crèche* that a friend of mine has started in Kentish Town. And now I'm trying to cultivate a sense of humour in Evelina."

"It will be difficult, won't it?" said Mary, trying hard to take an interest.

"Never mind. It's what women ought to cultivate above all other things, especially the poorer classes. With a keen sense of the ridiculous, they would never fall in love at all; and as to improvident marriages, they wouldn't exist. If you could see the baby's father!—a pudding-faced boy, who helps in a tiny cheesemonger's shop down there. She 'walked out' with him for two years. He is now nearly nineteen. It is all very well to smile, but it is terrible—for the woman. In the evening, when she has done her work, she lights the lamp in my little sitting-room (everything is quite simple, you know; only I've got a few books, and the tiny Corot from my den at Ives Court, and the Rossetti drawings), and then I read aloud while she knits. I read comic things—Dickens, Mark Twain, and so on; and when the poor girl laughs, I feel that I have scored one. She isn't much more than a child, you know, and she has such a good heart. I think she likes to talk to me; she tells me her little story."

"A story," repeated Mary; "she has a story then?"

"Oh! a common one enough down there," answered Alison. " She drifted into the East End, from Essex, about three years ago, and is a country girl who got a place as drudge-of-all-work in a family of ten, in the Mile End Road. Her master was pleased to make love to her when his wife and eight children had gone for the day to Southend; Evelina ran out of the house, leaving her box behind, and never dared to go back. My dear, these London idyls are not pretty. She is, however, beginning to show a faint sense of the ridiculous. I believe I shall make a sensible person of Evelina."

Mary raised her head, for she had been listening mechanically, with her eyes fixed on the ink-spots on her father's desk, the desk on which his hand had so often rested. But it was impossible not to feel cheered by Alison's whimsical yet energetic personality. She looked so bright, so alert, so capable, as she stood there, in her pretty black gown and her rakish hat, a little askew with the wind.

"By the bye, did I tell you the adventures I had on my visit to the Blaythewaites? My dear, it was only by the intervention of Providence that I didn't have to dine the first night in my tailor-gown. Of course, I went down third-class—"

"That's because you are saving for Evelina's baby, I suppose," interrupted Mary.

"And so," went on Alison, taking no notice of the interruption, "and so the footman never thought of looking for me there. They all drove off without me, and my basket trunk, with my favourite white gown in it, got taken off with some other people to another place about five miles off. However, it was got back in time, and when I told my little story at dinner to Sir Horace, he was immensely amused, though I'm sure Lady Blaythewaite thought I was graduating for a lunatic asylum. People who don't know me well always do."

"Did you tell Sir Horace Blaythewaite about the workman's flat—and Evelina?" said Mary, laughing. Alison was already at the door, trying on her hat firmly.

"You know I never talk about that," she said, flushing up. "Why, it would look like a pose—as if I thought myself better than other people. And I couldn't bear anyone to say that I had 'taken up slumming.' You know how I detest the whole attitude of the upper and middle classes toward the poor. Lifting the lids of people's saucepans and routing under their beds for fluff are not to my taste. Why, district visiting is nothing less than a gross breach of manners—a little worse than electioneering, if that's possible. I'm just going up," she said, giving a rakish twist to her velvet hat-strings, "to the *crèche* in Kentish Town to see Evelina's baby. I'm going on the top of one of those charming trams. I told Worth when I was in Paris that I always went on the tops of omnibuses, and he designed me this little frock on purpose. It's pretty, isn't it, but a little too *ingénue* for me? It smacks of the Comédie Française. I think I see Reichemberg in it," said Alison, doubtfully smoothing down the folds of her loose bodice. "Now you've got to promise to come and dine with me in Portman Square. We shall have the house to ourselves. Good-bye. Eight o'clock!"

"Nonsense! It's very sweet of you, but I can't possibly go," cried Mary down the passage.

In another instant she was gone, and the house seemed blank and empty again. But trying not to think of her sorrow, Mary went steadily on with the proofs.

A Cross Line

George Egerton

From Keynotes 1893

THE RATHER FLAT notes of a man's voice float out into the clear air, singing the refrain of a popular music-hall ditty. There is something incongruous between the melody and the surroundings. It seems profane, indelicate, to bring this slangy, vulgar tune, and with it the mental picture of footlight flare and fantastic dance into the lovely freshness of this perfect spring day.

A woman sitting on a felled tree turns her head to meet its coming, and an expression flits across her face in which disgust and humorous appreciation are subtly blended. Her mind is nothing if not picturesque; her busy brain, with all its capabilities choked by a thousand vagrant fancies, is always producing pictures and finding associations between the most unlikely objects. She has been reading a little sketch written in the daintiest language of a fountain scene in Tanagra, and her vivid imagination has made it real to her. The slim, graceful maids grouped around it filling their exquisitely-formed earthen jars, the dainty poise of their classic heads, and the flowing folds of their draperies have been actually present with her; and now?—why, it is like the entrance of a half-tipsy vagabond player bedizened in tawdry finery—the picture is blurred. She rests her head against the trunk of a pine tree behind her, and awaits the singer. She is sitting on an incline in the midst of a wilderness of trees; some have blown down, some have been cut down, and the lopped branches lie about; moss and bracken and trailing bramble, fir-cones, wild rose bushes, and speckled red "fairy hats" fight for life in wild confusion. A disused quarry to the left is an ideal haunt of pike, and to the right a little river rushes along in haste to join a greater sister that is fighting a troubled way to the sea. A row of stepping-stones crosses it, and if you were to stand on one you would see shoals of restless stone loach "Beardies" darting from side to side. The tails of several ducks can be seen above the water, and the paddle of their balancing feet, and the gurgling suction of their bills as they search for larvae can be heard distinctly between the hum of insect, twitter of bird, and rustle of stream and leaf. The singer has changed his lay to a whistle, and presently he comes down the path a cool, neat, grey-clad figure, with a fishing creel slung across his back, and a trout rod held on his shoulder. The air ceases abruptly, and his cold grey eyes scan the seated figure with its gipsy ease of attitude, a scarlet shawl that has fallen from her shoulders forming an accentuative background to the slim roundness of her waist.

Persistent study, coupled with a varied experience of the female animal, has given the owner of the grey eyes some facility in classing her, although it has not supplied him with any definite data as to what any one of the species may do in a given circumstance. To put it in his own words, in answer to a friend who chaffed him on his untiring pursuit of women as an interesting problem:

"If a fellow has had much experience of his fellow-man he may divide him into types, and, given a certain number of men and a certain number of circumstances, he is pretty safe on hitting on the line of action each type will strike; 't aint so with woman. You may always look out for the unexpected, she generally upsets a fellow's calculations, and you are never safe in laying odds on her. Tell you what, old chappie, we may talk about superior intellect; but, if a woman wasn't handicapped by her affection, or need of it, the cleverest chap in Christendom would be just a bit of putty in her hands. I find them more fascinating as problems than anything going. Never let an opportunity slip to get new data—never!"

He did not now. He met the frank, unembarrassed gaze of eyes that would have looked with just the same bright inquiry at the advent of a hare, or a toad, or any other object that might cross her path, and raised his hat with respectful courtesy, saying, in the drawling tone habitual with him—

"I hope I am not trespassing?"

"I can't say; you may be, so may I, but no one has ever told me so!"

A pause. His quick glance has noted the thick wedding ring on her slim brown hand, and the flash of a diamond in its keeper. A lady decidedly. Fast? perhaps. Original? undoubtedly. Worth knowing? rather.

"I am looking for a trout stream, but the directions I got were rather vague; might I—"

"It's straight ahead, but you won't catch anything now, at least not here, sun's too glaring and water too low, a mile up you may, in an hour's time."

"Oh, thanks awfully for the tip. You fish then?"

"Yes, sometimes."

"Trout run big here?" (what odd eyes the woman has, kind of magnetic.)

"No, seldom over a pound, but they are very game."

"Rare good sport isn't it, whipping a stream? There is so much besides the mere catching of fish. The river and the trees and the quiet sets a fellow thinking—kind of sermon—makes a chap feel good, don't it?"

She smiles assentingly. And yet what the devil is she amused at he queries mentally. An inspiration. He acts upon it, and says eagerly:

"I wonder—I don't half like to ask—but fishing puts people on a common footing, don't it? You knowing the stream, you know, would you tell me what are the best flies to use?"

"I tie my own, but—"

"Do you? how clever of you! wish I could," and sitting down on the other end of the tree, he takes out his fly book, "but I interrupted you, you were going to say?"

"Only," stretching out her hand (of a perfect shape but decidedly brown) for the book, "that you might give the local fly-tyer a trial, he'll tell you."

"Later on, end of next month, or perhaps later, you might try the oak-fly, the natural fly you know; a horn is the best thing to hold them in, they get out of anything else—and put two on at a time."

"By Jove, I must try that dodge!"

He watches her as she handles his book and examines the contents critically, turning aside some with a glance, fingering others almost tenderly, holding them daintily and noting the cock of wings and the hint of tinsel, with her head on one side; a trick of hers he thinks.

"Which do you like most, wet or dry fly?" (she is looking at some dry flies.)

"Oh," with that rare smile, "at the time I swear by whichever happens to catch most fish. Perhaps, really, dry fly. I fancy most of these flies are better for Scotland or England. Up to this March-brown has been the most killing thing. But you might try an "orange -grouse," that's always good here; with perhaps a "hare's ear" for a change—and put on a "coachman" for the evenings. My husband (he steals a side look at her) brought home some beauties yesterday evening."

"Lucky fellow!"

She returns the book. There is a tone in his voice as he says this that jars on her, sensitive as she is to every inflection of a voice, with an intuition that is almost second sight. She gathers up her shawl. She has a cream-coloured woollen gown on, and her skin looks duskily foreign by contrast. She is on her feet before he can regain his, and says, with a cool little bend of her head: "Good afternoon, I wish you a full basket!"

Before he can raise his cap she is down the slope, gliding with easy steps that have a strange grace, and then springing lightly from stone to stone across the stream. He feels small, snubbed someway, and he sits down on the spot where she sat and, lighting his pipe, says "check!"

She is walking slowly up the garden path. A man in his shirt sleeves is stooping amongst the tender young peas. A bundle of stakes lies next him, and he whistles softly and all out of tune as he twines the little tendrils round each new support. She looks at his broad shoulders and narrow flanks; his back is too long for great strength, she thinks. He hears her step, and smiles up at her from under the shadow of his broad-leafed hat.

"How do you feel now, old woman?"

"Beastly. I've got that horrid qualmish feeling again. I can't get rid of it."

He has spread his coat on the side of the path and pats it for her to sit down.

"What is it" (anxiously)? "if you were a mare I'd know what to do for you. Have a nip of whisky?"

He strides off without waiting for her reply and comes back with it and a biscuit, kneels down and holds the glass to her lips.

"Poor little woman, buck up! You'll see that'll fix you. Then you go by-and-by and have a shy at the fish."

She is about to say something when a fresh qualm attacks her and she does not. He goes back to his tying.

"By Jove!" he says suddenly, "I forgot. Got something to show you!"

After a few minutes he returns carrying a basket covered with a piece of sacking. A dishevelled-looking hen, with spread wings trailing and her breast bare from sitting on her eggs, screeches after him. He puts it carefully down and uncovers it, disclosing seven little balls of yellow fluff splashed with olive green. They look up sideways with bright round eyes, and their little spoon bills look disproportionately large.

"Aren't they beauties (enthusiastically)? This one is just out," taking up an egg, "mustn't let it get chilled." There is a chip out of it and a piece of hanging skin. "Isn't it funny?" he asks, showing her how it is curled in the shell, with its paddles flattened and its bill breaking through the chip, and the slimy feathers sticking to its violet skin.

She suppresses an exclamation of disgust, and looks at his fresh-tinted skin instead. He is covering basket, hen, and all—

"How you love young things!" she says.

"Some. I had a filly once, she turned out a lovely mare! I cried when I had to sell her, I wouldn't have let any one in God's world mount her."

"Yes, you would!"

"Who?" with a quick look of resentment.

"Me!"

"I wouldn't!"

"What! you wouldn't?"

"I wouldn't!"

"I think you would if I wanted to!" with a flash out of the tail of her eye.

"No, I wouldn't!"

"Then you would care more for her than for me. I would give you your choice (passionately), her or me!"

"What nonsense!"

"May be (concentrated), but it's lucky she isn't here to make deadly sense of it." A humble-bee buzzes close to her ear, and she is roused to a sense of facts, and laughs to think how nearly they have quarrelled over a mare that was sold before she knew him.

Some evenings later, she is stretched motionless in a chair, and yet she conveys an impression of restlessness; a sensitively nervous person would feel it. She is gazing at her husband, her brows are drawn together, and make three little lines. He is reading, reading quietly, without moving his eyes quickly from side to side of the page as she does when she reads, and he pulls away at a big pipe with steady enjoyment. Her eyes turn from him to the window, and follow the course of two clouds, then they close for a few seconds, then open to watch him again. He looks up and smiles.

"Finished your book?"

There is a singular soft monotony in his voice; the organ with which she replies is capable of more varied expression.

"Yes, it is a book makes one think. It would be a greater book if he were not an Englishman. He's afraid of shocking the big middle class. You wouldn't care about it."

"Finished your smoke?"

"No, it went out, too much fag to light up again! No (protestingly), never you mind, old boy, why do you?"

He has drawn his long length out of his chair, and, kneeling down beside her, guards a lighted match from the incoming evening air. She draws in the smoke contentedly, and her eyes smile back with a general vague tenderness.

"Thank you, dear old man!"

"Going out again?" negative head shake.

"Back aching?" affirmative nod, accompanied by a steadily aimed puff of smoke, that she has been carefully inhaling, into his eyes.

"Scamp! Have your booties off?"

"Oh, don't you bother, Lizzie will do it!"

He has seized a foot from under the rocker, and, sitting on his heels, holds it on his knee, whilst he unlaces the boot; then he loosens the stocking under her toes, and strokes her foot gently.

"Now, the other!" Then he drops both boots outside the door, and fetching a little pair of slippers, past their first smartness, from the bedroom, puts one on. He examines the left foot; it is a little swollen round the ankle, and he presses his broad fingers gently round it as one sees a man do to a horse with windgalls. Then he pulls the rocker nearer to his chair and rests the slipperless foot on his thigh. He relights his pipe, takes up his book, and rubs softly from ankle to toes as he reads.

She smokes and watches him, diverting herself by imagining him in the hats of different periods. His is a delicate-skinned face with regular features; the eyes are fine, in colour and shape with the luminous clearness of a child's; his pointed beard is soft and curly. She looks at his hand,—a broad strong hand with capable fingers,—the hand of a craftsman, a contradiction to the face with its distinguished delicacy. She holds her own up with a cigarette poised between the first and second fingers, idly pleased with its beauty of form and delicate nervous slightness. One speculation chases the other in her quick brain; odd questions as to race arise; she dives into theories as to the why and wherefore of their distinctive natures, and holds a mental debate in which she takes both sides of the question impartially. He has finished his pipe, laid down his book, and is gazing dreamily, with his eyes darkened by their long lashes, and a look of tender melancholy in their clear depths, into space.

"What are you thinking of?" There is a look of expectation in her quivering nervous little face.

He turns to her, chafing her ankle again.

"I was wondering if lob-worms would do for—"

He stops. A strange look of disappointment flits across her face and is lost in an hysterical peal of laughter.

"You are the best emotional check I ever knew," she gasps.

He stares at her in utter bewilderment, and then a slow smile creeps to his eyes and curves the thin lips under his moustache, a smile at her.

"You seem amused, Gipsy!"

She springs out of her chair and seizes book and pipe; he follows the latter anxiously with his eyes until he sees it laid safely on the table. Then she perches herself, resting her knees against one of his legs, whilst she hooks her feet back under the other—

"Now I am all up, don't I look small?"

He smiles his slow smile. "Yes, I believe you are made of gutta percha."

She is stroking out all the lines in his face with the tip of her finger; then she runs it through his hair. He twists his head half impatiently, she desists.

"I divide all the people in the world," she says, "into those who like their hair played with, and those who don't. Having my hair brushed gives me more pleasure than anything else; it's delicious. I'd *purr* if I knew how. I notice (meditatively) I am never in sympathy with those who don't like it; I am with those who do. I always get on with them."

"You are a queer little devil!"

"Am I? I shouldn't have thought you would have found out I was the latter at all. I wish I were a man! I believe if I were a man, I 'd be a disgrace to my family."

"Why?"

"I'd go on a jolly old spree!"

He laughs: "Poor little woman, is it so dull?"

There is a gleam of devilry in her eyes, and she whispers solemnly—

"Begin with a D," and she traces imaginary letters across his forehead, and ending with a flick over his ear, says, "and that is the tail of the y!"

After a short silence she queries—

"Are you fond of me?" She is rubbing her chin up and down his face.

"Of course I am, don't you know it?"

"Yes, perhaps I do," impatiently; "but I want to be told it. A woman doesn't care a fig for a love as deep as the death-sea and as silent, she wants something that tells her it in little waves all the time. It isn't the love, you know, it's the being loved; it isn't really the man, it's his loving!"

"By Jove, you're a rum un!"

"I wish I wasn't then. I wish I was as commonplace as—. You don't tell me anything about myself (a fierce little kiss), you might, even if it were lies. Other men who cared for me told me things about my eyes, my hands, anything. I don't believe you notice."

"Yes I *do*, little one, only I think it."

"Yes, but I don't care a bit for your thinking; if I can't see what's in your head what good is it to me?"

"I wish I could understand you, dear!"

"I wish to God you could. Perhaps if you were badder and I were gooder we'd meet halfway. *You* are an awfully good old chap; it's just men like you send women like me to the devil!"

"But you are good (kissing her), a real good chum! You understand a fellow's weak points. You don't blow him up if he gets on a bit. Why (enthusiastically), being married to you is like chumming with a chap! Why (admiringly), do you remember before we were married, when I let that card fall out of my pocket? Why, I couldn't have told another girl about her. She wouldn't have believed that I *was* straight. She'd have thrown me over. And you sent her a quid because she was sick. You are a great little woman!"

"Don't see it! (she is biting his ear). Perhaps I was a man last time, and some hereditary memories are cropping up in this incarnation!"

He looks so utterly at sea that she has to laugh again, and, kneeling up, shuts his eyes with kisses, and bites his chin and shakes it like a terrier in her strong little teeth.

"You imp! was there ever such a woman!"

Catching her wrists, he parts his knees and drops her on to the rug. Then, perhaps the subtle magnetism that is in her affects him, for he stoops and snatches her up and carries her up and down, and then over to the window and lets the fading light with its glimmer of moonshine play on her odd face with its tantalising changes. His eyes dilate and his colour deepens as he crushes her soft little body to him and carries her off to her room.

Summer is waning and the harvest is ripe for ingathering, and the voice of the reaping machine is loud in the land. She is stretched on her back on the short heather-mixed moss at the side of a bog stream. Rod and creel are flung aside, and the wanton breeze, with the breath of coolness it has gathered in its passage over the murky dykes of black bog water, is playing with the tail fly, tossing it to and fro with a half threat to fasten it to a prickly spine of golden gorse. Bunches of bog-wool nod their fluffy heads, and through the myriad in definite sounds comes the regular scrape of a strickle on the scythe of a reaper in a neighbouring meadow. Overhead a flotilla of clouds is steering from the south in a north-easterly direction. Her eyes follow them. Old time galleons, she thinks, with their wealth of snowy sail spread, riding breast to breast up a wide blue fjord after victory. The sails of the last are rose flushed, with a silver edge. Somehow she thinks of Cleopatra sailing down to meet Antony, and a great longing fills her soul to sail off somewhere too,—away from the daily need of dinner getting and the recurring Monday with its washing, life with its tame duties and virtuous monotony. She fancies herself in Arabia on the back of a swift steed; flashing eyes set in dark faces surround her, and she can see the clouds of sand swirl, and feel the swing under her of his rushing stride; and her thoughts shape themselves into a wild song,—a song to her steed of flowing mane and satin skin, an uncouth rhythmical jingle with a feverish beat; a song to the untamed spirit that dwells in her. Then she fancies she is on the stage of an ancient theatre, out in the open air, with hundreds of faces upturned toward her. She is gauze-clad in a cobweb garment of wondrous tissue; her arms are clasped by jewelled snakes, and one with quivering diamond fangs coils round her hips; her hair floats loosely, and her feet are sandal-clad, and the delicate breath of vines and the salt freshness of an incoming sea seem to fill her nostrils. She bounds forward and dances, bends her lissome waist, and curves her slender arms, and gives to the soul of each man what he craves, be it good or evil. And she can feel now, lying here in the shade of Irish hills, with her head resting on her scarlet shawl and her eyes closed, the grand, intoxicating power of swaying all these human souls to wonder and applause. She can see herself with parted lips and panting, rounded breasts, and a dancing devil in each glowing eye, sway voluptuously to the wild music that rises, now slow, now fast, now deliriously wild, seductive, intoxicating, with a human note of passion in its strain. She can feel the answering shiver of emotion that quivers up to her from the dense audience, spellbound by the motion of her glancing feet; and she flies swifter and swifter, and lighter and lighter, till the very serpents seem alive with jewelled scintillations. One quivering, gleaming, daring bound, and she stands with outstretched arms and passion filled eyes, poised on one slender foot, asking a supreme note to finish her dream of motion; and the men rise to a man and answer her, and cheer, cheer till the echoes shout from the surrounding hills and tumble wildly down the crags.

The clouds have sailed away, leaving long feathery streaks in their wake. Her eyes have an inseeing look, and she is tremulous with excitement; she can hear yet that last grand shout, and the strain of that old-time music that she has never heard in this life of hers, save as an inner accompaniment to the memory of hidden things, born with her, not of this time.

And her thoughts go to other women she has known, women good and bad, school friends, casual acquaintances, women workers,—joyless machines for grinding daily corn, unwilling maids grown old in the endeavor to get settled, patient wives who bear little ones to indifferent husbands until they wear out,—a long array. She busies herself with questioning. Have they, too, this thirst for excitement, for change, this restless craving for sun and love and motion? Stray words, half confidences, glimpses through soul-chinks of suppressed fires, actual outbreaks, domestic catastrophes,—how the ghosts dance in the cells of her memory! And she laughs, laughs softly to herself, because the denseness of man, his chivalrous, conservative devotion to the female idea he has created, blinds him, perhaps happily, to the problems of her complex nature. "Ay," she mutters musingly, "the wisest of them can only say we are enigmas; each one of them sets about solving the riddle of the *ewig weibliche*,—and well it is that the workings of our hearts are closed to them, that we are cunning enough or *great* enough to seem to be what they would have us, rather than be what we are. But few of them have had the insight to find out the key to our seeming contradictions,—the why a refined, physically fragile woman will mate with a brute, a mere male animal with primitive passions, and love him; the why strength and beauty appeal more often than the more subtly fine qualities of mind or heart; the why women (and not the innocent ones) will condone sins that men find hard to forgive in their fellows. They have all overlooked the eternal wildness, the untamed primitive savage temperament that lurks in the mildest, best woman. Deep in through ages of convention this primeval trait burns,—an untamable quantity that may be concealed but is never eradicated by culture, the keynote of woman's witchcraft and woman's strength. But it is there, sure enough, and each woman is conscious of it in her truth telling hours of quiet self-scrutiny; and each woman in God's wide world will deny it, and each woman will help another to conceal it,—for the woman who tells the truth and is not a liar about these things is untrue to her sex and abhorrent to man, for he has fashioned a model on imaginary lines, and he has said, "So I would have you!" and every woman is an unconscious liar, for so man loves her. And when a Strindberg or a Nietzche arises and peers into the recesses of her nature and dissects her ruthlessly, the men shriek out louder than the women, because the truth is at all times unpalatable, and the gods they have set up are dear to them—"

"Dreaming, or speering into futurity? You have the look of a seer. I believe you are half a witch!" And he drops his gray-clad figure on the turf; he has dropped his drawl long ago in midsummer.

"Is not every woman that? Let us hope I'm for my friends a white one."

"A-ah! Have you many friends?"

"That is a query! If you mean many correspondents, many persons who send me Christmas cards, or remember my birthday, or figure in my address book,—no."

"Well, grant I don't mean that!"

"Well, perhaps, yes. Scattered over the world, if my death were belled out, many women would give me a tear, and some a prayer; and many men would turn back a page in their memory and give me a kind thought, perhaps a regret, and go back to their work with a feeling of having lost something that they never possessed. I am a creature of moments. Women have told me that I came into their lives just when they needed me; men had no need to tell me, I felt it. People have needed me more than I them. I have given freely whatever they craved from me in the way of understanding or love; I have touched sore places they showed me, and healed them,—but they never got at me. I have been for myself, and helped myself, and borne the burden of my own mistakes. Some have chafed at my self-sufficiency, and have called me fickle,— not understanding that they gave me nothing, and that when I had served them their moment was ended, and I was to pass on. I read people easily, I am written in black letter to most—"

"To your husband?"

"He," quickly,—"we will not speak of him; it is not loyal."

"Do not I understand you a little?"

"You do not misunderstand me."

"That is something."

"It is much!"

"Is it?" searching her face. "It is not one grain of sand in the desert that stretches between you and me, and you are as impenetrable as a sphinx at the end of it. This," passionately, "is my moment, and what have you given me?"

"Perhaps less than other men I have known; but you want less. You are a little like me,—you can stand alone; and yet, I) her voice is shaking, "have I given you nothing?"

He laughs, and she winces; and they sit silent, and they both feel as if the earth between them is laid with infinitesimal electric threads vibrating with a common pain. Her eyes are filled with tears that burn but don't fall; and she can see his some way through her closed lids, see their cool grayness troubled by sudden fire, and she rolls her handkerchief into a moist cambric ball between her cold palms.

"You have given me something, something to carry away with me,—an infernal want. You ought to be satisfied: I am infernally miserable. You," nearer, "have the most tantalizing mouth in the world when your lips tremble like that. I—What! can you cry? You?"

"Yes, even I can cry."

"You dear woman!" pause; "and I can't help you?"

"You can't help me; no man can. Don't think it is because you are you I cry, but because you probe a little nearer into the real me that I feel so."

"Was it necessary to say that?" reproachfully; "do you think I don't know it? I can't for the life of me think how you, with that free gypsy nature of yours, could bind yourself to a monotonous country life, with no excitement, no change. I wish I could offer you my yacht; do you like the sea?"

"I love it; it answers one's moods."

"Well, let us play pretending, as the children say. Grant that I could, I would hang your cabin with your own colors, fill it with books (all those I have heard you say you care for), make it a nest as rare as the bird it would shelter. You would reign supreme. When your highness would deign to honor her servant, I would come and humor your every whim. If you were glad, you could clap your hands and order music, and we would dance on the white deck, and we would skim through the sunshine of Southern seas on a spice-scented breeze. You make me poetical. And if you were angry, you could vent your feelings on me, and I would give in and bow my head to your mood. And we would drop anchor, and stroll through strange cities,—go far inland and glean folklore out of the beaten track of everyday tourists; and at night, when the harbor slept, we would sail out through the moonlight over silver seas. You are smiling,—you look so different when you smile; do you like my picture?"

"Some of it!"

"What not?"

"You!"

"Thank you."

"You asked me. Can't you understand where the spell lies? It is the freedom, the freshness, the vague danger, the unknown that has a witchery for me,—ay, for every woman!"

"Are you incapable of affection, then?"

"Of course not. I share," bitterly, "that crowning disability of my sex; but not willingly,—I chafe under it. My God! if it were not for that, we women would master the world! I tell you, men would be no match for us! At heart we care nothing for laws, nothing for systems; all your elaborately reasoned codes for controlling morals or man do not weigh a jot with us against an impulse, an instinct. We learn those things from you,—you tamed, amenable animals; they are not natural to us. It is a wise disposition of Providence that this untamableness of ours is corrected by our affections. We forge our own chains in a moment of softness, and then," bitterly, "we may as well wear them with a good grace. Perhaps many of our seeming contradictions are only the outward evidences of inward chafing. Bah! the qualities that go to make a Napoleon— superstition, want of honor, disregard of opinion, and the eternal I—are oftener to be found in a woman than a man. Lucky for the world, perhaps, that all these attributes weigh as nothing in the balance with the need to love, if she be a good woman; to be loved, if she is of a coarser fibre."

"I never met any one like you; you are a strange woman!"

"No, I am merely a truthful one. Women talk to me—why? I can't say; but always they come, strip their hearts and souls naked, and let me see the hidden folds of their natures. The greatest tragedies I have ever read are child's play to those I have seen acted in the inner life of outwardly commonplace women. A woman must beware of speaking the truth to a man; he loves her the less for it. It is the elusive spirit in her, that he divines but cannot seize, that facinates and keeps him."

There is a long silence; the sun is waning and the scythes are silent, and overhead the crows are circling,—a croaking, irregular army, homeward bound from a long day's pillage.

She has made no sign, yet so subtilely is the air charged with her that he feels but a few moments remain to him. He goes over and kneels beside her, and fixes his eyes on her odd, dark face. They both tremble, yet neither speaks. His breath is coming quickly, and the bistre stains about her eyes seem to have deepened, perhaps by contrast, as she has paled.

"Look at me!"

She turns her head right round and gazes straight into his face; a few drops of sweat glisten on his forehead.

"You witch woman! what am I to do with myself? Is my moment ended?"

"I think so."

"Lord, what a mouth!"

"Don't! oh, don't!"

"No, I won't. But do you mean it? Am I, who understand your every mood, your restless spirit, to vanish out of your life? You can't mean it! Listen!—are you listening to me? I can't see your face; take down your hands. Go back over every chance meeting you and I have had together since I met you first by the river, and judge them fairly. To-day is Monday: Wednesday afternoon I shall pass your gate, and if—if my moment is ended, and you mean to send me away, to let me go with this weary aching—"

"A-ah!" she stretches out one brown hand appealingly, but he does not touch it. *"Hang something white on the lilac bush!"*

She gathers up creel and rod, and he takes her shawl, and wrapping it round her holds her a moment in it, and looks searchingly into her eyes, then stands back and raises his hat, and she glides away through the reedy grass.

Wednesday morning she lies watching the clouds sail by. A late rose-spray nods into the open window, and the petals fall every time. A big bee buzzes in and fills the room with his bass note, and then dances out again. She can hear his footstep on the gravel. Presently he looks in over the half window,—

"Get up and come out,—'t will do you good; have a brisk walk!"

She shakes her head languidly, and he throws a great soft, dewy rose with sure aim on her breast.

"Shall I go in and lift you out and put you, 'nighty' and all, into your tub?"

"No!" impatiently. "I'll get up just now."

The head disappears, and she rises wearily and gets through her dressing slowly, stopped every moment by a feeling of faintness. He finds her presently rocking slowly to and fro with closed eyes, and drops a leaf with three plums in it on to her lap.

"I have been watching four for the last week, but a bird, greedy beggar, got one this morning early: try them. Don't you mind, old girl, I'll pour out my own tea!"

She bites into one and tries to finish it, but cannot. "You are a good old man!" she says, and the tears come unbidden to her eyes, and trickle down her cheeks, dropping on to the plums, streaking their delicate bloom.

He looks uneasily at her, but doesn't know what to do; and when he has finished his breakfast he stoops over her chair and strokes her hair, saying, as he leaves a kiss on the top of her head, "Come out into the air, little woman; do you a world of good!"

And presently she hears the sharp thrust of his spade above the bee's hum, leaf rustle, and the myriad late summer sounds that thrill through the air. It irritates her almost to screaming point; there is a practical non-sympathy about it; she can distinguish the regular one, two, three, the thrust, interval, then pat, pat, on the upturned sod. To-day she wants some one, and her thoughts wander to, and she wonders what, the gray-eyed man who never misunderstands her, would say to her. Oh, she wants some one so badly to soothe her; and she yearns for the little mother who is twenty years under the daisies,—the little mother who is a faint memory strengthened by a daguerreotype in which she sits with silk-mittened hands primly crossed on the lap of her moiré gown, a diamond brooch fastening the black-velvet ribbon crossed so stiffly over her lace collar, the shining tender eyes looking steadily out, and her hair in the fashion of fifty-six. How that spade dominates over every sound! and what a sickening pain she has, an odd pain; she never felt it before. Supposing she were to die, she tries to fancy how she would look; they would be sure to plaster her curls down. He might be digging her grave—no, it is the patch where the early peas grew, the peas that were eaten with the twelve weeks' ducklings: she remembers them, little fluffy golden balls with waxen bills, and such dainty paddles,—remembers holding an egg to her ear and listening to it cheep inside before even there was a chip in the shell. Strange how things come to life! What! she sits bolt upright and holds tightly to the chair, and a questioning, awesome look comes over her face; and then the quick blood creeps up through her olive skin right up to her temples, and she buries her face in her hands and sits so a long time.

The maid comes in and watches her curiously, and moves softly about. The look in her eyes is the look of a faithful dog, and she loves her with the same rare fidelity. She hesitates, then goes into the bedroom and stands thoughtfully, with her hands clasped over her breast. She is a tall, thin, flat-waisted woman, with misty blue eyes and a receding chin. Her hair is pretty. She turns as her mistress comes in, with an expectant look on her face. She has taken up a nightgown, but holds it idly.

"Lizzie, had you ever a child?"

The girl's long left hand is ringless; yet she asks it with a quiet insistence, as if she knew what the answer would be, and her odd eyes read her face with an almost cruel steadiness. The girl flushes painfully, and then whitens; her very eyes seem to pale, and her under lip twitches as she jerks out huskily,–

"Yes!"

"What happened to it?"

"It died, M'am."

"Poor thing! Poor old Liz!"

She pats the girl's hand softly, and the latter stands dumbly and looks down at both hands, as if fearful to break the wonder of a caress. She whispers hesitatingly,—

"Have you—have you any little things left?"

And she laughs such a soft, cooing little laugh, like the chirring of a ring-dove, and nods shyly back in reply to the tall maid's questioning look. The latter goes out, and comes back with a flat, red-painted deal box, and unlocks it. It does not hold very much, and the tiny garments are not of costly material; but the two women pore over them as a gem collector over a rare stone. She has a glimpse of thick-crested paper as the girl unties a packet of letters, and looks away until she says tenderly,—

"Look, M'am!"

A little bit of hair inside a paper heart. It is almost white, so silky and so fine that it is more like a thread of bog-wool than a baby's hair; and the mistress, who is a wife, puts her arms round the tall maid, who has never had more than a moral claim to the name, and kisses her in her quick way.

The afternoon is drawing on; she is kneeling before an open trunk, with flushed cheeks and sparkling eyes. A heap of unused, dainty lace trimmed ribbon-decked cambric garments are scattered around her. She holds the soft, scented web to her cheek and smiles musingly; and then she rouses herself and sets to work, sorting out the finest, with the narrowest lace and tiniest ribbon, and puckers her swarthy brows, and measures lengths along her middle finger, and then gets slowly up, as if careful of herself as a precious thing, and half afraid.

"Lizzie!"

"Yes, M'am!"

"Wasn't it lucky they were too fine for every day? They will be so pretty. Look at this one with the tiny valenciennes edging. Why, one nightgown will make a dozen little shirts,—such elfin-shirts as they are too; and Lizzie!"

"Yes, M'am!"

"Just hang it out on the lilac-bush,—mind, the lilac-bush!"

"Yes, M'am!"

"Or, Lizzie, wait: I'll do it myself!"

VIRGIN SOIL

GEORGE EGERTON

From DISCORDS 1894

THE BRIDEGROOM IS waiting in the hall; with a trifle of impatience he is tracing the pattern of the linoleum with the point of his umbrella. He curbs it, and laughs, showing his strong white teeth, at a remark of his best man, then compares the time by his hunter with the clock on the stairs. He is florid, bright-eyed, loose-lipped, inclined to stoutness, but kept in good condition. His hair is crisp, curly, slightly gray; his ears peculiar, pointed at their tops like a faun's. He looks very big and well-dressed, and, when he smiles, affable enough.

Upstairs a young girl, with the suns of seventeen summers on her brown head, is lying with her face hidden on her mother's shoulder; she is sobbing with great childish sobs, regardless of reddened eyes and the tears that have splashed on the silk of her gray going-away gown.

The mother seems scarcely less disturbed than the girl. She is a fragile-looking woman with delicate fair skin, smoothly parted thin chestnut hair, dove-like eyes, and a monotonous piping voice. She is flushing painfully, making a strenuous effort to say something to the girl,—something that is opposed to the whole instincts of her life.

She tries to speak, parts her lips only to close them again, and clasp her arms tighter round the girl's shoulders; at length she manages to say, with trembling, uncertain pauses,—

"You are married now, darling, and you must obey," she lays a stress upon the word, "your husband in all things—there are—there are things you should know—but—marriage is a serious thing, a sacred thing—" with desperation. "You must believe that what your husband tells you is right—Let him guide you—tell you—"

There is such acute distress in her usually unemotional voice that the girl looks up and scans her face, her blushing, quivering, faded face. Her eyes are startled,—fawn-like eyes, as her mother's; her skin, too, is delicately fair: but her mouth is firmer, her jaw squarer, and her piquant, irregular nose is full of character. She is slightly built, scarcely fully developed in her fresh youth.

"What is it that I do not know, mother? What is it?" with anxious impatience. "There is something more—I have felt it all these last weeks in your and the others' looks—in his, in the very atmosphere—but why have you not told me before—I—" Her only answer is a gush of helpless tears from the mother, and a sharp rap at the door, and the bridegroom's voice, with an imperative note that it strikes the nervous girl is new to it, that makes her cling to her mother in a close, close embrace, drop her veil, and go out to him.

She shakes hands with the best man, kisses the girl friend who has acted as bridesmaid,—the wedding has been a very quiet one,—and steps into the carriage. The Irish cook throws an old shoe after them from the side door; but it hits the trunk of an elder-tree, and falls back on to the path, making that worthy woman cross herself and mutter of ill omens and bad luck to follow,—for did not a magpie cross the path first thing this morning when she went to open the gate; and wasn't a red-haired woman the first creature she clapped eyes on as she looked down the road?

Half an hour later the carriage pulls up at the little station, and the girl jumps out first. She is flushed, and her eyes stare helplessly as the eyes of a startled child, and she trembles with quick running shudders from head to foot. She clasps and unclasps her slender gray-gloved hands so tightly that the stitching on the back of one bursts.

He has called to the station-master, and they go into the refreshment-room together. The latter appears at the door, and, beckoning to a porter, gives him an order.

She takes a long look at the familiar little place. They have lived there three years, and yet she seems to see it now for the first time; the rain drips, drips monotonously off the zinc roof, the smell of the dust is fresh, and the white pinks in the borders are beaten into the gravel.

Then the train runs in, a first-class carriage, marked "engaged," is attached, and he comes for her. His hot breath smells of champagne, and it strikes her that his eyes are fearfully big and bright, and he offers her his arm with such a curious amused proprietary air that the girl shivers as she lays her hand in it.

The bell rings, the guard locks the door, the train steams out, and as it passes the signal-box, a large, well-kept hand, with a signet-ring on the little finger, pulls down the blind on the window of an engaged carriage.

Five years later, one afternoon on an autumn day, when the rain is falling like splashing tears on the rails, and the smell of the dust after rain fills the mild air with freshness, and the white chrysanthemums struggle to raise their heads from the gravel path into which the sharp shower has beaten them, the same woman—for there is no trace of girlhood in her twenty-two years—slips out of a first-class carriage; she has a dressing-bag in her hand.

She walks with her head down, and a droop in her shoulders; her quickness of step is due rather to nervous haste than elasticity of frame. When she reaches the turn of the road, she pauses, and looks at the little villa with the white curtains and gay-tiled window-boxes. She can see the window of her old room, distinguish every shade in the changing leaves of the creeper climbing up the south wall, hear the canary's shrill note from where she stands.

Never once has she set foot in the peaceful little house, with its air of genteel propriety, since that eventful morning when she left it with him; she has always framed an excuse.

Now, as she sees it, a feeling of remorse fills her heart, and she thinks of the mother living out her quiet years, each day a replica of the one gone before, and her resolve weakens; she feels inclined to go back. But the waning sun flickers over the panes in the window of the room she occupied as a girl; she can recall how she used to run to the open window on summer mornings, and lean out, and draw in the dewy freshness and welcome the day; how she has stood on moonlight nights, and danced with her bare white feet in the strip of moonlight, and let her fancies fly out into the silver night,—a young girl's dreams of the beautiful, wonderful world that lay outside.

A hard, dry sob rises in her throat at the memory of it, and the fleeting expression of softness on her face changes to a bitter disillusion.

She hurries on, with her eyes down, up the neat gravelled path, through the open door, into the familiar sitting-room.

The piano is open, with a hymn-book on the stand; the grate is filled with fresh green ferns; a bowl of late roses perfume the room from the centre of the table. The mother is sitting in her easy-chair, her hands folded across a big white Persian cat on her lap; she is fast asleep. Some futile lacework, her thimble, and bright scissors are placed on a table near her.

Her face is placid; not a day older than that day five years ago. Her glossy hair is no grayer, her skin is clear; she smiles in her sleep. The smile rouses a sort of sudden fury in the breast of the woman standing in her dusty travelling-cloak at the door, noting every detail in the room. She throws back her veil, and goes over and looks at herself in the mirror over the polished chiffonniere,—scans herself pitilessly. Her skin is sallow, with the dull sallowness of a fair skin in ill-health, and the fringe of her brown hair is so lacking in lustre that it affords no contrast. The look of fawn-like shyness has vanished from her eyes; they burn sombrefully and resentfully in their sunken orbits; there is a dragged look about the mouth, and the keynote of her face is a cynical disillusion. She looks from herself to the reflection of the mother, and then, turning sharply, with a suppressed exclamation, goes over, and, shaking the sleeping woman not too gently, says,—

"Mother, wake up; I want to speak to you!"

The mother starts with frightened eyes, stares at, the other woman as if doubting the evidence of her sight, smiles, then cowed by the unresponsive look in the other face, grows grave again, sits still, and stares helplessly at her, finally bursting into tears with a,—

"Flo, my dear, Flo, is it really you?"

The girl jerks her head impatiently, and says dryly,—

"Yes, that is self-evident. I am going on a long journey. I have something to say to you before I start! Why on earth are you crying?"

There is a note of surprised wonder in her voice, mixed with impatience.

The older woman has had time to scan her face, and the dormant motherhood in her is roused by its weary anguish. She is ill, she thinks, in trouble! She rises to her feet. It is characteristic of the habits of her life, with its studied regard for the observance of small proprieties, and distrust of servants as a class, that she goes over and closes the room-door carefully.

This hollow-eyed, sullen woman is so unlike the fresh girl who left her five years ago that she feels afraid. With the quiet selfishness that has characterized her life, she has accepted the excuses her daughter has made to avoid coming home, as she has accepted the presents her son-in-law has sent her from time to time. She has found her a husband well-off in the world's goods, and there her responsibility ended. She approaches her hesitatingly; she feels she ought to kiss her; there is something unusual in such a meeting after so long an absence; it shocks her, it is so unlike the one she has pictured; she has often looked forward to it, often,—to seeing Flo's new frocks, to hearing of her town life.

"Won't you take off your things? You will like to go to your room?"

She can hear how her own voice shakes; it is really inconsiderate of Flo to treat her in this strange way.

"We will have some tea!"—she adds.

Her color is coming and going, the lace at her wrist is fluttering. The daughter observes it with a kind of dull satisfaction; she is taking out her hat pins carefully. She notices a portrait in a velvet case upon the mantelpiece; she walks over and looks at it intently. It is her father,—the father who was killed in India in a hill skirmish when she was a little lint-locked maid barely up to his knee. She studies it with new eyes, trying to read what man he was, what soul he had, what part of him is in her, tries to find herself by reading him. Something in his face touches her, strikes some underlying chord in her, and she grinds her teeth at a thought it rouses.

"She must be ill, she must be very ill," says the mother, watching her. "To think I daren't offer to kiss my own child!" She checks the tears that keep welling up, feeling that they may offend this woman who is so strangely unlike the girl who left her. The latter has turned from her scrutiny of the likeness, and sweeps her with a cold, criticising look as she turns towards the door, saying,—

"I *should* like some tea; I will go upstairs and wash off the dust."

Half-an-hour later the two women sit opposite one another in the pretty room. The younger one is leaning back in her chair, watching the mother pour out the tea, following the graceful movements of the white, blue-veined hands amongst the tea-things; she lets her wait on her. They have not spoken, beyond a commonplace remark about the heat, the dust, the journey.

"How is Philip, is he well?" the mother ventures to ask, with a feeling of trepidation; but it seems to her that she ought to ask about him.

"He is quite well; men of his type usually are. I may say he is particularly well just now; he has gone to Paris with a girl from the Alhambra!"

The older woman flushes painfully, and pauses, with her cup halfway to her lips, and lets the tea run over unheeded on to her dainty silk apron.

"You are spilling your tea," the girl adds, with malicious enjoyment.

The woman gasps, "Flo, but Flo, my dear, it is dreadful! What would your poor father have said! *No wonder* you look ill, dear. How shocking! Shall I—ask the vicar to—to remonstrate with him?"

"My dear mother, what an extraordinary idea! These little trips have been my one solace. I assure you I have always hailed them as lovely oases in the desert of matrimony, resting-places on the journey! My sole regret was their infrequency. That is very good tea; I suppose it is the cream!"

The older woman puts her cup on the tray, and stares at her with frightened eyes and paled cheeks.

"I am afraid I don't understand you, Florence! I am old-fashioned," with a little air of frigid propriety; "I have always looked upon matrimony as a sacred thing. It is dreadful to hear you speak this way; you should have tried to save Philip—from—from such a shocking sin."

The girl laughs, and the woman shivers as she hears her. She cries,—

"I would never have thought it of Philip! My poor dear, I am afraid you must be very unhappy!"

"Very," with a grim smile; "but it is over now, I have done with it. I am not going back!"

If a bomb had exploded in the quiet, pretty room the effect could hardly have been more startling than her almost cheerful statement. A big bee buzzes in and bangs against the lace of the older woman's cap, and she never heeds it; then she almost screams,—

"Florence, Florence, my dear, you can't mean to desert your husband! Oh, think of the disgrace, the scandal, what people will say, the," with an uncertain quaver, "the sin. You took a solemn vow, you know, and you are going to break it—"

"My dear mother, the ceremony had no meaning for me; I simply did not know what I was signing my name to, or what I was vowing to do. I might as well have signed my name to a document drawn up in Choctaw. I have no remorse, no prick of conscience at the step I am taking; my life must be my own. They say sorrow chastens,—I don't believe it; it hardens, embitters. Joy is like the sun, it coaxes all that is loveliest and sweetest in human nature. No, I am not going back."

The older woman cries, wringing her hands helplessly,—

"I can't understand it. You must be very miserable to dream of taking such a serious step."

"As I told you, I am. It is a defect of my temperament. How many women really take the man nearest to them as seriously as I did?—I think few. They finesse, and flatter, and wheedle, and coax; but truth there is none. I couldn't do that, you see, and so I went to the wall. I don't blame them, it must be so, as long as marriage is based on such unequal terms, as long as man demands from a wife as a right what he must sue from a mistress as a favor,—until marriage becomes for many women a legal prostitution, a nightly degradation, a hateful yoke under which they age, mere bearers of children conceived in a sense of duty, not love. They bear them, birth them, nurse them, and begin again, without choice in the matter, growing old, unlovely, with all joy of living swallowed in a senseless burden of reckless maternity, until their love,—granted they started with that,—the mystery, the crowning glory of their lives, is turned into a duty they submit to with distaste, instead of a favor granted to a husband who must become a new lover to obtain it."

"But men are different, Florence; you can't refuse a husband, you might cause him to commit sin."

"Bosh, mother! he is responsible for his own sins; we are not bound to dry-nurse his morality. Man is what we have made him; his very faults are of our making. No wife is bound to set aside the demands of her individual soul for the sake of imbecile obedience. I am going to have some more tea!"

The mother can only whimper,—

"It is dreadful! I thought he made you such an excellent husband; his position, too, is so good, and he is so highly connected."

"Yes, and it is as well to put the blame in the right quarter. Philip is as God made him; he is an animal with strong passions, and he avails himself of the latitude permitted him by the laws of society. Whatever of blame, whatever of sin, whatever of misery is in the whole matter rests *solely and entirely* with you, mother!" the woman sits bolt upright, "and with no one else. That is why I came here,—to tell you that. I have promised myself over and over again that I would tell you. It is with you, and you alone, the fault lies."

There is so much of cold dislike in her voice that the other woman recoils, and whimpers piteously,—

"You must be ill, Florence, to say such wicked things. What have I done? I am sure I devoted myself to you from the time you were little. I refused," dabbing her eyes with her cambric handkerchief, "ever so many good offers.

There was young Fortescue in the Artillery, such a good-looking man, and such an elegant horseman, he was quite infatuated about me; and Jones—to be sure he was in business, but he was most attentive. Every one said I was a devoted mother. I can't think what you mean, I—."

A smile of cynical amusement checks her.

"Perhaps not. Sit down, and I'll tell you."

She shakes off the trembling hand, for the mother has risen and is standing next to her, and pushes her into a chair, and paces up and down the room. She is painfully thin, and drags her limbs as she walks.

"I say it is your fault, because you reared me a fool, an idiot, ignorant of everything I ought to have known,—everything that concerned me and the life I was bound to lead as a wife,—my physical needs, my coming passion, the very meaning of my sex, my wifehood and motherhood to follow. You gave me not one weapon in my hand to defend myself against the possible attacks of man at his worst. You sent me out to fight the biggest battle of a woman's life,—the one in which she ought to know every turn of the game,— with a white gauze," she laughs derisively, "of maiden purity as a shield."

Her eyes blaze, and the woman in the chair watches her as one sees a frog watch a snake when it is put into its case.

"I was fourteen when I gave up the gooseberrybush theory as the origin of humanity, and I cried myself ill with shame when I learned what maternity meant, instead of waking with a sense of delicious wonder at the great mystery of it. You gave me to a man,—nay, more, you told me to obey him, to believe that whatever he said would be right, would be my duty,—knowing that the meaning of marriage was a sealed book to me, that I had no real idea of what union with a man meant. You delivered me body and soul into his hands, without preparing me in any way for the ordeal I was to go through. You sold me for a home, for clothes, for food; you played upon my ignorance,—I won't say innocence; that is different. You told me, you and your sister and your friend, the vicar's wife, that it would be an anxiety off your mind if I were comfortably settled—"

"It is wicked of you to say such dreadful things!" the mother cries. "And besides," with a touch of asperity, "you married him willingly; you seemed to like his attentions—"

"How like a woman! What a thorough woman you are, mother! The good old-fashioned kitten, with a claw in her paw! Yes, I married him willingly; I was not eighteen, I had known no men; was pleased that you were pleased, and, as you say, I liked his attentions. He had tact enough not to frighten me, and I had not the faintest conception of what marriage with him meant. I had an idea," with a laugh, "that the words of the minister settled the matter. Do you think that if I had realized how fearfully close the intimacy with him would have been that my whole soul would not have stood up in revolt, the whole woman in me cried out against such a degradation of myself?" Her words tremble with passion, and the woman who bore her feels as if she is being lashed by a whip. "Would I not have shuddered at the thought of him in such a relationship, and waited, waited until I found the man who would satisfy me body and soul, to whom I would have gone without any false shame, of whom I would think with gladness as the father of a little child to come, for whom the white fire of love or passion, call it what you will, in my heart would have burned clearly, and saved me from the feeling of loathing horror that has made my married life a nightmare to me,—ay, made me a murderess in heart over and over again? This is not exaggeration. It has killed the sweetness in me, the pure thoughts of womanhood; has made me hate myself and hate you. Cry, mother, if you will; you don't know how much you have to cry for. I have cried myself barren of tears. Cry over the girl you killed," with a gust of passion. "Why didn't you strangle me as a baby? It would have been kinder. My life has been a hell, mother. I felt it vaguely as I stood on the platform waiting; I remember the mad impulse I had to jump down under the engine as it came in to escape from the dread that was chilling my soul. What have these years been? One long crucifixion; one long submittal to the desires of a man I bound myself to in ignorance of what it meant. Every caress," with a cry, "has only been the first note of that. Look at me!" stretching out her arms. "Look at this wreck of my physical self! I wouldn't dare to show you the heart or the soul underneath. He has stood on his rights; but do you think if I had known, that I would have given such insane obedience from a mistaken sense of duty as would lead to this? I have my rights too, and my duty to myself. If I had only recognized them in time—

"Sob away, mother, I don't even feel for you; I have been burned too badly to feel sorry for what will only be a tiny scar to you,—I have all the long future to face, with all the world against me. Nothing will induce me to go back. Better anything than that. Food and clothes are poor equivalents for what I have had to suffer; I can get them at a cheaper rate. When he comes to look for me, give him that letter. He will tell you he has only been a uxorious husband, and that you reared me a fool. You can tell him, too, if you like, that I loathe him, shiver at the touch of his lips, his breath, his hands; that my whole body revolts at his touch; that when he has turned and gone to sleep, I have watched him with such growing hatred that at times the temptation to kill him has been so strong that I have crept out of bed and walked the cold passage in my bare feet until I was too benumbed to feel anything; that I have counted the hours to his going away, and cried out with delight at the sight of the retreating carriage!"

"You are very hard, Flo; the Lord soften your heart! Perhaps," with trepidation, "if you had had a child—"

"Of his—that indeed would have been the last straw—No, mother."

There is such a peculiar expression of satisfaction over something; of some inner understanding, as a man has when he dwells on the successful accomplishment of a secret purpose, that the mother sobs quietly, wringing her hands,—

"I did not know, Flo, I acted for the best; you are very hard on me!"

Later, when the bats are flitting across the moon, and the girl is asleep,—she has thrown herself half-dressed on the narrow white bed of her girlhood, with her arms folded across her breast, and her hands clenched,—the mother steals into the room. She has been turning over the contents of an old desk; her marriage certificate, faded letters on foreign paper, and a bit of Flo's hair cut off each birthday, and a sprig of orange-blossom she wore in her hair. She looks faded and gray in the silver light, and she stands and gazes at the haggard face in its weary sleep. The placid current of her life is disturbed, her heart is roused, something of her child's soul-agony has touched the sleeping depths of her nature. She feels as if scales have dropped from her eyes, as if the instincts and conventions of her life are toppling over, as if all the needs of protesting women of whom she has read with a vague displeasure have come home to her. She covers the girl tenderly, kisses her hair, and slips a little roll of notes into the dressing-bag on the table, and steals out, with the tears running down her cheeks.

When the girl looks into her room as she steals by when the morning light is slanting in, she sees her kneeling, her head with its straggling gray hair bowed in tired sleep; it touches her: life is too short, she thinks, to make any one's hours bitter; she goes down, and writes a few kind words in pencil, and leaves them near her hand, and goes quickly out into the road.

The morning is gray and misty, with faint yellow stains in the east, and the west wind blows with a melancholy sough in it, the first whisper of the fall,— the fall that turns the world of nature into a patient suffering from phthisis. Delicate season of decadence, when the loveliest scenes have a note of decay in their beauty, when a poisoned arrow pierces the marrow of insect and plant, and the leaves have a hectic flush, and fall, fall and shrivel and curl in the night's cool; and the chrysanthemums, the "goodbye summers" of the Irish peasants, have a sickly tinge in their white. It affects her, and she finds herself saying, "Wither and die, wither and die, make compost for the loves of the spring, as the old drop out and make place for the new, who forget them, to be in their turn forgotten." She hurries on, feeling that her autumn has come to her in her spring, and a little later she stands once more on the platform where she stood in the flush of her girlhood, and takes the train in the opposite direction.

At the Heart of the Apple

George Egerton

From Symphonies 1897

It matters little in what precise latitude, but somewhere on the south coast of Norway, there lies an island in a short, wide fjord, one of the many that cut into the coast like the irregular teeth in a broken comb.

Solitude is its dominant expression, an atmosphere of restfulness that is rarely marred save by the encroachment of a stray pleasure cutter "out of its bearings," that may sail up for a little way, only to bear back and bend round the tongue of land with which the island is connected,—in winter by ice, in summer by a roughly constructed bridge,—to pursue her course up the west fjord. This is long and wide, dotted with numerous rocky islets; landing-stages for the landing of produce, tiny verdant *"sletten"*—our "slades," in old English,—fat with herbage, and stray homesteads, can be seen on either side as one glides up toward the prosperous town with saw and pulp mills at the head of it.

The peninsula-like strip of land to which the island is joined belongs to the owner of the latter, an Englishman, who uses the roughly made road upon it as a means of transit to the market town. Notices prohibit trespassers, and so it and the island are unvisited. The latter is of about ten acres, six of which afford good pasture for the cow and sturdy little Hallingah mare; the rest is well wooded. At the time of my story, it boasted of a tiny landing-stage, and hidden in the trees, a long, low farm-house with roof of blue glazed tiles; a turret room with a large window looking seawards had been added to the older building. A stable, sheds, and tiny farmyard lay at the back of it, and a neglected herb garden ran along one side. Gooseberry and currant bushes sadly in need of pruning, and some hardy apple-trees struggled to bear in it, all the trees on the island inclined one way before the blasts of the wind. Birds had come from the mainland, and built for many springs in perfect freedom; colonies of half-wild ducks had hatched out their young unmolested, and taken them for trial trips up the fjord.

One January day a little maid with a grave face came down to the edge of the ice-bound island in the company of a solemn black-and-tan hare hound. She was a quaint little person; a costly seal-skin coat reached the end of her frock, and when it gaped as she moved, it showed a pinafore of coarse blue-and-white check; a coarsely knitted scarlet cap was pulled down over her ears, and a mane of tangled, red-brown, elf locks fell beneath it to her shoulders; gaiters made by finishing off a pair of grey worsted stockings at the ankles came to the top of her clumsy boots. All her movements were deliberate; she fastened her skates carefully, stepped on to the ice and tested them; but once satisfied she darted forward as if transformed. She curved like a swallow, a sort of sprite in woollen, across the frozen fjord. The grave little maid became a demon of motion, curving, swaying, swinging round, first on one foot, then on the other in giddy circles; cutting backwards, making figures, giving herself to the enjoyment of her skill.

Her cheeks tingled, her eyes sparkled as she skimmed in flying curves ever farther from the island towards the turn to the other fjord, where the ice became rough and ran up in curling ridges from the wave-wash in wreaths of frozen froth. She had never been so far from the island before, and the alert, seeking spirit of the child had longed, yet feared, to explore her surroundings. The fjord she came to stretched as far as her eye could see, a glistening roadway breasted with steel blue ice, its sides flanked with pines and firs, their branches bending under a fringe of sparkling icicles, every rocky fissure pendent with stalactites.

She seated herself upon a boulder, the dog at her feet, and sat, a quaint little figure, her chin in the palms of her hands, gazing with wondering eyes up the frozen waterway. What lay up there at the end of it? She has seen so little, and yet in the picture books in the master's room there were figures of ladies, and men, and gardens full of flowers and big buildings. Peter has often told her of the great towns where the people crowd as thickly as the sea mews, or the birds speeding southward when autumn comes. Her lips curved tenderly as she thought of Peter,—Peter with his odd, twinkling eyes and shaggy beard! The days would be long without Peter. Sigrid is deaf, and never speaks, and never smiles, just works always; sometimes she makes her sit and learn to card wool with a tiny carding-board, and knit and spin; and at times when she has looked up she has found her eyes resting upon her with a puzzled look, not like Peter's one bit—what wonderful things he has told her! When the wild geese fly overhead and give tongue like a pack of aerial hounds, he whispers tales of the Valkyrie; and in summer when the rainbow arches across the sky from the end of the land to the selvage of the sea, Peter knew that it was burning all afire to keep the frost giants out of Jötunheim. And he had signs for everything. He knew too the crevices where the wagtail laid their eggs; the haunt of the fly orchids, the "spraint" of lynx and badger in the snow; the folk lore of all the plants and insects; a medley of the curious and superstitious, inextricably mixed with facts.

The child's unusually keen, unspoiled intelligence travelled back, as her quick thoughts danced inconsequently through her memory. She wondered what "the England" was like, and the people in it with whom she lived before she was brought to the island, a little child of three summers. Peter couldn't tell her, for he and Anna had only been there one year when the master came with her. Sigrid was deaf, and cross, and talked English to the master when he wrote on the slate. Sigrid made her say the names of all the things in the house and yard in English, so that she might not forget them. She felt a burning desire to know all about it. Anna had been kind to her; she had been happy up in Anna's warm room over the stable. Anna used to kiss her, and make her little cakes with currants in them, and sometimes bake an apple as well. But two winters ago Anna went to bed; she can remember so well how Peter was away for half a day, and came back with a fat, little man with funny glasses on his nose, like tiny round windows, and a fur-lined coat; how he went up to Anna and came down shaking his head as he got into the sleigh, and went across the bridge again.

Next day she couldn't go up; Sigrid stopped her, and she sat and watched Peter planing white-pine planks, whilst the tears ran down his cheeks and made drops on his beard as he drilled holes for the screws in the funny-shaped box he had made; and how roughly he had sworn at her because she began to dance amongst the curly shavings with Grip, the hare hound. Then two strange men in blue jerseys, and leather jackets, and rabbit-fur caps came and helped to put the box on a sledge, and Sigrid covered it with fur branches, and Peter sat up and drove away through the snow, with only one bell at the horse's collar. But Anna never was seen again; perhaps Draugen, the water fury, with a face like a seal and the mew of an angry cat, took her away to the floating islands, that disappear when ships come nigh. The faces of those three men are the only strange ones she has ever seen, except that of Knut the Finn, who comes with a boat at times to sell crockery and tins. The dog moved uneasily, and the child lifted her head quickly, for she was keen in hearing as Heimdal, who could hear the grass grow in the meadows, and the wool on the backs of the sheep. A voice pierced the still, clear air sweetly,—a boy's soprano, shouting the words of a student's song, a song of comradeship and brave deeds. She listened and watched as if spellbound; there was nothing of fear, but much of wonder in the expectant look. The notes rang gladder, louder, and a lad of fourteen sped forward with rapid curves, watching his feet as he sang. The dog growled, the child held him by the scruff of the neck; the song stopped with a check as the boy saw them. An amazed look flitted across his face,—an ugly, clever face, with merry, inquisitive eyes, and a mass of thick fair curls clustering closely to his head; when he smiled a dimple showed in his chin, and his teeth gleamed whitely.

"Hullo!" he cried; "what have we here?"

His quick eyes took in the incongruous parts of her dress; the great solemn grey eyes, with their thick fringe of lashes; the odd, irregular features and look of intense expression that sat so oddly on the little face. He raised his cap humourously.

"Good day, Frost Fairy; all hail!"

The child made no answer, only clutched the dog more firmly; the boy glided closer.

"Have you no tongue in your country, then?"

She thrust it out between her strong little teeth, then drew it shyly back. The boy broke into an infectiously happy laugh.

"Well, you are not deaf, anyway. But seriously, what is your name, if a common mortal may ask?"

"My name," very slowly, with a precise enunciation, "is Evir."

"Humph, and what else?"

"Only Evir now; Anna used to call me Little Elf."

"Discriminating person, Anna; but you must have another; what is your father's name?"

She knitted her straight black brows in perplexity; the lad added, "Or your mother's?"

"I haven't any, I don't know what you mean. I know a mother duck—"

The boy looked intently at her, then sat down on the boulder with an evident determination of discovering if she were quite normal.

"Do you know what *I* am?"

"Yes," slowly; "you are a young man. I never saw one before, except in pictures. I've only seen," counting on her fingers, "four besides Peter; and they all had beards, and one had glass windows on his eyes."

"How old are you?"

"Peter says I am nine."

"Where do you live?"

She pointed behind her to the mouth of the fjord.

"Round there; but," with uneasiness, "I must go back; Peter will be vexed. I only skated round here because I wanted to see where he goes to fetch things in the boat in the summer."

"And who is Peter when he is at home?"

She answered with the same slow consideration, and the lad's merry eyes grew grave as he listened. His thoughts flew to the jolly parsonage home, with the nine noisy girls and boys, who made the rafters ring with quarrels and laughter. He found by adroit questioning that Peter went to town every week for provisions; that Sigrid got some of her clothes, some were sent by the "master's" orders. He grew more and more amazed as he discovered that she was ignorant of the simplest relationships in life, or of religion except of the curious, half-superstitious, half-pagan form of it that Peter had evolved in his solitude or picked up in his wanderings, or half Biblical, such as she had gleaned from listening as Sigrid read aloud to herself on Sundays; and Sunday meant to her the day on which less work was done than other days, no more.

She told of the master, who came now and then, and of how Peter kept her out in the shed, or up in the loft, so that she rarely saw him; of the wonderful pictures and pretty things in his room that Sigrid let her look at in his absence; of the cow "Primrose" that had a little calf last spring, and many other incidents of her daily life.

He put his arm round her from a sudden impulse of tenderness and pity for this most solitary of little mortals, with no playmates, no soul to speak to except Peter, whom he mentally decided was crazed, and the deaf woman who spoke without expecting any answer. A sudden thought struck him; he took a book out of his pocket saying to himself:—

"It's an awful shame." Then to her, "Do you know what this is?"

"Yes, a book; I like picture ones best. The master has a lot, full of birds and plants. I know some of them. Peter says the little black marks are letters that tell about the pictures; I don't see how they can. I've thought and thought about it; I wish I could make them out."

"Poor little mite! I'll tell you what; in May when the summer is coming, I shall be home for the long vacation, and I'll teach you to read. You quaint little thing, you wouldn't be so lonely then, would you?"

The wistful, odd face, with the eager eyes, her slow tones, and repressed old ways, roused an interest in the boy. There seemed to him to be a certain romance about this solitary little mortal in medley of homespun and fine feathers. He said pityingly:—

"The dusk will soon fall; I must be getting back. You too, you sprite; I'll watch you skate to the point. Adjö, then, mysterious Princess, till the summer!"

He kissed her awkwardly, and patted her back patronisingly, as he did to little Aagot, the youngest at home. She looked back at the turn, where the ice curled up in ridges like dirty white feathers, balanced herself for a second, waved her hand, and vanished. Then the gliding song of the skates and the glad voice of the boy once more made music up the Rowan fjord.

A day came when the frost king grew aweary of holding the earth and water in his icy hands, so he relaxed his stark grip unexpectedly, causing the ice to cry out with a sharp, crackling rend, that told of its rapid dissolution. Then the spring whispered mystically, and thus it came to pass that little Evir witnessed a wonderful transformation scene; for though one day the snow still covered the earth in tarnished whiteness, the next it had vanished, leaving only shreds and rags of its mantle in the hollows and under the bushes. There was a gurgle of trickling water, the gushing music of the melting snows, the rhythmic trickle of a thousand rivulets, as they slid to the fjord, like the cooing of infants in content; the wild hyacinths peered out in the woods, the breeze blossoms danced airily, and all the tender leaflets shot forth and lisped of spring.

The little maid clapped her hands and danced, no sun on Easter day more merrily, until Peter thought she must surely be "elfshot," and watched her anxiously. She hailed each token of its coming with delight, from the discovery of a brood of ducklings bobbing round their mother, like floating balls of yellow down, in a tiny round of clear water, to the distant bleat of kids, and the bell music of the cattle on the main-land.

May gave way graciously to June, the wild strawberry blossoms peered out, and the rock heartsease, "step-mother-flowrets," as Peter called them, nodded their wise little faces from their stony harbourage. She sat, hour after hour, with Grip at her side, watching the point of the land with anxious eyes. Then a great doubt troubled her; perhaps, after all, he would not come that way; she had not told him where she would meet him, and the rock upon which they had sat would surely be covered with water.

During the dark days since they had met, she had often peered at the little black signs crawling, like files of ants, from the middle of the book towards the edges, until her eyes had ached. She dare not venture to row round there, because Peter was always about, as the master was expected; she must wait until he had come, and tied flies, and got ready his tackle, and seen to things for the summer, and gone again.

He came; the weeks dragged very slowly. Then, at length, one day he was to leave. She hid in the wood, and watched Peter and the man with the squint eye and the leather jacket prepare the big boat and row him round the point. She laughed gaily, and danced to the shadow of the pine needles, bobbing in answer to the touch of the sea breeze. Then she went up to the house and into the big kitchen, with the black oaken beams and quaint chairs,—seat and back hewn out of one solid block, with letters and date glistening in tarnished gold amongst the gaudily painted scrollwork. The deaf woman turned as she came in, and pointed to her dinner of rice porridge and milk.

"Peter won't be back till to-morrow." The child nodded. "Don't stay out after six, Miss Evir; you are growing big now, and must not run so wild; you must do some sewing."

Sinking her voice, she muttered: "I can't think what the master means to do with her; Peter's no fit companion for her."

The girleen finished her meal, whistled to the little hound, crossed the roughly built pilebridge, and mounted the uneven stony road. Once before only had Peter let her go a piece of the way with him; there seemed to be a tacit understanding that she was to stay upon the island.

It was a wondrous adventure; she observed every plant and tree with interest; a silver birch and a tiny yellowish-grey bird, such as she had not seen on the island, were objects of delightful freshness; over there she knew each plant and stone by heart. She turned aside at a bend in the road, and sprang, like a chamois, from rock to boulder, to try and get a glimpse of the Rowan fjord. The ascent was difficult, for the sodden leaves from last year's fall, and the wet club-moss, made her feet slip, until she reached a strip of fir wood, with a thread of blue shining beyond it. She darted on, then dropped behind a barberry bush, seizing Grip by the collar, and peered cautiously down. She gave a cry of delight. An ice schooner was drawn taut to the main-land, on the other side of the fjord, for the rocks sank perpendicularly into the water. Block after block of ice, cut into crystal squares, came slithering down the ice race on to the deck of the trim craft. Peter had told her how the women and children row about the tarns in autumn, and pick up every twig and leaf, so that the ice may not be flawed, and so lessened in value; then, when it is strong enough to bear, how a man cuts it into equidistant lines with an ice plough, and another man divides it crosswise with a pick into squares, so that it can be raised in blocks and stored in the ice-house until the summer, when the ships come and fetch it away to other countries. The tapering masts, delicate tracery of the rigging, and painted wooden figurehead of a lady enchanted her. How regularly the blocks fell, as if set in motion by machinery; first one sees them appear high up on the ridge, flashing like a bit of spar amongst the rocks, growing bigger and bigger as they descend. A man on the deck was singing in English; she could understand a few of the words. Further on she could see Peter and the other man pulling steadily up the fjord; they would soon be hidden behind an island. She clambered lower down between the rocks and ferns and grey-blue lichens. She knew from a tree on the opposite side, a fir-tree that had been dislodged, and fallen between a fissure in the rock, and grew head downwards over the water, that she must be near the place where she had met him in the ice days. She peered down. The boy was sitting in a boat, with a book upon his knee.

The little face lit up with the grave smile so much her own; she took a wooden flute, with plated stops, out of her pocket. Peter had shown her how to play; she could imitate most of the birds, and she had picked out many a wild melody that came to her out of the world of nature and fancy in which she moved. The colour flooded her little face as she put it to her mouth; then the boy's own song of brave deeds and true comradeship, filtered liquidly through the sounds of the young summer.

The lad started, listened, lifted his head, loosened the boat, backwatered deftly, and espied her. She stood with her heavy locks fluttering in the breeze, a slight little figure in a blue homespun gown, girt with an untanned leather belt, fastened by a silver clasp, such as the peasants wear; a scarlet crape kerchief, with silk fringe, was knotted about her shoulders, and she looked down at him with laughter-lit, mischievous eyes as she played. He ran the boat in, fastened it, and began to climb up to her, waving his cap gleefully. Some sudden shyness seized her; she darted behind a pine tree, and peered round the trunk; he sprang after her, seized her by the arm, and pulled her forth, looking at her quizzically. Her deep-set grey eyes smiled up to him with a frank charm.

"I've been watching for you for several days. I thought you had been spirited away by some of your fairy friends; to-morrow I should have gone round to the island."

"Oh, you must never do that, it would spoil everything; I couldn't come. *He* has been here, and only went a while ago!"

"You mean the master, as you call him; was he in a boat with two men and some baggage?"

She nodded.

"You have grown, elf; you are taller. I often thought of you; the winter seemed long this year, and so much can happen in a few months. Did you wonder if I'd come?"

She smiled an assent.

"Don't you want to know my name?—Einar Stang. You can call me Einar."

He slung a satchel off his back and opened it.

"I have brought a primer and some other books. You can hide them some place. If I once set you going you'll be able to get along alone. "

He opened the book, laid it upon a flat stone, and they set to work at the alphabet. And so every day for a month. With few intermissions the boat was tied to the tree stump, and the two heads bent over a book The keen, unspoiled intelligence of the child proved intensely receptive. Her quick eye and ear, trained, perforce, for lack of other pastime, to notice each detail of the life of plant, and bird, and fish, in her surroundings, had developed a wonderful, visual memory. Once she had seen a word and named it, she never forgot it again. The primer was discarded for an easy reading book, and the child's delighted wonder at the rhyme and beat of some simple verses in it led the lad to teach her a folk-song now and then.

July had yet a few days to riot, when he failed to come. She waited for three days, standing up on the highest rock, shading her eyes from the fierce sun with patient hand, watching the fjord unceasingly. The fourth day found her listening with misery-filled eyes for the plash of oars, a tense strain disfiguring her little face. Noon came and went; she lay with her face hidden upon her folded arms, worn out with watching. The rattle of falling pebbles roused her, she sat up and gripped the carved, wooden haft of the sheath knife she carried peasant fashion at her hips; thus he found her. She sprang to her feet with a sob of relief, and flew to him, straining her arms about his neck.

"I thought you had gone, Einar, never to come again; oh, I could have killed myself, I just could!"

The boy stroked back her hair with soothing words, and sat down pulling her to his side; he opened his satchel.

"See, I have brought you a parcel of books this time, and a piece of the mother's cake, and some fruit syrup. You've been crying, you dear little one! I couldn't come before because—Well, let us eat our lunch first. I have something to tell you."

He sat with his arm round her, and watched her divide the cake, taking the smaller half herself. She barely tasted her portion; her eyes wandered to his face, as if trying to read what he had to tell her; the quick intuition that was the essence of her nature filled her with forebodings.

"Listen, childie; I'm afraid I shall not be able to come again. My father has got a larger parish, a long way north, and we are to move at once. Then I am going to the University, and perhaps it may be years before I shall be able to come here again. Don't hide your face, childie; you must be a brave little maid, and try not to forget anything I have taught you, and learn as much as you can. I have brought you a few books, and a dictionary. I'll show you how to find the meaning of words in it, and," with a shy lowering of voice, "a New Testament. I have written something in it, but you must find that out for yourself later on. See, here is a copy book. I have put all the written letters under the printed ones that you know now, and set headlines in these others; you can learn to write this way, and when you know all the letters spell out what it is, eh? Try and learn as much as you can, and when you are grown up ask that man what he means to do with you. Don't cry, Evir; don't, little sis. I do want you so to be jolly on our last day. Cheer up, and play me one of your queer tunes!"

The child cried, sharply:—

"I couldn't, Einar, oh, I couldn't!" and buried her head on his shoulder, and sat crying quietly for a long time, only stirring once to stoop and kiss his hand fiercely.

"Poor little girl, I'm so sorry. I'm afraid I must go now, childie."

He raised her face and started at the impress of pain sealed upon it, and realised that the grief of this little being with her concentrated, suppressed emotions was different from the quick passionate crying of his little sisters; the tears running down her cheeks splashing into big drops as they fell, the hard, voiceless convulsion of her breast was like the crying of a deaf mute. He tried to console her, in an awkward, boyish way, coaxed a smile from her in good-bye and left her. He looked back from the bend in the road; the pathetic little figure, with the wistful eyes, following him hungrily, hurt him; he bounded back and kissed her again.

Five years slipped by with no change other than the intermarriage of the seasons. The girl at fifteen promised to grow into a glorious woman, tall and strong, yet fine-boned and lithe; she had developed early, and showed every sign of precocious womanhood. Amongst the anæmic, retarded girls of a city, she might have passed easily for a woman grown.

There was something fawn-like in her questioning bright eyes, something untamed in the poise of her dart-like figure and easy movements; she suggested a wild doe. She had pored over the books in the "master's" room, conned dictionary after dictionary; a Norsk English lexicon had proved a treasure trove.

There was not one novel, not one romance amongst them; of books on birds and beasts and fishes and plants with their lore, there were many. Costly plates enabled her to find those in her immediate neighbourhood. She spent hours watching them court and brood and build; she knew their sex, noted the beauty of colour or form in the male, the duller garb of the female; the miracle of sex, underlying every natural law, its individual working in the propagation of the young, was no mystery to her, and consequently no subject for prurient musing; but of love or marriage, moral or social laws, or the ordinary relationships of so-called civilised life, she was more ignorant than any savage; she had not even a rudimentary sense of family, possessed no totem.

She was a thing of absolute health, every muscle, every fibre sound, every nerve strung to the right key,—a creature of instinct, pure and simple, quick with natural impulses, always acting from them, uninfluenced by any system founded on social expediency; a young female animal with her basic instincts intact.

A classical dictionary gave her imagination a jerk, and the pine trees held a new meaning, since Attis lurked in them, with ever-growing hair and ever-moving little finger,—but only for a brief spell; she leaned to the concrete, as all unspoiled, simple women do; poetry and abstract imaginings being more to the man. The courtships of the birds, the domestic economy of the little red ants, interested her far more than the loves of Zeus.

A year before, Sigrid's health had failed, and so it came to pass that the girl took her share in the household management She went to the lambing, assisted at the coming of the little white calf, saw naught of evil in God's world, and knew no single cause for shame. The elder woman had softened much with her waning strength; she sat with her Bible on her knee, her faded eyes following the girl's movements, with the wistful admiration that age gives so grudgingly to youth.

At times the girl's germinant womanhood disturbed her in a subtle way, although she was ignorant of definite desires, nor thought of her future with man as a possible factor in it.

Chance—or is it ever chance?—gave a new trend to her thoughts. One afternoon in the late spring, she stood patting some cakes into shape while Sigrid baked them on an iron griddle, when Knut the Finn entered the big kitchen. He bore his usual fardel of tin ware, cottons, pins, buttons, and hair combs. Sigrid hailed him with a welcome; Knut had an extraordinary faculty for making the deaf woman hear. He nodded respectfully to the girl.

"Good day, good day there!" shrieked Sigrid, "indeed, but it's good to see you. I want a milk pan badly, and Peter never gets the right needles. Sit down there, Knut. You'll have some ale, some bread and cheese, or some coffee; it's just cooked."

"Thank you, Sigrid, indeed I thank you, but my woman's with me, and she's none too strong yet. I'll make bold to ask if I may take her some hot coffee. I'll take ale myself, thank you."

The girl could not recall having ever seen a woman's face, except those of Anna and Sigrid. She felt an overpowering desire to see the pedlar's woman; she said eagerly:—

"Certainly, Knut; but stay where you are, I'll fetch her."

She flushed with eagerness and darted down to the boat, a broad, flat bottomed craft with one mast and a dirty white sail. As she drew near, the woman who had stepped out and seated herself upon the landing-stage, turned and looked at her. Then she rose and muttered an awkward good day.

She was stout limbed, with small deep set eyes above high cheek bones, fair, freckled skin, with pink cheeks and red fuzzy hair curling off her forehead.

The girl eyed her closely, guessing her age. Then she did a singular thing; she ran to the end of the stage, knelt down, and gazed steadily at her own reflection in the water, looked back to the other woman, made a mental comparison, and then stood up proudly with a sigh of content.

"You are to come to the house and take some coffee; your man says so,— you can leave your bundle in the boat."

The woman chuckled softly, and pressed the object under her shawl more closely to her breast; a stir and faint cry resulted.

"Thank you, Miss, it's my baby; I'll take it with me!"

Again, as once on the ice, the girl knit her straight brows in perplexity.

"Oh! Peter has told me of babies; Anna's died. I've never seen the young things of men and women; may I look? I'd like to."

The other woman looked curiously at the tall, straight girl, with the signs of early maturity, who spoke so simply of never having seen one of the commonest things in the world. She sat down and untied the knot of the shawl in which she carried it.

The girl looked on with her hands clasped tightly behind her back; then she stooped and touched it with her forefinger. The sun showed up the tiny hairs, cobweb-fine, silk-soft as those on a leaf of silverweed, that covered its forehead and cheeks, the clumsy nose and pursy lids and rose-flushed skin.

"Why, it's as soft as a mullein leaf!" she cried.

The mother lifted a dimpled hand, and pointed out the nails, and unrolled the swaddling cloths and showed the little feet. The air struck coldly; it contracted all its pink toes as if about to grip something, stirred, and opened dim eyes, that blinked vacantly with a helpless appeal in them. Then she wrapped it up carefully, with hushsome gutturals. The girl kept silent,—a tumult of foreign thoughts surged through her mind; then, as the mother rose to her feet and looked at her questioningly she said softly:—

"I never imagined them one bit like that. It's very small and helpless, strangely helpless!"

Arrived at the house she sat and watched Sigrid nurse it. The old woman was quite excited; she took it to the light, tickled its upper lip with her finger, declaring that it smiled. When it cried the mother put it to her breast and let it suck until it fell back satisfied, and dropped asleep with a pearl of milk on its lips. Then the girl stole out and unloosing her boat, rowed away from the island, with long, steady strokes, amusing look upon her face; and after that day, all the early summer through, the solitary figure in the boat might be seen gliding about the fjords, or sometimes resting tethered amongst the rocks, whilst her flute sent thrills of melody, quick with yearning, through the warm air; her unrest and vague desires made her venture ever further from the island.

In a sheltered bay in one of the neighbouring fjords, a tent had been pitched, and an easel, bearing a large canvas, might be seen on the strand near it. Sometimes a man sat and painted; more often he lay amidst the bracken and smoked. Once as he lay there the singular notes came rippling landwards. He listened lazily, then, as they died away, he rose to his feet and shading his eyes with his hand gazed out to sea. He could see the boat; the girl was plainly visible. She paddled in, fastened the boat-chain round a large stone, and stood looking about her. He watched her go to the canvas and compare the half-finished picture with the landscape; then she walked to the door of the tent and looked in; as she turned from it, he advanced and met her. She came to a dead stop as she saw him, drew her breath sharply, and scrutinised him gravely, then smiled, with her hands clasped upon her breast. Something in the attitude arrested the words upon his lips,—a laughing query meant for an inquisitive peasant girl, as he at first assumed her to be. What a strange girl! The shy yet fearless look in her wonderful eyes, her dignity of form and carriage, puzzled him. He could think of nothing to say. Why did the *Huldre* stare at him so? he felt uncomfortable under her close scrutiny. He raised his hat and said, as he felt, banally enough:—

"Good day, strange maid from the sea!"

"Good day, strange young man!" she replied slowly and gravely. He started at the few words; the voice was pure metal in timbre, the idiom unmistakably that of a peasant. It reassured him; he thought with amusement of his hesitation in addressing her, and his natural insolent familiarity with women reasserted itself.

"I welcome you, Huldre. It was getting deuced slow. What can I offer you in the way of refreshment?"

He fastened the flap of the tent door aside and invited her to enter. She stepped in, and sat down, without any trace of embarrassment, upon a camp stool, examining the things strewn about with alert, observant eyes, that turned to him every now and then. They troubled him somewhat; their fearlessness was of quite a different order from the boldness of a light o' love peasant girl. He cut a slice of cake and poured out some wine. She tasted it, made a grimace, and spilled it calmly on the ground.

"It's very nasty, I can't drink it. I like milk better."

He laughed, filled a cup out of a pitcher, and came close to her as she took it. He gathered a handful of her hair in his hand; it divided into heavy locks as it hung below her waist, and the light caught one as he lifted it, and burnished it to red gold.

"Your hair is very beautiful, you *are* like a Huldre, are you sure you are not one?"

She hesitated, expression was more difficult than ever; since she had learned to read she sought for words.

"Yes, Peter says they have a cow's tail that swings when they dance."

"Let me make sure—" said the man, as he laughed boisterously, with a rich, deep note in his voice, and caught her by the skirt. She sprang aside with blazing eyes, doubled her strong little fist, and struck him between the eyes,—from some undefinable instinct of self-preservation, not in any way connected with modesty. The blow brought smarting tears to his eyes; he swore and called her a wild-cat; seized her wrists and held them. She stood still, knowing herself powerless, but glared at him undauntedly. He tried a new wile; he dropped her hands, sat down, and held his own over his eyes. One smarted as he stooped; he let it fill with water.

"Your hand is strong, Huldre, I can't see with this eye."

A brief silence, during which he watched her covertly through his fingers; she stood irresolutely, biting her apron; then she stooped and pulled down his hand, turned his head round to the light, lifted up the eyelid and examined it anxiously. Then she let her hands fall to her sides and burst into a ringing peal of laughter.

"Why it's nothing, you man, nothing. Dabble it with water, the salt will cure it!"

Before he could divine her intent, she sped down to the shore, slipped the chain, and rowed out, paused, keeping the boat steady by lightly moving the oars, and laughed wickedly at him. He could see her perfect teeth as she threw her head back.

"Come back, you wood-cat!" he called coaxingly. "I won't touch you, I promise."

A long derisive whistle was her only response. She was pulling against a current, and bent her back to her work; in a few seconds she had vanished, leaving the impression with him of an incarnation as wholesomely fresh as a sea breeze, as wildly sweet as the heath bells that grew further up in the mountain woods.

Days passed; often the man's eyes turned seawards. Then one day as he sat before his easel, he laid aside his brush and listened; he was obsessed by a strange presence; he felt as if eyes were watching him from behind some rock or tree; surely that was the echo of her flute in the wood above. He sprang to his feet, the notes died away, as a peal of mocking laughter came floating down. "The jade has bewitched me," he cried, impatiently. "I can't work, I'll cross to Olas and borrow a boat."

He put his things away and taking a stout stick, went inland, up the roughly cut path through the resinous pine and fir woods. He got back late, heated and tired, for he had come by boat; the boy from the farm was to return by the road. He had questioned him about all the girls in the neighbourhood, without identifying the water pixy of the mocking laugh and elusive charm. As he opened the flap of the tent, the perfume of brier roses came pleasantly to him; he struck a match, lit the lamp that hung to the centre-pole and looked about him.

Some one had been at work during his absence. The bed was made, the floor strewn with pine-needles, the crockery washed, and all the litter of papers and cans cleared away. A fresh home-made loaf, a can of cream, and a wooden bowl of wild strawberries stood on the box that served as a table. The perfume came from a spray of roses fastened above the couch.

"By Jove, the pixy again!"

Next day no sound disturbed his restless quiet. The morning of the day after, he rowed out in the direction which she had taken; he rounded a narrow tongue of land, came to the mouth of a wide fjord, with many rocky islets, numerous tiny creeks and sheltered coves, but no sign of girl or of a habitation. He explored, until the sun scorched, and struck off the rock, with a white, blinding glare, blistering the paint of his boat, and making his head ache; his hands, too, began to blister. No faintest breeze ruffled the water; it was as if the sun had gone to sleep up there, and the winds held their breath for fear of waking him. He rowed back in a fury of impatience; the first thing that met his eyes as he landed was a row of bath towels and socks spread to dry upon the rocks. He ran into the tent eagerly; everything in spotless order, a spray of barberries in place of the roses—no girl.

"Damn the tantalising witch," he muttered as he examined his blistered palms ruefully; "she must have come by land."

So the comedy played itself merrily for several days; once he followed the unmistakable lure of her flute up to the woods, and sat there, waiting for her to appear like a dryad through the tangle of sweet wild honeysuckle, and the stems of the witch-beams, or the silver birches with the sprays of feathery green foliage crossing their satin-flecked trunks, like dappling flights of green butterflies. A badger peered at him round a tree, birds grew bolder as he sat motionless, hopped down on to the lower branches, with cheeky chirps and flits of tail, and blinked at him out of their round eyes; all sorts of insects and tiny vermin peered at him; the whole quiet wood seemed alive with eyes. They oppressed him; he fell asleep. The sun had veered when he awoke; he rose, yawned wearily, and went down again; he broke into a run as he topped the decline, for a boat was just vanishing round the point. After that he stuck doggedly to his work for three days. On the afternoon of the fourth he rowed out, determined to explore every creek and islet in the neighbourhood. He darted in and out round the islands to no purpose; then let himself drift slowly on a current that rounded a tongue of land. It carried him through a ring of rocks into a shorter, wider fjord: "Eureka!" he cried exultantly, for before him, rocking gently in her boat, sat the girl dabbing for whiting. He watched her bait the droppers with bits of mussel, sink the line carefully, and then sit patiently with a loop over her extended forefinger, waiting for the jerk of the bite, that is so tantalisingly imperceptible to unpractised fishers. Jerk! She wound the line deftly round a board; a flash of struggling silver; another; the third fell back, and she caught the fourth as it loosened, and added it to the glistening heap in the flat tub filled with sea water at her feet.

He was forced to unship oars, as the current was carrying him on to a half-sunken rock. She heard him, turned her head quickly over her shoulder,—one shy, wild look,—dropped the tackle into the boat, seized her oars, and paused with an almost imperceptible hesitation as to the direction which she should take, then rowed rapidly and steadily towards the opening through which he had drifted. He gave a sigh of relief, but soon clenched his teeth obstinately as he realised that she was bent on getting away from him. He knew little of boating, but he had dwelt so much on her for days and nights—the nights were worst, when the smell of the roses and leaves she fastened above his couch disturbed him cruelly, and the sense of her past presence worried him in a tantalising way—that he pursued her. The currents ran strongly, his breath grew laboured. "The little devil must be made of steel, or else she knows every inch of the way," he muttered. The brine clung to his beard, he sneezed violently too, and let go one oar, only just saving it by a frantic clutch; but the distance grew between them ever greater.

Suddenly he swung round, and began to row back with his head down. His knowledge of women stood him in good stead. Pursue her and she will flee, either from a desire to escape (and then if you catch her, she is not yours) or from a love of being caught; give up the chase and she will seek you, for at heart she always craves you, and is lonely without you; but the ineradicable first instincts always at war in her make her yield more gladly to the captor who dominates, than to the suitor who pleads submissively.

He pulled slowly, making for his temporary home. She overtook him at the mouth of the bay. He could hear her breath coming quickly as she swept alongside. He stole a look at her; her cheeks were glowing, her eyes met his with a smile lurking in their depths. He met them indifferently, with no response in his own. He fastened the boat and inspected his hands without noticing her at all; the new blisters had broken, and the old ones were rubbed raw again. She watched him in some concern, ran her boat in, stepped out and reached him with a bound; She touched his arm gently; he held out his hands to her.

"It's your fault; see what you have done! I can't work till they get well."

"I'll cure them. I'll bring you something; I never saw such soft skin," there is a note of contempt in her voice; "everything hurts it; it's like the woman's baby."

"Not everything hurts,—you do, you sea witch!"

She looked puzzled; something in his eyes startled her. She stepped back, holding her palms to her breast, and as he put out his hand suddenly, she turned to fly; but he was too fleet of foot and more at home on land. He caught her before she reached the wood, bent her waist back upon his arm, and held her forcibly. Her wild eyes looked up desperately, with a strange enquiry in them; she flushed darkly as she met his; then she bent swiftly and caught his hand in her teeth. He drew his breath, stood still, and waited for the sting of the grip; he felt her teeth tighten as if to bite, then loosen as suddenly, and she burst into a fit of passionate weeping, with her face turned down on to his arm. After that each day saw her boat tied to the flat stone; and on many silver nights, when the moon played hide and seek behind the errant clouds with her own reflection in the mirror of the sea, the girl glided noiselessly out from the island, and the man waited at the tent door.

A wild autumn trod in the wake of the late summer. Sigrid had become more helpless and dependent; lately she had taken to watching the girl as she went about her work or bent over her books in the evenings. This was during the first days of the winter. At length Christmas came to a white world, covered with snow, not crisp and sparkling, but dull, like a dirty shroud, with a sky above like a leaden coffin lid.

On Christmas eve, as Peter was hoisting the corn sheaf for the birds, she hobbled to the door and called him, bidding him follow her to the master's room, shutting the door carefully behind them. In a little while the man came out with his lips trembling under his ragged gray moustache. He walked slowly to the woodshed, and sat down on a block, and thought, in a dazed kind of way. From that day forth they both watched the girl, until she felt their eyes haunt her when she woke in the dark; she was conscious of every look of wonder they exchanged as she sang softly, whilst she span, quaint melodies with a hushful croon in them. One evening she made a fine picture as she sat in the big gloomy kitchen; the open door of the great oven carpeting the floor in front of it with a rich patch of red; the full-rigged ship on the top of the tall clock riding rhythmically on the rampant waves in time to its steady tick. The bright copper coffee kettle sent a fragrant steam from its spout; she stopped her wheel abruptly, got up, and wrote a few words on a slip of paper, then laid it on the psalm book in Sigrid's lap, leaning heavily over the back of the curiously carved oak settle, as the old woman read it. She read it slowly, her withered cheek went a shade duller, her eyelids twitched nervously, and she moistened her lips as if they had become suddenly dry. The girl took the paper again, wrote a few words more, and gave it back to her. The woman muttered a reply without raising her eyes.

The girl counted slowly on her fingers, saying:—

"This is January!"

Then she took down a coloured almanac that Peter had brought with the Christmas stores, and traced the months eagerly, setting a thumbnail dent against each one as she ticked it off. When she came to April she marked it deeply, and pointed it out to the old woman, with so radiant a smile that the latter shook with nervous non-understanding, whilst the helpless tears welled in her faded eyes and dimmed the glasses of her brass-rimmed spectacles. The girl patted her unsightly old hands, swollen and veined and shrivelled, with the yellow-brown splotches, like exaggerated freckles, upon their backs; she smoothed the wisp of flaxen white hair that straggled from under the closefitting black stuff cap. Something had tempered her wildness rarely of late. That night, when she slept, Peter and Sigrid sat at the table, laboriously concocting a letter to be taken to the post town next day. A cockerel out in the shed had crowed twice before they sealed it; then Sigrid muffled herself in an old fur cloak, and Peter held a lantern, so that the rays fell upon the ground in front of each hobbling step she took up the path to the stable. She groaned as she climbed up the ladder leading to the room that was once Anna's, of blessed memory. They turned over the contents of the green wooden chest with the name, letters, and marriage date of the dead woman painted in orange and red scrolls upon the lid, and took out some things that smelled of camphor, lavender, and mustiness. The letter Peter posted went first to England, then to Algiers, only to be sent back to London, to lie and wait until the owner of the name it carried should return from some unknown destination.

Meanwhile the snows melted up in Norway with the waning of the April moon; the cattle scented spring in their stalls, and tugged at their head ropes; the kids bleated incessantly; perhaps their mothers had told them of the world outside, or hereditary memories of grass and green things worked in their shaggy heads. Peter had fetched the doctor with the beard, now white; and when the master did come one afternoon, the wail of a child in Sigrid's arms met him as he entered the kitchen.

Later on in the evening the young mother came to his room, in obedience to a behest through Peter; she stood quietly near the door, waiting for him to speak.

"Sit down, girl," pointing to a chair.

"No, I'll stand; I must go to the child if it cries."

She was examining him with absolutely calm eyes. He had started as she entered, for she was a glorified edition of her mother,—the mother who had thrown him over for a wastrel, and then, on her death-bed, had left him the child of the marriage with a characteristically sentimental letter. Well, the girl had actually no claim on him; he had provided her with food and shelter, and the years had slipped by somehow. Now he realised, with dismay, that he had failed in every way to do his self-imposed duty by her. He had left her in a living grave, with unlettered peasants, and she had probably given herself to the first fisherman who had crossed her path; yet—a pile of books and some cheap copy books lay on the table in front of him. She flushed as she saw them, and a look of dismay crept into her eyes; she had forgotten them when her pains came on so suddenly.

The keen eyes behind the glasses noted it. He had been looking them through before he sent for her,—the copy books, with the headlines written over and over again with patient striving to perfection, letter by letter, word by word.

"You are how old?"

"Peter says I am fifteen."

"Good God, a mere child!"

After a pause, pointing to the book:—

"You wrote these?"

She nodded her head.

"Humph, as you have taken down these books, I suppose you can read; not that I think it likely you understand much of them."

"I think I can. I find the meanings of the words in the dictionary."

"Indeed; and may I ask you where you acquired this knowledge?"

"From Einar Stang."

"So. Mr. Peter then has added lying to his varied accomplishments. He tells me no one has visited the island." He put out his hand for the bell. "Did Mr. Einar also father the brat?"

The girl did not seem to grasp his last remark; she stepped forward to deter him from ringing the bell, saying quickly:—

"Peter didn't know anything about it. I went over," with a sweep of hand in the direction of the main-land, "to skate. I met Einar, and he was sorry for me; he taught me how to learn. That was five summers ago. I haven't seen him since."

It was not possible to doubt the truth of her statement. She poised her head to listen; the attitude reminded him of a startled gemsbok; the faint cry of the child echoed through the house.

"I can't stay; he wants me!" she said simply, and darted from the room.

Weeks passed, yet the master stayed on. The girl-mother became each day a more attractive study; sometimes he went out to the kitchen and watched her at work; sometimes he sent for her on the pretext of a question as to some local plant or bird. Always she leant against the door lintel, listening for the child's cry.

She proved a never-failing delight to him, this child woman, with her absolutely fresh, unspoiled nature, all her basic instincts intact; a genetic creature, fashioned of the right ground-stuff for the renewal of life in man by the formation of new strong individuals,—in her physiological structrue a "driftnatur,"—quick to laugh, quick to be grave, with no conscious personality, a thing of perfect health, sound in mind and body, all her apperceptions unconfused by the scrapment system of modern education.

Her mother had made him shrink from women, as a gun-shy setter from the report of a firearm. He had spent his early manhood in visiting out-of-the-way places, in the pursuit of rare plants and curious beetles. Now he was tired, and had a craving for human sympathy; his men pals had put voluntary hobbles on their feet and mortgages upon their time in the shape of wives and families; he was very lonely. She offered fresh interest; for that he was grateful. He desired to develop her keen intelligence, but the way was beset with difficulties. The child was a bar to every plan he formed for her future.

He had soon discovered how absolute and complete was her ignorance of all social laws. He wrote, in stress of mind, to his sister, who had married an Anglo-Norwegian, with large interests in forests and timber-floating; for he hoped, with the short-sightedness of a man knowing little of women, that she might be able to make the girl understand things as they looked to the world outside.

He had tried to prepare her for the advent of his sister. She had listened at first with indifference, then with quickened interest as he hinted at some possible arrangement for her future. Her eyes had darkened, and she clutched the child closer to her breast, never letting it out of her sight from that hour; she spoke, too, less than ever.

Fru Alfred Hagen arrived; she gave one the idea of a freshly painted three-master with new sails. She had bright hard eyes, white teeth, a rich colour that never varied, and a steady, gliding gait.

Common-sense, and a keen appreciation of the world's values were perhaps her strongest points.

The interview was characteristic, and inevitable in its brevity. Fru Alfred found herself faced by a blank non-comprehension of all the things that were to her the essentials of life. It irritated her; the one thing for which commonsense, worldly folks can never make allowance is temperament, or nature. She had spoken, as she thought, kindly, and the girl had sat and listened. She had touched, with a delicacy that was, by the way, entirely thrown away, upon the identity of the father; the mother declared herself entirely ignorant of his name even, and she was forced to believe her. At length her patience gave way, and she dwelt with some harshness of term on the shame of the whole affair, and the disastrous result of the action seen by the world's eyes. The words conveyed nothing whatever to the girl's intelligence. She listened in patient silence, with knitted brows and watchful eyes. Then she spoke to her of her future, and her brother's desire to educate her, and proposed that the child should be put out to nurse with a niece of Sigrid's, an honest peasant woman in the Hollingdal. After all, it was not so uncommon as it ought to be, and no one need know.

"You mean to send him to strange people, and leave him with them altogether?"

"Yes; it is done every day. The daughter of a friend of mine got into trouble last year, and it was so well managed that no one is any the wiser." Emboldened by the girl's silence she waxed confident and confessed that she had already taken the initiative steps in the matter. This brought the interview to a somewhat unexpected close. The girl laid the boy carefully down and "went" for her in the most literal way, with the instinct of a wild cat in defence of its offspring. She slapped her face as a set off, and then shook her to breathlessness, seized the child, got into her boat, and rowed out to the fjord, declaring that she would not return until that unnatural beast left the island.

The "master" had been a silent spectator until called to active interference in the last scene. Having rescued Fru Alfred, his dormant sense of humour awoke in him, and he laughed unrestrainedly at the upshot of their diplomacy. He endeavoured to soothe her ruffled dignity.

"She is in the right, after all, Susan; all our expedient reasonings don't weigh a doit in the balance with her instincts. I'm sorry to have brought you on a fruitless journey, my dear, but I'm hanged if I won't leave her unspoiled. If I don't mistake, she'll come through all right."

The episode cost him some thousands of kroners; for he could scarcely refuse to meet an overdue draft in connection with a pulp mill, an item, after all, in a country where most of the capital of going concerns floats on paper, and one or two bankruptcies are rather cogent arguments for ultimate success in business.

He found it more difficult to allay the girl's suspicions; she refused to land. Peter took her food and rugs to the boat, and the "master," more anxious than he cared to own even to himself, paced the little strip of wood and listened to her crooning lullabies to the child as they rocked in the boat through the translucent star-flecked summer light. Fru Hagen left in the forenoon.

Seven years more stole away; the farm house on the island had a wing added to its sheltered side, a bridge communicated with the main-land, and the road there had been widened and well laid.

One hot July day, the flag hung limply round the new white flag-staff, the sea barely lisped as it touched the rocks, not a leaf rustled, one seemed to see the air quiver whitely with the intense heat; it would have been unbearable but that now and then a breath of cooler air tickled the land gently, as if blown in playful caress by some gracious ocean spirit.

The chuckling, gleeful shriek of a little lad, and the bell-like voice of a woman chiding him patiently, broke the drowsy quiet.

He was standing upon the wooden ledge of a bathing-house in a shady nook at the water's edge, and a woman, floating in the water, was trying to coax him into it. The urchin pretended to drop in, then shrieked with laughter each time she turned expectantly, only to find him still there.

"Don't be tiresome, Sonnikin; do come!"

"No, let me ride on your back like the picture in the book; you might!"

The woman swam close to the ledge, lifted her beautiful glistening shoulders out of the water, turning her back to enable him to put his arms round her neck, and grip her under the armpits with his sturdy legs; this done, she let herself slide gently out crying:—

"Let go your arms, boy, as I swim out; rest your hands flat on my shoulders and sit straight; grip tight, and don't be afraid if you slip off."

The two perfect nude figures might have reconciled a pessimist to hope for humanity,—the bronze head of the woman, and the quince- coloured head of the laddy, closely, crisply curled, like the hair on the neck of a retriever puppy; supple strength, skilled grace, her white arms cleaving the water for her beautiful body to follow; the gay laughter of the child, the half-frightened catch of his breath, as the water caught his breast when he slipped to the small of her back; the clear deep eyes of exquisite hazel filled with content that looked out so fearlessly under her level brows.

After a while they clambered out of the water; the urchin escaped from her grasp and running away, rolled himself like a frolicksome puppy, in the dry, soft moss that filled a space between the rocks.

Soon she came out of the bathing box and called to him; her hair fell like a glorious mantle below her waist, the half-short sleeves of a print jacket showed the rarely perfect modelling of her forearms, egg-white, to where the slight, strong wrists joined the brown hands so daintily.

"A boat, mother, with a man in it!" he called, paying no heed to her summons, running further from her.

She walked slowly after him, to find him, his chubby hands clasped behind his back, looking questioningly up in his father's face.

The man looked at her as she advanced, took a step towards her, then paused.

She called the boy to her with the note in her voice that he had learned to obey; he went and leant his head against her knees, looking shyly round; thus she stood with her hand upon his head waiting for the man to speak.

His eyes warmed as he looked at them, too thorough an artist not to seize every detail of the picture before him: the sea in the background; the shadowy rays of the fir spines flecking the ground at the feet of this perfect woman, so strangely developed from the wild child girl who had given herself so unquestioningly to him that summer ago; the little lad with the seal of his own features set upon the round rosy face. The instinct of possession awoke in him; it struck him that life might hold a new meaning.

Her cold eyes, her unembarrassed dignity disconcerted him, as once before; he tried to think of something apt to say, feeling wretchedly unsure of his ground. The child had been looking impatiently from her to him; suddenly he darted after a yellow butterfly. That broke the spell.

"I see you haven't forgotten me, Huldre."

He took a step forward.

"He's a grand little chap! I am glad," with a break in his voice, "that he is ours!"

He broke off, for she smiled as he spoke, and something in her face arrested his thought. She said gravely:—

"No, I have not forgotten you, but you mistake when you say *ours; he is mine!*"

"How? I—"

"Simply, you have no claim on him, that is all; he is mine absolutely. That is the compensation the world offers the woman if she'd only recognise it. I've often thought what I'd say if I met you. I'll tell you now. To me he would be just as dear, ay, perhaps dearer, if he were a cripple or an idiot, though my pride might suffer. I don't think you would be so eager to claim us if his beauty and," drawing herself up with a glorious flush, "mine did not rouse you. I don't want to be claimed. I like it best so. I am one of the race of women, and they are many, to whom the child is first—the man always second. He fills life for me, and I should be jealous of your claim on him. Marriage does not attract me; indeed, except as a means of making me a mother when I chose, I would loathe it."

"O-oh!—yet you had some affection for me that summer, I know you had. I never met any one like you since; I have never had the same feeling for any of them as I had for you, Huldre, I swear it."

"No? As a matter-of-fact I didn't know what you call affection meant, and I don't know now."

"How could I know? You don't understand how a man—"

"Oh, but I do," she interrupted, "and I am sorry for you in a way. I wish you would go away now; talking won't change anything."

"No, perhaps not. Yet I'd like, now that I've seen you, to make it right if I can. You can't take what is me out of him!" with an exultant tone.

"No, but I need not develop it. It is the me in him I love. I have no use for you. He satisfies me, you would only trouble me; and, besides, you are not the kind of man I would give a right over him; that is all."

She caught the child as she spoke, and half turned to go.

"I am sorry for you, indeed I am, sorry for many men like you; you haven't learnt yet to divide women into the mere women and the mere mothers. I'd hate to share him, that is the truth; I'd be horribly jealous of interference."

"Is that your last word?"

His voice shook with anger, and his face had gone white.

She bowed her head mutely, without looking at him, only called the child.

"Come, my son, come home, you must be hungry!"

"You are an unnatural beast, you!" cried the man, breaking off with a shake in his voice.

"Perhaps, but I think not."

"I may kiss him I suppose—"

She let the child go; he stood a mutinous manikin, with a scowl on his face. His father bent and lifted him up and held him a moment with a keen pang of self-pity, then put him down gently, and read her face searchingly to find it quietly unemotional as before.

He turned and strode away; anger against this, to him, enigmatical woman of the steady eyes and quiet face full of possibilities of warmth, aching wish for the possession of the little son so like himself, warred in him as he stepped into the boat. He let the lad in it row him out, and sat with his head in his hand.

The Z note of the dancing flies, the lazy kiss of the water, the regular plash, swish, trickle, plash, swish, trickle of the oars, the call of the riotous summer came mockingly to him; and as the boat turned the point the shrill tone of a little lad's voice calling, "Mother!" echoed from the rocks behind him.

SUGGESTED READING

FICTION

Jude the Obscure by Thomas Hardy

The Odd Women by George Gissing

The Story of an African Farm by Olive Scheriner

Diana of Crossways by George Meredith

The Wing of Azrael by Mona Caird

Keynotes by George Egerton

Discords by George Egerton

The Story of a Modern Woman by Ella Hepworth Dixon

The Heavenly Twins by Sarah Grand

Our Manifold Nature; Stories from Life by Sarah Grand

The Woman Who Did by Grant Allen

Dracula by Bram Stoker

NON-FICTION

Foster, Shirley. *Victorian Women's Fiction: Marriage, Freedom, and the Individual*, St. Martin's Press, 2000.

Heilmann, Ann. *New Woman Fiction: Women Writing First-Wave Feminism*, Palgrave Macmillan, 2000.

Mangum, Teresa. *Married, Middlebrow, and Militant: Sarah Grand and the New Woman Novel*, University of Michigan Press, 1998.

Purdue, Melissa and Stacey Floyd. *New Woman Writers, Authority and the Body*, Cambridge Scholars Publishing, 2009.

Sutherland, Gillian. *In Search of the New Woman: Middle-Class Women and Work in Britain, 1870–1914*, Cambridge University Press, 2015.

Young, Emma and James Bailey. *British Women Short Story Writers: The New Woman to Now*, Edinburgh University Press, 2015.

Lightning Source UK Ltd.
Milton Keynes UK
UKHW04f0616241018
331108UK00001B/191/P